A Basic Bahá'í Chronology

A BASIC BAHÁ'Í CHRONOLOGY

Glenn Cameron

with Wendi Momen

GR

GEORGE RONALD • OXFORD

GEORGE RONALD, Publisher
46 High Street, Kidlington, Oxford OX5 2DN

British Library Cataloguing in Publication Data

A catalogue record for this book is available from the British Library

ISBN 0-85398-404-2

Typesetting and cover design by Leith Editorial Services, Abingdon, Oxon, UK

Printed and bound in Great Britain by Biddles Ltd, Guildford and King's Lynn, England

Contents

A Note from the Publisher

A Basic Bahá'í Chronology is a reference book intended to serve the needs of readers, authors, students and researchers. Much effort has gone into making it as accurate as possible. However, there are difficulties in dating some events, particularly in the early period, to which the reader's attention is drawn.

Moojan Momen notes in *The Bábí and Bahá'í Religions, 1844-1944: Some Contemporary Western Accounts* that

> . . . many of those who could have provided the most detailed knowledge of important episodes have died without recording their memoirs. Much of what was written in the way of historical accounts was recorded many years after the events took place. Thus most of *Nabíl's Narrative* is the record of what Nabíl and his informants at a relatively advanced age could remember of events that had occurred in their youth. Similarly the histories of the Bahá'í Faith in various localities in Persia that we have at present were mostly recorded in the 1930s on the instructions of Shoghi Effendi by elderly believers recalling events that had occurred many years previously. Thus, not surprisingly, both *Nabíl's Narrative* and these other histories are often inaccurate with regard to dates (for no one can be expected to remember the exact date of an event that occurred twenty or thirty years previously).

Further difficulties arise in the fixing of Muslim dates, used in the Middle East, and their translation to Gregorian dates. John Walbridge in *Sacred Acts, Sacred Space, Sacred Time* notes that the Muslim month

> . . . begins on the first day after the new moon is sighted by reliable witnesses. Because the new moon is very close to the sun and is first seen just before sunset, it is difficult to predict exactly on which of two days the new month will begin . . . there are to this day regular disagreements about the beginning of the month . . . Because of this, conversions of Muslim dates to Gregorian dates are subject to a one-day error.

Owing to these considerations, some events are recorded in the present volume as having taken place *circa* a particular month or year. Where sources disagree on the date of an event, the date found most widely in Bahá'í literature is the one used in the *Chronology*, with the alternatives mentioned in the sub-section of the entry entitled *Notes*.

A chronology is necessarily a selection of events: no one book could contain every single thing that occurs. *A Basic Bahá'í Chronology* attempts to include those events essential to the development of the Bahá'í Faith as we today understand it, as well as many which are less important but nonetheless fascinating. No doubt future historians will point to many omissions, as events often take on significance only in retrospect and may be excluded here because we do not yet appreciate their importance.

Life does not occur in neat blocks of time. Events unfold, sometimes over long periods, and have effects long into the future. Similarly, people do many things in their lives. The index to *A Basic Bahá'í Chronology* enables the reader to follow many events and people over time.

Details of each event are kept short but many are followed by a number sources so that the reader may read about the event in a variety of contexts. Where no source has been given, details have generally been supplied by national spiritual assemblies or their chroniclers in correspondence too copious to mention but for which we are extremely grateful.

A Basic Bahá'í Chronology highlights the interplay of the forces of darkness and light that so characterize the history of the Bahá'í Faith. The expansion of the religion stands out in bold relief against a backdrop of constant persecution, particularly in the land of its birth. Crises strike almost simultaneously with victories, minor and major, while setbacks in one place are counterbalanced by spurts of growth in another.

Another feature of the development of the Bahá'í Faith underscored by the *Chronology* is the different phases of its expansion. Before the turn of the 20th century almost all the action takes place in the Middle East. Then, suddenly, the scene shifts to North America and to Europe in the early years of the century as the Faith draws new believers from these continents. As the century moves on, however, the scene shifts again, now to South America and more far-flung corners of the planet – Australia, Asia. Then in the 1950s comes the burst of teaching work that takes the Faith to the whole world, and we see the scene shift once again, this time to Africa and the Pacific, rivals in the race to win new converts to the Faith of God. In the 1960s and 1970s Bahá'í youth begin to make a huge impact on the development of the Faith; women's activities become significant in the 1970s and 1980s; while vast numbers of people begin to enrol in the Faith from the 1960s onwards. In the 1980s Bahá'ís around the world become involved in social and economic development projects and peace initiatives, and the external affairs activities of the Faith begin to blossom even as the Iranian Bahá'í community is effectively silenced. The arts are used more widely to teach the Faith, while increasing efforts are made to reach out to the indigenous peoples of the world, to professionals of all kinds, to people of capacity and leaders of thought. Then in the late 1980s and 1990s come the dramatic changes in Eastern Europe and the former Soviet bloc countries, enabling the last of the territories of the world to be opened to the Bahá'í Faith and their national spiritual assemblies to be formed.

A Basic Bahá'í Chronology merely provides the skeleton for this pageant. The reader is encouraged not only to read more thoroughly the history of the Bahá'í Faith but to participate more fully in its unfolding drama.

Abbreviations and Bibliography

The following abbreviations are used in the references to entries in *A Basic Bahá'í Chronology*. In general, figures following an abbreviation denote the page number or numbers, e.g. AB7, 9 refers to Balyuzi's *'Abdu'l-Bahá*, pages 7 and 9. Where a title is in multiple volumes, such as *Bahá'í World*, a colon separates the title and volume number from the page numbers. Thus BW18:16 refers to *Bahá'í World*, volume 18, page 16 (see individual books below for further examples). Occasionally a colon is used in a reference for clarity, e.g. 239D:65 refers to Allan Ward's *239 Days*, page 65.

239D Ward, Allan L. *239 Days*. Wilmette, Ill.: Bahá'í Publishing Trust, 1979.

AB Balyuzi, H. M. *'Abdu'l-Bahá*. Oxford: George Ronald, 1971.

ABMM Momen, Moojan. *'Abdu'l-Bahá*. Manuscript.

ADJ Shoghi Effendi. *The Advent of Divine Justice*. Wilmette, Ill.: Bahá'í Publishing Trust, 1990.

AVI Nakhjavání, Violette. *Amatu'l-Bahá Visits India*. New Delhi: Bahá'í Publishing Trust, 1984.

AWH The Universal House of Justice. *A Wider Horizon: Selected Messages of the Universal House of Justice 1983-1992*. Riviera Beach, FL: Palabra Publications, 1992.

B Balyuzi, H. M. *The Báb*. Oxford: George Ronald, 1973.

BA Shoghi Effendi. *Bahá'í Administration*. Wilmette, Ill.: Bahá'í Publishing Trust, 1968.

BBD Momen, Wendi. *A Basic Bahá'í Dictionary*. Oxford: George Ronald, 1989.

BBIC *Bahá'u'lláh*. A statement prepared by the Bahá'í International Community Office of Public Information. London: Bahá'í Publishing Trust, 1991.

BBR Momen, Moojan. *The Bábí and the Bahá'í Religions, 1844-1944, Some Contemporary Western Accounts*. Oxford: George Ronald, 1981.

BBRSM Smith, Peter. *The Bábí and Bahá'í Religions.* Cambridge: Cambridge University Press, 1987.

BEL Collins, William. *Bibliography of English-Language Works on the Bábí and Bahá'í Faiths, 1844-1985.* Oxford: George Ronald, 1990.

BFA1 Stockman, Robert. *The Bahá'í Faith In America,* vol. 1. Wilmette, Ill.: Bahá'í Publishing Trust, 1985.

BFA2 Stockman, Robert. *The Bahá'í Faith in America, Early Expansion, 1900-1912,* vol. 2. Oxford: George Ronald, 1995.

BHC *Bahá'í History Calendar.* Honolulu, Hawaii: Hawaii Bahá'í National Library.

BHP The Universal House of Justice. *Bahá'í Holy Places at the World Centre.* Haifa: Bahá'í World Centre, 1968.

BI Cooper, Roger. *The Bahá'ís of Iran.* No. 51, Minority Rights Group series. Feb. 1982.

BINS *Bahá'í International News Service.* Issued fortnightly by the Bahá'í World Centre. [Issues are indicated by edition number followed by page number; thus BINS210:8 refers to *Bahá'í International New Service,* number 210, page 8.]

BK *Bahíyyih Khánum.* Haifa: Bahá'í World Centre, 1982.

BKG Balyuzi, H. M. *Bahá'u'lláh, The King of Glory.* Oxford: George Ronald, 1980.

BN *Bahá'í News.* A monthly publication of the National Spiritual Assembly of the United States. [Figures following 'BN' refer to volume number and page number, thus BN596:14 refers to *Bahá'í News,* volume 596, page 14.

BNE Esslemont, J. E. *Bahá'u'lláh and the New Era.* London: Bahá'í Publishing Trust, 1974.

BR Smith, Peter. *The Bahá'í Religion: A Short Introduction to its History and Teachings.* Oxford: George Ronald, 1988.

BW *Bahá'í World.* Prepared under the supervision of the National Spiritual Assembly of the United States and Canada with the approval of Shoghi Effendi or prepared by the Universal House of Justice. [Figures appearing after 'BW' refer to volume numbers, thus BW8:25 refers to *Bahá'í World*, volume 8, page 25. From 1992-3, *Bahá'í World* is dated year by year rather than by volume number. Thus BW92-3:6 refers to *Bahá'í World*, 1992-3, page 6.]

BWMF Balyuzi, H. M. *Bahá'u'lláh, The Word Made Flesh*. Oxford: George Ronald, 1963.

CB Taherzadeh, Adib. *The Covenant of Bahá'u'lláh*. Oxford: George Ronald, 1992.

CBM Matthews, Gary L. *The Challenge of Bahá'u'lláh*. Oxford: George Ronald, 1993.

CF Shoghi Effendi. *Citadel of Faith*. Wilmette, Ill.: Bahá'í Publishing Trust, 1980.

CH Blomfield, Lady. *The Chosen Highway*. Wilmette, Ill.: Bahá'í Publishing Trust, 1975.

CT Rutstein, Nathan. *Corinne True*. Oxford: George Ronald, 1987.

GTT Shoghi Effendi. *Guidance for Today and Tomorrow*. London: Bahá'í Publishing Trust, 1953

DB Nabíl-i-A'ẓam. *The Dawn-Breakers*, Wilmette, Ill.: Bahá'í Publishing Trust, 1970.

DG Shoghi Effendi. *Directives from the Guardian*. New Delhi: Bahá'í Publishing Trust, 1973.

DH Ruhe, David. S. *Door of Hope*. Oxford: George Ronald, 1983.

DJEE Momen, Moojan. *Dr. J. E. Esslemont*. London: Bahá'í Publishing Trust, 1975.

DJT *The Diary of Juliet Thompson*. Los Angeles: Kalimát Press, 1983.

DM Muhájir, Irán Furútan. *Dr Muhájir, Hand of the Cause of God, Knight of Bahá'u'lláh*. London: Bahá'í Publishing Trust, 1992.

DND Shoghi Effendi. *Dawn of a New Day*. New Delhi: Bahá'í Publishing Trust, 1970.

DP Whitmore, Bruce W. *The Dawning Place.* Wilmette, Ill.: Bahá'í Publishing Trust, 1984.

EB Balyuzi, H. M. *Eminent Bahá'ís in the Time of Bahá'u'lláh.* Oxford: George Ronald, 1985.

EGB Balyuzi, H. M. *Edward Granville Browne and the Bahá'í Faith.* London: George Ronald, 1970.

ER Weinberg, Robert. *Ethel Jenner Rosenberg,* Oxford: George Ronald, 1995.

ESW Bahá'u'lláh. *Epistle to the Son of the Wolf.* Wilmette, Ill.: Bahá'í Publishing Trust, 1971.

FGM Vader, John Paul. *For the Good of Mankind: August Forel and the Bahá'í Faith.* Oxford: George Ronald, 1984.

G Bahá'u'lláh. *Gleanings from the Writings of Bahá'u'lláh.* Wilmette, Ill.: Bahá'í Publishing Trust, 1983.

GAP *Green Acre on the Piscataqua.* Eliot, Maine: Green Acre Bahá'í School Council, 1991.

GBF Rabbaní, Rúḥíyyih. *The Guardian of the Bahá'í Faith.* London: Bahá'í Publishing Trust, 1988.

GPB Shoghi Effendi. *God Passes By.* Wilmette, Ill.: Bahá'í Publishing Trust, 1970.

GT Hofman, David. *George Townshend.* Oxford: George Ronald, 1983.

HLS Rutstein, Nathan. *He Loved and Served.* Oxford: George Ronald, 1982.

I Khianra, Dipchand. *Immortals.* New Delhi: Bahá'í Publishing Trust, 1988.

KA Bahá'u'lláh. *The Kitáb-i-Aqdas.* Haifa: The Bahá'í World Centre, 1992.

KAN Notes to *The Kitáb-i-Aqdas.*

KB Balyuzi, H. M. *Khadíjih Bagum.* Oxford: George Ronald, 1981.

KI Bahá'u'lláh. *Kitáb-i-Íqán.* Wilmette, Ill.: Bahá'í Publishing Trust, 1989.

L Heller, Wendy. *Lidia.* Oxford: George Ronald, 1985.

LANZ Shoghi Effendi. *Letters from the Guardian to Australia and New Zealand.* Sydney, Australia: Bahá'í Publishing Trust, 1970.

LDG1&2 Shoghi Effendi. *The Light of Divine Guidance: The Messages from the Guardian of the Bahá'í Faith to the Bahá'í's of Germany and Austria.* Hofheim-Langenhaim: Bahá'í-Verlag, 1982.

LOG Hornby, Helen, comp. *Lights of Guidance.* New Delhi: Bahá'í Publishing Trust, 1983.

MA Shoghi Effendi. *Messages to America.* Wilmette, Ill.: Bahá'í Publishing Trust, 1947.

MAP Phelps, Myron H. *The Master in 'Akká.* Los Angeles: Kalimát Press, 1985.

MBW Shoghi Effendi. *Messages to the Bahá'í World.* Wilmette, Ill.: Bahá'í Publishing Trust, 1971.

MC *The Ministry of the Custodians, 1957-1963: An Account of the Stewardship of the Hands of the Cause.* Haifa: Bahá'í World Centre, 1992.

MF 'Abdu'l-Bahá. *Memorials of the Faithful.* Wilmette, Ill.: Bahá'í Publishing Trust, 1971.

MH Mehrabhani, R. *Mullá Ḥusayn, Disciple at Dawn.* Los Angeles: Kalimát Press, 1987.

MKBM Ma'ani, Baharieh. *Muníríh Khánum.* Manuscript.

MMBA Momen, Moojan. *Mullá 'Alí Basṭámí.* Manuscript.

MMNF Momen, Moojan. *The Núrí Family.* Manuscript.

MR Garis, M. R. *Martha Root: Lioness at the Threshold.* Wilmette, Ill.: Bahá'í Publishing Trust, 1983.

MRHK Zinky, Kay, comp. *Martha Root, Herald of the Kingdom.* New Delhi: Bahá'í Publishing Trust, 1983.

MS Salmanpour, Manuchehr. *Arabia.* Manuscript.

MUHJ The Universal House of Justice. *Messages from the Universal House of Justice 1968-1973.* Wilmette, Ill.: Bahá'í Publishing Trust, 1976.

OC *One Country*. A publication of the Bahá'í International Community Office of Public Information.

PDC Shoghi Effendi. *The Promised Day is Come*. Wilmette, Ill.: Bahá'í Publishing Trust, 1951.

PH Seow, Jimmy Ewe Huat. *The Pure in Heart: The Historical Development of the Bahá'í Faith in China, Southeast Asia and Far East*. Sydney: Bahá'í Publications Australia, 1991.

PP Rabbaní, Rúḥíyyih. *The Priceless Pearl*. London: Bahá'í Publishing Trust, 1969.

PSBW Whitehead, O. Z. *Portraits of Some Bahá'í Women*. Oxford: George Ronald, 1996.

PT 'Abdu'l-Bahá. *Paris Talks*. London: Bahá'í Publishing Trust, 1995.

PUP 'Abdu'l-Bahá. *The Promulgation of Universal Peace*. Wilmette, Ill.: Bahá'í Publishing Trust, 1982.

RB1 Taherzadeh, Adib. *The Revelation of Bahá'u'lláh*, vol. 1. Oxford: George Ronald, 1974.

RB2 Taherzadeh, Adib. *The Revelation of Bahá'u'lláh*, vol. 2. Oxford: George Ronald, 1977.

RB3 Taherzadeh, Adib. *The Revelation of Bahá'u'lláh*, vol. 3. Oxford: George Ronald, 1983.

RB4 Taherzadeh, Adib. *The Revelation of Bahá'u'lláh*, vol. 4. Oxford: George Ronald, 1987.

RG Braun, Eunice. *A Reader's Guide: The Development of Bahá'í Literature in English*. Oxford: George Ronald, 1986.

RR Amanat, Abbas. *Resurrection and Renewal*. London: Cornell University Press, 1989.

RSLG Garrigues, Stephen L. *Rúmí*. Manuscript.

SA Walbridge, John. *Sacred Acts, Sacred Space, Sacred Time*. Oxford: George Ronald, 1996.

SB Furútan, 'Alí-Akbar. *Stories of Bahá'u'lláh.* Oxford: George Ronald, 1986.

SBBH1 Momen, Moojan, ed. *Studies in Bábí and Bahá'í History*, vol. 1. Los Angeles: Kalimát Press, 1982.

SBBH2 Cole, Juan R. and Momen, Moojan, eds. *Studies in Bábí and Bahá'í History: From Iran East & West.* Los Angeles: Kalimát Press, 1984.

SBBR5 Momen, Moojan, ed. *Studies in the Bábí and Bahá'í Religions: Studies in Honor of the Late Hasan M. Balyuzi.* Los Angeles: Kalimát Press, 1988.

SBR Whitehead, O. Z. *Some Bahá'ís to Remember.* Oxford: George Ronald, 1983.

SDC 'Abdu'l-Bahá. *The Secret of Divine Civilization.* Wilmette, Ill.: Bahá'í Publishing Trust, 1990.

SDH Faizi, A. Q. *The Delight of Hearts: Memoirs of Ḥájí Mírzá Ḥaydar-'Alí.* Los Angeles: Kalimát Press, 1980.

SE Giachery, Ugo. *Shoghi Effendi.* Oxford: George Ronald, 1973.

SEBW Whitehead, O. Z. *Some Early Bahá'ís of the West.* Oxford: George Ronald, 1976.

SI Momen, Moojan. *An Introduction to Shí'í Islam.* London: Yale University Press, 1985.

SS Braun, Eunice. *From Strength to Strength.* Wilmette, Ill.: Bahá'í Publishing Trust, 1978.

SUR Gail, Marzieh. *Summon Up Remembrance.* Oxford: George Ronald, 1987.

SW *Star of the West*, vols. 1-14. rpt. Oxford: George Ronald, 1978. [Figures appearing after 'SW' refer to volume and number; thus SW6,13:101 refers to *Star of the West*, volume 6, number 13, page 101. Some are identified merely by a volume number, thus SW13:277 refers to *Star of the West*, volume 13, page 277.]

SWAB 'Abdu'l-Bahá. *Selections from the Writings of 'Abdu'l-Bahá.* Haifa: Bahá'í World Centre, 1978.

SWB Báb, The. *Selections from the Writings of the Báb.* Haifa: Bahá'í World Centre, 1976.

TB Bahá'u'lláh. *Tablets of Bahá'u'lláh revealed after the Kitáb-i-Adqas*. Haifa: Bahá'í World Centre, 1978.

TDP 'Abdu'l-Bahá. *Tablets of the Divine Plan*. Wilmette, Ill.: Bahá'í Publishing Trust, 1980.

TMW Morrison, Gayle. *To Move the World*. Wilmette, Ill.: Bahá'í Publishing Trust, 1982.

TN 'Abdu'l-Bahá. *A Traveller's Narrative*. Wilmette, Ill.: Bahá'í Publishing Trust, 1980.

TR Sims, Barbara R. *Traces that Remain*. Japan: Bahá'í Publishing Trust, 1989.

UD Shoghi Effendi. *Unfolding Destiny of the British Bahá'í Community*. London: Bahá'í Publishing Trust, 1981.

V Honnold, Annamaire. *Vignettes from the Life of 'Abdu'l-Bahá*. Oxford: George Ronald, rev. ed. 1991.

VV Braun, Eunice. *From Vision to Victory*. Oxford: George Ronald, 1993.

WG The Universal House of Justice. *Wellspring of Guidance*. Wilmette, Ill.: Bahá'í Publishing Trust, 1976.

WOB Shoghi Effendi. *The World Order of Bahá'u'lláh*. Wilmette, Ill.: Bahá'í Publishing Trust, 1991.

WT 'Abdu'l-Bahá. *The Will and Testament of 'Abdu'l-Bahá*. Wilmette, Ill.: Bahá'í Publishing Trust, 1971.

ZK Khadem, Javidukht. *Zikrullah Khadem, The Itinerant Hand of the Cause of God*. Wilmette, Ill.: Bahá'í Publishing Trust, 1990.

Other Sources Cited

'Abdu'l-Bahá in Canada. Ontario: Bahá'í Distribution Canada, 1962.

Faizi, A. Q. *Milly: A Tribute to Amelia E. Collins.* Oxford: George Ronald, 1977.

Freeman, Dorothy. *From Copper to Gold: The Life of Dorothy Baker.* Oxford: George Ronald, 1984.

Gail, Marzieh. *Khánum: The Greatest Holy Leaf.* Oxford: George Ronald, 1982.

Hatcher, John S. *From the Auroral Darkness: The Life and Poetry of Robert Hayden.* Oxford: George Ronald, 1984.

Hein, Kurt John. *Radio Bahá'í Ecuador.* Oxford: George Ronald, 1988.

Khursheed, Anjam. *The Seven Candles of Unity.* London: Bahá'í Publishing Trust, 1991.

Labíb, Muhammad. *The Seven Martyrs of Hurmuzak.* Oxford: George Ronald, 1981.

Momen, Moojan. *Selections from the Writings of E. G. Browne.* Oxford: George Ronald, 1987.

Sears, William and Quigley, Robert. *The Flame: The Story of Lua.* Oxford: George Ronald, 1972.

Szanto-Felbermann, Renée. *Rebirth: The Memoirs of Renée Szanto-Felbermann.* London: Bahá'í Publishing Trust, 1980.

Vick, Holly Hanson. *Social and Economic Development: A Bahá'í Approach.* Oxford: George Ronald, 1989.

West, Marion. *Letters from Bonaire.* Oxford: George Ronald, 1990.

1753

In the year Birth of <u>Sh</u>ay<u>kh</u> Aḥmad Aḥsá'í in the village of Muṭayrafí in the Aḥsá region, the hinterland of Baḥrayn.

1771

In the year Birth of Fatḥ-'Alí <u>Kh</u>án (later <u>Sh</u>áh) in <u>Sh</u>íráz.

Fatḥ-'Alí <u>Sh</u>áh

1778

c. 1778 Birth of Siyyid Muḥammad Riḍay-i-Shírází, the father of the Báb.

1783

c. 1783 Birth of Mírzá 'Abbas-i-Iriváni, later Prime Minister Ḥájí Mírzá Áqásí, in Máh-kú.

1796

c. Mar Áqá Muḥammad Khán, leader of the Qájárs, proclaims himself Sháh of Persia; beginning of Qájár dynasty.

1797

In the year Birth of Siyyid Káẓim-i-Rashtí, in Rasht.

17 Jun Assassination of Muḥammad Sháh in Ádharbáyján.

c. Aug Crown Prince Fatḥ-'Alí Mírzá assumes leadership of Persia.

1798

21 Mar Fatḥ-'Alí Khán is crowned second Qájár Sháh during Naw-Rúz festival.

1799

21 Mar Fatḥ-'Alí Sháh's son, 'Abbás Mírzá (aged 9), is designated Crown Prince of Persia.

1806

c. 1806 Birth of Mírzá Muḥammad Taqí Khán-i-Farahání, later Prime Minister of Persia, in Hizávih.

1808

5 Jan Birth of Muḥammad Mírzá (later Sháh), son of Crown Prince 'Abbás Mírzá and grandson of Fatḥ-'Alí Sháh.

1812

c. 1812 Birth of Mullá Muḥammad-'Alíy-i-Zanjání, Ḥujjat.

1813

c. 1813 Birth of Muḥammad Ḥusayn-i-Bushrú'í (Mullá Ḥusayn).

1817

In the year Shaykh Aḥmad travels to Persia and visits Shíráz and Ṭihrán. He is in Ṭihrán when Bahá'u'lláh is born. [DB13]

The birth of Fáṭimih Umm-Salamih, Ṭáhirih (the Pure One), Qurratu'l-'Ayn (Solace of the Eyes), Zarrín-Táj (Crown of Gold). [BBD220; GPB7, 73, 75]

c. 1817 Birth of Hand of the Cause Mullá Abu'l-Ḥasan-i-Ardikání (Ḥájí Amín), in Ardikán, near Yazd.

12 Nov **Birth of Mírzá Ḥusayn-'Alíy-i-Núrí (Bahá'u'lláh).**

- He is of royal Persian blood, a descendant of Zoroaster and the Sásáníyán kings of Persia through Yazdigird III, the last king of that dynasty. Through His mother He is a descendant of Abraham through Katurah and Jesse. [BW8:874; GPB94; RB1:305]
- He is born in Ṭihrán. His father is Mírzá 'Abbás whose ancestral home is Tákur in the province of Núr. His father is also known as Mírzá Buzurg in royal circles. [BKG13; RB1:7]
- His mother is Khadíjih Khánum. [BBD127; BBRSM57–8]
- He is born at dawn. [LOG353]

1817–1819

See also *For biblical reference see* LOG378. *See* RB1:304 *for extracts from Shoghi Effendi re: His station. See* BBD39, GPB157–8 *for a condensed history.*

1818

May Birth of Mullá Zaynu'l-'Ábidín (Zaynu'l-Muqarrabín), Apostle of Bahá'u'lláh, in Najafábád.

1819

In the year Death of Shaykh 'Alí, son of Shaykh Aḥmad. Shaykh Aḥmad considers this loss as a sacrifice for 'the 'Alí whose advent we all await'. [MH24]

1819–31 'Abdu'lláh Páshá becomes the governor of 'Akká in 1819. In 1832 when the Egyptians take 'Akká he surrenders and is taken to Egypt. He is freed in 1840 when the area reverts to Turkish rule. [BBD5]

20 Oct **Birth of Siyyid 'Alí-Muḥammad (the Báb), before dawn, in Shíráz.** [B32; CH13; DB72]

- The Primal Point (Nuqṭiy-i-Úlá). [BBD185]
- The Promised One of Islam, the Qá'im. [BBD188]
- Siyyid-i-Dhikr (Lord of Remembrance). [BBD212]
- His mother is Fáṭimih-Bagum (Zajra Bagum). [B33, 46; KB20; RB2:382]
- His father is Mírzá Muḥammad Riḍá. [BW4:234–5; LOG351; SE206; TN4]
- He is a direct heir of the House of Háshim and descended thus from Muḥammad and through Him from Abraham. [BW8:874]
- Designations of the Báb include 'Abdu'dh-Dhikr (Servant of the Remembrance), Bábu'lláh (the Gate of God) and Ḥaḍrat-i-A'lá (His Holiness the Most Exalted One). [BBD1, 30, 93]

Notes *See* B32 *and* TN4 *for discussion of the date of His father's death.*

See also   *See* DB28–30. *See* DB75 *for the extent of His schooling. See* DB75 N1 *for His education.*

1820

In the year   Birth of <u>Kh</u>ádíjih Bagum (daughter of Mírzá 'Alí, a merchant of <u>Sh</u>íráz), first wife of the Báb, in <u>Sh</u>íráz.

Birth of Ásíyih <u>Kh</u>ánum (Navváb), first wife of Bahá'u'lláh, in Yálrúd. The only daughter of Mírzá Ismá'íl.

The Mansion at Bahjí

1821

'Abdu'lláh Pá<u>sh</u>á builds the Mansion at Bahjí. [BBD5, 42]

1822

In the year Birth of Mírzá-'Alíy-i-Bárfurú<u>sh</u>í (Quddus), the 18th Letter of the Living.

1823

c. 1823 Bahá'u'lláh's father dreams that his son is swimming in a sea with multitudes of fish clinging to the strands of His hair. He relates this dream to a soothsayer, who prophesies that Bahá'u'lláh will achieve supremacy over the world. [DB199–20]

Mi<u>sh</u>kín-Qalam

1825

c. 1825 Birth of Áqá Ḥusayn-i-Iṣfahání (Mi<u>sh</u>kín-Qalam), Apostle of Bahá'u'lláh and well-known calligrapher, in <u>Sh</u>íráz.

1826

27 Jun Passing of Shaykh Aḥmad-i-Aḥsá'í, the leader of the Shaykhís, in Ḥaddíyyih near Medina near the tomb of Muḥammad, at approximately 75 years. He is buried in the cemetery of Baqí' in Medina. [B2; MH20]

- At his passing Siyyid Káẓim-i-Rashtí becomes his designated successor. [BBD12]

Notes BBD12 *says it was 1828 and he was 81 years old.*

See also *See* CH11 *and* MH20 *for three chief articles of faith of the Shaykhís. See* BBRSM8 *for a brief account of his life. See* MH22 *for a picture.*

1828

In the year Passing of Mírzá Muḥammad Riḍá, the father of the Báb.

- The Báb is placed in the care of His maternal uncle, Ḥájí Mírzá Siyyid 'Alí, Khál-i-A'ẓam (the Most Great Uncle). He is a leading merchant of Shíráz and is the first, after the Letters of the Living, to embrace the new Cause in that city. He is one of the Seven Martyrs of Ṭihrán. [BBD14]

Notes *According to Mírzá Abu'l-Faḍl-i-Gulpáygání, the Báb was still an infant and had not yet been weaned when His father passed away.* [DB72]

Defeat of the Persians at the hands of the Russians. [BBRSM55]

1829

29 Mar Birth of Áqá Muḥammad-i-Qá'iní (Nabíl-i-Akbar), Apostle of Bahá'u'lláh, in Naw-Firist, near Bírjand.

1830

In the year Mullá Ḥusayn leaves his home in Mashhad to pursue his religious studies in Karbalá. [MH113]

c. 1830 Marriage of Ṭáhirih to her cousin Mullá Muḥammad, the son of Mullá Taqí.

c. 1830–1 Birth of Ḥájí Mírzá Muḥammad Taqí Afnán (Vakílu'd-Dawlih), maternal uncle of the Báb, who supervised and largely paid for the building of the Mas͟hriqu'l-Ad͟hkár in 'Is͟hqábád.

Ḥájí Mírzá Muḥammad Taqí Afnán, Vakílu'd-Dawlih, centre

1831

c. 1831 Birth of Mírzá Yaḥyá (Ṣubḥ-i-Azal), half brother of Bahá'u'lláh.

17 Jul Birth of Náṣiri'd-Dín Mírzá, later Sh͟áh.

29 Jul Birth of Nabíl-i-A'ẓam, Muḥammad-i-Zarandí, Apostle of Bahá'u'lláh.

1831–40 Egyptian occupation of 'Akká. [BBR202; DH128]

1834

9 Sep The end of the reign of Fatḥ-'Alí Sh͟áh and the accession of Muḥammad Sh͟áh. [B7; BBD83, 164; BBR153, 482]

Ḥájí Siyyid Muḥammad-Ḥusayn,
Maḥbúbu'sh-Sh͟uhadá'
('Beloved of Martyrs')

• Fifty-three sons and 46 daughters survive Fatḥ-'Alí Sh͟áh. [B7]

• After his accession Muḥammad Sh͟áh executes the Grand Vizier, the Qá'im Maqám, the man who has raised him to the throne. He then installs his tutor, Ḥájí Mírzá Áqásí, to the office (1835). [B10–11]

See also *See* BBD164 *for picture. See* B11–122 *for the relationship between the Sh͟áh and his new Grand Vizier, Ḥájí Mírzá Áqásí. For details on the life of Ḥájí Mírzá Áqásí see* BBD19.

Ḥájí Mírzá Áqásí

1835

In the year Birth of Mírzá Áqá Ján-i-Kash͟hání (Kh͟adímu'lláh), Apostle of Bahá'u'lláh and His amanuensis.

Birth of Ḥájí Siyyid Muḥammad-Ḥusayn, Maḥbúbu'sh͟-Sh͟uhadá' ('Beloved of Martyrs'), in Iṣfahán.

Oct Marriage of Mírzá Ḥusayn-'Alí to Ásíyih Kh͟ánum. [BKG23; RB1:382]

c. Nov Ḥájí Mírzá Áqásí becomes Prime Minister of Persia.

1837

In the year Birth of Ḥájí Siyyid Muḥammad-Ḥasan, Sulṭánu'sh-Shuhadá' ('King of Martyrs'), in Iṣfahán.

c. 1837 Birth of Mírzá Muḥammad Muṣṭáfáy-i-Baghdádí, Apostle of Bahá'u'lláh, in Iraq.

Ḥájí Siyyid Muḥammad-Ḥasan,
Sulṭánu'sh-Shuhadá' ('King of Martyrs')

1838

In the year Manúchihr Khán is appointed Governor of Iṣfahán. [BBR167]

1839

In the year Passing of Mírzá Buzurg. His body is taken to Najaf, Iraq. [BBD49; BKG17; BNE23–4; MBW175]

Defeat of Persia at the hands of the British. [BBRSM55]

Mírzá Buzurg, father of Bahá'u'lláh

1840

In the year The British fleet take 'Akká from the Egyptians. [BBR202]

1841

In the year Siyyid 'Alí Muḥammad (the Báb) goes to Najaf and Karbalá where He attends the lectures of Siyyid Kázim-i-Rashtí, Shaykh Aḥmád's successor. He remains here for about a year. [B42–4; MH25; RB3:254; SBBH15]

- The followers of Shaykh Aḥmad number about 100,000 in Iraq alone. [MH25]

Notes BBRSM13 *says the Báb went to Najaf and Karbalá in 1839/40.*

1842

In the year Birth of Ḥájí Akhúnd (Mullá 'Alí-Akbar Shahmírzádí), who was named a Hand of the Cause by Bahá'u'lláh.

Aug The marriage of Siyyid 'Alí Muḥammad (the Báb) in Shíráz to Khadíjih-Bagum. [B46; BBD28, 127; BKG402; RB2:382]

See also *See* B80 *for a reproduction of the marriage certificate.*

1843

In the year Birth of Aḥmad, son of the Báb. He dies shortly after he is born. [B46]

See also *See* DB74 *for a picture of his resting-place.*

The Báb dreams that He drinks a few drops of blood from the wounds of the martyred Imám Ḥusayn. After this dream He feels that the Spirit of God has taken possession of His soul. [BBRSM14; DB253]

The sacking of the holy city of Karbalá at the hands of the Turks. [BBRSM55]

31 Dec Passing of Siyyid Káẓim-i-Rashtí, the disciple and chosen successor of Shaykh Ahmad, in Karbalá. Because Siyyid Káẓim designated no successor, within a short period of time the Shaykhí school was split into several factions. The two largest were grouped around Siyyid 'Alí Muḥammad and Ḥájí Mullá Muḥammad Karím Khán

Kirmání. The first faction moved away from the outward practice of Islam towards a development of inner realities and ultimately a new revelation. The second emphasized the continuing role of the Prophets and the Imáms and sought acceptance from the Shí'í majority which had formerly excommunicated Shaykh Aḥmad and Siyyid Kázim. [BBD126–7; MH26; SBBH1; TB6]

See also *See* BBRSM9 *for a brief account of his life and the Shaykhí school under his leadership. See* MH28 *for a picture. See* DB43–5, MH46–7 *for an account of a warning of his passing.*

Iran in the Nineteenth Century

1844

In the year Birth of Mírzá Abu'l-Faḍl-i-Gulpáygání, Apostle of Bahá'u'lláh, in Gulpáygán.

22 Jan Mullá Ḥusayn returns to Karbalá after a journey of two years in Persia. He has been on a mission in Iṣfahán and Mas͟hhad where he has successfully defended the views of his master, Siyyid Káẓim, before the leading clerics of those cities. [MH49]

- After a period of mourning and 40 days of prayer and fasting in the vicinity of the shrine in Najaf he sets out for Persia in the company of his brother and his nephew, following the last wishes of Siyyid Káẓim that his followers quit Karbalá and search for the Promised One. The party go to Bús͟hihr and then on to S͟híráz. [MH50–3]

7 Feb Birth of S͟hayk͟h Káẓim-i-Samandarí, Apostle of Bahá'u'lláh, in Qazvin.

S͟hayk͟h Káẓim-i-Samandarí,
Apostle of Bahá'u'lláh

1844

c. Apr Khadíjih Bagum apparently recognizes her husband as the promised Qá'im 'sometime before the Báb declared His mission'. He bids her to keep this knowledge concealed. [DB191–2; KB10–14]

22 May **Declaration of the Báb's Mission**

Two hours and eleven minutes after sunset Siyyid 'Alí-Muḥammad makes His declaration to Mullá Ḥusayn-i-Bushrú'í. He reveals the first chapter of the Qayyúmu'l-Asmá' (the Commentary on the Súrih of Joseph). The entire text will later be translated by Ṭáhirih. [B19–21; BBD190–1; BBRSM14–15; BKG28; BW12:85–8; BWMF16; DB52–65; GPB23, 73; MH56–71; SBBH17]

The House of the Báb, where He made His declaration to Mullá Ḥusayn

- This text was the most widely circulated of all the Báb's writings and came to be regarded as the Bábí Qur'án for almost the entirety of His mission. [BBRSM32]
- Bahá'u'lláh has described this book as being 'the first, the greatest, and mightiest of all books' in the Bábí Dispensation. [GPB23]
- See SBBH1:14 for a possible explanation for Mullá Ḥusayn's presence in Shíráz at this time.
- See BBRSM42–3 and DB57 for a list of signs by which the Promised One could be known.

- This date marks the end of the Adamic Cycle of approximately six thousand years and the beginning of the Bahá'í Cycle or Cycle of Fulfilment. [BBD9, 35, 72; GPB100]

- The beginning of the Apostolic, Heroic or Primitive Age. [BBD35, 67]

- See BBD113, DB383 and MH for information on Mullá Ḥusayn-i-Bushrú'í.

- See MH86–7 for an explanation of the implication of the word 'Báb' to the Shí'í Muslims.

- Three stages of the Báb's Revelation:

    1. He chooses the title 'Báb' and Mullá Ḥusayn is given the title Bábu'l-Báb (the gate of the Gate).

    2. In the second year of the Revelation (from His confinement in the house of His uncle in Shíráz) He takes the title of Siyyid-i-Dhikr (dhikr means 'remembrance of God') and gives the title 'Báb' to Mullá Ḥusayn. At Fort Ṭabarsí Mullá Ḥusayn is called 'Jináb-i Báb' by his companions.

    3. At His public declaration the Báb declares Himself to be the promised Qá'im. [MH87–8]

23 May The birth of 'Abdu'l-Bahá in Ṭihrán at midnight. [AB9]

- He is known as 'Abbás Effendi outside the Bahá'í community.

- Bahá'u'lláh gives Him the titles Ghuṣn-i-A'ẓam (the Most Great Branch), Sirru'lláh (Mystery of God) and Áqá (the Master). [BBD2, 19, 87, 89]

- Sarkár-Áqá (the Honourable Master) is a title of 'Abdu'l-Bahá. [BBD201]

- He Himself chose the title 'Abdu'l-Bahá (Servant of Bahá) after the passing of Bahá'u'lláh. [BBD2]

Jul–Aug Forty days after the Declaration of the Báb, the second Letter of the

Living, Mullá 'Alíy-i-Basṭámí, has a vision that leads him to Mullá Ḥusayn and he accepts the Báb. Sixteen others recognize Siyyid 'Alí-Muḥammad as the Promised One. The 18 are later designated 'Letters of the Living'. [B21–7; DB63–71, 80–2; MH73–81, MH121; SBBH1:16–17]

- See RB2:145–6 for the fate of the Letters of the Living.

- See B26–7, BBD138, DB80–1, MH81 for a list of the Letters of the Living.

- See BBRSM24–5 for more on the Letters of the Living.

- See BBRSM24–5 for a discussion of the special places occupied by Quddús, Mullá Ḥusayn and Ṭáhirih.

11 Aug The Báb sends Mullá 'Alíy-i-Basṭámí to Najaf and Karbalá to proclaim His Cause among the Shaykhís. In Najaf Mullá 'Alí delivers a letter from the Báb to Shaykh Muḥammad-Ḥasan Najafí, the leading Shí'í divine and the keeper of the shrines in Iraq. [BBRSM15; DB87–91; SBBH20–1]

- The Shaykh's rejection of the claim leads to violent debate. Mullá 'Alí is taken to Baghdád and imprisoned there. After a public trial, a joint tribunal of Sunní and Shí'í 'ulamá, he is sent to Istanbul. He is the first martyr of the Bábí Dispensation. It is significant that Mullá Ḥasan Gawhar, a leading figure of the Sháykhí school, participated in the condemnation as it marks the first major challenge to Bábism from a Shaykhí leader. [B27, 37–8, 58; BBR83–90; BBRSM 17; BKG31; DB90–2; MMBA]

c. Aug The intention of the Báb is to introduce the new Revelation slowly so as not to cause estrangement. [BBRSM14–16, 36; SWB119]

- The Báb addresses the Letters of the Living, giving each a specific task. [DB92–4; MH82–6; SBBH1:19]

- To Mullá Ḥusayn He assigns the task of delivering a Tablet to Bahá'u'lláh in Ṭihrán and going to the court of the Sháh to apprise him of the Báb's cause. Mullá Ḥusayn is not able to gain access to the Sháh. [B48–57; BBRSM15; BKG32–3; CH22–3; DB85–7, 97; MH90–2, 102]

• See DB99 for the story of Mullá Ja'far, the sifter of wheat, who is the first to embrace the Cause of the Báb in the city of Iṣfahán.

• See MH96 for information on Munírih, future wife of 'Abdu'l-Bahá.

• After Iṣfahán, Mullá Ḥusayn visits Káshán, about 130 miles from Iṣfahán. He then goes to Qum, about 100 miles from Káshán. After Qum he goes to Ṭihrán. [MH98–101]

• See B53–6; DB104–7, MH104–11 for the delivery of the Báb's Tablet to Bahá'u'lláh.

• Mullá Ḥusayn does not meet Bahá'u'lláh on this occasion. [MH110]

• Mullá Ḥusayn carries to Ṭihrán a Tablet revealed by the Báb for Muḥammad Sháh. This is the first of a number of unsuccessful attempts to enlist his aid. [BBRSM20–1; MH102; SWB13]

• See RB2:303, 'The Báb . . . sent Tablets to only two monarchs of His day – Muḥammad Sháh of Persia and Sulṭán 'Abdu'l-Majíd of Turkey.'

On receiving the Tablet of the Báb, Bahá'u'lláh accepts His Cause. He immediately journeys to Mázindarán, His native province, to promote the Cause of the Báb. [BKG39–40; BW8:782; DB109; TN35]

Mullá Ḥusayn leaves for Khurásán, winning supporters for the Báb's Cause while there.

• He writes to the Báb regarding these new believers and Bahá'u-'lláh's immediate response to the Báb's Revelation. [B56, DB128–9, MH118]

• See MH121–2 for a discussion of the speed of Mullá Ḥusayn's journey before the letter was dispatched to the Báb.

9 Sep The Báb, Quddús (Ḥájí Mullá Muḥammad-'Alíy-i-Bárfurúshí) and the Báb's Ethiopian servant, Mubarak, leave Shíráz for Búshihr en route to Mecca. The journey takes ten days. [B57; DB129; MH119]

30 Sep The Báb receives the letter from Mullá Ḥusayn giving Him details of his journey and meeting with Bahá'u'lláh. [MH118–19]

Notes *Nabíl indicates that the Báb received the letter on 9 October (26 Ramaḍan) and that it was a deciding factor in His decision to undertake the pilgrimage.* [DB126–7, 129] *Balyuzi says soon after the Báb received the letter, 'in the month of September' He left Shíráz'.* [B57]

See MH119 *for a discussion of this discrepancy.*

2 or 3 Oct The Báb departs on His pilgrimage. [B57; MH119, 121]

- He instructs His followers to await His arrival in Karbalá. [DB86, 87; MH122; SBBH1:23]
- He has been awaiting the letter from Mullá Ḥusayn before starting on His pilgrimage. [DB123; MH117]
- The vessel taking the Báb to Jiddah is probably the Arab sailing-boat named *Futúḥ-ar-Ras'úl.* [B69]

c. Dec The Báb and His companions arrive in Jiddah after a rough sea voyage of two months. There they put on the garb of the pilgrim and proceed to Mecca by camel. [B71; DB129, 132]

- See B69–71 and DB130–1 for a description of the voyage.
- Quddús walks from Jiddah to Mecca. [B71, DB132, GPB9]

12 Dec The Báb arrives in Mecca and performs the rites of pilgrimage in company with 100,000 other pilgrims. [GPB9]

- See B70 and SA107–8 for the timing, rites and significance of the pilgrimage.

20 Dec The Báb offers 19 lambs as a sacrifice in the prescribed manner, distributing the meat to the poor and needy. [B71; DB133]

c. 20 Dec The Báb makes a declaration of His mission by standing at the Ka'bih and repeating three times that He is the Qá'im.

- He makes an open challenge to Mírzá Muḥammad-Ḥusayn-i-Kirmání, known as Muḥíṭ, of the Shaykhí school and sends an invitation to the Sharíf of Mecca to embrace the new Revelation. The Sharíf is too busy to respond. [B73–4; BW12:89; DB134–8; GPB9, 89]

1845

c. 1845 Birth of Mírzá 'Alí-Muḥammad-i-Khurásání, later known as Ibn-i-Aṣdaq, Hand of the Cause.

c. Jan Crowds gather in Karbalá in response to the Báb's summons, among them Ṭáhirih. [B162; BBRSM15, 215; SBBH1:22]

10 Jan The beginning of the Islamic new year. Messianic fervour grows, particularly among Shaykhís. [BBRSM15]

13 Jan The trial of Mullá 'Alíy-i-Basṭámí in Baghdád. [B64; BBRSM15, 215; SBBH21, 22]

c. 13 Jan A *fatwá* is issued in Baghdád against both Mullá 'Alíy-i-Basṭámí and the Báb, condemning the Báb, who is unnamed in the *fatwá*, to death as an unbeliever.

16 Jan The Báb arrives in Medina from Mecca. [KHUT BÍY-I-JIDDIH]

- He reveals 'The Epistle between Two Shrines' en route. [B73–4]
- He stays 27 days. [MS2]

Notes B75 *and* DB140 *indicate that the Báb arrived 10 January. The Research Department at the Bahá'í World Centre states that the date 16 January accords with the Báb's own writings.* [REPORT 20 JAN 1994]

12 Feb The Báb leaves Medina for Jiddah. [MS2]

27 Feb The Báb leaves Jiddah. [MS2]

- He disembarks at Muscat and remains there for two months, awaiting news of the outcome of Mullá 'Alíy-i-Basṭámí's trial. [MS2]
- He sends a letter to the Imám of Muscat. [MS2]

Notes SBBH23 *says the Báb left Jiddah on 4 March.*

c. 16 Apr Mullá 'Alíy-i-Basṭámí is removed from his prison cell in Baghdád and taken to Istanbul, where he is sentenced to hard labour in the imperial naval dockyard.

c. late Apr/ early May The Báb returns to Búshihr. He sends Quddús to Shíráz with a letter addressed to His uncle Ḥájí Mírzá Siyyid 'Alí who embraces his nephew's Cause. The Báb also entrusts Quddús with a treatise entitled Khaṣá'il-i-Sab'ih ('the Seven Qualifications') and promises him his impending martyrdom. [B77–8; DB142–3; MS2]

Notes B77 *and* GPB10 *say the Báb arrived in Búshihr in Feb-Mar.;* SSBH1:23 *says 15 May.*

- Before leaving on pilgrimage the Báb had stated that He would return to Karbalá and asked His followers to congregate there. An explanation in part for the large following that have gathered there is the messianic expectation associated with the year 1261, a thousand years after the Twelfth Imám's disappearance in 260 AH. This gathering is perceived as a threat by the authorities. [BBRSM15, 45, 216; DB157–8; SBBH1:23, 32]

- The Báb changes His plan to meet His followers in Karbalá and instructs them to go to Iṣfahán instead. A number abandon Him, regarding this as *badá'* 'alteration of divine will'. [BBRSM16; DB158; MH125; SBBH23]

- Some speculate that He did not go to Karbalá to avoid conflict and sedition. Many Bábís had gone to Karbalá armed in preparation for holy war, 'jihád'. [BBRSM21–2; SBBH1:23]

Jun Quddús meets Mullá Ṣádiq-i-Muqaddas in Shíráz. Mullá Ṣádiq, following instructions received in a Tablet from the Báb, sounds the call to prayer using the additional words provided by the Báb. [B78; DB144]

- This provokes a public commotion. [B78; DB145; BBRSM16]

23 Jun The governor of Fárs, Ḥusayn Khán, has Quddús, Mullá Sádiq-i-Khurásání, Mullá 'Alí-Akbar-i-Ardistání and Mullá Abú-Ṭálib arrested, tortured and expelled from Shíráz. [B78; BBR69; BW18:380; DB145–8; GPB11]

- See B78–84 and BBR169–71 for background on Ḥusayn Khán.

Notes B78 *says that Mullá Abú-Ṭálib was not among the group.*

The governor orders that the Báb be arrested and brought to Shíráz. [B84; BW18:380; DB148–50; GPB11]

• The Báb leaves Bú<u>sh</u>ihr for <u>Sh</u>íráz on an unknown date. [B105]

28 Jun Prince Dolgorukov is appointed Russian ambassador to Ṭihrán. He was previously first secretary of the Russian legation at Istanbul. He arrives in Ṭihrán in January 1846.

30 Jun The Báb meets the soldiers of the governor of Fárs who had been sent to arrest Him at Dálakí, some 40 miles northeast of the city. He is escorted to <u>Sh</u>íráz. [B84, 105; BBR170; BBRSM216; DB148–9; GPB11; TN6]

Notes DB150 *says the Báb travelled 'free and unfettered', 'before His escort'.* BBRSM16 *implies the Báb returned to <u>Sh</u>íráz by Himself in July and that He was placed under house arrest on arrival.*

c. 7 Jul The Báb is publicly interrogated, struck in the face and later released into the custody of His maternal uncle Ḥájí Mírzá Siyyid 'Alí. [B85–9; BBRSM216; DB150–1; GPB11]

Notes B105 *says it must have taken the Báb another week at least to reach <u>Sh</u>íráz;* SBBH1:24 *says He arrived in <u>Sh</u>íráz in early July.*

Jul and months following The Báb is told to attend a Friday gathering at the Mosque of Vakíl to appease the hostility and the curiosity of some of the residents of <u>Sh</u>íráz and to clarify His position. The exact date of His attendance is unknown. He makes a public pronouncement that He is neither the representative of the Hidden Imám nor the gate to him, that is, His station is higher. [B94–8; DB151–7]

• see DB152 for pictures of the above mosque.

Upon hearing the news of the confinement of the Báb, Mullá Ḥusayn and his companions leave Iṣfahán where they have been awaiting further instructions and travel to <u>Sh</u>íráz. Mullá Ḥusayn is able to meet secretly with the Báb several times in the house of His uncle. The Báb sends word to the remainder of His followers in Iṣfahán to leave and travel to <u>Sh</u>íráz. [B102–3; MH128–9]

After a time the presence of Mullá Ḥusayn in <u>Sh</u>íráz threatens to cause civil unrest. The Báb instructs him to go to <u>Kh</u>urásán via Yazd and Kirmán and tells the rest of the companions to return to Iṣfahán. [B90, 102–3; DB170; MH130]

• This time, described as the 'most fecund period' of the Báb's ministry, marks the birth of the Bábí community. [B89–90]

The Sháh sends one of the most learned men in Persia, Siyyid Yaḥyáy-i-Dárábí, surnamed Vaḥíd, to investigate the claims of the Báb. He becomes a follower of the Báb. As a result of his conversion most of the inhabitants of the town of Nayríz later become Bábís. [B90–4; BBD216; BBRSM41; CH21; DB171–7; GPB11–12; TN7–8]

Another learned scholar, Muḥammad-'Alíy-i-Zanjání, surnamed Ḥujjat, becomes a believer after reading only one page of the Qayyúmu'l-Asmá'. Several thousand of his fellow townspeople become Bábís. [B100–2; BBD111; BBRSM16; GPB12]

Mírzá Aḥmad-i-Azg̲h̲andí, yet another learned man, who had compiled traditions and prophecies concerning the expected Revelation, becomes a believer as well. [GPB12–13]

In Karbalá Ṭáhirih revives the remnant of the Bábí community there. She is considered a part of the radical element of S̲h̲ayk̲h̲í-Bábís because she believes that the S̲h̲ayk̲h̲í tradition has been abrogated by the new Revelation. The new Bábí movement causes the S̲h̲ayk̲h̲í leaders to unite in their opposition to the Báb and to redefine the nature of the school, toning down its more controversial teachings and moving back towards mainstream S̲h̲í'ism. [BBRSM16–18]

In Kirmán, Karím K̲h̲án, the leading S̲h̲ayk̲h̲í cleric, has a number of Bábís expelled from the city and writes a number of refutations. The first, *Isháqu'l-Báṭil* (*The Crushing of Falsehood*) is published in July. This causes some Bábís to dissociate themselves from S̲h̲ayk̲h̲ism. [BBRSM17–18]

1 Nov *The Times* of London carries an item on the arrest and torture of Quddús, Mullá Ṣádiq-i-K̲h̲urásání, Mullá 'Alí-Akbar-i-Ardistání and Mullá Abú-Ṭálib in S̲h̲íráz in June. This is the first known printed reference to the Revelation. A similar article is reprinted on 19 November. [B76–7; BBR4, 69]

30 Dec The Báb's birthday falls on the first day of the mourning observance for the Imám Ḥusayn. Ṭáhirih, who is in Karbalá with the widow of Siyyid Káẓim-i-Ras̲h̲tí, instructs her relatives and the Bábís to dress in bright clothing and joyously celebrate the Báb's birth. This causes a considerable disturbance, even among the Bábís. Ṭáhirih is arrested and expelled from the city. [RR305, SA217]

1846

In the year The birth of Bahíyyih Khánum, the Greatest Holy Leaf, eldest daughter of Bahá'u'lláh and Navváb, and sister of 'Abdu'l-Bahá, in Ṭihrán. She is later designated by Shoghi Effendi 'the outstanding heroine of the Bahá'í Dispensation'. [BBD42; GPB108]

• For a description of her nature see BK42–3.

Bahíyyih Khánum, circa 1890

Many Bábís go to Shíráz and meet the Báb. [B103]

Ṭáhirih is sent back to Baghdád from Karbalá. She is lodged first in the house of Shaykh Muḥammad Shibl and then in the house of the Muftí of Baghdád. During her time in Iraq she enlists a considerable number of followers and makes a number of enemies among the clergy. [B162; DB271]

Jan Prince Dolgorukov arrives in Ṭihrán as Russian ambassador.

summer The Báb bequeaths all His possessions to His mother and His wife and reveals a special prayer for His wife to help her in times of sorrow. He tells his wife of His impending martyrdom. He moves to the house of His uncle Ḥájí Mírzá Siyyid 'Alí. He tells the Bábís in Shíráz to go to Iṣfahán. [GPB14; KB21–2; TB103–5]

23 Sep The governor, Ḥusayn Khán, threatened by the Báb's rising popularity, orders His arrest. The chief constable, 'Abdu'l-Ḥamíd Khán, takes the Báb into custody and escorts Him to the governor's home but finds it abandoned. He takes the Báb to his own home and learns that a cholera epidemic has swept the city and that his sons have been stricken. At the chief constable's insistence the Báb cures the boys by requesting they drink some of the water with which He has washed His own face. 'Abdu'l-Ḥamíd resigns his post and begs the governor to release the Báb. He agrees on condition the Báb leaves Shíráz. The incident proves to be Ḥusayn Khán's undoing: the Sháh dismisses him from office shortly after. [B104–5; BBRSM55; DB194–7; GPB13; TN9]

• See BBR170–1 and DB197 for the fate of Ḥusayn Khán.

Notes DB196–7 *says 'Abdu'l-Ḥamíd Khán had only one ill son.*

23–4 Sep The Báb departs for Iṣfahán after a sojourn in Shíráz of less than 15 months. [B105–6; BBRSM216; BW18:380; TN9]

Notes TN9 *says that the Báb left Shíráz 'the morning after' the night He saved the children from cholera;* B105 *says he left 'in the last days of September'.*

Sep–Oct On His approach to the city the Báb writes to Manúchihr Khán, the governor-general of Iṣfahán, and asks him for shelter. The governor requests that Siyyid Muḥammad, the Imám-Jum'ih of Iṣfahán, accommodate Him. During His stay of 40 days the Báb impresses His host as well as the governor. [B109–10, 13; DB199–202, 208]

• See B108–9 for information on Manúchihr Khán.

c. Nov Manúchihr Khán arranges a meeting between the Báb and the clerics to silence their opposition. After the encounter, about 70 of them meet and issue a death-warrant. [B112–13; DB205–9]

c. Feb–Mar 1847 The Sháh had already instructed Manúchihr Khán to send the Báb to Ṭihrán. The governor, fearing for the safety of the Báb, devises a scheme to have the Báb escorted from Iṣfahán but returned secretly to his own residence. The Báb remains there for four months with only three of His followers apprised of His whereabouts. These four months are described as having been the calmest in His Ministry. [B113–16; DB209–11, 213; TN9–11]

- It is during His six-month stay in Iṣfahán that the Báb takes a second wife, Fáṭimih, the sister of a Bábí from that city. [RB1:249]

The governor offers all of his resources to try to win the Sháh over to His Cause but the Báb declines his offer saying that the Cause will triumph through the 'poor and lowly'. [B115–16; DB212–13]

Dec Mullá 'Alíy-i-Basṭámí dies in Istanbul naval dockyards. He is the first martyr of the Bábí Dispensation.

1847

Feb–Mar The passing of Manúchihr Khán. His death had been predicted by the Báb 87 days earlier. The governor had made the Báb the beneficiary of his vast holdings, estimated to be 40 million francs, but his nephew Gurgín Khán appropriated everything after his death. [B116; DB213–14]

- Before the death of Manúchihr Khán the Báb instructed His followers to disperse. [B115; DB213–14]

Gurgín Khán, in his role as the new governor, informs the Sháh that the Báb is in Iṣfahán and has been sheltering with Manúchihr Khán. The Sháh orders that the Báb be taken to Ṭihrán incognito. The Báb, escorted by Nuṣayrí horsemen, sets out for Ṭihrán soon after midnight. [B116, 118; DB215–16; TN11]

22 Feb Birth of Thornton Chase, designated the first American Bahá'í, in Springfield, Massachusetts.

21 Mar En route to Ṭihrán the Báb spends three nights in Káshán in the home of Ḥájí Mírzá Jání, a noted resident of that city who had realized in a dream that the Báb would be his quest. [B118; DB217–22]

28 Mar The Báb and His escort arrive at the fortress of Kinár-Gird, 28 miles from Ṭihrán. Muḥammad Big, the head of the escort, receives a message from Ḥájí Mírzá Áqásí, the prime minister, telling him to take the Báb to Kulayn to await further instructions. [B119; DB225–6; GPB16]

29 Mar The Báb arrives in Kulayn where He stays for 20 days. [B120; DB227; TN11]

1 Apr The Báb receives a letter and gifts from Bahá'u'lláh in Ṭihrán. The letter cheers His heart, which has been despondent since His arrest and departure from Shíráz. [B120; DB227; GPB67–8]

c. 1–17 Apr One night the Báb disappears and is found the next morning on the road coming from the direction of Ṭihrán. A look of confidence has settled on Him and His words have a new power. [B120–1; DB228–9]

c. 17 Apr The Báb sends a letter to the Sháh requesting an audience. [B121; DB229; TN11]

Apr The Báb receives a courteous message from the Sháh, who, on the advice of his prime minister, Ḥájí Mírzá Áqásí, assigns Him to the fortress of Máh-Kú in the province of Ádharbáyján. The Báb is taken to Máh-Kú via Tabríz. [B121–2, 124; DB229–32; GPB16; TN11–12]

Notes *Some accounts maintain that the prime minister intervened in the correspondence between the Báb and the Sháh.*

En route to Tabríz the Báb writes to various people, including the Grand Vizier, the father and uncle of Ṭáhirih, and Ḥájí Sulaymán Khán. Ḥujjat learns of this last and sends a message to the Bábís of Zanján to rescue the Báb. The Báb declines their assistance. [B124–5; DB235–6]

- See B126 for an account of the Báb's demonstration to His guards that He could have escaped had He so wished.

c. May Birth of Fáṭimih (Munírih) Khánum, wife of 'Abdu'l-Bahá, in Iṣfahán.

c. May–Jun The Báb arrives in Tabríz, en route to Máh-Kú. He remains for 40 days and is well received by the general populace. He spends His time in seclusion, being allowed only two visitors. [B127–8; DB237–40; GPB18; TN12]

Jul The Báb arrives at the prison fortress of Máh-Kú (the Open Mountain). [B128; BW18:380]

Máh-Kú. The castle prison is at the base of the overhanging rock above the village.

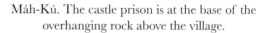

- See B128, BBD142 and DB243–4 for descriptions of Máh-Kú, its environs, fortress and inhabitants.

Jul–Apr 1848 The people of Máh-Kú show marked hostility to the Báb on His arrival. Later they are won over by His gentle manners and His love. They congregate at the foot of the mountain hoping to catch a glimpse of Him. [B129; DB244–5]

At the beginning of the Báb's incarceration the warden 'Alí Khán keeps the Báb strictly confined and allows no visitors. He has a vision of the Báb engaged in prayer outside of the prison gates, knowing that the Báb is inside. He becomes humble and permits the Bábís to visit the Báb. [B129–31; DB245–8]

1847

The winter the Báb spends in Máh-Kú is exceptionally cold. [DB252]

Many of the Báb's writings are revealed in this period. [GPB24–5]

- It was probably at this time that He addressed all the divines in Persia and Najaf and Karbalá, detailing the errors committed by each one of them. [GPB24]

- He revealed nine commentaries on the whole of the Qur'án, the fate of which is unknown. [GPB24]

- He revealed the Persian Bayán, containing the laws and precepts of the new Revelation in some 8,000 verses. It is primarily a eulogy of the Promised One. [BBD44–5; BBRSM32; BW12:91 GPB24–5]

- The Báb began the composition of the 'smaller and less weighty' Arabic Bayán. [B132; BBD45; GPB25]

- He stated in the Bayán that, to date, He had revealed some 500,000 verses, 100,000 of which had been circulated. [BBRSM32, GPB22]

- In the Dalá'il-i-Sab'ih (Seven Proofs) the Báb assigned blame to the seven powerful sovereigns then ruling the world and censured the conduct of the Christian divines who, had they recognized Muḥammad, would have been followed by the greater part of their co-religionists. [BBD63; BW12:96; GPB26]

- The Báb wrote His 'most detailed and illuminating' Tablet to Muḥammad Sháh. [GPB26]

spring–summer Ṭáhirih's activities in Iraq so alarm some Bábís of Káẓimayn that they agitate against her. Siyyid 'Alí Bishr writes to the Báb in Máh-Kú on their behalf. The Báb replies praising Ṭáhirih, causing the Káẓimayn Bábís to withdraw from the Faith. [B163]

- Among those Ṭáhirih meets in Baghdád is Ḥakím Masíḥ, a Jewish doctor who years later becomes the first Bahá'í of Jewish background. [B165]

Ṭáhirih is sent back to Persia by Najíb Páshá. She is accompanied by a number of Bábís; they make a number of stops along the way, enrolling supporters for the Cause of the Báb. [B163–4; BBRSM216]

Notes *Ma'ani says Ṭáhirih left Baghdád early in 1847.*

- In Kirand 1,200 people are reported to have volunteered to follow her. [BI64; DB272; TN20]

Notes BI64 *says the number is 12,000;* DB272 *says it was 1,200.*

- In Kirmánsháh she is respectfully received by the 'ulamá. [BI64; DB272]

Ṭáhirih arrives in Hamadán. Her father has sent her brothers here to persuade her to return to her native city of Qazvín. She agrees on condition that she may remain in Hamadán long enough to tell people about the Báb. [BI65; DB273]

- MF180 says Ṭáhirih remained in Hamadán for two months.

Aug Ṭáhirih sends Mullá Ibráhim Maḥallátí to present to the chief mujtahid of Hamadán her dissertation in defence of the Bábí Cause. Maḥallátí is attacked and severely beaten.

c. Aug–Sep On her departure from Hamadán Ṭáhirih asks most of the Arab Bábís travelling with her to return to Iraq. [BI65; DB273]

Arrived in Qazvín, Ṭáhirih refuses her estranged husband's attempts at reconciliation and lives with her father. Her father-in-law, Ḥájí Mullá Taqí, feels insulted and denounces the Shaykhís and Bábís. [BI66; DB273–6]

Meanwhile, Mullá Ḥusayn is residing in Mashhad, in Khurásán, where he has been since returning from Shíráz in 1845. The leader of a local rebellion wishes to enlist the Bábís on his side and seeks a meeting with Mullá Ḥusayn. To avoid entanglement in the affair, Mullá Ḥusayn decides to make a pilgrimage to Máh-Kú. [TB56; DB254–5; MH133–5]

As an act of piety, he makes the whole 1,200-mile journey on foot. Along the route he visits the Bábís and in Ṭihrán meets secretly with Bahá'u'lláh. No account of their interview survives. In Qazvín, Mullá Ḥusayn meets Ṭáhirih for the first time. [DB255; MH137]

Sep or Oct The murder of Ḥájí Mullá Muḥammad Taqí, the powerful uncle of Ṭáhirih, by Mullá 'Abdu'lláh of Shíráz. [BI66; BBRSM216; DB276–8]

Notes BBRSM22 *says the murder took place towards the end of October.*

- Mullá 'Abdu'lláh indicatew that he was 'never a convinced Bábí'. [DB276]

Oct–Nov Ṭáhirih is accused of instigating the assassination of her uncle and is confined to her father's house while about 30 Bábís are arrested. Four, including the assassin, are taken to Ṭihrán and held in the house of Khusraw Khán. [BKG41; BW18:380; DB276–8]

Nov–Dec Bahá'u'lláh, who is living in Ṭihrán, visits the detainees and gives them money. [BKG41; DB278–9; GPB68]

Mullá 'Abdu'lláh confesses to the murder of Ḥájí Mullá Muḥammad Taqí and is helped to escape. [BKG41–2; DB278]

- See BKG42 for why Bahá'u'lláh was thought to have engineered his escape.

Bahá'u'lláh is imprisoned for a few days for having assisted in Mullá 'Abdu'lláh's escape.

- This was Bahá'u'lláh's first imprisonment. [BKG41; BW18:380; DB585]

Shaykh Ṣáliḥ-i-Karímí, one of the imprisoned Bábís, is publicly executed in Ṭihrán.

- He is the first to suffer martyrdom on Persian soil. His remains are interred in the courtyard of the shrine of the Imán-Zádih Zayd in Ṭihrán. [B166; BW18:380; DB280]

The remaining captives are returned to Qazvín. Ḥájí Asadu'lláh-i-Farhádí is secretly put to death in prison. Mullá Ṭáhir-i-Shírází and Mullá Ibráhím-i-Maḥallátí are also put to death. [B166; BW18:380; DB280–3]

Note DB280–3 *says 'the rest of' the detainees were put to death by the relatives of Ḥájí Mullá Muḥammad Taqí.*

1848

In the year The birth of Mírzá Midhí, 'the Purest Branch', the son of Bahá'u-'lláh and Navváb. [BBD155]

Bahá'u'lláh plans Ṭáhirih's escape, giving the task to Mírzá Hádíy-i-Farhádí, the nephew of Ḥájí Asadu'lláh-i-Farhádí. Ṭáhirih is rescued and escorted from Qazvín to Bahá'u'lláh's home in Ṭihrán. [B:167; BKG42; DB284–5; MF199]

- While she is in Bahá'u'lláh's home she is visited by Vaḥíd and challenges him by saying 'Let deeds, not words, be our adorning!' [DB285; MF200]

- After a few days Bahá'u'lláh sends Ṭáhirih to a place of safety before sending her on to Khurásán. [DB286–7; GPB68]

Notes *Ma'ani says this was the house of Mírzá Áqá Khán-i Núrí, who was then living in Káshán as an exile. His sister acted as Ṭáhirih's hostess until she left for Badasht.*

20 Mar Mullá Ḥusayn and his companion, walking from Mashhad, arrive at Máh-Kú on the eve of Naw-Rúz. The Báb meets them at the gate and together they celebrate Naw-Rúz, the fourth after the declaration of the Báb. Mullá Ḥusayn stays the night at the fortress. He remains with the Báb for nine days. [B:131; DB257, 262; MH138, 143]

Notes MH137 *says Mullá Ḥusayn arrived in Tabríz on 21 March.*

- See DB255–7 for story of the dream of 'Alí Khán, the prison warden, preceding the arrival of Mullá Ḥusayn at Máh-Kú. From this time on the pilgrims are allowed unrestricted access to the Báb. [DB258]

- The warden requests that the Báb marry his daughter. [DB259; MH143]

30 Mar Mullá Ḥusayn departs for Mázindarán, setting out on foot as the Báb has directed. [DB260; MH144]

- The Báb tells him to visit the Bábís in Khuy, Urúmíyyih, Marághih, Milán, Tabríz, Zanján, Qazvín and Ṭihrán before proceeding to Mázindarán. In Mázindarán he is to find 'God's hidden treasure'. [DB260; MH144]

- In Ṭihrán he again meets Bahá'u'lláh. [DB261; MH148]

9 Apr The Báb is removed from Máh-Kú.

- Ḥájí Mírzá Áqásí is alarmed by the developments at Máh-Kú and orders that the Báb be moved to Chihríq. [B131; DB259; GPB19–20]

- The Báb's presence in Máh-Kú, so close to the Russian frontier, is also a cause for concern for the Russian government. Prince Dolgorukov, the Russian Minister in Ṭihrán, asks that He be removed. It is likely that this request was made in 1847 but not carried out until now. [B131; BBR72; TN13]

- The Báb had been in Máh-Kú for nine months. [DB259]

10 Apr The Báb is transferred to the fortress of Chihríq, 'Jabal-i-Shadíd' (the Grievous Mountain) into the custody of Yaḥyá Khán, a brother-in-law of Muḥammad Sháh. [BR72; BBRSM216; GPB19]

The prison at Chihríq

- He remains here for two years. [BBD55; BBR73; GPB27]

- He is subjected to a more rigorous confinement than He had been at Máh-Kú and the warden is harsh and unpredictable. [B135; DB302]

Apr–Jul The presence of the Báb in Chihríq attracts much notice. Eventually Yaḥyá Khán softens his attitude to the Báb. [B135; DB303]

- Excitement among local people eclipses that of Máh-Kú. [GPB20]
- Many priests and government officials become followers, among them Mírzá Asadu'lláh of Khuy, surnamed Dayyán. [B136; DB303; GPB20]
- So many Bábís come to Chihríq that they cannot all be housed. [B135]
- See B136 for story of the inferior honey.
- A dervish, a former navváb, arrives from India after having seen the Báb in a vision. [B137; DB305; GPB20]
- The Báb reveals the Lawḥ-i-Ḥurúfat (Tablet of the Letters) in honour of Dayyán. [DB304; GPB27]

late spring Mullá Ḥusayn goes to the house of Quddús in Bárfurúsh, Mázindarán, and realizes that the 'hidden treasure' is his recognition of the station of Quddús. [DB261–5; MH148–54]

Mullá Ḥusayn proceeds to Mashhad and builds a 'Bábíyyih', a centre for the Bábís, as instructed by Quddús. He and Quddús take up residence in it and begin to teach the Bábí religion. [DB260–7 MH157–8]

- See DB288–90 and MH158–68 for the result of this effort.
- Among those who come to the Bábíyyih is Sám Khán, the chief of police. [MH158]
- See MH156 for a picture of the Bábíyyih.

summer Quddús leaves Mashhad for Badasht. Mullá Ḥusayn is prevented from attending. He is invited to stay in the camp of the soldiers garrisoned in the area to control a local revolt. The invitation amounts to a confinement but he is able to teach the soldiers while so confined. [BKG50; DB290; MH165–6]

Notes MH160 *says that it was at this time that the Báb wrote to all the believers in Persia and Iraq* *instructing them to go to the aid of Mullá Ḥusayn and Quddús in the 'Land of Khá (Khurásán).* DB269ff *implies this letter was written in 1845.*

c. 26 Jun – 17 Jul **The Conference of Badasht**

Bahá'u'lláh, who hosts and directs the event, rents three gardens, one for Quddús, another for Ṭáhirih and the third for Himself. [BI68; GPB31, 68; MF200]

The conference coincides with the removal of the Báb to Tabríz for interrogation in July.

It is held near the village of Sháhrúd. [BBRSM23; DB292]

- 'The primary purpose of that gathering was to implement the revelation of the Bayán by a sudden, a complete and dramatic break with the past – with its order, its ecclesiasticism, its traditions, and ceremonials. The subsidiary purpose of the conference was to consider the means of emancipating the Báb from His cruel confinement in Chihriq.' [BBRSM23; BKG43; DB297–8; GPB31, 157]

Notes BI67 *says that the Bábís did not come to Badasht to make plans to rescue the Báb.*

It is attended by 81 believers and lasts 22 days. [BKG43–4, 46; DB292–3; GPB31–2]

Each day Bahá'u'lláh reveals a Tablet, and on each believer He confers a new name. Each day an Islamic law is abrogated. [DB293; GPB32]

- See BKG44–5, DB293 and MF201 for the story of the central event, Ṭáhirih's confrontation with Quddús and removal of her veil.

See also BI67–9; BBD31–2; BBRSM46; BKG43–7; DB292–8; RB2:353.

c. 17 Jul The Bábís leave Badasht for Mázindarán. They are attacked by a mob of more than 500 outside the village of Niyálá. [BI70–1; BKG46–7; BW18:380; DB298; GPB68]

Bahá'u'lláh travels to Núr with Ṭáhirih. He entrusts her into the care of Shaykh Abú-Turáb-i-Ishtahárdí, to be taken to a place of safety. [BKG48; DB299]

- Bahá'u'lláh travels to Núr 'in easy stages'. By September He is in Bandar-Jaz. [BKG48]

Jul After three months in Chihríq, the Báb is taken under escort to Tabríz for trial. [B137; BW18:380; TN14]

- En route He stops in Urúmíyyih where the governor tests the Báb by offering Him an unruly horse to ride. The local people take away His bath water. [B138; BBR74; DB309–11]

- A sketch of the Báb is made there and later two copies of the portrait are made in water colour. The sketch and one of the water colours are now in the International Archives. [B138–9]

c. Jul Quddús is arrested and taken to Sárí where he is placed under house arrest in the home of Mírzá Muḥammad-Taqí, a leading cleric. [B171; BKG50; DB300]

Ṭáhirih is arrested and is later taken to Ṭihrán where she is held in the home of Maḥmúd Khán, the Kalántar of Ṭihrán, until her martyrdom in August 1852.

Mullá Ḥusayn leaves the army camp near Mashhad where he has been a guest of a brother of the Sháh. He plans to make a pilgrimage to Karbalá. While making preparations for the journey he receives a Tablet from the Báb instructing him to go to Mázindarán to help Quddús, carrying a Black Standard before him. He is also instructed to wear the Báb's own green turban and to take the new name Siyyid 'Alí. [B171; BKG50; DB324; MH174]

21 Jul Mullá Ḥusayn and his companions leave Mashhad for Mázindarán. They will arrive in September. [BBRSM26, 216]

ast week in Jul The Báb arrives in Tabríz and is brought before a panel of which the 17-year-old Crown Prince Náṣiri'd-Dín Mírzá is the president. The Báb publicly makes His claim that He is the Qá'im. This claim has also been announced to those gathered at Badasht. [B140–7; BBR157; BBRSM23, 216; BW18:380; DB314–20; GPB21–2; TN14]

- This constitutes the formal declaration of His mission. [GPB22]

- The purpose of the public forum is to force the Báb to recant His views; instead He takes control of the hearing and embarrasses the clergy. After considerable argument and discussion, they decide He is devoid of reason. [GPB22]

The Báb is bastinadoed. [B145; BBD44; DB320; GPB22; TN14–15]

- This is the first formal punishment He receives. [BBRSM20]
- He is first attended by an Irish physician, Dr William Cormick, to ascertain His sanity. Cormick is the only Westerner to meet Him. [B145; BBR74–5, 497–8; DBXXXII–XXXIII]

The clergy issue a *fatwá* or legal pronouncement against the Báb condemning Him to death for heresy, but to no purpose as the civil authorities are unwilling to take action against Him. [BBRSM19–20]

Jul–Sep Mullá Ḥusayn and his companions, marching to Mázindarán, are joined by Bábís who had been at Badasht as well as newly-converted Bábís. [B171–2]

- Their numbers swell into hundreds, possibly 300 and beyond. [B172; BKG50]
- The Black Standard is raised on the plain of Khurásán. [B171, 176–7; BBD46; BBRSM52; MH175]
- The Black Standard will fly for some 11 months. [B176–7; DB351]
- See DB326 and MH177–83 for details of the journey.
- See MH182 for Mullá Ḥusayn's prophecy of the death of Muḥammad Sháh.

Aug The Báb is taken back to Chihríq, where He remains until June/July 1850. [B147; DB322; TN15]

Notes B147 *says He must have arrived in the first days of August.*

- On His return the Báb writes a denunciatory letter to Ḥájí Mírzá Áqásí. He sends it to Ḥujjat in Ṭihrán, who delivers it personally. [B147; DB323; GPB27]
- The Báb completes the Arabic Bayán. [BBD45; GBP25]

Sep Bahá'u'lláh is in Bandar-Jaz. An edict comes from Muḥammad Sháh ordering His arrest. [BKG49–50; BW18:381]

- The Russian agent at Bandar-Jaz offers Him passage on a Russian ship at anchor there but He refuses. [BKG50]

Birth of Ḥájí Mírzá Ḥasan, Adíb, Hand of the Cause and Apostle of Bahá'u'lláh, in Ṭáliqán.

Mírzá Ḥasan, known as Adíb

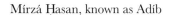

1 Sep Birth of August Forel, renowned entomologist and Bahá'í, in Switzerland.

4 Sep The death of Muḥammad Sháh. [BBR153–4]

- This precipitates the downfall of the Grand Vizier, Ḥájí Mírzá Áqásí. [B147; BBD19; BBR156]

- For details of his life, fall and death, see BBR154–6 and BKG52–5.

- The edict for Bahá'u'lláh's arrest is rendered null. [BKG50; BW18:381]

12 Sep The accession of Náṣiri'd-Dín Sháh at Tabríz. [BBR482]

- He is 17 years old. [BBR158; GPB37]

- He ruled from 1848 to 1 May 1896 when he was assassinated on the eve of his jubilee. [BBD168; BBR482]

- The first four years of his reign were marked by the 'fiercest and bloodiest of the persecutions of the religion of the Báb and Bahá'u'lláh'. During the whole of his reign there were 'sporadic persecutions and, in at least some cases, he himself was directly responsible for the death of the martyrs'. [BBR157]

- For the first time in the Faith's history the civil and ecclesiastical powers banded together in a systematic campaign against it, one that was to 'culminate in the horrors experienced by Bahá'u'lláh in the Síyáh-Chál' and 'His subsequent banishment to Iraq'. [GPB37]

- See BBRSM25 for an explanation of why the Bábí religion was a challenge to the secular regime.

- See SB86 for a reason for Náṣiri'd-Dín Sháh's cruelty towards the Bábís and Bahá'ís.

- See RB3:201 for an explanation of his lengthy reign.

- He chose as his prime minister Mírzá Taqí Khán-i-Faráháni, known as a great reformer and a founder of modern Iran. [BBD221; BBR160]

- It was not until the spring of 1849 that the new regime was in firm control.

10 Oct Mullá Ḥusayn and his company arrive near Bárfurúsh. The Sa'ídu'l-'Ulamá, threatened by their presence, has stirred up the townspeople, who go out to meet them. Some three or four miles from the city they clash and seven of Mullá Ḥusayn's companions are killed. [B172; BW18:381; DB329–31; MH192–3]

Notes MH188 *says that the journey from Mashhad had taken 83 days.*

In the ensuing battle, the townspeople are worsted. They beg for peace and a truce is agreed. [B172; DB336; MH197]

• It was here that Mullá Ḥusayn cut a man, a musket and a tree with one blow from his sword. [B172; DB330–1; MH193]

Mullá Ḥusayn and his companions take shelter in a caravanserai. Three young men who mount the roof to raise the call to prayer are each met with a bullet and killed. Mullá Ḥusayn gives the command to attack the townspeople, who are again routed. [BW18:381; DB337–8; MH201–5]

Mullá Ḥusayn and his companions are offered safe passage by the town's leaders if they will leave Bárfurúsh. They agree but are attacked by their escort, Khusraw-i-Qádí-Kalá'í and his hundred men. [B172; DB338–42; MH206–9]

12 Oct The band of 72 Bábís take refuge in the shrine of Shaykh Ṭabarsí which is located about 14 miles southeast of Bárfurúsh and prepare it for siege. [B173; BBRSM26; BW18:381; DB344–5]

Oct–May 1849 The siege of the Shrine of Shaykh Ṭabarsí.

The shrine of Shaykh Ṭabarsí

- See BBD217, BW18:381, DB345–413 and MH221–85 for chronicle of events.

- The episode lasts seven months. [BBRSM26; BW18:381]

- See BBRSM26 for the Bábís' intentions.

- See DB343–5 for pictures and DB348, MH217–18 for sketches.

- See MH212 for a diagram of the fortifications.

- Bahá'u'lláh visits the fortress and approves the fortifications. [BKG51, DB347–9; MH227]

- He advises Mullá Ḥusayn to seek the release of Quddús. Mullá Ḥusayn sets out immediately and secures the release of Quddús, who has been in detention for 95 days. [B173; BKG51; DB349–50; MH227]

- Quddús arrives towards the end of the year. [B173]

- See DB352–4 for the entry of Quddús into Shaykh Tabarsí. His arrival brings the number of Bábís in the shrine to 313. [DB354]

Notes BBRSM26 *and* MH233–4 *say that the number of defendants rose to 500–600 individuals.*

- 37 per cent of the identified participants were of the 'ulamá class. [BBRSM50]

- The siege begins with the arrival of 'Abdu'lláh Khán's forces on 19 December.

19 Oct Entry of Náṣiri'd-Dín Sháh into Ṭihrán. [BBR482]

Notes MH240 *says it took him 45 days to travel to Ṭihrán to occupy his father's throne.*

Mírzá Taqí Khán-i-Faráhání takes up post as prime minister. [BBR 482]

early Dec Bahá'u'lláh sets out from Ṭihrán with 11 companions to reinforce the Bábís at Shaykh Ṭabarsí. Nine miles from the fort they are arrested and taken to the town of Ámul, where they are held prisoner in the home of the deputy governor. This is Bahá'u'lláh's second imprisonment. He intervenes to spare His companions the bastinado and He alone receives it.

- When the governor returns to his home he orders that Bahá'u'lláh and His companions be released and arranges a safe conduct for them to Ṭihrán. [B174; BBD44; BKG56–60; BW18:381; DB369–76; GPB68; SB7]

- See BKG57 and DB70 for pictures.

19 Dec The siege of the Shrine of Shaykh Ṭabarsí begins with the arrival of 'Abdu'lláh Khán's forces. [BW18:381]

Notes DB361 *says this was 1 December.*

- There are about 12,000 troops. [MH245]

- The supply of bread and water to the fort is cut. A rainfall replenishes the water supply and ruins the munitions of the government forces. Snow further hampers the army's movement. [DB361, MH243]

21 Dec The Bábís, led by Quddús, make a mounted attack on the army. All of the officers are killed including 'Abdu'lláh Khán. A number of soldiers are drowned as they retreat into the Tálár River. About 430 soldiers are killed but no Bábís; one Bábí is wounded. [BW18:381; DB361–3; MH243–6]

- For the next 19 days the defenders dig a moat. [DB363]

1849

In the year Bahá'u'lláh marries his second wife, Fáṭimih Khánum Mahd-i-'Ulyá (1828–1904), His cousin, the daughter of Malik-Nisá Khánum (Mírzá Buzurg's sister) and Mírzá Karím-i-Namadsáb.

Notes *According to one source, she was married to the famous cleric Mírzá Muḥammad Taqí 'Allámi-yi-Núrí and widowed before Bahá'u'lláh married her.*

early Jan Arrival of Mihdí-Qulí Mírzá and 3,000 royal troops in the vicinity of the shrine of Shaykh Ṭabarsí. [B173–4; BW18:381; DB363]

• He sets up camp and his headquarters in the village of Vás-Kas. [DB363]

11 Jan Quddús and Mullá Ḥusayn lead a night attack on the encamped army. Two hundred and two Bábís disperse the camp. [BW18:381; BD365; MH254]

Notes DB 368 *says this occurred on 21 December 1848.*

• Mihdí-Qulí Mírzá flees barefoot. [DB366]

• Mullá Ḥusayn's sword is broken in the attack and he uses Quddús's. His companions bring him the abandoned sword of Mihdí-Qulí Mírzá. [DB367; MH257]

At daybreak the soldiers mount a counter-attack. [DB367; MH258–9]

• In this encounter Quddús is wounded in the mouth and is rescued by Mullá Ḥusayn who disperses the enemy using the sword of Mihdí-Qulí Mírzá in one hand and that of Quddús in the other. [B174; DB367; MH258–9]

27 Jan The arrival of reinforcements for the besiegers under the leadership of 'Abbás-Qulí Khán-i-Láríjání. [BW18:381; DB378–9; MH263]

• This is the third army to be mustered.

• The water supply is again cut off and Mullá Ḥusayn orders that a well be dug and a bath constructed. [DB379; MH263]

1 Feb The well is completed. Mullá Ḥusayn performs his ablutions and puts on clean clothes and the turban of the Báb. [DB379; MH264–6]

2 Feb Soon after midnight, Mullá Ḥusayn leads a charge of 313 men that again routs the king's army. He is struck in the chest by a bullet and dies. His body is carried back to the fort and buried. Ninety other Bábís are also wounded, about 40 of whom die. [B174; BW18:381; DB379–82; MH266–70]

• Mullá Ḥusayn is 36 years old at the time of his death. [DB383; MH272]

• See DB382–3 for an account of his life.

- See DB415–16 for an account of the heroics of Mullá Ḥusayn.

- See DB381–2 and MH265–70 for an account of the death and burial of Mullá Ḥusayn.

- See SDH13–14 for an account of his death by Mihdí-Qulí Mírzá.

- Seventy-two of the original 313 inhabitants of the fort had been martyred by this time. [DB382]

- It takes the army 45 days to reassemble its forces. [DB384; MH277]

c. 11 Mar On learning through a traitor of the death of Mullá Ḥusayn, 'Abbás-Qulí Khán launches a fresh attack on the fort. [DB384–6]

Notes DB386 *says this was 10 days before Naw-Rúz.*

- Nineteen Bábís led by Mírzá Muḥammad-Báqir overcome the attackers. [DB386–8]

27 Mar Renewed forces under Mihdí-Qulí Mírzá encamp in the neighbourhood of the fort, build fortifications and begin to bombard the shrine. [BW18:381; DB390–3]

Notes DB391 *says this was the ninth day after Naw-Rúz.*

c. end Mar The army continues to fire on the shrine for a few days. Mírzá Muḥammad-Báqir and 18 others attack the new fortifications and destroy some of them. [DB393–4]

early Apr Sulaymán Khán-i-Afshar arrives with more troops. [BW18:381]

26 Apr A charge by the forces of Sulaymán Khán is repulsed by 37 Bábís led by Mírzá Muḥammad-Báqir. [BW18:381; DB395–6]

- A few days later some of the Bábís leave the fort on the promise of Mihdí-Qulí Mírzá that they will be returned to their homes. As soon as they are outside the fort they are put to death. [DB396–9]

9 May Mihdí-Qulí Mírzá sends an emissary to the fort to invite two representatives to his camp to conduct negotiations. On the strength of assurances written on a Qur'án, Quddús leaves the fort and enters the Prince's camp. [B175; BW18:381; DB399–400]

10 May   The end of the siege of the fort at <u>Sh</u>ay<u>kh</u> Ṭabarsí. Two hundred and two Bábís are tricked into leaving the shrine. [BW18:381]

Notes   DB400 *says they accompanied Quddús.*

• They are not conducted to their homes as promised but are set upon by the Prince's soldiers. Some are killed, others sold into slavery. The fortifications around the shrine are razed to the ground. [DB403–4; MH283]

• See DB414–29 for a list of the martyrs of Ṭabarsí.

11 May   Quddús is taken to Bárfurú<u>sh</u> and handed over to the priests. [DB408]

16 May   Quddús is tortured and, in the public square, he is struck down with an axe, dismembered and burnt. [B176; BBD191; BW18:381; DB409–13; MH283–4]

• As he dies he begs God's forgiveness for his foes. [DB411; MH284]

• His remains are gathered and buried by a friend. [B176; DB413]

• See GPB49–50 for the rank and titles of Quddús.

c. Jun–Jul   The Báb, in prison in the castle of <u>Ch</u>ihríq, learns of the massacre at <u>Sh</u>ay<u>kh</u> Ṭabarsí and the martyrdom of Quddús. He is so overcome with grief that He is unable to write or dictate for a period of six months. [DB411, 430]

Notes   DB430 *says he languished in despondency and sorrow for five months.*

1 Aug   Death of Ḥájí Mírzá Áqásí at Karbalá. [B147; BBD19; BBR156]

26 Nov   The Báb sends Mullá Ádí-Guzal to the graves of Quddús and Mullá Ḥusayn to make a pilgrimage on His behalf. [DB431]

1850

early weeks   Vaḥíd clashes with the authorities in Yazd. He escapes and makes a missionary journey through Fárs. [B178–9; DB466–71; BBRSM28, 216]

Notes *B178 says this took place in the early weeks of 1850; B204–5 says Lt-Col Sheil reported it to London in February; BBRSM28, 216 says it was January or February; DB466 sets it at Naw-Rúz 1850 and DB468 says that the siege carried on for 40 days.*

See BBR106–9 for the various dates assigned to this event and for the difficulties in dating it.

15 Jan Mullá Ádí-Guzal arrives in Mázindarán and carries out the Báb's request. [DB432]

14 Feb Fourteen Bábís are arrested as a result of the actions of an informer. [BBRSM28; BW18:381]

19 or 20 Feb Martyrdom of the Seven Martyrs of Ṭihrán. Seven of the Bábís are executed in Ṭihrán on the false charge of having plotted to kill the Grand Vizier. [B182–5; BBD225; BBR100–5; BBRSM28, 216; BKG71; BW18:381; DB462; GPB47–8]

- See BBD225, BBR100 and BW18:381 for a list of their names.
- Three of the victims are so eager to be martyrs that they ask the executioner if they can be the first to die. [B183; BBD225; GPB47]
- Their bodies are left in the public square for three days. [BBD225; GPB47]
- See GPB47–8 for the chief features of the episode.
- The martyrs are the 'Seven Goats' referred to in Islamic traditions that were to 'walk in front' of the promised Qá'im. [GPB47–8]
- See B206–7 and BBR100–5 for the accounts of the event and responses of Prince Dolgorukov and Lt-Col Sheil.

spring The house of Vaḥíd in Yazd is attacked by crowds and pillaged. The crowd is dispersed by Mullá Muḥammad-Riḍá. Vaḥíd leaves Yazd. [BW18:381; DB466–75]

Notes *See comments under 'early weeks' above.*

13 May– c. 2 Jan 51 Zanján upheaval. A quarrel among children escalates into opposition and hostility towards Ḥujjat. [B185; DB540–1]

• Ḥujjat had converted a sizeable proportion of the town. Tension mounted between the Bábís and the 'ulamá. [BBR114]

• See BW18:381 for a chronicle of events.

See also B185–8, 209–13; BBD111, 245; BBR114–26; BBRSM28, 216; DB527–81; GPB44–5; TN24–5.

16 May Martyrdom of Shaykh Muḥammad-i-Túb-Chí in Zanján. [BBR115; DB542–3]

19 May The Governor sends a mob against Ḥujjat, which is dispersed by Mír Ṣaláḥ. The Governor sends to Ṭihrán for reinforcements and the town Zanján is split into two camps. [BW18:381]

• See BBD245 and GPB45 for the story of Zaynab, the Bábí woman who dressed as a man and defended the barricades.

27 May–21 Jun First Nayríz upheaval.

Vaḥíd travels from Yazd towards Shíráz, eventually coming to Nayríz. He goes to the Mosque of Jum'ih where he ascends the pulpit and proclaims the Cause of God. The Governor makes moves against him and Vaḥíd orders his companions to occupy the fort of Khájih. The siege that follows lasts a month. [B178, 204–5; BBR109–13; BW18:381]

• See BW18:381 for a chronicle of events.

• See RB1:325–31 for the story of Vaḥíd. See also GPB50, K1223.

See also B178–82; BBD171; BBR109–13; BBRSM28, 216; DB485–99; GPB42–4; RB1:264; TN24–5.

c. Jun Mírzá Taqí Khán determines to execute the Báb to halt the progress of His religion. On his orders the Báb is taken from Chihríq to Tabríz. [B152; BBR76–7; GPB51]

• His guard takes Him on a circuitous, much longer route through Urúmíyyih where His presence is noted by American missionaries. [B152; BBR73, 76]

• Forty days before the Báb was to leave Chihríq He collected all His documents, Tablets, pen cases, seals and His agate rings, and put them in a coffer. He entrusted it to Mullá Báqir, one of the Letters of the Living, and instructed him to deliver it to His secretary. The secretary is instructed to proceed to Ṭihrán to deliver the box to 'Jináb-i-Bahá', that is, Bahá'u'lláh. [B151–2; DB504–5; TN25–6]

- When the box is opened they find a Tablet in the form of a pentacle with 500 verses consisting of derivatives of the word 'Bahá'. [B151–2; DB504–5; TN25–6]

17 Jun At Nayríz, Vaḥíd receives a message from the Governor offering a truce and a promise of safety written on the Qur'án. He, together with five attendants, leaves the fortress and is received into the camp of his enemies where he is entertained with great ceremony for three days. [B180–1; BW18:381]

21 Jun End of the first Nayríz upheaval. [BBRXXIX, 112]

- Vaḥíd is forced to write to his companions in the fortress to assure them that a settlement has been reached. The Bábís leave the fort, are set upon and killed. [B181; BW18;381]

24 Jun The severed heads of 13 Bábís arrive in Shíráz from Nayríz. They are raised on lances and paraded through the town. [B182; BW18:381]

29 Jun Vaḥíd is martyred in Nayríz. [B182; BW18:381; DB495, 499; GPB42; RB1:265]

- See DB494 for details of his martyrdom.

- His body is dragged through the streets to the accompaniment of drums and cymbals. [RB1:265]

The Báb arrives in Tabríz. [BBR76]

Notes BBRXXIX *says He arrived on 19 June.*

8 Jul The Báb, divested of His turban and sash, is taken on foot to the barracks in Tabríz. Mírzá Muḥammad-'Alíy-i-Zunúzí, Anís, throws himself at the feet of the Báb and asks to go with Him. [B153; DB507]

- That night the Báb asks that one of His companions kill Him, rather than let Him die at the hands of His enemies. Anís offers to do this but is restrained by the others. The Báb promises that Anís will be martyred with Him. [B154–5; DB507–8]

9 Jul **Martyrdom of the Báb**

In the morning the Báb is taken to the homes of the leading clerics to obtain the death-warrants. [B155; DB508]

- The warrants are already prepared. [B155–6; DB510]

- Anís's stepfather tries to persuade him to change his mind. Anís's young son is also brought to 'soften his heart' but Anís's resolve remains unshaken. [B156–7; DB509–10]

At noon the Báb and Anís are suspended on a wall in the square in front of the citadel of Tabríz. They are shot by 750 soldiers in three ranks of 250 men. [B157; DB512]

- When the smoke clears the Báb is gone and Anís is standing, unharmed, under the nail from which they were suspended. The Báb, also unhurt, is found back in his cell completing His dictation to His secretary. [B157–8; DB512–13]

- See BBD200–1 and DB510–12, 514 for the story of Sám Khán, the Christian colonel of the Armenian regiment which was ordered to execute the Báb.

The Báb and Anís are suspended a second time. A new regiment, the Náṣirí, has been found to undertake the execution. After the volley, the bodies of the Báb and Anís are shattered. [B158; DB514]

- See BBR77–82 for Western accounts of the event.

- The face of the Báb is untouched. [B158]

- At the moment the shots are fired a gale sweeps the city, stirring up so much dust that the city remains dark from noon until night. [B158; DB515]

- See CH239 and DH197 for the story of the phenomenon of the two sunsets.

At night, the bodies are thrown onto the edge of the moat surround-

The barrack square in Tabríz. The small x indicates the nail from which the Báb was suspended.

ing the city. Soldiers stand guard over them and, nearby, two Bábís, feigning madness, keep vigil. [B159; TN27]

See also B148–60, 202–3; BBD147; BBR77–82; DB510–17; GPB49–55; TN26–7.

10 Jul The Russian Consul has an artist make a sketch of the body of the Báb. [B159; DB518; TN28]

- See BBR43 for details of the drawing made by Consul Bakulin.

11 Jul The bodies are removed from the moat and taken to a silk factory. [B159–60; DB519]

- See B159–60, DB518–22 and TN27–8 for the story of the recovery of the bodies.

- The soldiers report that the bodies have been eaten by dogs. [B160; DB519]

Jul The Faith of the Báb has spread to two countries at this point, Iran and Iraq. [MBW147]

1850

25 Aug The arrival of 'Azíz <u>Kh</u>án-i-Mukrí, commander-in-chief of Iran's army, in Zanján where the fighting begun in May continues. He takes charge of the operation. [BBR119; BW18:382; DB556]

* For the story of A<u>sh</u>raf and his mother see DB562–3.

c. Aug Mullá Abu'l-Ḥasan-i-Ardikání (Ḥájí Amín), Hand of the Cause becomes a Bábí.

Notes *MM suggests it might have been 1851.*

3 Oct Two of Vaḥíd's companions are executed in <u>Sh</u>íráz.

Nov–Dec Muḥammad <u>Kh</u>án, the commander of the government forces at Zanján, tries to deceive Ḥujjat into surrender by drawing up a peace proposal. Ḥujjat, recalling Ṭabarsí and Nayríz, responds by sending children and old men to Muḥammad <u>Kh</u>án, who has them thrown into a dungeon. This signals the beginning of the final month-long siege at Zanján. [B186–7; DB564–8]

early Dec Ḥujjat is wounded in the arm. His companions lay down their arms and rush to his assistance. The royal forces take advantage of the lull to breach the fortifications. [B187; BBR121; DB569]

* About 100 women and children are taken captive. They are left exposed in the open for 15 days without food, shelter or appropriate clothing. [BBR121; DB569–70]

* The remaining Bábís, about 140, shelter in Ḥujjat's residence under fierce attack. [BBR121]

The bombardment of the fortress is stepped-up and Ḥujjat's house particularly targeted. Ḥujjat's wife and baby are killed. [B187 DB572–3]

29 Dec Ḥujjat dies of his wounds. [B187; BRR122; BW18:382]

Notes *DB573 says this was on 8 January 1851.*

1851

In the year Mullá Zaynu'l-'Ábidín (Zaynu'l-Muqarrabín), a prominent mujtahid, becomes a Bábí, in Najafábád.

c. 2 Jan End of the Zanján upheaval. [BW18:382]

- With the death of Ḥujjat the Bábí resistance weakens. A general assault by the royal forces ends the siege. [B187; BBR122; BW18:382; DB573–4]
- See B187 and DB574–7 for the fate of the survivors.
- See B187 and DB577–9 for the fate of Ḥujjat's body.
- About 1,800 Bábís were killed during the upheaval. [DB580, 598]

2 Mar Four Bábís brought from Zanján are execute in Ṭihrán. [BW18:382]

30 Apr Mullá Ḥasan-i-Faḍil is executed in Yazd when he refuses to recant. [BW18:382]

1 May Áqá Ḥusayn is blown from a cannon in Yazd. [BW18:382]

c. Jun Mírzá Taqí Khán meets with Bahá'u'lláh and tells Him that it would be advisable for Bahá'u'lláh to leave Ṭihrán temporarily. [BKG66; DB591]

A few days later, Bahá'u'lláh leaves Ṭihrán for Karbalá on pilgrimage. [BKG66; DB587]

23 Jul Áqá Muḥammad-Ṣádiq-i-Yúzdárání is beaten to death in Yazd after refusing to recant. [BW18:382]

Aug Bahá'u'lláh spends most of August in Kirmánsháh. [BKG67; DB591]

4 Aug Áqá 'Alí-Akbar-i-Hakkák is blown from a cannon after refusing to recant. [BW18:382]

28 Aug Bahá'u'lláh arrives in Karbalá via Baghdád on His pilgrimage. [BKG67; DB593; GPB70]

- See BKG68 and DB593–4 for those who became Bábís in Karbalá in this period.

Oct Shaykh Ḥasan-i-Zunúzí, the Báb's amanuensis, meets Bahá'u'lláh in the Shrine of the Imám Ḥusayn in Karbalá, as promised by the Báb. [BKG67–8]

c. Nov Siyyid Baṣír-Hindí, a blind Indian, is put to death by Ildirím Mírzá. [BW18:382]

- For details of his life see DB588–90.

13 Nov Mírzá Taqí Khán, the Amír-Niẓám, is dismissed from his post and told he is only in charge of the army. [BBR163; BKG71]

- He is succeeded by Mírzá Áqá Khán-i-Núrí. [BBRXXIX, 482; DB598]

1852

In the year Birth of Mírzá Buzurg-i-Khurasání (Badí'), Apostle of Bahá'u'lláh, in Mashhad.

Jan Mírzá Taqí Khán is killed in the public bath in Káshán by order of the Sháh on the instigation of the Sháh's mother and Mírzá Áqá Khán. [BBR164–5; BKG72]

- He chooses to have his veins opened and he bleeds to death. [BBR164; BKG72]

21 Feb Birth of Isabella Brittingham, prominent American Bahá'í teacher, in New York City.

c. Apr–May Bahá'u'lláh returns to Iran from Karbalá. [DB598]

- He is the guest of the Grand Vizier for one month. [BKG74; DB598–9]

summer Bahá'u'lláh stays at the summer residence of Ja'far-Qulí Khán, the brother of the Grand Vizier, in Afchih, Lavásán, near Ṭihrán. [BKG77; DB599]

15 Aug Attempt on the life of the Sháh. [BBR128; BBRSM:30; BKG74–5; DB599; ESW20; GPB62; TN29–30]

- See BKG74–5 for circumstances of the event.

- See BKG76 for the fate of the perpetrators.

- See BBR128–46 for reporting of the event in the West.

- Ja'far-Qulí Khán writes immediately to Bahá'u'lláh telling Him of the event and that the mother of the Sháh is denouncing Bahá'u'lláh as the 'would-be murderer'. Ja'far-Qulí Khán offers to hide Bahá'u'lláh. [BKG77; DB602]

16 Aug Bahá'u'lláh rides out towards the headquarters of the imperial army. He stops at Zargandih at the home of Mírzá Majíd Khán-i-Áhí, secretary to the Russian legation. [BKG77; DB603]

- Bahá'u'lláh is invited to remain in this home. [DB603]

- The Sháh is informed of Bahá'u'lláh's arrival and sends an officer to the legation to demand the delivery of Bahá'u'lláh into his hands. The Russian minister, Prince Dolgorukov, refuses and suggests that Bahá'u'lláh be sent to the home of the Grand Vizier. [BKG77; DB603]

Bahá'u'lláh is arrested. [BKG77; DB603]

days following 16 Aug For a few days after His arrest, Bahá'u'lláh is interrogated. [TN 31]

He is then taken 'on foot and in chains, with bared head and bare feet' to Ṭihrán where He is cast into the Síyáh-Chál. [BKG77; DB606–7; ESW20; GPB71; TN31]

- See BKG77–8 and DB606–8 for a description of Bahá'u'lláh's journey.

- See CH40–1 for the effect on Bahá'u'lláh's family.

16–22 Aug A large number of Bábís are arrested in Ṭihrán and its environs following the attempt on the life of the Sháh. A number are executed. [BBR134–5; BW18:382]

- Eighty-one, of whom 38 are leading members of the Bábí community, are thrown into the Síyáh-Chál. [BKG77]

The martyrdom of Ṭáhirih in Ṭihrán. [BBR172–3; BBRSM:30; BW18:382; BKG87; MF203]

- She is martyred in the Ílkhání garden, strangled with her own silk handkerchief which she has provided for the purpose. Her body is lowered into a well which is then filled with stones. [BBD220; DB622–8; GPB75]

- See GPB73–5 for a history of her life.

22–7 Aug After the initial executions, about 20 or more Bábís are distributed among the various courtiers and government departments to be tortured and put to death. [BBR135–6; BW18:382]

Aug In Mílán, Iran, 15 Bábís are arrested and imprisoned. [BW18:382]

Many Bábís are tortured and killed in the weeks following the attempt on the life of the Sháh. [BKG84]

- See BBR171 for the story of Maḥmud Khán, the Kalántar of Ṭihrán, and his role in the arrest and execution of the Bábís.

- See BKG84–93 for a description of the tortures and executions of Bábís. Thirty-eight Bábís are martyred.

- See BKG86–7 and DB616–21 for the torture and martyrdom of Sulaymán Khán. Holes are gouged in his body and nine lighted candles are inserted. He joyfully dances to the place of his execution. His body is hacked in two, each half is then suspended on either side of the gate.

- The persecutions are so severe that the community is nearly annihilated. The Bábí remnant virtually disappears from view until the 1870s. [BBRSM:30; EB269]

Aug–Dec Bahá'u'lláh's imprisonment in the Síyáh-Chál.

- See AB10–11, BBD211–12, BKG79–83, CH41–2, DB631–3, GPB109 and RB1:9 for a description of the prison and the conditions suffered by the prisoners.

- No food or drink is given to Bahá'u'lláh for three days and nights. [DB608]

- Bahá'u'lláh remained in the prison for four months. [CH41; ESW20, 77; GPB104; TN31]

- See CH42–3 for the effect of Bahá'u'lláh's imprisonment on His wife and children.

- 'Abdu'l-Bahá, as a child of eight, is attacked in the street of Ṭihrán. [DB616]

- See AB11–12, RB1:9 for 'Abdu'l-Bahá's account of His visit to His father.

- Bahá'u'lláh's properties are plundered. [CH41; RB1:11]

- See BBD4–5 and BKG94–8 for the story of 'Abdu'l-Vahháb-i-Shírazí who was martyred while being held in the Síyáh-Chál.

- See BBD190, 200 and ESW77 about the two chains with which Bahá'u'lláh was burdened while in the Síyáh-Chál.

- Bahá'u'lláh had some 30 companions. [BBIC:6]

- An attempt was made to poison Him. [BBIC:6; BKG99–100]

Bahá'u'lláh's half-brother Mírzá Yaḥyá flees to Tákur and goes into hiding. He eventually goes to Baghdád. [BKG90, 107]

Oct Bahá'u'lláh has a vision of the Maiden, who announces to Him that He is the Manifestation of God for this Age. [BBD142–3, 212; BKG82–3; ESW11–12, 21; GPB101–2; KAN62]

- This experience compares to the episode of Moses and the Burning Bush, Zoroaster and the Seven Visions, Buddha under the Bodhi tree, the descent of the Dove upon Jesus and the voice of Gabriel commanding Muḥammad to 'cry in the name of thy Lord'. [GPB101]

- The Báb repeatedly gave the year nine as the date of the appearance of 'Him Whom God shall make manifest'. The Declaration of the Báb took place in 1260 AH; year nine was therefore 1269 AH, which began in the middle of October when Bahá'u'lláh had been in prison for about two months. [CB46–7]

Dec   Bahá'u'lláh is released from the Síyáh-<u>Ch</u>ál.

- This was owing to: the efforts of the Russian Minister Prince Dolgorukov; the public confession of the would-be assassin; the testimony of competent tribunals; the efforts of Bahá'u'lláh's own kinsmen; and the sacrifices of those followers imprisoned with Him. [GPB104–5]

- See CH43–4 for the role of the Russian Consul in securing His release.

- See BKG101–2, CH44 and DB647–8 for the physical condition of Bahá'u'lláh on release.

- See BKG101, DB648–9 and GPB105 for the words of Bahá'u'lláh to Mírzá Áqá <u>Kh</u>án on His release.

- The Russian minister invited Bahá'u'lláh to go to Russia but Bahá'u'lláh chose instead to go to Iraq. It may be that He refused the offer because He knew that acceptance of such help would have been misrepresented as having political implications. [BBIC:8; DB650]

1853

12 Jan   Bahá'u'lláh and His family depart for Ba<u>gh</u>dád after a one month respite in the home of his half-brother Mírzá Riḍá-Qulí. During the three-month journey Bahá'u'lláh is accompanied by His wife Navváb, His eldest son 'Abdu'l-Bahá (9), Bahíyyih <u>Kh</u>ánum (7) and two of His brothers, Mírzá Músá and Mírzá Muḥammad-Qulí. They are escorted by an officer of the Persian imperial bodyguard and an official representing the Russian legation. [BKG102–5; GPB108]

Notes   CH44–5 *says the family had ten days after Bahá'u'lláh's release to prepare for the journey to Iraq.*

- 'Never had the fortunes of the Faith proclaimed by the Báb sunk to a lower ebb'. [DB651]

- This exile compares to the migration of Muḥammad, the exodus of Moses and the banishment of Abraham. [GPB107–8]

- See BKG104 and GPB108–9 for conditions on the journey.

Right: Mírzá Músá.
Far right: Muḥammad-Qulí

Mar Bahá'u'lláh and His companions arrive in Khániqayn, just across the Iraqi border, where they rest in a beautiful orchard to observe Naw-Rúz. [BKG105]

26 Mar Five Bábís, acting on their own initiative, murder the governor of Nayríz, providing the spark for the second Nayríz upheaval. [BBR147]

8 Apr Bahá'u'lláh and His family arrive in Baghdád. [BBR177; BKG106; GPB109; TN38]

- See BBR177–83 for conditions in Baghdád during this period.

- Shortly after the family's arrival in Baghdád Navváb gives birth to a son. [CB71; CH51–2]

summer Bahá'u'lláh reveals His station and mission to Mírzá Áqá Ján in Karbalá. [BKG109–11; GPB115–16]

Oct Second Nayríz upheaval. [BBR147–51; BBRSM:217; BW18:382; DB642–5]

- The new governor of Nayríz, Mírzá Na'ím-i-Núrí, arrests a large number of Bábís and pillages their properties. The Bábís take to the hills. [BW18:382]

Mírzá Áqá Ján

• See BW18:382 for a chronicle of events.

• See BBR147–51 for Western accounts.

31 Oct Some 600 female and 80 to 180 male Bábís are taken prisoner at Nayríz and marched to Shíráz, along with the heads of some 180 martyrs. This fulfils an Islamic prophecy concerning the appearance of the Qá'im indicating that the heads of the followers would be used as gifts. [BW18:382; KI245]

24 Nov The prisoners from Nayríz and the heads of the martyrs arrive in Shíráz. More Bábís are executed and their heads sent to Ṭihrán. The heads are later buried at Ábádih. [BW18:382]

1853 or 1854 Birth of Mírzá Muḥammad-'Alí, first son of Bahá'u'lláh and His second wife, Mahd-i-'Ulyá. [CB125]

- He was born in the first year of Bahá'u'lláh's arrival in Baghdád. [CB125]

Bahá'u'lláh reveals the Lawḥ-i Kullu'ṭ-ṭa'ám (Tablet of All Food). [BRSM:62; BKG112]

- The revelation of this Tablet points up Mírzá Yaḥyá's lack of ability. [BKG112]

1854

10 Apr Bahá'u'lláh suddenly leaves Baghdád and goes to Kurdistán. [BKG115; DB585; GPB120]

- Before He left, Bahá'u'lláh asked His family to look after Mírzá Yaḥyá during His absence. [CB70–1; CH50–1]

Apr–19 Mar 1856 Bahá'u'lláh lives for some time as a dervish in a cave on the mountain of Sar-Galú. He takes the name Darvísh Muḥammad-i-Írání to conceal His true identity. [BBD214–15; BBRSM:60–1; BKG116–19; GPB120–1; TN38–9]

- This action compares to Moses' going out to the desert of Sinai, to Buddha's retreat to the wilds of India, to Christ's walk in the wilderness and to Muḥammad's withdrawal to the hills of Arabia. [BKG114]

- Áqá Abu'l-Qásim-i-Hamadání was His only companion. Áqá Abu'l-Qásim was killed on a journey to collect money and provisions. [BKG116–17]

1854–1856

- It was during this time that Bahá'u'lláh revealed the poem *Qasídiy-i-'Izz-i-Varqá'íyyih.* It was composed of 2,000 couplets but Bahá'u'lláh allowed only 127 to be preserved. [BBD215; BKG118; GPB123]

- See BKG114, GPB117–19 and KI250 for reasons for Bahá'u'lláh's retirement.

- Before and during His absence no fewer than 25 people claimed to be the One promised by the Báb. [BBRSM29, 59; EB269; GPB125]

- See BKG115–19 and GPB120 for Bahá'u'lláh's activities while in Kurdistán.

- See KI248–51 for Bahá'u'lláh's own account of the episode.

- See BKG119–22 and GPB124–6 for the condition of the Bábí community in Baghdád during this period.

- The son born to Navváb shortly after the family's arrival in Baghdád became ill and died during Bahá'u'lláh's absence. [CB71; CH51–2]

See also SBBR2:1–28 *for Bahá'u'lláh's contact with Ṣúfís. See* BW12:528 *for an account of Daoud Toeg, who visited the caves of Sar-Galú and photographed them.*

1855

5 Mar Birth of John Henry Hyde Dunn, Hand of the Cause, in London.

15 Oct 1855 or 1856 Birth of Robert Turner, first black American Bahá'í.

1856

19 Mar Bahá'u'lláh returns from Kurdistán.

- From this time Bahá'u'lláh started to educate the believers in the principles of the Faith. [GPB127–8; TN39]

1856–8 Bahá'u'lláh's writings during this period are so prolific that in one hour He would reveal a thousand verses and in the course of one day the equivalent of the Qur'án. He reveals a vast number of works and then commands that hundreds of thousands of verses be destroyed. [BBRSM62–3; BKG167; GPB137–8]

1856 to Mar 1857 The Anglo-Persian War. [BBR165, 263]

1856–63 It is in this period that Bahá'u'lláh reveals the *Seven Valleys* in response to a request from a Ṣúfí, Shaykh Muḥyi'd-Dín, the Qáḍí of Khániqayn, whom He may have met in Kurdistán. In it Bahá'u'lláh describes the stages of the mystical life. [BBD206 BBRSM:64; SA150]

- For details of the composition and content of the *Seven Valleys* see SA150–7.

c. 1856–7 Birth of Ṣamadíyyih Khánum, first daughter of Bahá'u'lláh and His second wife, Mahd-i-'Ulyá.

1857

c. 1857 Bahá'u'lláh reveals the *Four Valleys*, addressed to Shaykh 'Abdu'r-Raḥmán-i-Tálabání and describing four stages of the spiritual life. [SA157–8]

1858

In the year Bahá'u'lláh reveals the Hidden Words (Kalimát-i-Maknúnih), originally designated 'The Hidden Words of Fáṭimih', while walking along the banks of the Tigris. [BBD102; BKG159; GPB138–40]

Aug The dismissal of Mírzá Áqá Khán, the prime minister who had directed the persecution of the Bábís that followed the attempt on the life of the Sháh.

1860

c. 1860 Mírzá Midhí, the son of Bahá'u'lláh, is taken from Ṭihrán to join his family in Baghdád. He is about 12 years old. [RB3:205]

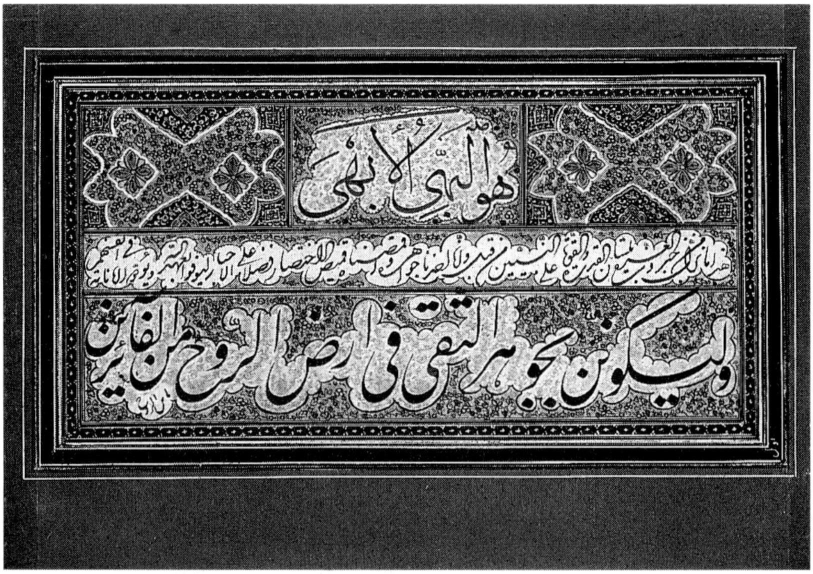

A calligraphic rendering of the Hidden Words

• He travels with the second wife of Bahá'u'lláh, Mahd-i-'Ulyá. [MMNF]

In the year Birth of Shaykh Muḥammad-'Alíy-i-Qá'iní, Apostle of Bahá'u'lláh, in Naw Firist, near Birjand. [EB273]

1861

c. 1861 'Abdu'l-Bahá writes the *Sharḥ-i Kuntu Kanzan Makhfiyan*, the commentary on the Islamic tradition 'I was a Hidden Treasure . . .' for 'Alí Shawkat Páshá. He is reported to be 17 years old at the time. [AB14]

Ḥájí Ákhúnd (Mullá 'Alí-Akbar-i-Shahmírzádí), Hand of the Cause, becomes a Bábí in Mashhad. [EB266]

Mullá Ṣádiq-i-Muqaddas-i-Khurásání (Ismu'lláhu'l-Aṣdaq), a Bábí and father of Ibn Aṣdaq, meets Bahá'u'lláh in Baghdád and becomes a follower. [BKG18]

25 Jun Death of Sulṭán 'Abdu'l-Majíd and accession of Sulṭán 'Abdu'l-'Azíz to the Ottoman throne. [BBR485]

Notes BKG139 *says this was 14 August.*

Ḥájí Á<u>kh</u>und

1862

In the year Bahá'u'lláh reveals the *Kitáb-i-Íqán*, 'a comprehensive exposition of the nature and purpose of religion'. [BBD134, 162; BKG159; BBIC10; BBRSM64–5; GPB138–9; RB1:158]

Sulṭán 'Abdu'l-Azíz

• The Tablet is revealed in answer to four questions put to Bahá'u'lláh by Ḥájí Mírzá Siyyid Muḥammad, a maternal uncle of the Báb. [BBD134, 162; BKG163–5; RB1:158]

• It is revealed in the course of two days and two nights. [BBD134; BKG165; GPB238; RB1:158]

• The original manuscript, in the handwriting of 'Abdu'l-Bahá, is in the Bahá'í International Archives. [BKG165; RB1:159]

• It is probably the first of Bahá'u'lláh's writings to appear in print. [BKG165; EB121]

• For a discussion of the circumstances of its revelation, its content and major themes see RB1:153–97.

Some Bábís are imprisoned in Ṭihrán. [BW18:382]

'Abdu'l-'Alí Khán-i-Marághi'í is killed in Ṭihrán on the order of Náṣiri'd-Dín Sháh. [BW18:382]

c. 1862 Bahá'u'lláh sends a ring and cashmere shawl to His niece, Shahr-Bánú, the daughter of Mírzá Muḥammad-Ḥasan, in Ṭihrán to ask for her hand in marriage to 'Abdu'l-Bahá. Shahr-Bánú's uncle, acting in place of her dead father, refuses to let her go to Iraq. [BKG342–3]

c. Mar–Jun Birth of Sádhijíyyih, second daughter of Bahá'u'lláh and His second wife, Mahd-i-'Ulyá.

1862–8 Ḥájí Mírzá Muḥammad-'Alí, a cousin of the Báb, lives in Shanghai during this period. This is the first record of a Bábí or Bahá'í living in China. [PH24]

- From 1870 he lived in Hong Kong dealing as a merchant and was joined by his brother, Ḥájí Mírzá Muḥammad Ḥusayn. [PH24]

1863

1863 or earlier Colonel Sir Arnold Burrowes Kemball, the British Consul-General in Baghdád, offers Bahá'u'lláh the protection of British citizenship and offers Him residence in India or anywhere of Bahá'u'lláh's choosing. [BBR183, 234; BBRSM65; GPB131]

- Bahá'u'lláh declines the invitation, preferring to remain in Ottoman lands. [GBP131]
- See BBR183, 508 for details on Kemball; see BBR160–1 for a picture.

c. Jan The governor of Baghdád, Námiq Páshá, receives the first of 'five successive commands' from 'Álí Páshá, the Grand Vizier of Turkey, to transfer Bahá'u'lláh to Constantinople. This order is ignored by the governor, who is sympathetic to Bahá'u'lláh. In the next three months, four more orders will be received and similarly ignored before the governor is compelled to comply. [BKG154; GPB131]

Mar Bahá'u'lláh celebrates the two-week festival of Naw-Rúz at the Mazra'iy-i-Vashshásh, a farm along the river Tigris, not far from His house in Baghdád. [BKG154; GPB147; SA163]

26 Mar Bahá'u'lláh reveals the Tablet of the Holy Mariner on the fifth day of Naw-Rúz. [BKG154; GPB147; RB1:228; SA163]

- The Tablet is recited by Mírzá Áqá Ján. [RBI:228]

- See GPB147 and RBI:228 for the effect on those present.

- See RBI:228–44 and SA163–5 for descriptions of the Tablet and analyses of its content.

- Immediately after it is chanted Bahá'u'lláh orders the tents to be folded and everyone to return to the city. [GBP147; RBI:228–9; SA163]

- The party has not yet left when a messenger arrives from Námiq Pá<u>sh</u>á summoning Bahá'u'lláh to the governorate the next day to receive the invitation to go to Constantinople. [RBI:229; SA163]

27 Mar Bahá'u'lláh meets the deputy governor in a mosque opposite the Government House and is given the letter summoning Him to Constantinople. [BKG154–5; GPB147–8; RBI:229]

- Námiq Pá<u>sh</u>á could not bring himself to meet Bahá'u'lláh and give Him this news. [BKG155; RBI:229]

- See BKG155–6 and GPB148 for the effect of this news on the believers.

- Bahá'u'lláh and His family had been given Ottoman citizenship by this time. [BBRSM66]

- See BKG156–8 for a list of those chosen by Bahá'u'lláh to migrate with Him.

- See TN50–3 for the story of the sedition behind Bahá'u'lláh's removal from Bag<u>h</u>dád.

See also BBD196; BBIC:13, *note* 68.

Apr Mírzá Yaḥyá flees Bag<u>h</u>dád, travelling to Mosul in disguise. [BKG158; RB252–5]

- Bahá'u'lláh advised him to go to Persia to disseminate the writings of the Báb. [RBI:252–3]

- Mírzá Yaḥyá abandoned the writings of the Báb and travelled surreptitiously to Constantinople. [ESW167–8; RB1:255]

• See ESW167 and RB1:253–4 for Yaḥyá's movements.

On learning that Bahá'u'lláh is to leave Baghdád, large numbers visit Him. The house is too small for the purpose. Najíb Páshá puts his garden-park, Najíbíyyih, at Bahá'u'lláh's disposal. [RB1:259]

18 Apr Birth of William Henry (Harry) Randall, Disciple of 'Abdu'l-Bahá, in Boston.

22 Apr–3 May **Declaration of Bahá'u'lláh in the Garden of Riḍván**

22 Apr Thirty-one days after Naw-Rúz, which in this year falls on 22 March, Bahá'u'lláh leaves His house for the last time and walks to the Najíbíyyih Garden, afterwards known as the Garden of Riḍván (Paradise).

• See BKG168, GPB149, RB1:260–1 and SA234–5 for details of His walk.

• For the first time, He wears a tall táj as a symbol of His station. [BBD221; BKG176; GPB152]

Bahá'u'lláh enters the Garden just as the call to afternoon prayer is being made. [GPB149; RB1:261]

On this day Bahá'u'lláh declares His mission to a few of His disciples. [RB1:260, 262]

• 'Of the exact circumstances . . . we, alas, are but scantily informed.' [BKG173; GPB153]

• For such details as are known, see BKG173–5 and GPB153.

• For the import of the event, see BKG169–73; G27–35; GBP153–5.

• This initiates the holy day of the First Day of Riḍván, to be celebrated on 21 April. [BBD196]

• This marks the end of the dispensation of the Báb and of the first epoch of the Heroic or Apostolic Age of the Bahá'í dispensation. [BBD72, 79]

On the same day Bahá'u'lláh makes three important statements to His followers:

1. He forbids the use of the sword.

2. He states that no other Manifestations will appear before one thousand years. This is later reiterated in the Kitáb-i-Badí' and in the Kitáb-i-Aqdas.

3. He states that, as from this moment, all the names and attributes of God are manifested within all created things, implying the advent of a new Day. [RB1:278–80]

On the afternoon of Bahá'u'lláh's arrival at the Garden He reveals the Lawḥ-i-Ayyúb for Ḥájí Muḥammad-i-Taqíy-i-Nayrízí. [SA239]

During the 12 days in the Riḍván Garden Bahá'u'lláh confides to 'Abdu'l-Bahá that He is 'Him Whom God shall make manifest'. [CH82]

• See CH82–3 for the effect of this announcement on 'Abdu'l-Bahá.

30 Apr Bahá'u'lláh's family joins Him in the Garden. [BKG175; RB1:281; SA235]

• This initiates the holy day of the Ninth Day of Riḍván, to be celebrated on 29 April. [BBD196]

3 May Bahá'u'lláh leaves the Garden of Riḍván.

• This initiates the holy day the Twelfth Day of Riḍván, to be celebrated on 2 May. [BBD196]

• As He is about to leave He reveals a Tablet addressed to Áqá Mírzá Áqá in Shíráz. It brings relief and happiness to those who receive it. [EB222]

• His leaving is accompanied by symbolic signs of His station: He rides a horse rather than a donkey and wears a tall táj. [BBD221; BKG176]

• See BKG175–6, GPB155 and RB1:281–2 for descriptions of the scenes that accompanied His departure.

A táj belonging to Bahá'u'lláh

Bahá'u'lláh and His party arrive at Firayját, three miles away on the banks of the Tigris. [BKG176]

- They remain here for seven days. [BKG176]
- See BKG for a description of activities during this period.

9 May Bahá'u'lláh and His party leave Firayját for Istanbul. [GPB156; SA235]

- The journey takes 110 days. [GPB156]
- For the details of the journey see BKG176–96; GPB156–7; SW13:277.
- See BKG180 for a map of the journey.
- For the number of people on the journey see BKG179 (72), GPB156 (26 plus members of His family plus guards), RB2:5–6 (54) and SW13:277 (72).
- As the party draws close to Sámsún on the Black Sea Bahá'u'lláh reveals the Súriy-i-Hawdaj. [BKG195; RB2:6]
- The party remains in Sámsún for seven days. [GPB157]

13 Aug Bahá'u'lláh and His party depart from Sámsún by steamer for Istanbul. [BKG196; GPB157]

1863

16 Aug Bahá'u'lláh and His party arrive at Constantinople. [BKG197; GPB157; RB2:1]

16 Aug–1 Dec Bahá'u'lláh resides in Constantinople. [BKG197, 204; GPB157–61]

- See BKG197–204 for an account of Bahá'u'lláh's stay.

- Among the works Bahá'u'lláh reveals in Constantinople is Mathnaví-i-Mubárak. [RB2:29–54]

News is brought to Bahá'u'lláh by Shamsí Big of the possibility that He will be transferred to Adrianople. [BKG199]

Bahá'u'lláh refuses to leave, on pain of martyrdom, but Mírzá Yaḥyá and his comrades, cowardly and fearful, persuade Him to go. [BKG201–3]

Sulṭán 'Abdu'l-'Azíz issues an edict banishing Bahá'u'lláh to Adrianople. [GPB159–60; RB2:57]

- See BBIC:34, *note* 68, BKG201 and GPB159 for reasons for the edict.

On the same day Bahá'u'lláh reveals the Lawḥ-i-'Abdu'l-'Azíz-Va-Vukalá, a Tablet addressed to the Sulṭán. When the Grand Vizier peruses it he turns pale. The text of this Tablet is lost. [BKG206; GPB160]

c. Aug–Nov Death of Sádhijíyyih, 18-month-old daughter of Bahá'u'lláh and Mahd-i-'Ulyá. Her body is buried in a plot of land outside the Ádirnih Gate of Constantinople. [BKG203]

19 Oct Bahá'u'lláh reveals the Tablet of the Bell (Subḥánika-Yá-Hú). [BKG206; BW14:632; RB2:18]

1 Dec Bahá'u'lláh and His companions leave Istanbul for Adrianople. [BKG204; GPB 161; RB2:427]

- The journey takes twelve days. [BKG204; GPB161]

- See BKG204–5, GPB161 and RB2:62 for the rigours of the journey. The winter is extremely cold and the travellers are not clad for freezing weather.

12 Dec Bahá'u'lláh and His companions arrive in Adrianople. [BKG206; GPB161; RB2:62]

- This is the furthest point from His native land that Bahá'u'lláh reaches and the first time in known history that a Manifestation of God had lived on the European continent. [BKG217]

- See BKG218–19, 221–2; GPB161–2 and MRHK179–96 for a description of the houses Bahá'u'lláh lives in during this period.

- See BKG219–20 for the hardships of the first winter.

1864

In the year Birth of Mírzá Hádí Shírází, the father of Shoghi Effendi, in Shíráz.

27 Mar Birth of A. L. M. Nicolas, who later becomes an important European scholar on the life and teachings of the Báb, in Rasht. [BBR516]

Apr Sulaymán Páshá, a Ṣúfí, succeeds Muḥammad Pásháy-i-Qibrisí as Governor of Adrianople. Both are admirers of Bahá'u'lláh. [BBR487; BKG254]

Upheaval at Najafábád.

- Several hundred Bahá'ís are arrested by Shaykh Muḥammad-Báqir (later stigmatized as 'the Wolf' by Bahá'u'lláh) and taken to Iṣfahán to be put to death. He is dissuaded from this plan by other 'ulamá of Iṣfahán. Two of the prisoners are executed, 18 are sent to Ṭihrán and the remainder are sent back to Najafábád where they are severely beaten. Those sent to Ṭihrán are put in a dungeon but released after three months by the Sháh. Two of these are beaten then executed upon their return from Ṭihrán on the order of Shaykh Muḥammad-Báqir. [BBD213; BBR268–9; BW18:382]

15 Aug Birth of Mírzá Ḍiyá'u'lláh, the third son of Bahá'u'lláh and Mahd-i-'Ulyá. [BKG222]

Dec Death of Governor Sulaymán Páshá of Adrianople. He is succeeded by 'Arif Páshá, who is not well-disposed to Bahá'u'lláh and His followers. [BBR487]

Shaykh Muḥammad-Báqir, 'the Wolf'

1865

In the year French diplomat Joseph Comte de Gobineau publishes *Religions et les Philosophies dans l'Asie Centrale*, over half of which is devoted to a study of the Bábí movement. [BBR17]

Mírzá Kazem-Beg of St Petersburg University publishes *Bab Babidy*, the first Western book written entirely on the subject of the Bábí religion. [BBR26]

c. 1865 Bahá'u'lláh reveals the Arabic Tablet of Aḥmad (Lawḥ-i-Aḥmad) for Aḥmad, a believer from Yazd. [RB2:107]

- See RB2:107–66 for the story of Aḥmad.
- See RB2:119–26 for an analysis of the Tablet.
- Shoghi Effendi states that the Tablet has a special potency and significance. [DG60]

About a year after Bahá'u'lláh's arrival in Adrianople Mírzá Yaḥyá poisons Bahá'u'lláh. [BKG225; GPB165]

- Bahá'u'lláh is ill for a month following this and is left with a shaking hand for the rest of His life. [BKG225; GPB165]
- Bahá'u'lláh is attended by a foreign doctor named Shíshmán who dies shortly after seeing Him. Bahá'u'lláh intimated that the doctor had sacrificed his life for Him. [BKG225; GPB166]
- This event takes places after the revelation of the Tablet of Aḥmad.

See also *For Yaḥyá's instigation of the attempt on Bahá'u'lláh's life in the public bath see* BKG227–30, CB82–3, GPB166 *and* RB2:158–61. *For Yaḥyá's poisoning of Bahá'u'lláh's well see* GBP166.

Mar Death of former Prime Minister Mírzá Áqá Khán, in Qum. He is buried at Karbalá. [BBR165]

1866

c. Mar Bahá'u'lláh reveals the Súriy-i-Amr (Súrih of Command) for Mírzá Yaḥyá. [CB84; GBP166]

- This is the formal announcement to the nominee of the Báb of the station of 'Him Whom God shall make manifest' and a summons for him to pay allegiance to His Cause. [CB83–4; RB2:161]
- Mírzá Yaḥyá responds by claiming that he is the recipient of a divine revelation and all must turn to him. [BKG230; CB84; GPB166–7; RB2:162]

Bahá'u'lláh reveals the Lawḥ-i-Bahá in honour of Khátún Ján, a believer and close friend of Ṭáhirih. [RB2:171, 179]

- It was probably revealed just before He took up residence in the house of Riḍá Big. [RB2:171]
- This is the first Tablet in which Bahá'u'lláh uses the term 'people of Bahá' to refer to His followers, to distinguish them from the 'people of the Bayán'. [RB2:179]

Mar Khurshíd Páshá takes up the governorship of Adrianople. [BBR487; BKG233]

1866

10 Mar Bahá'u'lláh and His family withdraw from the house of Amru'lláh, the residence shared with the exiles, and go to the house of Riḍá Big. [BKG230; GPB167; RB2:162]

- He stays in this house for about one year. [GPB168]
- See BKG235 for a description of the house of Riḍá Big.

Bahá'u'lláh goes into isolation for two months. He orders that all of the family's goods should be divided. The companions are to choose between Himself and Azal. This has become known as the 'Most Great Separation'. [BBRSM67; BKG230–2; GPB167–8; RB2:162]

- See BKG231–2, GPB167 and RB2:163 for the effect of this.
- See BBRSM59–60 for a description of Azal's leadership.

10 Mar–c. Mar 1867 Bahá'u'lláh reveals numerous Tablets in the months that follow.

- See GBP170–1 for a description of the number of verses revealed every day.
- See BKG245 and GPB171 for list of Tablets revealed before Bahá'u'lláh's arrival in the house of 'Izzat Áqá.

14 Nov The 'star-fall' of 1866. [RB2:270, 422–6]

- The falling of stars is predicted in MATT. 24:29.
- For Bahá'u'lláh's reference to this see ESW131–2.
- For the symbolism of falling stars see KI41.

Dec About a hundred Bahá'ís are arrested in Tabríz following a disturbance in which a Bábí is killed. [BBR251–3; BW18:382]

1 Dec Birth of Marion Jack, prominent Bahá'í travel teacher, pioneer and artist, known affectionately as 'General Jack' for her services to the Bahá'í community, in Saint John, New Brunswick.

- See LDG1:217 for information on her pioneer work.

1867

In the year Birth of Mírzá Badí'u'lláh, fourth son of Bahá'u'lláh and Mahd-i-'Ulyá. [BKG247]

11 Jan Three Bahá'ís are executed in Tabríz. Their arrest is precipitated by conflict and rivalry between the Azalís and the Bahá'ís. [BBR252–3; BKG237–8; BW18:382–3; RB2:61]

Notes BW18:382 *says this was 8 January.*

Jan or Feb Mírzá Muḥammad-'Alí, a Bahá'í physician, is executed in Zanján. [BBR253; BKG238; BW18:383]

Áqá Najaf-'Alíy-i-Zanjání, a disciple of Ḥujjat, is executed in Ṭihrán. [BBR254; BW18:383]

c. Mar Bahá'u'lláh moves back to the now empty house of Amru'lláh. [GPB168]

- He stays for about three months. [GPB 168]

Notes BKG239 *says that within six months of Bahá'u'lláh's return to the house the owner sold it.*

Apr An appeal by 53 Bahá'ís in Baghdád addressed to the United States Congress arrives at the American Consulate in Beirut. [BBR265]

c. Jun Bahá'u'lláh rents the house of 'Izzat Áqá. [BKG239; GPB168]

- See BKG241 for a description of this house.

c. Aug Bahá'u'lláh refuses to draw the allowance granted Him by the Ottoman government. [RB2:327]

- Mírzá Yaḥyá twice petitions the government to convince it that he ought to be the recipient of the allowance. [RB2:327]
- Bahá'u'lláh sells some of His belongings to provide the necessities for Himself and His dependents. [RB2:327]

Sep Mírzá Yaḥyá, prodded on by Mír Muḥammad, challenges Bahá'u-'lláh to a public confrontation in the mosque of Sulṭán Salím, thinking that He will not accept. In the end, it is Mírzá Yaḥyá who does not appear. [BKG239–41; GPB168–9; RB2:291–300]

- The incident gains Bahá'u'lláh respect in the eyes of the people. [RB2:289]

- See RB2:304 for a picture of the mosque.

Sep 1867–Aug 1868 Bahá'u'lláh reveals the Súriy-Mulúk (Súrih of Kings). [BKG245; GPB171–2; RB2:301]

- This is described by Shoghi Effendi as 'the most momentous Tablet revealed by Bahá'u'lláh', in which He, 'for the first time, directs His words collectively to the entire company of the monarchs of East and West'. [GPB171]

- See GPB172–5 and RB2:301–25 for a description of the content of the Tablet.

Bahá'u'lláh reveals the Kitáb-i-Badí', the Munájátháy-i-Ṣíyám (Prayers for Fasting), the first Tablet to Napoleon III, the Lawḥ-i-Sulṭán written to Náṣiri'd-Dín Sháh, and the Súriy-i-Ra'ís. [BKG245; GBP172]

- See RB2:370–82 for details of the Kitáb-i-Badí'.

Bahá'u'lláh reveals the Súriy-i-Ghuṣn (Tablet of the Branch) in which 'Abdu'l-Bahá's future station is foreshadowed. [BBD218; BKG250; GPB177]

- See RB2:338–9 for a description of the Tablet.

In this period the extent of the Faith is enlarged, with expansion in the Caucasus, the establishment of the first Egyptian centre and the establishment of the Faith in Syria. [GPB176]

The greeting 'Alláh-u-Abhá' supersedes the Islamic salutation and is simultaneously adopted in Persia and Adrianople. [BKG250; GPB176]

The phrase 'the people of the Bayán', which now denotes the followers of Mírzá Yaḥyá, is discarded and is supplanted by the term 'the people of Bahá'. [BKG250; GBP176]

Nabíl-i-A'ẓam is despatched to Iraq and Iran to inform the Bábís of the advent of Bahá'u'lláh. He is further instructed to perform the rites of pilgrimage on Bahá'u'lláh's behalf in the House of the Báb and the Most Great House in Baghdád. [BKG250; EB224; GPB176–7]

• For details of his mission see EB224–7.

• On hearing Nabíl's message, the wife of the Báb, Khadíjih Khánum, immediately recognizes the station of Bahá'u'lláh. [EB225]

• For the rites of the two pilgrimages performed by Nabíl see SA113–15.

Bahá'u'lláh addresses a Tablet to Mullá 'Alí-Akbar-i-Shahmírzádí and Jamál-i-Burújirdí in Ṭihrán instructing them to transfer secretly the remains of the Báb from the Imám-Zádih Ma'ṣúm, where they were concealed, to some other place of safety. [GPB177]

The first pilgrimages to the residence of Bahá'u'lláh take place. [GPB177]

Persecutions begin anew in Ádharbáyján, Zanján, Níshápúr and Ṭihrán. [GPB178]

1868

In the year Áqá 'Abdu'r-Rasúl-i-Qumí, the water carrier at the House of Bahá'u'lláh at Baghdád, is murdered. [BKG247–8; RB2:332–3; SA143]

• Badí' takes his place. [BKG296]

Notes RB2:333 *says this took place towards the end of Bahá'u'lláh's stay in Adrianople.*

Bahá'ís in Bushrúyyih, Khurásán, are attacked and several are injured. [BW18:383]

Ḥájí Mírzá Ḥaydar-'Alí and six other prominent Bahá'ís are arrested in Cairo for being Bahá'ís. They are banished to Khartoum, where Ḥaydar-'Alí will spend the next 9 years in confinement. [BBR257; BKG250; GBP178]

• For the story of his life see RB2:438–50.

Ḥájí Mullá 'Alí-i-Akbar-i-Shahmírzádí (later Hand of the Cause Ḥájí Ákhúnd) is imprisoned in Ṭihrán as a Bahá'í on the order of Mullá 'Alí Kání. This is the first of many imprisonments. [EB266]

Ḥájí Mírzá Ḥaydar-'Alí

• He was imprisoned so often that 'Abdu'l-Bahá later said of him that at the first sign of disturbances, he would 'put on his turban, wrap himself in his 'abá and sit waiting' to be arrested. [MF11]

Group and individual photographs are taken of the Bahá'í and Azalí exiles in Adrianople, including one of Bahá'u'lláh.

Apr Seven Bahá'ís in Constantinople are arrested and interrogated by a commission of inquiry whose mandate it is to verify the claims of Bahá'u'lláh and Mírzá Yaḥyá. [BKG250–2; GPB179; MF99–100; RB2: 328–9]

• See RB2:329–32 for the conduct of the interrogations.

• Among those arrested is Mis͟hkín-Qalam, the calligrapher. He is particularly distraught because he is not allowed pen or paper. Eventually these are given to him. [BKG252]

c. May Bahá'u'lláh sends Nabíl-i-A'ẓam to Cairo to enquire after Ḥájí Mírzá Ḥaydar-'Alí. He is thrown into prison and befriends a Christian cellmate, Fáris Effendi, who soon becomes a Bahá'í. [BKG248, 265–6; EB268; GPB178]

Bahá'ís in Adrianople. Standing, left to right: Áqá Muḥammad-Qulí-i-Iṣfahání, Mírzá Naṣru'lláh-i-Tafri<u>sh</u>í, Nabíl-i-A'ẓam, Mírzá Áqá Ján, Mi<u>sh</u>kín-Qalam, Mírzá 'Alíy-i-Sayyáḥ, Áqá Ḥusayn-i-Á<u>sh</u><u>ch</u>í and Áqá 'Abdu'l-<u>Gh</u>affár-i-Iṣfahání. Sitting, left to right: Mírzá Muḥammad-Javád-i-Qazvíní, Mírzá Mihdí, 'Abdu'l-Bahá, Mírzá Muḥammad-Qulí (with, presumably, one of his children) and Siyyid Mihdíy-i-Dahijí. Sitting on the floor, left to right: Majdi'd-Dín (son of Mírzá Músá) and Mírzá Muḥammad-'Alí (half-brother of 'Abdu'l-Bahá)

- See BKG265–8 for an account of Nabíl's arrest and imprisonment.

- Fáris Effendi is probably the first Christian to become a Bahá'í. [RB3:10]

c. 7 Jun Nabíl has a dream in which Bahá'u'lláh appears to him in his cell and assures him that he will have reason to rejoice within the next 81 days. [BKG267]

c. Jul Principal Bahá'ís in Ba<u>gh</u>dád are arrested by the Turkish authorities and exiled to Mosul. [BBR265; BKG247; CH129–30; RB2:333]

- About 70 people are exiled. [GPB178; RB2:334]

- See BKG184 for an illustration of Mosul.

- See BKG183 for a description of the city.

- See RB2:334 for the hardships suffered by the exiles.

- They remained in Mosul for some 20 years until Bahá'u'lláh advised the community to disband. Their hardship was lessened by generous contributions from the King of Martyrs and the Beloved of Martyrs. A charity fund was established, the first fund of that kind in any Bahá'í community. [RB2:334–6]

c. 21 Jul Mírzá Abu'l-Qásim-i-Shírází is arrested in Egypt and money extorted from him. [BBR257–8; BKG243; GPB178]

26 Jul Sulṭán 'Abdu'l-'Azíz issues a firmán condemning Bahá'u'lláh to perpetual banishment. [BKG283–4; GPB179, 186; RB2:401–2]

- See RB2:402 for a list of those included in the edict.

- Bahá'u'lláh's property in Baghdád, valued at £50,000, is confiscated. [BBR196; BBRSM68]

- The Persian ambassador in Constantinople informs the Persian consuls in Iraq and Egypt that the Turkish government has withdrawn its protection from the Bábís and that they are free to do with them as they please. [GPB180]

- The Válí of Adrianople, Khurshíd Páshá, refuses to enforce the edict and leaves, ostensibly on urgent business, to a remote place. [BKG253; GPB180]

Notes BKG261, GPB181 *and* RB2:403 *indicate that it was not until the party reached Gallipoli that they were informed that their ultimate destination was 'Akká.*

BBD40 *says that it was because of the disloyal Mírzá Yaḥyá's plotting against Bahá'u'lláh that the Turkish authorities condemned Him to perpetual imprisonment in 'Akká.*

Aug Mullá Muḥammad-Riḍá, Riḍá'r-Rúḥ, is poisoned in Yazd. [BW18:383]

One morning without warning Bahá'u'lláh's house is surrounded by soldiers. The inhabitants are rounded up and taken to government headquarters. They are told to make ready for their departure for Gallipoli. [BKG255; GPB179; RB2:403]

• The Consuls of European powers offer assistance to Bahá'u'lláh and are prepared to ask the intervention of their governments. Bahá'u'lláh refuses these offers. [BKG255, 257–8]

Notes *Western accounts of this incident suggest that Bahá'u'lláh asked for such assistance.* [BBR187–91]

• The next day the goods of the Bahá'ís are sold or auctioned for very low prices. [BKG255, 258]

12 Aug Bahá'u'lláh and His family and companions, escorted by soldiers, set out for Gallipoli. [BKG260; GPB180; RB2:409]

15 Aug The Bahá'ís imprisoned in Constantinople arrive in Gallipoli to be exiled with Bahá'u'lláh's party. [BKG260]

16 Aug They arrive in Gallipoli on the fifth day. [BKG260]

Notes GPB180 *says it was a four-day journey.*

• They remain there for three nights. [BKG263; GPB181]

Notes BKG261 *says they were there for 'a few days'.*

21 Aug Bahá'u'lláh and His companions leave Gallipoli on an Austrian-Lloyd steamer. [BKG263; GPB182; RB2:411]

• See BKG270 for map of the journey.

• Towards sunset the same day the steamer touches on Madellí and stops for a few hours. It continues on to Smyrna the same night. [BKG264]

22 Aug Soon after sunrise the ship arrives at Smyrna. [BKG264]

• It stays for two days. [BKG264; GPB182]

• The illness of Mírzá Áqáy-i-Ká<u>sh</u>ání necessitates his removal to the hospital. He dies soon after and is buried in Izmír. [BKG264–5; GPB182]

23 Aug The steamer leaves Smyrna at night for Alexandria, which she gains on a morning two days later. [BKG265]

1868

26 Aug The steamer carrying Bahá'u'lláh docks at Alexandria, early in the morning. [BKG265; RB3:6]

• The exiles change ships, again onto an Austrian-Lloyd. [BKG265]

27 Aug Several exiles go ashore to make purchases. One passes by the prison house where Nabíl is detained. Nabíl, watching from the roof of his prison cell, recognizes him. [BKG265, 267; RB3:6]

28 Aug Nabíl and Fáris Effendi write letters to Bahá'u'lláh which are delivered by a Christian youth. The youth returns with a Tablet from Bahá'u'lláh and gifts from 'Abdu'l-Bahá and Mírzá Mihdí. [BKG267–8; RB3:6–7]

The ship bearing Bahá'u'lláh leaves Alexandria for Port Said. [BKG268]

29 Aug In the morning the ship arrives in Port Said. At nightfall it travels on to Jaffa. [BKG268]

30 Aug The ship arrives at Jaffa at sunset. At midnight the ship leaves for Haifa. [BKG168]

31 Aug The ship arrives in Haifa in the early morning. [BKG269; GPB182; RB3:11]

The sea gate into 'Akká

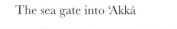

The stairway up which Bahá'u'lláh climbed to His cell in the Most Great Prison

- Bahá'u'lláh and His companions – 70 in all – disembark and are taken ashore in sailing boats. [RB3:11]

- Mírzá Yaḥyá and the four Bahá'ís arrested at Constantinople, including Mishkín-Qalam, are sent to Famagusta in Cyprus. [BKG268; GPB179]

- One of the Bahá'ís, Áqá 'Abdu'l-Ghaffár, throws himself into the sea when he learns he is to be separated from Bahá'u'lláh. [BKG269; GPB182]

A few hours later Bahá'u'lláh's party is put aboard a sailing vessel and taken to 'Akká. [RB3:12]

- See CH66 for Bahíyyih Khánum's account of the journey.

The exiles land in 'Akká to begin a confinement in the citadel that is to last two years, two months and five days. [BBR205; BKG169; DH12; RB3:11]

- See BKG277–9 for a list of the exiles. Two others joined them immediately after arrival. [BBR205]

- See BR205–6 for 'Abdu'l-Bahá's account of the journey of exile.

- See RB2:2 and RB3:21 for prophecies regarding Bahá'u'lláh's exile to 'Akká.

- See BKG271–4 and DH17–24 for a history of 'Akká before the arrival of Bahá'u'lláh.

- See DH26–8 and GPB186–7 for a description of the exiles' walk to the prison.

- See GPB186–7 for Bahá'u'lláh's description of the citadel and the conditions there on His arrival.

- See BKG275–7 for Áqá Riḍá's description of the citadel and the conditions there.

- See DH30–1 for a description of the citadel building and the accommodation used by Bahá'u'lláh.

- The first night the exiles are refused both food and drink. [GPB187]

- Afterwards each prisoner is allocated three loaves of stale black bread as a daily food ration plus filthy water. [GBP187]

- Three of the exiles die soon after arrival. Soon after their death Bahá'u'lláh reveals the Lawḥ-i-Ra'ís, the second Tablet to 'Alí Pá<u>sh</u>á. [BKG283; GPB187; RB3:20, 34]

- See BKG317–21 and CH250–1 for the story of the Azalís who were confined to 'Akká with the exiles.

- See BBRSM69–70 for details on the system of communications used between the Holy Land and the Bahá'í communities.

3 Sep The firmán of the Sulṭán 'Abdu'l-'Azíz condemning Bahá'u'lláh to life imprisonment is read out in the Mosque of Al-Jazzár. [BKG284–5; GPB186; RB3:18]

- See BKG283–4, 286; GBP186, RB2:402 and RB3:18 for the terms of the edict.

- See RB3:18–19 for 'Abdu'l-Bahá's response.

- See BKG283–8, RB3:19–20 for conditions of life in the barracks

'Akká, showing the Mosque of Al-Jazzár on the right

5 Sep Mírzá Yaḥyá and his family arrive in Famagusta along with four Bahá'ís. [BBR306]

- See BBR306 for the names of the Bahá'ís and their fate.
- Mírzá Yaḥyá arrives with his entire family but without a single disciple or even a servant. [BBR306]

c. Oct Nabíl is released from prison in Egypt and departs for 'Akká. [BKG290–1; RB3:57]

- He visits Cyprus on the way. [BKG291]

30 Oct Christoph Hoffman, founder of the Templers, and Georg David Hardegg, his principal lieutenant, land in Haifa. Hardegg remains in Haifa to head the colony, while Hoffman goes to Jaffa to found a colony there. [BBD224; BBR204, 215–16; DH133]

Notes DH139 *and* GPB277 *say this was 1863.*

- See BBR215–18 for the relationship between Bahá'u'lláh and the Templers.
- Bahá'u'lláh several times stayed in the houses of the colony. [BBR234]
- See BBR236–9 for articles written about the Bahá'ís by Templers.

1868–1869

end Oct Nabíl enters 'Akká in disguise but is recognized and after three days is thrown out of the city. [BKG290–1; GPB188; RB3:57]

- He spends the next four months wandering about Haifa, Mount Carmel and the Galilee waiting for another opportunity to enter 'Akká. [BKG290–1; RB3:57]

1868–70 During this period Bahá'u'lláh reveals a number of Tablets to rulers including the Lawḥ-i-Ra'ís to 'Alí Pá<u>sh</u>á, His second Tablet to Napoleon III and Tablets to Czar Alexander II, Queen Victoria and Pope Pius IX. [BBD13]

- President Grant of the United States is in office when Bahá'u'lláh addresses a Tablet to the 'Rulers of America and the Presidents of the Republics therein'. [BFA1:80N]

Right: Czar Alexander II
Far right: Pope Pius IX

1869

1869–72 A great famine occurs in Iran in which about 10 per cent of the population dies and a further 10 per cent emigrates. [BBRSM86; GPB233]

In the year Franz Josef, Emperor of Austria and King of Hungary, makes a pilgrimage to Jerusalem but fails to enquire after Bahá'u'lláh. [KAN116]

Early in the year Ḥájí Amín-i-Iláhí arrives in 'Akká from Iran and is the first pilgrim to see Bahá'u'lláh. [DH33]

• He is 'only able to do so in the public bath, where it had been arranged that he should see Bahá'u'lláh without approaching Him or giving any sign of recognition'. This is the bath of Al-Jazzár. [DH33; GBP817]

The 17–year-old Áqá Buzurg-i-Nís͟hápúrí, Badí', arrives in 'Akká having walked from Mosul. He is able to enter the city unsuspected. [BKG297; RB3:178]

• He is still wearing the simple clothes of a water bearer. [BKG297]

• For the story of his life, see BKG294–7 and RB3:176–9.

Badí' sees 'Abdu'l-Bahá in a mosque and is able to write a note to Him. The same night Badí' enters the citadel and goes into the presence of Bahá'u'lláh. He meets Bahá'u'lláh twice. [BKG297; RB3:179]

• For his transformation see RB3:179–82.

Badí' asks Bahá'u'lláh for the honour of delivering the Tablet to the S͟háh and Bahá'u'lláh bestows it on him. [BKG297; RB3:182]

• The journey takes four months; he travels alone. [BKG298]

• For the story of the journey see BKG297–300 and RB3:184.

• For the Tablet of Bahá'u'lláh to Badí' see BKG299 and RB3:175–6.

Feb Nabíl makes a second attempt to enter 'Akká. He is able to remain for 81 days and meets Mírzá Áqá Ján and others but does not see Bahá'u'lláh. [BKG291; RB3:57]

Notes DH35 *says Nabíl spent 81 days in the citadel from 21 March to 9 June 1870.*

1 May Nabíl meets Bahá'u'lláh. [RB3:57]

12 May Birth of Clara Davis Dunn, Hand of the Cause, in London.

Jul Badí' delivers the Tablet of Bahá'u'lláh to the S͟háh. He is tortured and executed. [BBRXXXIX; BKG300; BW18:383; RB3:184–6]

Áqá Buzurg-i-Ní<u>sh</u>ápúrí, Badí‘

• For details of his torture and martyrdom see BKG300, 304–7 and RB3:186–91.

• For the account of the French Minister in Ṭihrán see BBR254–5.

Badí' under guard

- He is given the title Fakhru'sh-Shuhadá' (Pride of Martyrs). [BKG300]

- Shoghi Effendi listed him among the Apostles of Bahá'u'lláh. [BW3:80–1]

- For the effect on Bahá'u'lláh of the martyrdom of Badí' see BKG300 and GPB199.

See also BKG293–314; GPB199, RB3:172–203; TN58–9.

25 Dec A mob attacks the Bahá'ís in Fárán, Khurásán, Iran, and two are severely beaten. [BW18:383]

1870

In the year Battle of Sedan. Napoleon III suffers defeat at the hands of Kaiser Wilhelm I. He goes into exile in England, where he dies in 1873.

• Bahá'u'lláh refers to this in KA86.

Napoleon III

Náṣiri'd-Dín Sháh makes a pilgrimage to the shrines in Iraq. In preparation for his visit the Bahá'ís are rounded up, arrested and exiled. [BBR267; BBRSM90; BKG441]

• See BKG441–3 for details of the exile.

In Zanján, Áqá Siyyid Ashraf is arrested, condemned to death as a Bábí and executed. [BWG470]

• He is the son of Mír Jalíl, one of the companions of Ḥujjat who was martyred in Ṭihrán at the end of the Zanján episode. [BKG470]

• He was born during the siege at Zanján. [BKG470]

• His mother was brought to prison to persuade him to recant his faith but she threatened to disown him if he did so. [BBD25; BKG470; ESW73–4; GPB199–200]

• See GI35–6 for Bahá'u'lláh's Tablet concerning Ashraf and his mother.

'Údí Khammár completes the restoration and expansion of the mansion at Bahjí originally built by 'Abdu'lláh Páshá in 1821. [BBD42, 128; DH106–7]

• See DH107 for the inscription he places over the door.

14 Jan Birth of May (or Mary) Ellis Bolles, prominent American Bahá'í teacher, in Englewood, New Jersey.

22 Jun Mírzá Mihdí, the Purest Branch, falls through the skylight in the roof of the prison in 'Akká onto a crate lying on the floor below. [BKG311–12; GBP188; RB3:205]

• It was a normal practice for prisoners to go onto the roof in the summer evenings for fresh air. [RB3:205]

• He was chanting the verses of Bahá'u'lláh's Qaṣídiy-i-Varqá'íyyih. [RB3:206]

• He is so badly injured that his clothes have to be torn from him. [RB206]

• Bahá'u'lláh comes to him at His bedside and asks His son whether he wishes to live; the Purest Branch begs Bahá'u-'lláh to accept his life as a ransom for the opening of the gates of the prison to pilgrims. Bahá'u'lláh accepts this sacrifice. [BKG311–12; GPB188; RB3:208]

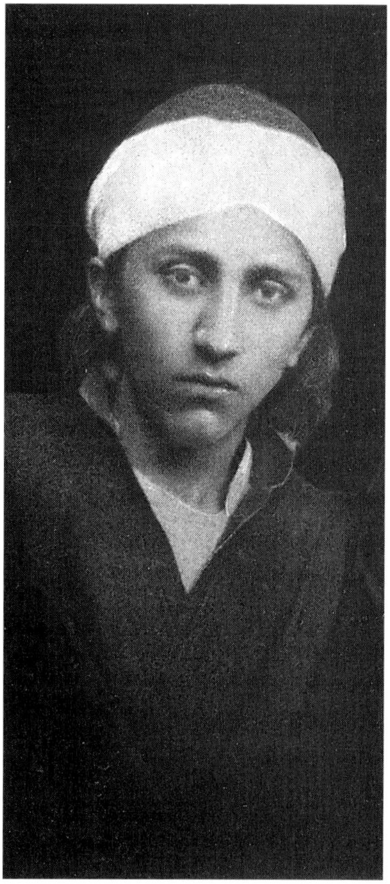

Mírzá Mihdí

23 Jun Mírzá Mihdí dies from his injuries 22 hours after his fall. [BKG311–12; GPB188; RB3:208]

• See BKG313, GPB188 and RB3:210 for the prayer of Bahá'u'lláh for His son.

• He is interred in the cemetery next to the shrine of Nabí Ṣáliḥ in 'Akká. [GBP188; RB3:209]

See also BBD155, BKG311–14, RB3:204–20.

Jul The Roman Catholic Vatican Council under Pope Pius IX formulates the doctrine of papal infallibility. Shortly afterwards Italian forces under Victor Emmanuel II attack the Papal States and seize and occupy Rome, virtually extinguishing the temporal sovereignty of the pope. [GPB227; PDC54]

29 Sep Mírzá 'Abdu'l-Ghaffár effects his escape from Cyprus and rejoins Bahá'u'lláh in 'Akká. [BBR306]

Oct Bahá'u'lláh is moved to the house of Malik in the Fákhúrah quarter, in the western part of 'Akká. [BBRXXIX, 209; BKG315; GPB189; RB3:221]

• Movements of troops required use of the barracks. [BKG315; RB3:221]

• Bahá'u'lláh's occupation of this house lasts three months. [BBR209–10; BKG315; GPB189]

• This is four months after the death of the Purest Branch. [BKG315; GPB189; RB3:221]

1870–1 Franco-Prussian War.

• See KA90 for Bahá'u'lláh's reference to this and KAN121 for 'Abdu'l-Bahá's interpretation.

1871

In the year Muḥammad-Ḥasan Khán-i-Káshí dies in Burújird, Iran, after being bastinadoed. [BW18:383]

Three Bahá'ís are executed in Shíráz. [BW18:383]

c. Jan Bahá'u'lláh is moved to the house of Khavvám, across the street from the house of Malik. [BBR209–10; BKG315; GPB189]

• His occupation of this house lasts a few months. [BKG319]

c. May Bahá'u'lláh is transferred to the house of Rábi'ih. [GPB189]

• His occupation of this house lasts four months. [BKG319; DH38–9]

mid-1871 'Údí Khammár, a wealthy Maronite Christian merchant, and his family move into the recently restored mansion at Bahjí, leaving their 'Akká house empty. [BKG316–17; DH203]

4 Aug Shaykh 'Alíy-i-Sayyáḥ, one of the Bahá'ís imprisoned in Cyprus, dies. [BBR306]

Sep Bahá'u'lláh is transferred to the house of 'Údí Khammár in 'Akká. [BBD109; BKG317; DH39, 203; GPB189]

• The house is so small that 13 people of both sexes occupy one room. The remainder of Bahá'u'lláh's companions take up residence in other houses and the Khán-i-'Avámíd. [GBP189]

• Bahá'u'lláh's occupation of this house lasts two years. [BKG319]

• See BKG317 for the initial response of His neighbour, Ilyás 'Abbúd.

• See DH201–3 for abiography of 'Údí Khammár.

1 Nov Birth of 'Lua' Getsinger (Lucinda Louisa Aurora Moore), Disciple of 'Abdu'l-Bahá, Herald of the Covenant and Mother Teacher of the West.

end of the year Bahá'u'lláh reveals the Lawḥ-i-Qad Iḥtaraqa'l-Mukhliṣun (Fire Tablet). [BKG321–2; RB3:226–31]

1872

In the year Restoration of the House of the Báb begins at the request of Khadíjih Bigum. On its completion she takes up residence there. [EB232]

Bahá'u'lláh calls Munírih Khánum (Fáṭimih Khánum) to 'Akká to marry 'Abdu'l-Bahá. She travels to Shíráz where she stays with the wife of the Báb then travels to Mecca for the pilgrimage. From Mecca she travels to 'Akká. [MKBM]

Above: The house of ‘Údí Khammár

Below: Khán-i-‘Avámíd

Notes DH45 *says she was called to the Holy Land in December 1871 to January 1872.*

BKG347 *says she performed the pilgrimage in February 1873.*

• See CH84–7 for Munírih Khánum's own account of the journey.

Birth of Joseph H. Hannen, a Disciple of 'Abdu'l-Bahá.

c. 1872 Birth of Thomas Breakwell, considered the first English Bahá'í, in Woking, Surrey, England.

22 Jan Three Azalís, among them Siyyid Muḥammad-i-Iṣfahání, the Antichrist of the Bahá'í Revelation, are murdered by seven Bahá'ís. [BBD163; BKG325–6; DH41; GPB189; RB3:235]

• Bahá'u'lláh is taken to the Governorate where He is interrogated and imprisoned for 70 hours. [BKG327; GBP190; RB3:237]

• 'Abdu'l-Bahá is thrown into prison and kept in chains the first night. Twenty-five of the companions were also imprisoned and shackled. [BKG328; GBP190; RB3:237]

• See BKG331, GPB191 and RB3:238 for the effect of the murders on the local population.

• Ilyás 'Abbúd puts a barricade between his house and the house of 'Údí Khammár, where Bahá'u'lláh lives. [BKG331; GPB191]

• See BKG330, DH44 and RB3:239 for the fate of the murderers, who are imprisoned for seven years.

10 Aug Birth of Martha Root, Hand of the Cause and itinerant Bahá'í teacher, in Richmond, Ohio.

22 Nov Muḥammad-Báqir-i-Maḥallátí, one of the Bahá'ís imprisoned in Cyprus, dies. [BBR306]

• This leaves Mishkín-Qalam as the only Bahá'í in Cyprus. [BBR306]

last months Munírih Khánum arrives in 'Akká. She stays in the house of Mírzá Músá for several months. [MKBM]

Notes BKG347 *suggests she arrived some time after February 1873.*

1873

In the year

Aḥmad Big Tawfíq (Aḥmad Bey) becomes Mutaṣarrif of 'Akká. [BBD12, 20; BBR487; DH126–9; GPB192]

- His governorship lasts two years. [BKG337]
- This 'sagacious and humane governor' meets 'Abdu'l-Bahá and is greatly impressed by Him. The governor peruses some of the writings, which also impress him. [BKG334; GPB191]
- In response to a request for permission to render Bahá'u'lláh some service, the suggestion is made to him to restore the disused aqueduct built to bring water into 'Akká, 'a suggestion which he immediately arose to carry out'. [DH52; GBP192]

See also

See DH126–9 *for history of the aqueduct. See* BKG333–4 *for information on Aḥmad Big Tawfíq.*

The aqueduct, just above Bahjí

Ibn-i-Abhar is arrested in Ṭihrán and imprisoned for 14 months and 15 days. [BW18:383]

Birth of Hippolyte Dreyfus, the first French Bahá'í, in Paris. Named by Shoghi Effendi a Disciple of 'Abdu'l-Bahá.

early part Bahá'u'lláh completes the revelation of the Kitáb-i-Aqdas in the southeast corner room of the house of 'Údí Khammár. [BBD132; BKG351; DH46; GPB213; RB3:275; SA248]

- This date is confirmed by the book's reference to the fall of Napoleon III in 1870. [SA248]
- There is some evidence to suggest that parts of the Kitáb-i-Aqdas were revealed as early as 1868. [SA16–17]

The room in the house of 'Údí Khammár in which the Kitáb-i-Aqdas was revealed

- For the significance of the Kitáb-i-Aqdas see BKG351–3, BW15:87–91, GPB213–15 and RB3:275–399.

- For analyses of its significance, content and application, see RB3:275–399 and SA248–52.

c. Mar Ilyás 'Abbúd offers to provide a room in his house for 'Abdu'l-Bahá and Munírih Khánum after their marriage. He furnishes a room, opens a doorway into it through the dividing wall and presents it to Bahá'u'lláh for 'Abdu'l-Bahá's use. [BKG348; DH45]

8 Mar Marriage of 'Abdu'l-Bahá to Munírih Khánum.

Notes DH45 *says the marriage took place in late August or September 1872.*

- See CH87–90, DH45–6 and RB2:208–9 for details of the wedding.

- For the story of Munírih Khánum's life see RB2:204–9.

- She was the daughter of Mírzá Muḥammad-'Alíy-i-Nahrí by his second wife. [BBD165; GPB130; RB2:204]

- See BBD166, BKG340–1, DB208–9 and RB2:203–4 for the story of her conception.

- See BKG344, MA112–13 and RB2:206–7 for the story of her first marriage.

- The marriage resulted in nine children, five of whom died in childhood: Ḥusayn Effendi (died 1887, aged two), Mihdí (died aged two-and-a-half), Ṭúbá, Fu'ádiyyih and Ruḥangíz. Four daughters grew to adulthood. The oldest of these was Ḍiyá'iyyih, who married Mírzá Hádí Shírází in 1895. Shoghi Effendi was their eldest child. The second daughter, Ṭúbá Khánum, married Mírzá Muḥsin Afnán. The third daughter of 'Abdu'l-Bahá, Rúḥá, married Mírzá Jalál, the son of Mírzá Muḥammad-Ḥasan, the King of Martyrs. The fourth daughter, Munavvar, married Mírzá Aḥmad. [ABMM]

7 Jun Birth of Amelia Engelder Collins, Hand of the Cause, in Pittsburgh, Pennsylvania.

late Bahá'u'lláh acquires the house of 'Abbúd. It is joined to the house of 'Údí Khammár to make one residence and Bahá'u'lláh moves to the side of the house previously occupied by 'Abbúd. [BBD106, 109; BKG319; DH51]

'Abdu'l-Bahá, taken in Adrianople

- He lives here for four years. [BBD106, 109; BKG319; DH51]
- See BBD1 for information on Ilyás 'Abbúd.

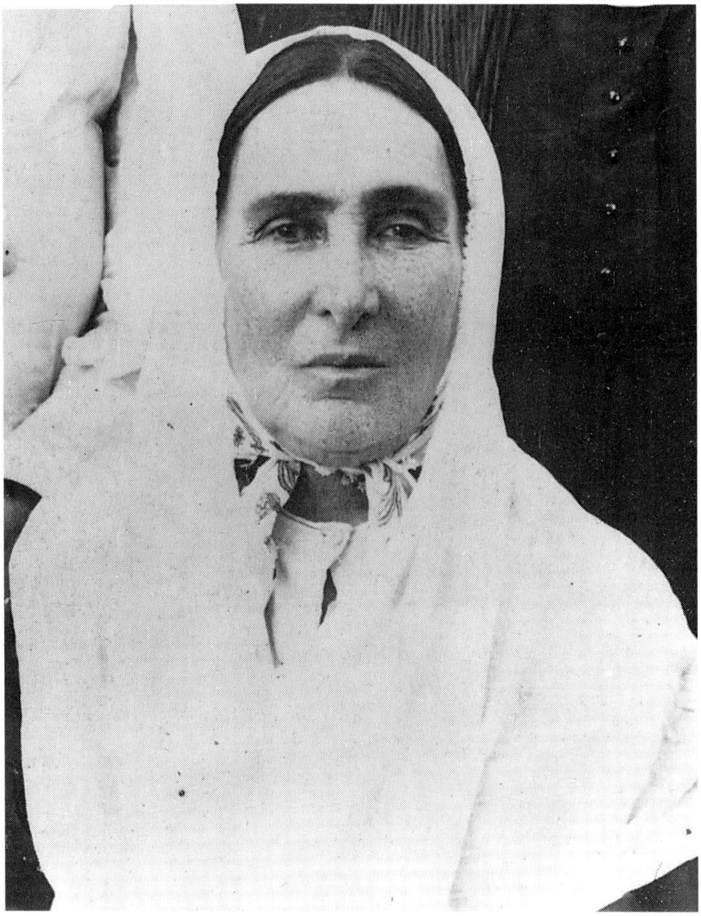

Munírih Khánum

latter part The existence of the Kitáb-i-Aqdas is made known to the Bahá'ís. [SA248]

1874

In the year Birth of William Sutherland Maxwell, Hand of the Cause of God, in Montreal.

Apr Shaykh Muḥammad-Báqir, the Wolf, has 20 or more Bahá'ís arrested in Iṣfahán. [BW18:383]

8 May The arrival of the eldest son of Náṣiri'd-Dín Sháh, Sulṭán-Mas'úd Mírzá, Ẓillu's-Sulṭán, arrives in Iṣfahán as governor. [BBR269]

Within a few days of the arrival of Ẓillu's-Sulṭán in Iṣfahán, a general persecution of Bahá'ís begins. [BBRXXXIX, 269–70]

- This can be traced to Shaykh Muḥammad Báqir, the 'Wolf'. [BBR270]
- For Western reports of this outburst see BBR 270–3.

19 May Birth of John Ebenezer Esslemont, Hand of the Cause of God, in Aberdeen, Scotland.

6 Jun Birth of Louis George Gregory, Hand of the Cause of God, at Charleston, South Carolina.

Ẓillu's-Sulṭán

1875

In the year The 'ulamá arouse the rabble against the Bahá'ís in Sidih, Iṣfahán. Several Bahá'ís are imprisoned, including Nayyir and Síná. [BW18:383]

'Abdu'l-Bahá writes *The Secret of Divine Civilization*, a treatise on the establishment of a just, progressive and divinely-based government. [SDCV]

- It was lithographed in Bombay in 1882. It was first published in English under the title *The Mysterious Forces of Civilization* in London in 1910. [SDCV]
- Shoghi Effendi calls it "Abdu'l-Bahá's outstanding contribution to the future reorganization of the world'. [WOB37]

Bahá'u'lláh sends Sulaymán Khán Ilyás, Jamál Effendi to India. [BW4:285; GPB195; MC155]

Jamál Effendi with a Burmese child

Notes BBRSM90, 193 *say he was sent in 1871 and left in 1878.* EB122 *says he reached Bombay in 1878 and stayed 11 years on the subcontinent.*

- His work helps establish Bahá'í communities in Bombay, Calcutta and Madras as well as in Burma. [BBRSM91; GPB225]
- Among those he teaches is Siyyid Muṣṭafá Rúmí, who later founds the Bahá'í community of Burma. [BW10:517]

See also EB120–1, 122–8 *and* MF 134–8.

'Abdu'l-Bahá rents a small garden near 'Akká for Bahá'u'lláh's use. [BBD196–7; DH95]

- See DH95 for its situation.
- This garden on the river Na'mayn is later named Riḍván by Bahá'u'lláh. [DH95]

Birth of Agnes Baldwin Alexander, Hand of the Cause, in Hawaii.

- She is a granddaughter of two of Hawaii's most famous missionary families, the Baldwins and the Alexanders.

16 Oct Birth of Ṭarázu'lláh Samandarí, Hand of the Cause of God, in Qazvín.

1876

Mírzá Mírzá Abu'l-Faḍl

In the year Six Bahá'ís are arrested in Ṭihrán and imprisoned for three months and 17 days. [BW18:383]

The conversion of Mírzá Abu'l-Faḍl Gulpáygání, a leading clerical philosopher. [BBRSM88; EB264]

- See EB263–5 for details of his life.
- See BKG 262 for details of his conversion.

14 Feb Birth of Keith Ransom-Kehler, Hand of the Cause and the first American Bahá'í martyr, in Kentucky.

30 May Sulṭán 'Abdu'l-'Azíz is deposed. [BBR485]

4 Jun 'Abdu'l-'Azíz either commits suicide or is assassinated. [BBD2; BBR485; GPB225]

- Bahá'u'lláh predicted his downfall in the Lawḥ-i-Fu'ád. [RB3:87]
- Bahá'u'lláh stated that the tyranny of Sulṭán 'Abdu'l-'Azíz exceeded that of Náṣiri'd-Dín

Sháh because the Sulṭán exiled Bahá'u'lláh to the Most Great Prison without any reason whereas the Sháh had reason to be fearful of the Bahá'ís because of the attempt on his life. [BKG412]

- Bahá'u'lláh addressed two Tablets to the Sulṭán including the Súriy-i-Mulúk (Tablet to the Kings) but he did not respond. [BBD2]

Accession of Murád V to the throne. [BBR485]

14 Jun Birth of George Townshend, Hand of the Cause of God, in Dublin.

31 Aug Deposition of Murád V. Accession of 'Abdu'l-Ḥamíd II.

Sulṭán 'Abdu'l-Ḥamíd II

1877

c. 1877 'Abdu'l-Bahá rents the house of Mazra'ih for Bahá'u'lláh's use. [BKG357; DH87; RB3:416]

In the year Birth of Siegfried Schopflocher, Hand of the Cause of God, in Germany.

spring 'Abdu'l-Bahá holds a banquet for the notables of 'Akká in a pine grove near Bahjí. [BKG358; DH54, 87]

- Permission is given him by its Christian owner, Jirjis al-Jamál. [DH54]
- The acceptance of the invitation by the notables signals the fact that the firmán of 'Abdu'l-'Azíz, though still in force, is a dead letter. [DH54; GPB193]

The pine grove at Bahjí

Jun Possibly the first visit of Bahá'u'lláh to the Riḍván Garden outside 'Akká. [BBD196–7; DH95; GPB193]

- See DH95–101 for a description of the garden and Bahá'u'lláh's use of it.

The Riḍván Garden, showing the two old mulberry trees and the spot on the right where Bahá'u'lláh customarily sat

• See CH96–8 for Ṭúbá Khánum's description of the garden.

3–10 Jun Bahá'u'lláh takes up residence at Mazra'ih. [BBD154]

• It takes the repeated pleadings of Shaykh 'Alíy-i-Mírí, the Muftí of 'Akká, to persuade Him to go. [BBD154; BKG358–9; GPB192–3]

Mazra'ih

- See BKG359 and DH89 for a description.

- Bahá'u'lláh resides here for two years with some members of His family while 'Abdu'l-Bahá, the Greatest Holy Leaf and Navváb continue to live in the House of 'Abbúd. [BBD13, 106; DH89–90]

- See CH136 for the reason why 'Abdu'l-Bahá did not live at Mazra'ih.

See also DH89–94.

Sep Ḥájí 'Abdu'l-Majíd-i-Ní<u>sh</u>ápúrí is executed in Ma<u>sh</u>had. [BW18:383]

Dec Mullá Káẓim-i-Tál<u>kh</u>un<u>ch</u>i'í is executed in Iṣfahán. [BBR273–4; BW18:383]

end Conversion of Siyyid Muṣṭafá Rúmí in Calcutta, where he is travelling with Jamál Effendi. [RSLG]

1877–8 War between Russia and Turkey, freeing some 11 million people from the Turkish yoke. Adrianople is occupied. [BKG262; GPB225]

- See BKG460 for the Siege of Plevna.

1878

In the year Siyyid Muṣṭafá Rúmí arrives in Burma with Jamál Effendi.

- He marries into a well-to-do Indo-Burman family of traders and settles in Rangoon, remaining in Burma to build up the Burmese community. [BW10:517; PH23]

- See BW10:517–18 and MC155 for his conversion of Daidanaw, the first all-Bahá'í village in the world outside Iran.

- See BW10:517–20 for an account of his life.

19 Feb Birth of George Adam Benke, German-Russian Bahá'í, who after his death was named by Shoghi Effendi as the first European Bahá'í martyr, in the Ukraine. [BW5:416–18]

12 Jul The British government takes over the administration of Cyprus. [BBR306]

1879

In the year 'Abdu'l-Bahá travels to Beirut at the invitation of Midḥat Pásh͟há, the Válí of Syria. [BKG378]

- 'Abdu'l-Bahá is still officially a prisoner of the Ottoman Empire. [BKG:379]
- Bahá'u'lláh reveals a Tablet marking the occasion. [BKG378–9; GPB243; TB227–8]
- Among the important figures 'Abdu'l-Bahá meets in Beirut are Midḥat Pásh͟há himself and S͟hayk͟h Muḥammad 'Abduh, the future Grand Muftí of Egypt. [BKG379]

Birth of Laura Clifford Barney, who compiled the table talks of 'Abdu'l-Bahá in *Some Answered Questions.*

c. 1879 Sárih K͟hánum, the faithful sister of Bahá'u'lláh, dies in Ṭihrán. She is buried a short distance from the city. [RB1:49–50]

12 Mar The arrest of Ḥájí Siyyid Muḥammad-Ḥasan, the 'King of Martyrs', and Ḥájí Siyyid Muḥammad-Ḥusayn, the 'Beloved of Martyrs'. [BBD130]

17 Mar The martyrdom of Ḥájí Siyyid Muḥammad-Ḥasan, the 'King of Martyrs', and Ḥájí Siyyid Muḥammad-Ḥusayn, the 'Beloved of Martyrs'. [BW18:383]

- Their martyrdom is instigated by Mír Muḥammad-Ḥusayn, the Imám-Jum'ih, stigmatized by Bahá'u'lláh as the 'she-serpent', who owes the brothers a large sum of money. [GPB200–1]
- S͟hayk͟h Muḥammad-Báqir, the 'Wolf', pronounces the death sentence on the two brothers and the Ẓillu's-Sulṭán ratifies the decision. [GPB201]
- The brothers are put in chains, decapitated and dragged to the Maydán-i-S͟háh for public viewing. [GPB201]
- For Western accounts of their martyrdom see BBR274–6.

See also BBD129–130, 193

- See BW11:594 for a picture of the memorial to the King and the Beloved of Martyrs.

summer An epidemic of plague breaks out in 'Akká and environs. Among others who feel its effects are 'Údí Khammár and his family, who leave the mansion at Bahjí. [BBD42, 128; BKG362; DH91, 203; GPB194]

20 Jun Mishkín-Qalam is given permission to move from Famagusta to Nicosia. [BBR307]

Sep Bahá'u'lláh moves to the empty mansion at Bahjí after two years' residence at Mazra'ih. [BBD42; BKG362]

- See BBD42 and GPB216 for a list of Tablets revealed by Bahá'u'lláh during His occupation of the mansion of Bahjí.

1880

early 1880s The first Zoroastrians become Bahá'ís, in Persia. [SBBH2:67]

- For information on these converts see SBBR2:67–93.

In the year Martyrdom of seven Bahá'ís in Sulṭánábád. [BW18:383]

- Three Bahá'ís are killed on the orders of Siyyid Muḥammad-Báqir-i-Mujtahid and a large number of Bahá'ís are thrown into prison. [BW18:383]
- Sayyidih Khánum Bíbí, an old lady, is sent to Ṭihrán and is strangled in prison. [BW18:383]

Birth of Ṭúbá Khánum, second daughter of 'Abdu'l-Bahá. [ABMM]

18 or 19 Jun Bahá'u'lláh visits the Druze village of Yirkih (Yerka). 'Abdu'l-Bahá joins Him for the last four nights. [DH123]

- See DH123 for other Druze villages visited by Bahá'u'lláh.

15 Aug Mishkín-Qalam addresses a petition to the High Commissioner of Cyprus begging to be released from his confinement. [BBR307]

- See BBR307–11 for consequences of this.

1881

In the year The Riḍván Garden and the Firdaws Garden are purchased in the name of Bahá'u'lláh. [BBD84, 196; DH95, 103]

- Most of the flowering plants in the Riḍván Garden are brought by pilgrims from Iran. [CH96]

24 Mar Mírzá Yaḥyá is granted freedom by the British administration of Cyprus. [BBR311]

- He asks for British citizenship or protection so that he may return to Iran or Turkey in safety but is denied it and so he stays on in Cyprus for the rest of his life. [BBR311]

1882

In the year Ibn-i-Aṣdaq is given the distinction Shahíd Ibn-i-Shahíd (Martyr, son of the martyr) by Bahá'u'lláh. [EB173]

Mírzá 'Alí-Muḥammad Varqá is arrested in Yazd. He is sent to Iṣfahán where he is imprisoned for a year. [BW18:383]

Prompted by the fear that Egypt will default on its enormous debts to European banks, the British invade Egypt and take over its administration. [BFA15]

15 Sep The death of Khadíjih-Bagum, the wife of the Báb, in Shíráz. [BBD127; EB235; KB35]

1882–3 The Ṭihrán Upheaval.

- A number of leading members of the Ṭihrán Bahá'í community are arrested and subsequently condemned to death. Some are confined for a period of 19 months in severe circumstances but the death sentences are not carried out. [BBR292–5; BW18:383]
- This is occasioned by the release of Bahá'u'lláh from strict confinement and the subsequent increase in the number of pilgrims from Iran causing an upsurge of Bahá'í activities, particularly in Ṭihrán. [BBR292–5]

Mírzá 'Alí-Muḥammad Varqá

1883

In the year Six Bahá'ís are arrested in Yazd and sent to Iṣfahán in chains. [BW18:383]

Four Bahá'ís are arrested in Sarvistán, Fárs, and sent to Shíráz where they are bastinadoed. [BW18:383]

19 Mar Sixteen Bahá'í traders of the bazaar are arrested in Rasht; three others are brought from Láhíján. [BW18:383]

15 Apr Birth in Goslar, Germany, of Dr Artur Eduard Heinrich Brauns, a prominent German Bahá'í, named by Shoghi Effendi a Disciple of 'Abdu'l-Bahá.

Aug Bahá'u'lláh travels to Haifa on the second of four known visits (His first is His brief stop there before travelling to 'Akká). [BBD94; DH109; GPB194]

- He stays in Bayt-i-Fanduq, a house in the German Templar colony. [BKG: 373–4; BPP173; DH109]

1884

In the year Birth of Valíyulláh Varqá, Hand of the Cause of God, in Tabríz.

Two Bahá'ís are imprisoned in Turshíz, Khurásán. [BW18:383]

1885

27 Mar Martyrdom of Mullá 'Alíy-i-Námiqí in Námiq, Turbat-i-Ḥaydarí, Khurásán. [BW18:383]

1886

In the year The death of the wife of Bahá'u'lláh, Ásíyih Khánum, entitled Navváb (the Most Exalted Leaf) in the House of 'Abbúd. [BBD170; BKG369; DH57, 213]

- See CB119–20 for comments on her nature and station and for Tablets revealed by Bahá'u'lláh in her honour.
- After her passing Bahá'u'lláh reveals a Tablet for her in which He calls her his 'perpetual consort in all the worlds of God'. [GPB108]
- See CB120–1 for 'Abdu'l-Bahá's commentary on *Isaiah* 54, which refers to Navváb.
- She is interred in the Bahá'í section of the Muslim cemetery. [BBD170; DH57, 81]

• Muḥammad-Yúsuf Páshá demands that 'Abdu'l-Bahá vacate the house of 'Abbúd even during Navváb's illness. [BKG369]

Ibn-i-Abhar (Mullá Muḥammad Taqí) travels to the Holy Land and is appointed a Hand of the Cause of God by Bahá'u'lláh. [BBD114; EB268]

Birth of Músá Banání, Hand of the Cause of God, in Baghdád.

Birth of Narayan Rao Sethji Vakil, the first Hindu to become a Bahá'í, in Surat, Gujarat, India.

c. 1886 'Abdu'l-Bahá writes *A Traveller's Narrative*. [TN40]

Ibn-i-Abhar

14 Sep Mishkín-Qalam leaves Cyprus on a Syrian vessel going direct to 'Akká. [BBR311]

1887

In the year Mírzá Músá, Áqáy-i-Kalím, the faithful brother of Bahá'u'lláh, dies in 'Akká. [BBD166; BKG369; DH57]

- He is buried in the Bahá'í section of the Muslim cemetery. [DH81]
- He was designated by Shoghi Effendi as one of the 19 Apostles of Bahá'u'lláh. [BBD166; BW3:80–1]

Karbalá'í Ḥasan Khán and Karbalá'í Ṣádiq are arrested in Sarvistán, Fárs, and imprisoned for two years before being killed in prison. [BW18:383]

Apr The first mention of the concept of 'Hand of the Cause' in Bahá'u'lláh's writings is within a Tablet revealed in honour of Ibn-i-Aṣdaq. [BBD115; EB173]

7 Apr Birth of Horace Holley, Hand of the Cause of God, in Torrington, Connecticut.

1887–8 E. G. Browne, the noted orientalist, spends 12 months in Persia. An important purpose of his journey is to contact the Bábís. [BBR29]

- For a list of his books and other works and his relationship with the Bahá'í Faith see BBR29–36.

See also BBD47; *Balyuzi,* EDWARD GRANVILLE BROWNE AND THE BAHÁ'Í FAITH *and Momen,* SELECTIONS FROM THE WRITINGS OF E. G. BROWNE.

1888

In the year Nabíl begins his chronicle, *The Dawn-Breakers: Nabíl's Narrative of the Early Days of the Bahá'í Revelation.* [DBXXXVII]

Jamál Effendi, accompanied by Ḥájí Faraju'lláh-i-Tafrishí, embarks on a long journey to the East visiting Burma, Java, Siam, Singapore, Kashmir, Tibet, Yarqand, Khuqand in Chinese Turkistan, and

Afghanistan. [EB123–4; PH22]

c. Jul–Aug Two Bahá'ís are arrested in Sarvistán, Fárs, and are sent to Shíráz, where one is imprisoned. [BW18:383]

23 Oct The martyrdom of Mírzá Ashraf of Ábádih in Iṣfahán. He is hanged, his body burnt and left hanging in the market. Later his body is buried beneath a wall. [BBRXXIX, 277–80; BW18:383; GPB201]

1889

Mar The first lecture in the West on the Bahá'í Faith ('Bábism') is given by E. G. Browne at the Essay Society, Newcastle, England.

Apr E. G. Browne gives a paper on the Bahá'í Faith ('Bábism') at the Royal Asiatic Society, London.

Jun E. G. Browne gives a paper on the Bahá'í Faith ('Bábism') at the Royal Asiatic Society, London.

Áqá Najafí, the 'Son of the Wolf', initiates a campaign against the Bahá'ís in Iṣfahán, Sidih and Najafábád. [BW18:383]

17 Jul Upheaval in Najafábád: Áqá Najafí, the 'Son of the Wolf', drives over a hundred Bahá'ís out of Sidih and Najafábád. They take sanctuary in the Telegraph Office and in the stables of the governor of Iṣfahán. [BW18:383]

- See BBR280–4 for Western reporting of the episode.

18 Jul The Bahá'ís are persuaded to leave the Telegraph Office after being assured that they will receive protection in their villages. [BW18:383]

Aug Bahá'ís of Sidih and Najafábád, having received no help or protection, go to Ṭihrán to petition the Sháh. [BW18:383]

8 Sep Ḥájí Muḥammad Riḍáy-i-Iṣfahání is martyred in 'Ishqábád. [BBRXXIX, 296–7; GPB202]

- Czar Alexander III sends a military commission from St Petersburg to conduct the trial of those accused of the murder. [AB109; GPB202]

- Mírzá Abu'l-Faḍl serves as chief Bahá'í spokesman at the trial. [AB109]

- Two are found guilty and sentenced to death, six others are ordered to be transported to Siberia. [AB109; BBR297; GPB203]

- Bahá'u'lláh attaches importance to the action as being the first time Sẖí'ís received judicial punishment for an attack on Bahá'ís. [BBRSM91]

- The Bahá'í community intercedes on behalf of the culprits and has the death sentences commuted to transportation to Siberia. [AB109; BBR297; GPB203]

- For Western accounts of the episode see BBR296–300.

19 Nov Birth of General Sẖu'á'u'lláh 'Alá'í, Hand of the Cause of God, in Ṭihrán.

1890

In the decade Bahá'í books are published for the first time, in Bombay and Cairo. [GPB195; SA250]

c. 1890 Nabíl presents his chronicle, *The Dawn-Breakers*, to Bahá'u'lláh and 'Abdu'l-Bahá for approval. [DBXXXVII]

In the year By 1890 about a thousand Bahá'ís have settled in 'Isẖqábád. [BBRSM91]

E. G. Browne is in 'Akká. Bahá'u'lláh is staying in the Templer colony in Haifa when he arrives. [BBR253]

Ḥájí Akẖúnd, Ḥájí Amín and Ibn-i-Abhar are arrested. Ḥájí Akẖúnd is imprisoned in Ṭihrán for two years; Ḥájí Amín is imprisoned in Qazvín for two years; and Ibn-i-Abhar is imprisoned in Ṭihrán for four years. [BW18:383–4]

Mírzá Maḥmúd-i-Furúgẖí is arrested in Furúgẖ and sent to Masẖhad. From there he is sent to Kalát-i-Nádírí where he is imprisoned for two years. [BW18:384]

In Ma<u>sh</u>had a mob sets out to kill Mírzá Ḥusayn-i-Bajistání but failing to find him they loot his shop. [BW18:384]

A number of people of the Jewish, Zoroastrian and Buddhist Faiths become Bahá'ís. [BBR248–9; GPB195]

Ibrahim George Kheiralla (<u>Kh</u>ayru'lláh) becomes a Bahá'í in Cairo under the tutelage of 'Abdu'l-Karím-i-Ṭihrání. [BFA1:19]

- It is probable that he is the first Bahá'í from Syrian Christian background. [BFA19]
- See BFA1:175 for pictures.

25 Feb Seven Bahá'ís from Sidih who had gone to Ṭihrán to petition the <u>Sh</u>áh for protection secure a decree from him permitting them to return home. When they try to enter Sidih they are killed. [BBRXXIX, 285–9; BW18:383]

Apr Bahá'u'lláh visits Haifa for a third time. [BBD94; BPP173; DH109; GPB194; RB4:351]

- He first stays near Bayt-i-Zahlán, near the town. [BKG374]
- He then moves to Oliphant House in the German colony. His tent is pitched on a piece of land opposite. [BKG374; BPP173]

15–20 Apr E. G. Browne is granted four successive interviews with Bahá'u'lláh at Bahjí. [BBD43; BBR225; BKG371; GPB193]

- See BBR225–32 for Browne's own account of the visit.
- See BBR229–31, BKG371–3 and DH110 for Browne's pen portrait of Bahá'u'lláh.
- Browne is given the manuscript of *A Traveller's Narrative* in the handwriting of Zaynu'l-Muqarrabín. [EGB54]

See also BFA1:44–5; *Balyuzi*, EDWARD GRANVILLE BROWNE AND THE BAHÁ'Í FAITH *and Momen*, SELECTIONS FROM THE WRITINGS OF E. G. BROWNE.

Aug–Sep Mullá Ḥasan and his two brothers are arrested and beaten in Sar<u>ch</u>áh, Bírjand. [BW18:383]

E.G. Browne in oriental robes

1891

In the year On the instructions of Bahá'u'lláh, the Kitáb-i-Aqdas is published for the first time in Bombay. [SA250]

- It is published in Arabic. [SA250]

A Traveller's Narrative is published in two volumes by the Cambridge University Press. [BBD226; EGB55]

Bahá'u'lláh reveals the Kitáb-i-'Ahd. [BBD32; CB142; GPB236–40]

- It was probably written at least one year before His Ascension. [CB142]
- Bahá'u'lláh alludes to it in *Epistle to the Son of the Wolf* as the 'Crimson Book'. [DG16; ESW32; GPB238]

- In it Bahá'u'lláh explicitly appoints 'Abdu'l-Bahá His successor, the Centre of the Covenant and the Expounder of the revealed word. [BKG420; GPB239]

See also BKG420–5; RB4:419–20.

Bahá'u'lláh reveals *Epistle to the Son of the Wolf*, addressed to Shaykh Muḥammad-Taqíy-i-Najafí (Shaykh Najafí), the son of Shaykh Muḥammad-Báqir. [BBD78, 164; BKG382; GPB219; RB4:368]

- It was revealed about a year before the ascension of Bahá'u'lláh. [GPB220]

- It was Bahá'u'lláh's 'last outstanding Tablet'. [BBD78; BKG382; GPB219]

- For an analysis of its content, themes and circumstances of its revelation, see RB4:368–412.

- For a study guide to the Tablet see RB4:433–40.

Bahá'u'lláh reveals the Tablet to the *Times* in which He recounts the circumstances of the martyrdoms in Yazd. [RB4:348–50]

15 Feb First public lecture in the West on the Bahá'í Faith, given by E. G. Browne at the Southplace Institute, London.

19 May The execution of the Seven Martyrs of Yazd. [BBRXXIX, BW18:384]

Seven Bahá'ís are executed on the order of the governor of Yazd, Jalálu'd-Dín-Dawlih, at the instigation of the mujtahid, Shaykh Ḥasan-i-Sabzivárí. [BW18:384]

- For their names see BW18:384.

- For details of the executions see GBP201–2.

- For Western reports of the episode see BBR301–5, 357–8.

See also RB3:194–6 *and* SBBH2:77.

summer Bahá'u'lláh visits Haifa for the fourth time. [BKG374; DH109; GPB194; RB4:351]

• He stays three months. [BBD94; BKG374; DH109; GPB194; RB4:351]

• He lives in the house of Ilyás Abyaḍ near the Templar colony, His tent pitched nearby. [BKG374; DH186]

• It is during this visit that Bahá'u'lláh points out to 'Abdu'l-Bahá the site for the Shrine of the Báb. [AB45; BKG374; DH134–5; GPB194]

• One day He pitches His tent a few hundred yards east of the Carmelite monastery and visits the monastery. [DH186]

• Bahá'u'lláh visits the cave of Elijah. [BKG375; DH174; RB4:351–2]

• He reveals the Lawḥ-i-Karmil (Tablet of Carmel), the 'Charter of the World Spiritual and Administrative Centres of the Faith' near the site of the future Mashriqu'l-Adhkár. [BBD118–19; BKG375; DH174; MBW63; RB4:352]

• For the text of this Tablet see BKG376–7, G14–17 and TB3–5.

• For an analysis of the text see RB4:353–67.

Jul–Aug Members of the Afnán family meet Bahá'u'lláh in Haifa. [BKG374, 406]

• For details of this visit see BKG406–13.

3 Oct Mullá Muḥammad-'Alíy-i-Dihábádí is martyred in Yazd. [BW18:384]

1892

In the year Mu'tuminu's-Salṭanih is poisoned in Ṭihrán on the orders of Náṣiri'd-Dín Sháh. [BW18:384]

8 May Bahá'u'lláh contracts a slight fever. [GPB221]

• See RB4:414–17 for the progress of this illness.

c. 24 May Bahá'u'lláh calls to His bedside all the believers, including many pilgrims, for their last audience with Him. [GPB222]

29 May **The Ascension of Bahá'u'lláh**

Bahá'u'lláh dies at Bahjí in His seventy-fifth year. [AB47; BBRXXIX, 233; BKG420; CB148; GPB221; RB4:411]

- For an account by Ṭúbá Khánum see CH105–9.
- Bahá'u'lláh has spent 23 years, 8 months and 29 (or 30) days in the Holy Land. [DH12]
- He passes away eight hours after sunset. [GPB221; UD170]
- The news of His passing is immediately communicated to Sulṭán 'Abdu'l-Ḥamíd by 'Abdu'l-Bahá: 'the Sun of Bahá has set'. [AB47; BKG420; GPB222]
- Shortly after sunset, on the very day of His passing, Bahá'u'lláh is buried beneath the floor of a room in the house adjacent to the mansion of Bahjí, the Qiblih of the Bahá'í Faith. [AB47; BBD211; BKG427; GPB222]
- See CB149 and RB4:149 for the effect of Bahá'u'lláh's ascension on 'Abdu'l-Bahá.
- See AB52–3, CB148–9 and RB4:148–9 for the theft of Bahá'u'lláh's cases containing His seals, papers and other items.
- See AB52–61, CB148–51 and RB4:148–54 for the Covenant-breaking activities of Bahá'u'lláh's family immediately following His death.
- See GPB222–3 for the mourning following the ascension of Bahá'u'lláh.
- At this time the Faith has spread to 15 countries. [MBW61]
- See BBR234–6 for a list of Europeans who met Bahá'u'lláh.

sometime after the ascension of Bahá'u'lláh

'Abdu'l-Bahá asks Nabíl to choose a number of passages from the writings of Bahá'u'lláh to be used as a Tablet of Visitation. This Tablet is also used at observances commemorating the Martyrdom of the Báb. [BBD234; BKG427; GPB222; RB4:419]

- For an analysis of this Tablet, see SA121–2.

'Abdu'l-Bahá rents the house now known as the Pilgrim House at Bahjí from its Christian owner Iskandar Hawwá', the husband of

The Shrine of Bahá'u'lláh as it appears today

'Údí Khammár's daughter Haní. [DH114, 226]

7 Jun On the ninth day after Bahá'u'lláh's passing the Will and Testament of Bahá'u'lláh, the Kitáb-i-'Ahd, is read at Bahjí before a large assembly in His Most Holy Tomb. [AB51–2; BBD132; CB150; DH113; GPB238; RB4:419–20]

• See CB150, 164 for the effect this has on the believers.

16 Jun 'Abdu'l-Bahá sends a message to the Bahá'ís of the world calling for steadfastness. [AB48–9; DH113]

- This is 'Abdu'l-Bahá's first message. [AB48–9; CH110]

- For the text of the message see AB48–9, CH110–11, DH113 and SWAB17–18.

The pilgrim house at Bahjí

summer 'Abdu'l-Bahá goes to Haifa and Mount Carmel and isolates Himself in a small apartment in the stone building west of the lower cave of Elijah. [DH59, 188]

Áqá Murtaḍá of Sarvistán, who has been in prison for five years, is executed in Shíráz. [BW18:384]

Anton Haddad arrives in the United States. [BFA1:26]

- He is probably the first Bahá'í to reach American soil. [BFA1:26]

6 Jul Death of Nabíl-i-Akbar, Hand of the Cause, Apostle of Bahá'u-'lláh, in Bukhárá. [EB115]

- The Lawḥ-i-Ḥikmat was addressed to him. [EB115]

- For details of his life see EB112–15.

20 Dec Ibrahim Kheiralla arrives in New York. [BBD129; BFA1:26; SSBH1:88]

- See BFA1 for Kheiralla's life, work for the Bahá'í Faith and defection.

1892–3 Nabíl, inconsolable at the death of Bahá'u'lláh, commits suicide by drowning himself in the sea. [AB56; BBD167; BKG427–8; DH81; EB270; GPB222]

- He leaves a note paying homage to 'Abdu'l-Bahá, writing the date of his death in the single Arabic word 'Gharíq' (drowned), the numerical value of which is 1310 AH (AD 1892–3). [MF35; RB1:205]

- See DH81 for his own epitaph.

- He is buried in the Muslim Cemetery near 'Akká. [DH81]

'Abdu'l-Bahá writes *Risáliy-i-Siyásiyyih* (Treatise on Politics). [ABMM]

1893

17 Jun Áqá Muḥammad-Riḍáy-i-Muḥammadábádí is killed by three men on the orders of two of the 'ulamá of Yazd. [BW18:384; GPB296]

- He is the first to suffer martyrdom in the ministry of 'Abdu'l-Bahá.

- See GPB296 for details of his martyrdom.

23 Sep First public reference in North America to the Bahá'í Faith.

- Reference was made to it in a paper entitled 'The Religious Mission of the English Speaking Nations' by Rev. Henry H. Jessup, a retired missionary from north Syria, read by Rev George A. Ford at the World Parliament of Religions in Chicago. [AB63–4; BBD241–2; BBR57; BFA1:32–3; BW2:230; GPB256; SBBH1:76, 88, 202]

- See AB63–4, BW2:169 for text.

1894

In the year Green Acre is founded by Sarah J. Farmer in the aftermath of the World Parliament of Religions. [BBRSM:104; BFA2:142–7; BW5:29; GPB261; SBBH1:125]

Two Bahá'ís are arrested and bastinadoed in Nishápúr. One dies seven days later, the other two years later. [BW18:384]

Nabíl-i-A'ẓam

Ḥájí Yárí, a Bahá'í of Jewish background, is arrested and imprisoned in Hamadán. [BW18:384]

A Bahá'í in Dastjirdán, Khurásán, Áqá 'Abdu'l-Vahháb Mukhtárí, is beaten and expelled from the village. [BW18:384]

Bahá'ís in Fárán, Khurásán, are beaten and Bahá'í homes are looted. [BW18:384]

Feb Ibrahim George Kheiralla settles in Chicago. [BFA1:XXVII]

- Owing to his work, the first Bahá'í community in North America is soon formed in Chicago. [BBRSM:100; BW10:179]

5 Jun Thornton Chase becomes a Bahá'í in Chicago. [BBD53; BFA1:35–6]

- He is designated by 'Abdu'l-Bahá the first American believer. [BBD53; GPB257]

- See BFAI:35 for his own account of how he became a Bahá'í.

- See BFAI:33–7 for other Americans who became Bahá'ís around the same time.

- He was given the name T͟hábit (Steadfast) by 'Abdu'l-Bahá. [BBD53; GPB257]

1895

In the year Mrs Kate C. Ives of Orleans, Cape Cod, Massachusetts becomes a Bahá'í, making her the first woman born in the United States to accept the Bahá'í Faith. [BFAI:37]

23 Jun Birth of Leonora Stirling Armstrong, pioneer American Bahá'í, regarded as the Mother of South America, in upstate New York.

c. summer Miss Marion Brown becomes a Bahá'í in London, the first European to accept the Bahá'í Faith. [BFAI:37]

1896

c. 1896 Mírzá Muḥammad-'Alí sends letters with misleading statements and calumnies against 'Abdu'l-Bahá, thus making widely known his Covenant-breaking activities. [CB151, 178]

In the year 'Abdu'l-Bahá is forced to withdraw from 'Akká to Tiberias owing to the accusations levelled against Him by Mírzá Muḥammad-'Alí. [SBBHI:77]

Ḍíyá'íyyih K͟hánum, the eldest daughter of 'Abdu'l-Bahá, marries Mírzá Hádí Afnán of S͟híráz. [BW4:234 (GENEALOGY); DH59–60]

- These are the parents of Shoghi Effendi.

- For a picture of Ḍíyá'íyyih K͟hánum see MA105.

Bahá'ís in Ḥiṣár, K͟hurásán are persecuted and imprisoned. [BW18:384]

Áqá Siyyid Mihdíy-i-Yazdí is martyred in Tabríz. [BW18:384]

Thornton Chase

Mullá Ḥasan Khazá'í is arrested in Khúzistán. [BW18:384]

15 Feb Birth of Leroy C. Ioas, Hand of the Cause of God, in Wilmington, Illinois.

19 Apr Náṣiri'd-Dín Sháh is assassinated on the eve of his jubilee. [BKG455]

Notes BBRXXIX *and* BBRSM219 *say it was 1 May.*

- His assassin is a follower of Jamálu'd-Din-i-Afghání, one of the originators of the Constitutional movement in Iran. [BBRSM87; GBP296]

Leroy Ioas

- For anaccount of his assassination see PDC67–8.
- See BKG430–55 for a history of his reign.
- He is succeeded by his son Muẓaffari'd-Dín. [GPB296]

See also CBM54–6.

1 May Martyrdom of Mírzá 'Alí-Muḥammad, Varqá, and his 12-year-old son Rúḥu'lláh, in Ṭihrán. [BBRXXIX]

- For the method of their martyrdom see GPB296.
- Their martyrdom is a consequence of the assassination of the Sháh, for which the Bahá'ís are erroneously blamed. [GPB296]
- For the story of their lives see MRHK405–22.
- For a Western account of the episode see BBR361–2.

See also BBD199, 234.

13 May Birth of Dr Ugo Giachery, Hand of the Cause of God, in Palermo, Sicily.

Jun–Jul Several Bahá'ís are beaten and four are imprisoned in Turbat-i-Ḥaydarí when two mujtahids stir up the townspeople against them. [BW18:384]

21 Jul Ḥájí Muḥammad Ṣádiq is stabbed to death in Turbat-i-Ḥaydarí. [BW18:384]

24 Jul Four Bahá'ís are executed in Turbat-i-Ḥaydarí on the order of the mujtahid. [BW18:384; BBR405]

Notes BBRXXIX *says the four Bahá'ís were martyred in August.*

Left to right: Varqá, Rúḥu'lláh, Mírzá Ḥusayn, Ḥájí Imán

Below right: Rúḥu'lláh, before his martyrdom

- These four together with Ḥájí Muḥammad Ṣádiq are known as the S͟huhadáy-i-K͟hamsih (Five Martyrs). [GPB296]

- Their martyrdom is the result of the assassination of the S͟háh, for which the Bahá'ís are erroneously blamed. [GPB296]

- For Western accounts of the episode see BBR405–6.

c. Oct 'Abdu'l-Bahá rents the former Governorate of 'Abdu'lláh Pás͟há in the northwest corner of the city of 'Akká at the inner moat. [BBD13, 108; DH60]

- He establishes it as His residence and as the home for His daughters, their husbands and families. [DH60]

See also BW16:104–6, DH60–4.

1897

c. 1897 Mírzá Áqá Ján, Bahá'u'lláh's amanuensis for 40 years, throws in his lot with Mírzá Muḥammad-'Alí and becomes a Covenant-breaker. [CB181]

Ugo Giachery

• For the story of his downfall see CB181–92.

In the year Ḥájí Mírzá Muḥammad-'Alí, the first Bahá'í to have settled in China, dies in Bombay on his way back to Shíráz. [PH24]

The Hands of the Cause appointed by Bahá'u'lláh are instructed by 'Abdu'l-Bahá to gather to begin the consultations regarding the future organization of the Bahá'í community in Ṭihrán.

• This gathering leads to the formation of the Central Spiritual Assembly of Ṭihrán in 1899. [BBD98, 114, 115; EB268]

Fifteen Bahá'ís are arrested in Saysán, Ádharbáyján. They are taken to Tabríz, imprisoned and fined. [BW18:384]

Three Bahá'ís are arrested in Nayríz on the orders of Áqá Najafi, the 'Son of the Wolf'. [BW18:384]

The homes of several Bahá'ís in Hamadán are looted and ransacked after complaints by Jews of the town against Bahá'ís of Jewish background. [BW18:384]

The Governorate of 'Abdu'lláh Pá<u>sh</u>á, outlined in white

Feb Six Bahá'ís are arrested in Mamaqán, Á<u>dh</u>arbáyján. Three are bastinadoed and three are imprisoned in Tabríz. [BW18:384]

24 Feb Birth of Jalal Khazeh (Jalál <u>Kh</u>áḍih), Hand of the Cause of God, in Ṭihrán.

1 Mar The birth of Shoghi Effendi, in the house of 'Abdu'lláh Pá<u>sh</u>á. [BBD208; BKG359; DH60, 214; GBF2]

- He is descended from both the Báb and Bahá'u'lláh: his mother is the eldest daughter of 'Abdu'l-Bahá; his father is an Afnán, a grandson of Ḥájí Mírzá Abu'l-Qásim, a cousin of the mother of the Báb and a brother of His wife. [CB280; GBF2]

- He is the <u>Gh</u>uṣn-i-Mumtáz, the Chosen Branch. [BBD87]

- 'Shoghi' means 'one who longs'. [CB281]

- 'Abdu'l-Bahá commands everyone, even Shoghi Effendi's father, to add the title 'Effendi' after his name. [CB281; GBF2]

- 'Abdu'l-Bahá gives him the surname Rabbani in the early years of his study in Haifa so that he will not be confused with his cousins, who are all called Afnán. Rabbani is also used by Shoghi Effendi's brothers and sister. [BBD191–2; DH60–1]

Jalal Khazeh

• See GBF6 for the schools he attends.

See also *Rabbani,* THE PRICELESS PEARL*; Rabbani,* THE GUARDIAN OF THE BAHÁ Í FAITH*;* *Giachery,* SHOGHI EFFENDI: RECOLLECTIONS.

21 May Lua Getsinger becomes a Bahá'í in Chicago. [BFA1:XXVII]

6 Jun Birth of Adelbert Mühlschlegel, Hand of the Cause of God, in Berlin.

1898

In the year 'Abdu'l-Bahá instructs that the remains of the Báb be brought from their hiding place in Ṭihrán to the Holy Land. [BBD209]

The Tarbíyat School for boys is established in Ṭihrán by the Bahá'ís. [BBD221]

The first anti-Bahá'í polemical tracts are published by Christian missionaries in Iran. [SBBH1:69]

Shoghi Effendi

Several Bahá'ís are arrested and imprisoned in Qazvín. [BW18:384]

Ḥájí Muḥammad is set upon and killed in Ḥiṣár, Khurásán. [BW18:384]

1 Jan Eighteen people become Bahá'ís in Kenosha, Wisconsin, following the visit of Kheiralla in the autumn of 1897. [BFA1:XXVIII]

- This marks the establishment of the third Bahá'í community in North America. [BFA1:110]

Feb Kheiralla arrives in New York and begins classes on the Bahá'í Faith. [BFA1:XXVIII, 116]

Lua Getsinger

Adelbert Mühschlegel

9 Feb Ḥájí Muḥammad-i-Turk is shot, beaten and then burned to death in a main street in Mas͟hhad by four religious students. [BBRXXX, 406; BW18:384]

• For Western accounts of the episode see BBR406–17.

Apr Nine Bahá'ís attending a Riḍván meeting are arrested, beaten and imprisoned in Hamadán. [BW18:384]

Jun In New York City, 141 people become Bahá'ís in the five months since Kheiralla's arrival. [BFA1:XXVIII, 125]

1 Jun Áqá G͟hulám-Ḥusayn-i-Banádakí is killed by a mob in Yazd after refusing to deny his faith. [BW18:384]

summer Phoebe Hearst becomes a Bahá'í in California through the efforts of Lua and Edward Getsinger. [BFA1:XXVIII, 139]

Notes BFA1:XXVIII *suggests this might have been August.*

20 Aug Jamál Effendi dies in 'Akká. [EB128]

22 Sep The first Western pilgrims depart for 'Akká, travelling via New York and Paris. [BFA1:XXVIII, 140–1, 230]

Phoebe Apperson Hearst

Notes SBBH1:93 *says this was July, based on Kheiralla's autobiography;* BFA1 *is based on a letter from Phoebe Hearst.*

- It is arranged by Phoebe Hearst, who had already planned a journey to Egypt for the autumn. [BFA1:140]
- There are 15 pilgrims in all. [AB68]

11 Nov Kheiralla arrives in 'Akká. [BFA1:XXVIII, 141]

- 'Abdu'l-Bahá confers titles on him: 'Bahá's Peter', the 'Second Columbus' and 'Conqueror of America'. [BFA1:142; GPB275; SBBH2:112]

13 Nov 'Abdu'l-Bahá commemorates Kheiralla's arrival by ending the period of mourning for Bahá'u'lláh and by opening His Tomb to pilgrims for the first time. [BFA1:142–3; SBBH2:112]

10 Dec The first Western pilgrims arrive in 'Akká. [AB68; BBD13; BBRXXX; DH214; GPB257]

- They divide themselves into three parties, using Cairo as a staging post. [AB68: BFA1:143; SBBH1:93]

The first Western pilgrims. Note Kheiralla in the centre and Robert Turner on the left

- See AB68–72; BFA2:9; DH61; GPB257, 259 for those included in the pilgrimage group.

- See BFA1:143–4 for those included in the first group.

- Among the group is Robert Turner, the first member of the black race to become a Bahá'í. [AB72; BBD227; BFA1:139; GPB259]

- 'Abdu'l-Bahá receives the pilgrims in the House of 'Abdu'lláh Pás͟há. [BBD13, 108; DH61]

- See AB68–71; BW16:104–5; CH235–6 and GPB257–9 for the pilgrims' responses to the pilgrimage.

- Edward Getsinger makes a recording of 'Abdu'l-Bahá chanting a prayer. [BFA1:160]

- The Getsingers returned from the pilgrimage with an Arabic copy of the Kitáb-i-Aqdas which was later translated by Anton Haddad. [BFA2:11]

c. 20 Dec The second group of Western pilgrims arrive in 'Akká, staying three days before returning to Cairo. [BFA1:145]

The House of
'Abdu'lláh Pá<u>sh</u>á

• See BFAI:145 for those included in this group.

21 Dec Birth of Dorothy Beecher Baker, Hand of the Cause of God.

1899

In the year Miss Olive Jackson of Manhattan becomes the first black American woman Bahá'í. [BFAI:126–7]

Dorothy Baker

The Serpent by Thornton Chase, an 18–page pamphlet on the image of the serpent in the Bible, is published in Chicago. This is probably the first published essay written by an American Bahá'í. [BFA2:26]

The Consulting Assembly of Ṭihrán, a forerunner of the National Spiritual Assembly, is established. [EB175–6]

- Four Hands of the Cause are permanent members; nine others are elected by special electors appointed by the Hands. [EB175–6]

Siyyid Muṣṭafá Rúmí and others carry to the Holy Land the marble casket made by the Bahá'ís of Mandalay to hold the remains of the Báb. [BW10:517]

31 Jan The remains of the Báb arrive in the Holy Land. [BBD209; DH66; GPB274]

- They are stored in the room of the Greatest Holy Leaf in the house of 'Abdu'lláh Pá<u>sh</u>á until the Shrine of the Báb is completed. [DH66]

Feb The first Tablets of 'Abdu'l-Bahá arrive in America. [BFA1:143]

The Consulting Assembly of Ṭihrán

• See BFA1:143 for the recipients.

c. Feb–Mar ʻAbdu'l-Bahá, accompanied by Kheiralla, lays the foundation stone for the Shrine of the Báb. [BFA1:xxviii, 142; BBD209; GPB275; SBBH2:112]

16 Feb The third group of Western pilgrims arrives in the Holy Land. [BFA1:145]

• See BFA1:145 for those in the group.

Birth of Hermann Grossmann, Hand of the Cause of God, in Rosario de Santa Fé, Argentina, into a family of German background.

spring On her return from pilgrimage, May Bolles establishes the first Bahá'í group on the European continent in Paris. [AB159; BBRSM:106; BFA2:151; GPB259; SBBH1:93]

• For those who became Bahá'ís in Paris, including Thomas Breakwell, the 'first English believer', and Hippolyte Dreyfus, the 'first Frenchman to embrace the Faith', see BFA2:151–2, 154–5; and GBP259.

9 Apr Upheaval at Najafábád. [BBRXXX, 426; BW18:384–5]

Hermann Grossman

• Mírzá Báqir-i-Há'í is arrested, several Bahá'ís are beaten and Bahá'í homes are looted in Najafábád. [BBR426; BW18:384–5]

• Some 300 Bahá'ís occupy the British telegraph office hoping that the Sháh will intervene on behalf of the Bahá'ís. [BBR427–8]

• For Western accounts of the episode see BBR426–30.

May A council board of seven officers, a forerunner of the Local Spiritual Assembly, is established in Kenosha. [BFA1:112; GPB260]

c. 1 May and period following Kheiralla returns to the United States from 'Akká. [BFA1:XXIX, 158]

• His ambitions to lead the Bahá'í Faith cause a crisis in the American Bahá'í community. [BFA1:158–67; GPB259–60; SBBH1:94, 239]

- In the coming months 'Abdu'l-Bahá dispatches successive teachers to heal the rift:

    - Ḥájí 'Abdu'l-Karím-i-Ṭihrání, who had taught Kheiralla the Faith, from c. 26 Apr to 5 Aug 1900. [BFA1:173–6; BFA2:17–29]

    - Ḥájí Ḥasan-i-Khurásání, from 29 Nov 1900 to Aug 1901. [BFA2:35, 38–9]

May Bolles

Bahá'ís of Paris
circa 1902

- Mírzá Asadu'lláh-i-Iṣfahání, from 29 Nov 1900 to 12 May 1902. [BFA2:VI, 35–43FF]

- Mírzá Abu'l-Faḍl, from Aug 1901 to Dec 1904. [BFA2:XV–XVI, 80–7; BW9:855–60]

- See BFA1:177–8 for lists of believers who sided with Kheiralla, left the Faith or remained loyal to 'Abdu'l-Bahá.

- See SBBH1:98–101 for Kheiralla's teachings.

See also BFA1:158–84; CB247–9.

summer Ethel Jenner Rosenberg accepts the Bahá'í Faith, the first English woman to become a Bahá'í in her native land. [AB73–4; ER39; GPB260; SBR20, 33; SEBW56]

See also *Weinberg,* ETHEL JENNER ROSENBERG*;* SEBW55–64.

Oct–Nov Stoyan Vatralsky, a Harvard educated, Bulgarian Christian, attacks the Bahá'ís, 'Truth-knowers', in a series of talks in a church in Kenosha, Wisconsin. [BFA1:XXIX, 114–15; SBBH2:111]

- By this time two per cent of the population of Kenosha are Bahá'ís. [BFA1:114]

19 Nov Birth of Yan Kee Leong, the first believer in Malaya, in Selangor, Malaysia.

3 Dec Charles Mason Remey becomes a Bahá'í in Paris through May Bolles. [BFA2:151–2]

1900

c. 1900 For the state of affairs in Haifa just after the turn of the century see CB223–4.

The Kitáb-i-Aqdas is translated by Anton Haddad. It is not published but circulates in typescript form. [BFA2:27; SA251]

Ethel Jenner Rosenberg

1900

A Bahá'í group is established in Italy. [BBRSM:106]

In the year *Tablets, Communes and Holy Utterances*, a collection of writings by Bahá'u'lláh, is published in the United States. [BFA2:26]

- It is the first prayer book and first compilation of Bahá'í writings published in the West. [BFA2:26]

- It was probably translated by Anton Haddad and published by the Behais Supply and Publishing Board. [BFA2:26]

Sarah Farmer puts Green Acre at the disposal of the Bahá'ís after her pilgrimage to 'Akká in 1900. [BFA2:144–5; GPB261]

- After 1900 Green Acre effectively became the site of the first Bahá'í summer school in the world, although it was not officially so until 1929. [BBRSM:104; BW5:29–30; SBBH1:125]

early part 'Abdu'l-Bahá begins to build the foundations of the Shrine of the Báb. [CB223]

Jan The Behais Publishing and Supply Board is created in Chicago. [BFA1:XXIX]

8 Mar At a meeting in Kenosha, Kheiralla publicly announces his doubts about 'Abdu'l-Bahá's leadership of the Bahá'í community. [BFA1:XXIX; SBBH1:96; SBBH2:117]

- He allies himself with Muḥammad-'Alí. [SSBH1:96]

- The Bahá'ís effectively divide into two camps. [SSBH1:96]

- For the changes to the Bahá'í community as a result of this see SSBH1:96–9 and SSBH2:117–20.

c. 16 Mar The Chicago community re-organizes by selecting a ten-member Board of Council. Neither Kheiralla nor any of his supporters are on the Board. [BFA1:XXIX, 170]

Apr Dr Yúnis Khán arrives in 'Akká to act as translator for 'Abdu'l-Bahá. He remains for nine years. [BW12:679]

26 Apr Ḥájí 'Abdu'l-Karím-i-Ṭihrání arrives in New York, the first Persian

Bahá'í to visit North America, to try to bring Kheiralla back into the Faith and to explain the basic teachings of the Faith to the American believers. He is accompanied by Mirza Sinore Raffie, his translator. [BFA173–6; BFA2:17–29]

5 Aug Ḥájí 'Abdu'l-Karím-i-Ṭihrání leaves the United States, his efforts to win Kheiralla back to the Faith having failed. [BFA176]

26 Nov Agnes Baldwin Alexander writes to 'Abdu'l-Bahá declaring her belief in Bahá'u'lláh. [BFA2:159; SBR176]

- She hears of the Bahá'í Faith from Charlotte Dixon while staying in a pension in Rome. [BFA2:159; SBR176]
- On returning to Hawaii in December 1901 she becomes the first Bahá'í to set foot in Hawaii. [BFA2:159–60; SBR177]

Agnes Alexander

1900–1901

29 Nov Ḥájí Ḥasan-i-Khurásání and Mírzá Asadu'lláh-i-Iṣfahání arrive in the United States to assist the Bahá'ís to deepen their knowledge of their Faith. [BFA2:VI, 35–43FF]

1901

1901–8 'Abdu'l-Bahá writes His Will and Testament over this seven-year period. [AB124–5, 484; BBD236]

- It is written in three parts. [AB124–5, 484; BBD236]
- It 'may be regarded as the offspring resulting from that mystic intercourse between Him Who had generated the forces of a God-given Faith and the One Who had been made its sole Interpreter and was recognized as its perfect Exemplar'. [GPB325]
- For an analysis of its content and its import see AB484–93 and GPB325–8.

In the year Arthur Pillsbury Dodge publishes his book *The Truth of It*, the first introductory book on the Bahá'í Faith written by a Western believer. [BFA2:93]

The Junaynih Garden northwest of Mazra'ih, owned by several Bahá'ís, is registered under the name of 'Abdu'l-Bahá and a brother. [BBD124]

William Hoar, one of the first Bahá'ís in America, is asked by 'Abdu'l-Bahá to meet with the Persian ambassador in Washington to request justice for the Bahá'ís of Iran, thus marking the beginning of the efforts of the American Bahá'í community to alleviate the persecution of their brethren. [BFA2:51]

22 Jan The passing of Queen Victoria.

- Of all the leaders addressed by Bahá'u'lláh only she is reputed to have made a courteous reply. [CBM47; PDC65]
- See CBM47–8 for Bahá'u'lláh's prophecy concerning the success of her reign.

May Ghulám-Riḍá is killed in Najafábád. [BW18:385]

15 May The Chicago Bahá'ís elect a nine-man Board of Council for a term of five years. [BFA2:XXV, 44–7]

20 May The number of members on the Board of Council is raised to 12. [BFA2:47]

24 May The name of the Chicago Board of Council is changed to the House of Justice. [BFA2:48]

- 'Abdu'l-Bahá requests that this name be changed a year later. [BFA2:49]

29 May The Bahá'í women of Chicago elect their own Board and hold the first business meeting of the 'Women's Auxiliary Board'. [BFA2:XV, 49–50]

Thomas Breakwell

summer Thomas Breakwell, an Englishman living in the United States, learns of the Bahá'í Faith in Paris from May Bolles. Within three days he becomes a believer and immediately writes to 'Abdu'l-Bahá. [AB74–5; BW7:707]

- For May Bolles's own account see SW7:707–11.
- He is the first male British Bahá'í. [BFA2:154]
- He is designated by Shoghi Effendi the 'first English believer'. [GPB259]
- He is the first Western Bahá'í to pay Ḥuqúqu'lláh. [BW7:710]

See also AB74–80; BFA2:154; SEBW65–72.

Hippolyte Dreyfus hears of the Bahá'í Faith from May Bolles in Paris and soon after accepts it. [AB81–2]

- He is designated by Shoghi Effendi

the 'first Frenchman to embrace the Faith'. [GPB259]

- He is the first European Bahá'í to visit Iran. [AB81]
- After his marriage to Laura Clifford Barney he adopts the surname Dreyfus-Barney. [AB81]

mid-Jul Ḥájí Ḥasan-i-Khurásání leaves the United States. [BFA2:38]

Aug Mírzá Abu'l-Faḍl arrives in North America. [BFA2:xv]

- See BFA2:80–7 and BW9:855–60 for accounts of his visit.

20 Aug Sulṭán 'Abdu'l-Ḥamíd re-imposes the restrictions confining 'Abdu'l-Bahá and His brothers within the walls of 'Akká. [AB94; CB226–7; DH67–8; GBP264]

- This is the result of mischief stirred up by Mírzá Muḥammad-'Alí. [AB92–5; CB227; GBP264]
- 'Abdu'l-Bahá is subjected to long interviews and detailed questioning. [AB95; GPB264–5]
- For the continued mischief and false allegations of the Covenant-breakers see CB227–30 and GBP265–7.
- 'Abdu'l-Bahá suspends the visits of the pilgrims for a time. [GBP267]
- He directs that all the Bahá'í writings in the possession of His family and secretaries be transferred to Egypt and has His mail re-directed through an agent in Egypt. [GBP267]
- For the work of 'Abdu'l-Bahá whilst in confinement 1901–8 see CB231–44 and GBP267–9.

Sep Thomas Breakwell goes on pilgrimage to 'Akká, the first English-man to do so. [BFA2:154; BW7:709]

- For an account of this pilgrimage see AB77 and BW7:710.

2 Nov Birth of John Robarts, Hand of the Cause of God, in Waterloo, Ontario, Canada.

Hippolyte Dreyfus

26 Nov The first celebration of the Day of the Covenant, the 'Master's Day', in North America. [BFA2:xv, 56; SA245]

26 Dec Agnes Alexander arrives back in Hawaii, the first Bahá'í to set foot in the islands. [BFA2:159–60]

1902

In the year The house in Bandar Anzalí in which Ḥájí Mírzá Ḥaydar-'Alí is staying is attacked and only the intervention of the governor saves the Bahá'í. [BW18:385]

In Shíráz, Ḥájí Abu'l-Ḥasan is beaten so severely on the order of the mujtahid that he dies a few months later from the effects. [BW18:385]

John Robarts

Pilgrims from the East and the West are once again permitted to visit 'Abdu'l-Bahá. [CB232]

Joseph Hannen, Disciple of 'Abdu'l-Bahá, and Pauline Hannen become Bahá'ís in Washington DC.

Bahá'í groups are established in Canada and in the Hawaiian Islands. [BBRSM:106–7; BFA2:160; SBBHI:135]

Shanghai is re-opened to the Bahá'í Faith by the arrival of two

Bahá'ís from 'Ishqábád, Áqá Mírzá Mihdí Rashtí and Áqá Mírzá 'Abdu'l-Baqí Yazdí, who open a branch of the Ummí'd company, an import-export firm. [PH25]

18 Mar Áqá Muḥammad-Zamá-i-Ṣabbágh and Siyyid Ja'far are executed in Isfandábád and Abarqú, Fárs. Several Bahá'ís are expelled from the town and another Bahá'í killed. [BW18:385]

8 May May Bolles marries Sutherland Maxwell in London and moves to Montreal. [BW8:635; GPB260]

Notes BFA2:156 *says they married 'late' in 1902.*

- Sutherland Maxwell becomes a Bahá'í in 1909. [BFA2:156]

10 May The Chicago House of Justice changes its name to the House of Spirituality. [BFA2:XV]

12 May Mírzá Asadu'lláh-i-Iṣfahání leaves the United States. [BFA2:VI]

13 Jun Thomas Breakwell dies from tuberculosis in Paris. [AB77; BBD46; SEBW70]

- 'Abdu'l-Bahá appears to know this without being told. [AB78–9; SEBW70]

- Shoghi Effendi designates him one of three 'luminaries shedding brilliant lustre on annals of Irish, English and Scottish Bahá'í communities'. [MBW174]

- See AB79, SEBW71–2 and SWAB187–9 for 'Abdu'l-Bahá's eulogy.

c. Sep Kanichi Yamamoto, the first Japanese to accept the Faith, becomes a Bahá'í in Hawaii. [BFA2:160; BW13:932; SBR179]

- He writes to 'Abdu'l-Bahá in Japanese. [SBR179]

See also BW13:931–3 *and* SBR176–86.

15 Sep Mírzá 'Azízu'lláh visits Count Leo Tolstoy, speaking to him at length about the history and teachings of the Faith and of the station of Bahá'u'lláh. [EB185; RB3:172–3]

Kanichi Yamamoto

- For Mírzá 'Azízu'lláh's own account of the interview see EB186–9.

- See BW10:569–70 for Tolstoy's response to the Faith.

10 Oct The Behais Supply and Publishing Board incorporates as the 'Bahai Publishing Society', a non-profit company. It is the first Bahá'í institution to be legally incorporated. [BFA2:XVI, 74]

12 Oct Birth of 'Abdu'l-Ḥamid Ishráq-Khávarí, Bahá'í scholar, author and translator, in Mashhad.

28 Nov Construction begins on the Mashriqu'l-Adhkár of 'Ishqábád with the laying of its cornerstone. [BFA2:116–17]

Notes BBRXXX *says this was 12 December. The discrepancy may lie in the use of two different calendars.*

- The foundation stone is laid in the presence of General Krupatkin, governor-general of Turkistán. [BFA2:116–17; GPB300]

- 'Abdu'l-Bahá commissions Ḥájí Mírzá Muḥammad-Taqí, the Vakílu'd-Dawlih, son of Ḥájí Siyyid Muḥammad, the uncle of the Báb for whom Bahá'u'lláh had revealed the Kitáb-i-Íqán, to be in charge of the project. [AB109]

- 'Abdu'l-Bahá Himself delineates the general design and a Russian architect, Volkov, plans and executes the details of the construction. [AB109–10]

Laying the foundation stone of the Mashriqu'l-Adhkár of 'Ishqábád. General Krupatkin is at the centre front

- A meeting hall and some of its dependencies had been built before 1900. [MDM11]

- Its dependencies include two Bahá'í schools, a travellers' hostel, a medical dispensary and Ḥazíratu'l-Quds. [BBD122; BBR442; BBRSM:91]

- For a Western account of this see BBR442–3.

- See jacket of BBR for a photograph of work on the Temple.

1903

In the year 'Abdu'l-Bahá commissions the restoration of the House of the Báb in Shíráz under the supervision of Áqá Mírzá Áqá, an Afnán and nephew of 'Abdu'l-Bahá. [AB108; EB236; GPB300]

Feb Mírzá Badí'u'lláh, the fourth surviving son of Bahá'u'lláh, writes to the Bahá'ís announcing his break with Muḥammad-'Alí and giving his loyalty to 'Abdu'l-Bahá. [AB102; GPB264]

- His letter gives details of the plots of Muḥammad-'Alí against 'Abdu'l-Bahá. [GPB264]
- This reconciliation is short-lived. [AB102]

7 Mar Inspired by the news of the 'Ishqábád Temple project, the Chicago House of Spirituality asks 'Abdu'l-Bahá for permission to construct a Mashriqu'l-Adhkár. [BFA2:XVI, 118; BW10:179; GPB348]

May Upheaval at Rasht. [BBRXXX, 373; BW18:385]

- See BW18:385 for a chronicle of events.

Upheaval at Iṣfahán. [BW18:385]

- See BW18:385 for a chronicle of events.
- The Bahá'ís take sanctuary at the Russian Consulate. [BBR376]
- For Western accounts of the episode see BBR377–85.

28 May A large mob gather outside the Russian Consulate in Iṣfahán and beat the Bahá'ís as they leave. One Bahá'í dies. [BW18:385]

30 May A letter from 'Abdu'l-Bahá is received by the Chicago House of Spirituality giving His approval for the building of a Mashriqu'l-Adhkár in North America. [BFA2:119]

7 Jun Eight days after 'Abdu'l-Bahá's first Tablet arrives, a second Tablet arrives from Him approving the project. [BW10:179; CT41; GPB262, 349; MBW142]

8 Jun Bahá'ís in Maláyir, Hamadán, are attacked, beaten and imprisoned.

Two are killed. [BW18:385]

Jun–Jul The Yazd Upheaval. [BBRXXX]

- See BW18:385–6 for a chronicle of events.
- This is said to be one of the bloodiest events to take place during the ministry of 'Abdu'l-Bahá.
- For Western responses see BBR385–98 and SBBH1:67.
- For details of the martyrdom of Ḥájí Mírzáy-i-Ḥalabí-Sáz during the upheaval see RB2:358–66.
- For the effect on Bahá'ís of Zoroastrian background see SBBH2:80.

1904

c. 1904 The birth of Zikrullah Khadem, Hand of the Cause of God, in Ṭihrán. [ZK3]

In the year At this point there are separate Spiritual Assemblies for the Jewish and Zoroastrian Bahá'ís in Hamadán and Ṭihrán. [BBRSM:151; CB371; CT33]

- See BW2:275–9 for a letter from the 'Israelitish' Bahá'í Assembly of Ṭihrán of November 1904.

A compilation of Bahá'í writings in English is published by the Board of Counsel of New York. [BW10:179]

Mahd-i-'Ulyá (Fáṭimih Khánum), the second wife of Bahá'u'lláh, dies. She and all her four surviving children are Covenant-breakers. [CB117]

Through the year the Covenant-breakers plot until the friendly governor of 'Akká is replaced by one hostile to 'Abdu'l-Bahá, Mírzá Muḥammad-'Alí stirring up opposition in certain elements of the population. [AB111; CB232]

- Newspapers in Egypt and in Syria write false reports about 'Abdu'l-Bahá. [AB111; CB232]

Zikrullah Khadem

- Mírzá Muḥammad-'Alí draws up an official indictment against 'Abdu'l-Bahá full of false accusations. [AB112; CB232]

These actions result in the arrival of a Commission of Inquiry, sent by Sulṭán 'Abdu'l-Ḥamíd. [AB112; CB233]

- The Commission summons 'Abdu'l-Bahá to answer the accusations levelled against Him and upon His replies the inquiry collapses. [AB113–14; CB233]

28 Oct Ali Kuli Khan marries Florence Breed, the first marriage between a Persian and a Western Bahá'í. [BFA2:147]

- For the details of this marriage see SUR223–20.

Dec Mírzá Abu'l-Faḍl leaves the United States. [BFA2:XVI]

1 Dec Sidney Sprague arrives in India. [BFA2:XVI]

- He is the first American Bahá'í travelling teacher in Asia. [BFA2:XVI]

1904–6 Laura Clifford Barney makes a number of extended visits to 'Akká in this period. She brings with her questions to ask 'Abdu'l-Bahá, the answers to which she notes down. These questions and answers result in the book *Some Answered Questions*. [AB81–2; BFA2:238]

- See AB81–2 for information about Laura Clifford Barney.

Laura Clifford Barney

- The translator during this period was Dr Yúnis Afrukhtih (Yúnis Khán), whose memoirs, not yet published in English, make a valuable contribution to the history of the Faith. [BW12:679–81]

- He arrived in 'Akká in 1900 and remained nine years. [BW12:679]

1905

In the year Agnes Alexander arrives in Alaska, the first Bahá'í travelling teacher to visit the territory.

A Bahá'í group is established in Germany. [BBRSM:107, 219]

A second Commission of Inquiry, under the chairmanship of 'Árif

Yúnis Khán

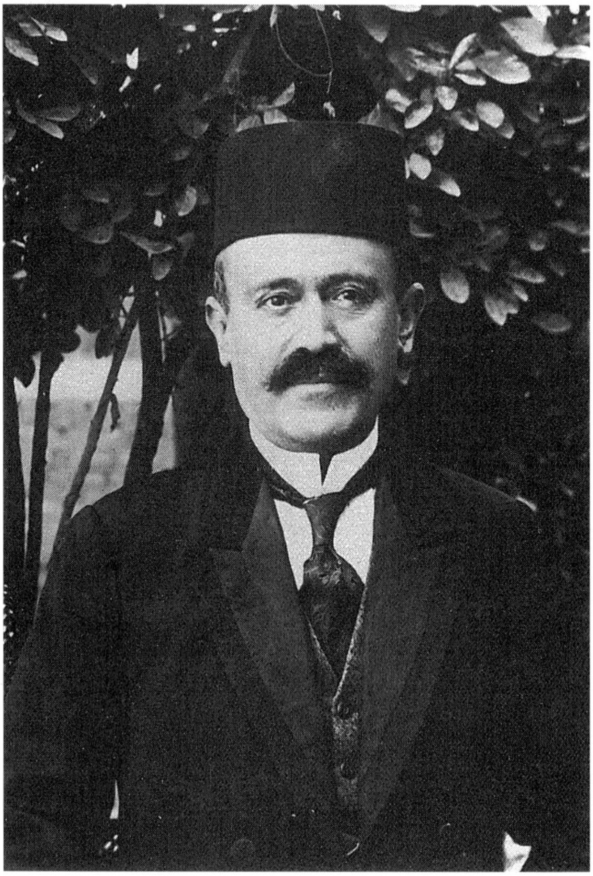

Bey, arrives in 'Akká further to investigate the charges laid against 'Abdu'l-Bahá. [AB117–25; BBR320–3; CB234–7; GPB269–71]

Notes *See* BBR322 *for difficulties in dating this event. All Bahá'í sources indicate that this took place in 1907 but documents in the Ottoman State Archives indicate that it took place in 1905.*

- The Commission returns to Turkey amid political upheavals and its report is put to one side. [AB122–3; CB237; GPB271]

c. 30 Mar Ḥájí Kalb-'Alí is shot and killed in Najafábád. [BW18:386]

29 Apr Birth of 'Alí-Akbar Furútan, Hand of the Cause of God, in Sabzivár, Khurásán.

23 May The first Nineteen Day Feast celebrated in the West is held in New York City. [BFA2:XVI, 245]

- It consists of a devotional portion and a social part. The administrative aspect of the Feast is developed in the 1930s. [BFA2:245; SA208]

1905–11 The 'Constitutional Revolution' takes place in Iran. [BBRSM:87, 219]

- The direct influence of the Bahá'ís in this movement was slight but many in Europe thought the Bahá'í influence was great. [BBR366]
- The Constitutional Movement fails to bring the Bahá'ís any benefit; rather, they suffer as a result. [BBR366–9]

1906

c. 1906 Birth of Abul-Qásim Faizi, Hand of the Cause of God, in Qum.

Mar Mrs Whyte, the wife of a well-known Scottish clergyman, makes a pilgrimage to 'Akká with Mary Virginia Thornburgh-Cropper. In answer to a letter Whyte leaves for 'Abdu'l-Bahá upon their departure, He reveals the Tablet the 'Seven Candles of Unity'. [AB361–2]

- See AB360–2 and SWAB29–32 for text of the Tablet.
- See AB355–9 and SBR20–1 for accounts of Mrs Whyte's pilgrimage.

Mary Virginia Thornburgh-Cropper

See also	Khursheed, THE SEVEN CANDLES OF UNITY.
summer	Bahá'ís in Sangsar, Khurásán, are persecuted such that they take to the hills. [BW18:386]
summer/ autumn	Hippolyte Dreyfus and Laura Barney visit Iran. [BFA2:XVI]
	• They are the first Western Bahá'ís to do so. [BFA2:XVI]
Oct–Nov	Several Bahá'ís in Sangsar and Shahmírzád are killed or injured by bullets; six Bahá'ís are arrested. [BW18:386]
10 Nov	Hooper Harris and Harlan Ober sail from Hoboken, New Jersey, for Naples and 'Akká en route to India. [BFA2:266]

• See BFA266–71 for details of the trip.

30 Dec The Constitution of Iran is re-established. The Bahá'ís are not included among the recognized religions. [BBR354; BI14; CB57; GPB298]

• For the prophecies of Bahá'u'lláh about the constitution see CBM56–8.

1907

In the year Hájar, an elderly Bahá'í woman, is shot dead in Nayríz. [BW18:386]

It is estimated that there are from 1000 to 1100 believers in North America by this date, with about 12 believers in Montreal and six Bahá'ís in other localities in Canada. [BFA2:230]

'Abdu'l-Bahá starts to move His family to the house that He has designed and built in the German colony at the foot of Mount Carmel in Haifa. [BBD107; DH145]

• Laura Clifford Barney helped to purchase the land for the house and to pay for its construction. [DH145]

• Some members of the family occupy it as early as February 1907, if not before. [DH145; GBF5–6]

Six rooms of the Shrine of the Báb are completed. [GBF103]

• See BBD8 and DH103–4 for information on Mullá Abú-Ṭálib, the master mason from Bákú, Ádharbáyján, who worked on the Shrine.

Lady Blomfield and her daughter Mary learn of the Faith at a reception in Paris. [CH1–2; ER95; SBR22; SEBW101]

• For accounts of Lady Blomfield's life see ER88–97 and SEBW101–10.

8 Jan The death of Muẓaffaru'd-Dín Sháh. [BBR354, 482]

19 Jan The accession of Muḥammad-'Alí Sháh to the throne of Iran. [BBR354, 482]

Left to right: Mírzá Maḥmúd Zargání, Hooper Harris, Harlan Ober and Hand of the Cause Ibn-i-Abhar in Bombay, 1907

- The Bahá'í community received some measure of protection under this regime. [BBRSM:97–8]

Feb Corinne True travels to 'Akká to present 'Abdu'l-Bahá with a scroll with the signatures of 800 Bahá'ís calling for construction to start on the American House of Worship. [CT51–3]

Notes BW13:847 *says the scroll contained over a thousand signatures.*

Lady Blomfield

Pritam Singh, an Assistant Master of Economics at Chiefs College in Lahore, accepts the Faith, the first Sikh to do so. [BFA2:269]

spring A census of religions in the United States counts 1280 Bahá'ís. [BFA2:XVI]

31 Mar The Bahá'í calendar is used in North America for the first time. [BFA2:247–8]

25 Apr Karbalá'í Sádiq is martyred in Tabríz. [BW18:386]

summer The first Universal Congress of Esperanto is held in Boulogne. [BW2:270]

1907–1908

19 Jul The Chicago 'Bahai Assembly' files an affidavit of incorporation, the first Bahá'í community to acquire legal status. [BFA2:278]

- The incorporation is in the name of the community rather than the governing body. [BFA2:278–9]

26 Nov The first national Bahá'í conference is held in America. [BFA2:XVI; BW10:179]

- At the invitation of the House of Spirituality of Chicago, nine Bahá'ís from various communities join some ten from the Chicago area at a one-day conference to foster national cooperation on the Temple project and to choose a suitable site for the Temple. [BFA2:280; CT78; GPB262, 349]

1908

In the year 'Abdu'l-Bahá's house in Haifa is completed. [BBD107]

'Alí Ádharí is martyred in Kirmán. [BW18:386]

The Kitáb-i-Aqdas and the Bahá'ís are attacked by Qavámu'l-Mulk from the pulpit of the Masjid-i-Naw in Shíráz. [BW18:386]

The outer structure of the House of Worship in 'Ishqábád is completed and the dome is in place. [AB110; EB267]

- The outer decoration will not be completed until 1919.
- For a description of the Temple, its gardens and environs see BW1:79–81, GPB300–1 and PUP71.

Mar *Some Answered Questions* is published in English. [AB82; BBD212–13; BFA2:238]

- The Persian edition is published the same year. [AB82]
- It is the only pilgrims' notes to be considered part of Bahá'í sacred literature. [BFA2:238; BW12:98–107]

9 Apr Two building plots for the future House of Worship are purchased in Wilmette for the sum of $2000. [BFA2:XVI; BW10:179; GPB262]

The House of 'Abdu'l-Bahá in Haifa

25 Apr Charles Mason Remey and Sidney Sprague sail from New York for Iran and Russia. [BFA2:289]

- For details of their journey see BFA2:289–95.
- In Ṭihrán Ṭá'irih Khánum, a Bahá'í woman with advanced ideas, hosts them at a meeting at which the women remove their veils. [BFA2:292–4]
- They give Ṭá'irih Khánum the address of Isabella Brittingham and the two women begin a correspondence. [BFA2:294]

The House of Worship at 'Ishqábád

Ṭá'irih Khánum

Jun Muḥammad-'Alí Sháh undertakes a successful *coup d'état* in Iran and abolishes the Constitution. [BBR369]

23 Jul The Young Turks issue a declaration demanding the restoration of the old constitution of Mihḍat Páshá and threatening the overthrow of the government. [AB123]

24 Jul The Constitution of Iran is restored to the people and all political and religious prisoners are set free. [AB123; BBD4; BBRXXX; CB237; DH71; GPB272]

- A cable is sent to Constantinople to enquire whether 'Abdu'l-Bahá is included in the amnesty. 'Abdu'l-Bahá is set free. [AB123; GPB272]

Notes BW2:22 *says that 'Abdu'l-Bahá walked free on 31 Aug.*

7 Sep The birth of Hasan Muvaqqar Balyuzi, Hand of the Cause of God. [SBBR5:XI]

1908–9 The Bahá'í Publishing Society is founded in Chicago. [BW10:179]

1909

In the year Sutherland Maxwell, Hand of the Cause of God, becomes a Bahá'í. [BFA2:156]

Karl Kruttner, a professor in Bohemia, becomes a Bahá'í, the first person to do so in the Austro-Hungarian empire.

c. Jan Isabella Brittingham organizes 12 Bahá'í women into a 'Unity Band' to write monthly to the 12 Bahá'í women's clubs formed in Iran. [BFA2:294]

Hasan Muvaqqar Balyuzi

Sutherland Maxwell

Mar Eighteen or 19 Bahá'ís are brutally assassinated in Nayríz when the Constitutionalists take control of the city. [BBR369; BW18:386; DH71, 138; GPB298; RB1:268]

21 Mar 'Abdu'l-Bahá lays the sacred remains of the Báb in their final resting place at the Shrine in Haifa. [AB126; BBD210; DH138; GBF103; GPB276]

- See AB126–30, CT84 and GPB273–8 for details of the occasion and its history.
- The Shrine is a simple rectangular structure of six rooms. [DH71, ZK284]
- The marble sarcophagus used for the remains of the Báb is a gift from the Bahá'ís of Rangoon. [AB129; MC155]

• For details of the sarcophagus see RB3:431.

The first American Bahá'í Convention opens in Chicago. [BFA2:XVII, 309; BW13:849; MBW142–3; SBBH1:146]

• It is held in the home of Corinne True. [CT82–3]

• It is attended by 39 delegates from 36 cities. [GPB262; SBBH1:146]

• The Convention establishes the 'Bahá'í Temple Unity', which is incorporated to hold title to the Temple property and to provide for its construction. A constitution is framed and an Executive Board of the Bahá'í Temple Unity elected. [BBD39; BBRSM:106; BW10:179; GPB349; PP397; SBBH1:146]

months following Mar Construction of the Eastern Pilgrim House in Haifa begins. [BBD178]

• Mírzá Ja'far Raḥmání, a believer from 'Ishqábád, is given permission by 'Abdu'l-Bahá to build it. [DH177]

• This is the first property to be granted tax exemption by the civil authorities. [GPB307]

Mar–Apr Bahá'ís of Námiq, Khurásán, are attacked and Kad-khudá Ismá'íl is killed. [BW18:386]

22 Apr Three Bahá'ís are killed in Ḥiṣár, Khurásán, and their wives seriously injured. [BW18:386]

27 Apr 'Abdu'l-Ḥamid II is deposed. [BBR486]

Accession of Muḥammad (-Rishád) V. [BBR486]

16 Jul After an armed revolt, Muḥammad-'Alí Sháh abdicates and the Iranian Constitution is resurrected. [BBR354, 482]

• The country soon deteriorates and anarchy prevails. It is effectively partitioned into two spheres of influence, British and Russian. [BBRSM:87]

18 Jul The accession of Aḥmad Sháh, the boy-king, to the throne of Iran. [BBR482; CBM57]

The Eastern Pilgrim House

28 Jul Bahá'ís in Námiq, Khurásán, are killed. [BW18:386]

20 Aug Birth of Paul Haney, Hand of the Cause of God, in Chicago.

- His given name is 'Abdu'l-Bahá, bestowed upon him by 'Abdu'l-Bahá Himself at his birth.

Nov Charles Mason Remey and Howard Struven leave the United States on the first Bahá'í teaching trip to circle the globe. [BFA2:348]

- They go to Hawaii, Japan, Shanghai, Singapore and to Burma, India and 'Akká. [BFA2:348–50]

8 Nov Ḥájí Ḥaydar, a leading Bahá'í of Najafábád, is shot and killed at Iṣfahán. [BBR432]

Notes BRXXX *and* BW18:387 *say this occurred on 5 November.*

- For Western accounts of the incident see BRR432–4.

25 Nov Dr Susan Moody arrives in Ṭihrán. She and four Persian Bahá'í doctors start the Sehat Hospital. [BFA2:360]

Young Paul Haney, with Grace Robarts

• Dr Sarah A. Clock arrives from Seattle in 1911 to assist her. [BFA2:361]

• Within a year of her arrival she opens the Tarbíyat School for Girls in Ṭihrán. [BBD221–2; BFA2:360–1]

Dec Charles Mason Remey and Howard Struven speak at the first Bahá'í public meeting held in Honolulu. [BFA2:348; SBR189]

1909–10 'Abdu'l-Bahá gradually moves His family from 'Akká to Haifa. [DH214]

Susan Moody, centre, with white hair, in Ṭihrán circa 1911

1910

c. 1910 Ghodsea Khanoum Ashraf (Qudsíyyih As͟hraf) arrives in the United States, the first Persian woman to travel to the country. [BFA2:358]

• See Ahmad Sohrab's letter to her in SW6,10:77–9.

In the year Charles Mason Remey and Howard Struven arrive in Shanghai and meet with Áqá Mírzá 'Abdu'l-Baqí Yazdí. They are probably the first Bahá'ís from the West to go to China. [PH25]

8 Jan The Persian-American Educational Society is inaugurated in Washington DC. [BFA2:xvii; 355–8]

• Its primary purpose is to assist the Tarbíyat School in Iran. [BFA2:357]

4 Mar Hand of the Cause of God 'Alí-Akbar-i-S͟háhmírzádí (Ḥájí Ák͟húnd) dies in Ṭihrán. [BBD14; EB266]

21 Mar The first issue of the *Bahai News* is published in Chicago. [BFA2:xvii; BW10:179]

Charles Mason Remey, left, and Howard Struven, right, pictured here with Bahá'ís of Mandalay, circa March 1910

- See BFA2:320–2, BW8:927 and SBBHI:116–17 for the magazine's development.

- The name is changed to *Star of the West* in volume two.

- It is the first Bahá'í magazine published in the West. [BBD214]

Aug Having moved all His family to Haifa, 'Abdu'l-Bahá Himself moves from the House of 'Abdu'lláh Páshá to His new home at 7 Haparsim (Persian) Street, Haifa. [BBD13, 107; DH145]

8 Aug Birth of Mary Sutherland Maxwell, Amatu'l-Bahá Rúḥíyyih Khánum, Hand of the Cause of God, in New York City.

10 Aug 'Abdu'l-Bahá departs for Ramleh, Egypt, accompanied by Shoghi Effendi. [BBRXXX; GPB280]

- After one month in Port Said He embarks for Europe but turns back to Alexandria owing to His health. [GPB280]

Mary Maxwell, Rúḥíyyih Khánum

- He remains in Ramleh, a suburb of Alexandria, for about one year. [GPB280]
- The Russian poet Isabel Grinevsky meets Him here. [MRHK348]

20 Sep Muḥammad-Ja'far-i-Ṣabbágh is martyred at Najafábád. [BW18:387]

1911

In the year A systematic teaching campaign is launched in India with the assistance of two American women and a 19-member teaching council is elected. [BBRSM:194 220]

Mírzá Ibráhím Khán, Ibtiháju'l-Mulk is killed near Rasht. [BW18:387]

3 May Aurelia Bethlen, a Hungarian who had come to the United States in 1892 and had become a Bahá'í in New York City about 1905, departs from San Francisco on the first around the world teaching trip undertaken by a Bahá'í woman. [BFA2:351–3]

Aug Ḥájí Muḥammad-Taqí Afnán, Vakílu'd-Dawlih, the cousin of the Báb largely responsible for the building of the House of Worship in 'Ishqábád, is buried in the newly acquired Bahá'í cemetery in Haifa, the earliest recorded burial in the cemetery. [BBD51; DH182]

The Bahá'í cemetery in Haifa

11 Aug The beginning of 'Abdu'l-Bahá's first Western tour. [AB139]

- 'Abdu'l-Bahá departs from Egypt with a party of four on the S.S. *Corsica* for Marseilles, Thonon-les-Bains and London. [AB139; GPB280; SBR22]

- See BW1:130 for a list of cities He visits between 1911 and 1913.

late Aug 'Abdu'l-Bahá stops briefly at Thonon-les-Bains on Lake Leman. [AB140; GPB280; SBR219]

4 Sep 'Abdu'l-Bahá arrives in London. [AB140; GBP280; SBR22, 148]

Notes CH149 *says He arrived 8 September.*

	• For details of His stay in England see AB140–58 and GPB283–5.
	• During His stay in London He has professional photographs of Himself taken. [SBR25]
See also	STAR OF THE WEST *volumes chronicle both the first and second Western journeys of 'Abdu'l-Bahá.*
10 Sep	'Abdu'l-Bahá gives His first public address in the West in the City Temple in London. [AB140; BW2:227; GPB283–4]
	• For the text of His talk see AB140–2.
	• For the words He wrote in the pulpit bible see AB145.
17 Sep	'Abdu'l-Bahá addresses the congregation of St John's, Westminster, His second address to a Western audience. [AB145; SBR8]
	• For text of His talk see AB147–8.
23–5 Sep	'Abdu'l-Bahá visits Bristol. [AB156]
30 Sep	'Abdu'l-Bahá addresses the Theosophical Society in London, His last talk in England on this visit. [AB152]
3 Oct	'Abdu'l-Bahá leaves London for Paris. [AB154; SBR25]
	• He remains in Paris for nine weeks. [AB159; GPB280]
	• For details of His visit see AB159–68.
	• For 'Abdu'l-Bahá's talks given in Paris see PT.
2 Dec	'Abdu'l-Bahá returns to Egypt. [AB167; GPB280; SBR25]

1912

c. 1912	Mishkín-Qalam dies in the Holy Land. [BBD157; EB272]
In the year	By this year at least 70 Bahá'í books and pamphlets have been produced in English. [BBRSM:103–4]

There are about two dozen Bahá'ís in Canada by this year. [BFA2:158]

Birth of 'Alí Muḥammad Varqá, Hand of the Cause of God, in Ṭihrán.

'Alí Muḥammad Varqá

Mírzá Muḥammad-'Alí, Mu'ínu't-Tujjár, and his wife are killed in Barfurúsh, Mázandarán. [BW18:387]

3 Jan In Sárí, Mázandarán, a mob attacks houses of Bahá'ís and four Bahá'ís are killed; a few days later another Bahá'í is killed. [BW18:387]

4 Feb Two Bahá'ís are killed in Máhfurúzak, Mázandarán. [BW18:387]

1912

25 Mar–17 Jun 1913	'Abdu'l-Bahá's second Western tour.
25 Mar	'Abdu'l-Bahá sails from Alexandria on the S.S. *Cedric* to New York via Naples. [AB171; GPB281]
	• 'Abdu'l-Bahá prefers the slower S.S. *Cedric* to the *Titanic*, about to make her maiden voyage. [AB171]
29 Mar	The S.S. *Cedric* stops at Naples.
	• Shoghi Effendi is taken off the ship owing to an eye infection. [AB171–2]
30 Mar	The S.S. *Cedric* leaves Naples for New York. [BHC93]
11 Apr	'Abdu'l-Bahá arrives in New York. [AB172; GPB281]
	• During His tour 'Abdu'l-Bahá visits 32 cities and makes numerous addresses of which 185 are recorded. [SBBH1:110]
	• For a chronological list of talks given by 'Abdu'l-Bahá while in North America see PUP473–8.
	• For details of His journey see AB171–339.
See also	*Ward,* 239 DAYS*; Balyuzi,* 'ABDU'L-BAHÁ*;* THE DIARY OF JULIET THOMPSON*; many editions of* STAR OF THE WEST *and numerous biographies of Bahá'ís of the time as well as other books carry information about 'Abdu'l-Bahá's travels and talks.*
14 Apr	'Abdu'l-Bahá speaks from the pulpit of the Church of the Ascension in New York. [239D:22–3]
20 Apr	'Abdu'l-Bahá arrives in Washington DC from New York by train. [239D:37–8; AB178; SBR78]
28 Apr	'Abdu'l-Bahá leaves Washington for Chicago. [239D:46; AB184; SBR 81]
	'Abdu'l-Bahá arrives in Chicago. [239D:47]
29 Apr	Mírzá Yaḥyá dies in Famagusta. [BBD243; BBR312]

- He had been deserted by most of his followers and is given a Muslim funeral. [BKG426; GPB233]

1 May 'Abdu'l-Bahá lays the cornerstone of the Mas͟hriqu'l-Ad͟hkár in Wilmette. [239D:51; AB186; GPB288, 349; MBW143]

'Abdu'l-Bahá addresses the Bahá'ís at the site of the Wilmette Mas͟hriqu'l-Ad͟hkár

- The cornerstone has been offered by Mrs Nettie Tobin. [AB186]
- 'Abdu'l-Bahá asks delegates from the various Bahá'í communities and Bahá'ís from different backgrounds each to dig the earth to lay the stone. [AB186–7]

5 May 'Abdu'l-Bahá meets with the Bahá'í children of Chicago. [PSBW 134–5]

6 May 'Abdu'l-Bahá leaves Chicago, arriving in Cleveland the same day. [239D:57; AB189]

7 May 'Abdu'l-Bahá leaves Cleveland for Pittsburgh, arriving the same day. [239D:63; AB189]

8 May 'Abdu'l-Bahá takes a morning train from Pittsburgh, arriving in Washington DC that night for His second visit to that city. [239D:64; AB189; SBR81]

'Abdu'l-Bahá with Bahá'í children in Lincoln Park, Chicago

11 May 'Abdu'l-Bahá leaves Washington for New York City, arriving the same day. [239D:64–5; AB190]

12 May 'Abdu'l-Bahá takes a ferry to New Jersey. He takes a train for Montclair where He addresses the congregation of the Unity Church before returning to New York to speak to the International Peace Forum. [239D:66; AB191]

13 May 'Abdu'l-Bahá, very unwell, attends a reception at the Hotel Astor. [239D:67; AB192]

14–16 May 'Abdu'l-Bahá attends the Conference on International Peace and Arbitration at Lake Mohonk, delivering an address on the first evening. [239D:67–9; AB193]

19 May 'Abdu'l-Bahá travels to Jersey City to speak in the Unitarian Church of which Howard Colby Ives is the pastor. [239D:70–1; AB194]

22 May 'Abdu'l-Bahá travels to Boston, arriving the same day. [239D:71; AB198]

Howard Colby Ives

23 May The Bahá'ís of Cambridge, Massachusetts, celebrate 'Abdu'l-Bahá's birthday with a cake bearing 68 candles. 'Abdu'l-Bahá addresses the group on the importance of the Báb. [239D:72; AB199]

26 May 'Abdu'l-Bahá leaves Boston and returns to New York, arriving in the evening. [239D:73; AB201]

28 May 'Abdu'l-Bahá and His party are evicted from their hotel because of the 'coming and going of diverse people' and the 'additional labours and troubles' caused to the staff. [239D:74]

31 May 'Abdu'l-Bahá travels to Fanwood, New Jersey. [239D:75; AB207]

1 Jun 'Abdu'l-Bahá returns to New York. [AB206]

- He has His first sitting for the portrait painted by Juliet Thompson. [DJT299]

Juliet Thompson, right, with Daisy Smythe

3 Jun 'Abdu'l-Bahá travels to Milford, Pennsylvania. [AB208]

4 Jun 'Abdu'l-Bahá returns to New York. [AB208]

8 Jun 'Abdu'l-Bahá arrives in Philadelphia. [239D:88; AB209]

10 Jun 'Abdu'l-Bahá leaves Philadelphia and returns to New York, arriving the same day. [239D:88; AB211]

19 Jun 'Abdu'l-Bahá names New York the 'City of the Covenant'. [239D:93; AB22; BBD55]

• See 239D:92–3 and DJT311–17 for a description of this event.

21 Jun 'Abdu'l-Bahá arrives in Montclair, New Jersey. [239D:97; AB221]

29 Jun 'Abdu'l-Bahá hosts a Unity Feast at the Wilhelm properties in West Englewood, New Jersey. [239D:102; AB223]

• For pictures of this event see 239D:100–1.

30 Jun 'Abdu'l-Bahá returns to New York after visiting Mr Topakyan, the Persian Consul General, in Morristown. [239D:103; AB225–6]

23 Jul 'Abdu'l-Bahá leaves New York, arriving in Boston the same day for His second visit. [239D:117; AB233]

25 Jul 'Abdu'l-Bahá leaves Boston, arriving in Dublin, New Hampshire, the same evening. [239D:117; AB233; SBR82]

16 Aug 'Abdu'l-Bahá journeys to Green Acre by car, arriving the same day. [239D:123; AB240]

• For 'Abdu'l-Bahá's activities while in Green Acre see AB240–51.

• For the story of Fred Mortensen see 239D:126–9 and AB247–51.

See also GREEN ACRE ON THE PISCATAQUA.

23 Aug 'Abdu'l-Bahá arrives in Malden, Massachusetts, for a week-long stay, making trips to Boston and Cambridge. [239D:131; AB251–2]

30 Aug 'Abdu'l-Bahá leaves Malden for Boston. He leaves Boston by train for Montreal, arriving at midnight. [239D:132; AB132; BW8:637]

• He stays in Montreal for ten days, living for four nights at the Maxwell residence. [239D:132]

See also 'ABDU'L-BAHÁ IN CANADA.

9 Sep 'Abdu'l-Bahá arrives in Buffalo by train from Montreal. [239D:139; AB265]

12 Sep 'Abdu'l-Bahá leaves Buffalo for Chicago, arriving the same day. [239D:142]

• He stays at the home of Corinne True. [239D:142; AB266]

15 Sep 'Abdu'l-Bahá leaves Chicago for Kenosha, Wisconsin. [239D:145; AB267]

• He misses His train and tells the Bahá'ís not to be concerned over this, as there is a good reason for it; travelling on the next train they come across the wreckage of the first, which has been in a collision. [239D:145; AB267]

16 Sep 'Abdu'l-Bahá leaves Chicago for Minneapolis, arriving the same night. [239D:146; AB273]

20 Sep 'Abdu'l-Bahá leaves Minneapolis for Omaha, Nebraska, arriving the same night. [239D:20]

Notes AB279 *says this was 21 September.*

21 Sep 'Abdu'l-Bahá visits Lincoln, Nebraska, then leaves for Denver. [239D:151]

23 Sep 'Abdu'l-Bahá arrives in Denver. [239D:152; AB280]

26 Sep 'Abdu'l-Bahá leaves Denver and arrives in Glenwood Springs, Colorado. [239D:158]

27 Sep 'Abdu'l-Bahá leaves Glenwood Springs for Salt Lake City. [239D:159]

Louisa Mathew and Louis Gregory, an interracial Bahá'í couple, are married in New York City. [239D:169]

28 Sep 'Abdu'l-Bahá arrives in Salt Lake City. [239D:159]

30 Sep Thornton Chase, the first American Bahá'í, Disciple of 'Abdu'l-Bahá, dies in California and is buried at Inglewood. [BBD71; BFA2:XVII]

1 Oct 'Abdu'l-Bahá arrives in San Francisco about midnight. [239D:165; AB286]

8 Oct 'Abdu'l-Bahá speaks at Stanford Junior University in Palo Alto. [239D:166; AB288]

Louis Gregory

• There are two thousand in the audience. [AB288]

14 Oct 'Abdu'l-Bahá visits Phoebe Hearst at her estate, at her invitation. [239D:168; AB307]

• She is estranged from the Faith but her invitation is sincere. [AB307–8]

16 Oct 'Abdu'l-Bahá returns to San Francisco. [AB308]

18 Oct 'Abdu'l-Bahá leaves San Francisco for Los Angeles, arriving the same day. [239D:169; AB309]

19 Oct 'Abdu'l-Bahá visits the grave of Thornton Chase in Inglewood. [239D:169; AB309]

- The purpose of His journey to Los Angeles is to visit the grave of Thornton Chase. [AB309]

21 Oct 'Abdu'l-Bahá leaves Los Angeles for San Francisco. [AB310]

25 Oct 'Abdu'l-Bahá leaves San Francisco for Sacramento, arriving at noon the same day. [239D:171]

26 Oct 'Abdu'l-Bahá leaves Sacramento for Denver. [239D:172; AB316]

28 Oct 'Abdu'l-Bahá arrives in Denver at midnight. [239D:175; AB316]

30 Oct 'Abdu'l-Bahá leaves Denver for Chicago. [239D:175]

31 Oct 'Abdu'l-Bahá arrives in Chicago. [239D:176]

4 Nov 'Abdu'l-Bahá leaves Chicago and arrives in Cincinnati the same day. [239D:179]

5 Nov 'Abdu'l-Bahá leaves Cincinnati for Washington DC. [239D:179]

6 Nov 'Abdu'l-Bahá arrives in Washington DC. [239D:179]

11 Nov 'Abdu'l-Bahá travels to Baltimore. On his return to New York He passes through Philadelphia, where He meets the Bahá'ís on the train platform. [239D:183; AB329]

12 Nov 'Abdu'l-Bahá arrives in New York at 1:00 a.m. [AB329]

18 Nov 'Abdu'l-Bahá visits the library of J. Pierpont Morgan and inscribes his album with a blessing for his philanthropy. [239D:186–7]

23 Nov A farewell banquet is held for 'Abdu'l-Bahá at the Great Northern Hotel in New York. [239D:187; AB331]

- The hotel does not allow the black Bahá'ís to attend. [239D:187]

24 Nov 'Abdu'l-Bahá and the white Bahá'ís serve the black Bahá'ís at a dinner at the Kinney's. [239D:187]

4 Dec 'Abdu'l-Bahá addresses His last meeting in North America. [239D:193; PUP462]

5 Dec 'Abdu'l-Bahá sails on the S.S. *Celtic* from New York to Liverpool. [239D:193–4; AB337; GPB281]

- For 'Abdu'l-Bahá's final words to the Bahá'ís, spoken while on board ship, see PUP468–70.

- For Ahmad Sohrab's account of the sea crossing see SW3,16:2.

Dec 1912 – Jun 1913 'Abdu'l-Bahá's second visit to Europe.

13 Dec 'Abdu'l-Bahá arrives in Liverpool aboard the S.S. *Celtic.* [AB343; SBR38]

16 Dec 'Abdu'l-Bahá leaves Liverpool for London. [AB343]

18 Dec E. G. Browne visits 'Abdu'l-Bahá in London. [AB346]

Ḥájí Abu'l-Ḥasan-i-Ardakání (Ḥájí Amín) arrives in London from Paris. [AB346–7]

22 Dec 'Abdu'l-Bahá attends a theatre performance for the first time, Alice Buckton's *Eager Heart.* [AB348]

31 Dec 'Abdu'l-Bahá visits Oxford to address a meeting at Manchester College. [AB352–4]

1913

In the year In 1913 'Abdu'l-Bahá writes to Dr Augur advising him to take the Bahá'í message to Japan.

Áqá Abu'l-Qásim-i-Isfandábádí is killed by two assailants in Qúzih-Kúh, Bavánát, Fárs. [BW18:387]

6 Jan 'Abdu'l-Bahá arrives in Edinburgh. [AB355, 363–8; SBR26]

10 Jan 'Abdu'l-Bahá returns to London. [AB368]

15 Jan 'Abdu'l-Bahá travels to Bristol. [AB369]

16 Jan 'Abdu'l-Bahá returns to London. [AB379]

1913

'Abdu'l-Bahá at the Woking Mosque

18 Jan 'Abdu'l-Bahá speaks at the Woking Mosque. [AB370]

21 Jan 'Abdu'l-Bahá leaves London for Paris. [AB371]

- The visit to Paris lasts 22 weeks. [AB372; SBR220]

'Abdu'l-Bahá at the Eiffel Tower

6 Feb 'Abdu'l-Bahá visits Versailles. [AB376]

30 Mar 'Abdu'l-Bahá travels from Paris to Stuttgart. [AB379]

- He tells His attendants to wear European dress and to discard their oriental headgear. [AB379]

- He does not tell the Bahá'ís of Stuttgart of His arrival in advance. [AB379]

7 Apr 'Abdu'l-Bahá travels to Bad Mergentheim to visit the hotel and mineral bath owned by Consul Schwarz, Disciple of 'Abdu'l-Bahá. [AB383]

8 Apr 'Abdu'l-Bahá returns to Stuttgart, then leaves in the evening for Budapest, changing trains in Vienna the next morning. [AB384]

9 Apr 'Abdu'l-Bahá arrives in Budapest. [AB384]

- For details of His visit see AB384–8 and MRHK362–70.

12 Apr 'Abdu'l-Bahá visits Arminius Vambéry, one of the most colourful figures of the nineteenth century. [AB286–7]

13 Apr 'Abdu'l-Bahá goes to the studio of Professor Robert A. Nadler to sit for a portrait. [AB387]

19 Apr 'Abdu'l-Bahá travels to Vienna, reaching the city in the evening. [AB388]

24 Apr 'Abdu'l-Bahá leaves Vienna and returns to Stuttgart, where He arrives in the early hours of the next morning. [AB389]

1 May 'Abdu'l-Bahá leaves Stuttgart and returns to Paris. [AB391]

13 May Birth of H. Collis Featherstone, Hand of the Cause of God, at Quorn, South Australia.

12 Jun 'Abdu'l-Bahá leaves Paris for Marseilles, arriving the same evening. [AB395]

13 Jun 'Abdu'l-Bahá leaves Marseilles on the S. S. *Himalaya* for Port Said. [AB395]

10 Jul 'Abdu'l-Bahá goes to Ismá'ílíyyah, where the weather is less humid. [AB399–400]

17 Jul 'Abdu'l-Bahá travels to Ramleh. [AB400]

23 Jul Lua Getsinger arrives at Port Said. [AB400]

1 Aug 'Abdu'l-Bahá, the Greatest Holy Leaf and the eldest daughter of 'Abdu'l-Bahá arrive in Egypt. [AB401]

14 Oct Daniel Jenkyn, from England, makes a two-week trip through the Netherlands, the first time a Bahá'í journeys to the country to teach the Faith. [SBR43–4]

Daniel Jenkyn

2 Dec 'Abdu'l-Bahá boards a Lloyd Triestino boat bound for Haifa. [AB 402]

5 Dec 'Abdu'l-Bahá arrives in the Holy Land. [AB402]

1914

In the year Hippolyte Dreyfus and Laura Barney travel around the world teaching the Faith. [BFA2:353]

The Great War (1914–18) breaks out in Europe.

9 Jan John Ferraby, Hand of the Cause of God, is born in Southsea, England.

John Ferraby

21 Jan Mírzá Abu'l-Faḍl-i-Gulpáygání, Apostle of Bahá'u'lláh, dies in Cairo. [AB404; BBD6–7]

- For a brief biography see EM263–5.

- His grave is next to that of Lua Getsinger in the Bahá'í cemetery in Cairo.

- His numerous works include *Hará'id* (The Peerless Gems) 1898; *The Brilliant Proof*, 1912; *Bahá'í Proofs*, 1902; and *Al-Duraru'l-Bahiyyih* (The Shining Pearls, published in English as *Miracles and Metaphors*), 1900. [BBD7]

Jun George Augur arrives in Japan. [BFA2:53; SBR191]

- He is the first Bahá'í to reside in the country. [SBR191]

- For a biography of George Augur see SBR187–98.

See also W2:42–4 *and Sims*, TRACES THAT REMAIN.

28 Jun The heir to the Austrian throne is assassinated in Sarajevo.

29 Jun 'Abdu'l-Bahá instructs the remaining pilgrims in the Holy Land to leave. [AB406]

Notes CH191 *says the American pilgrims left on the last boat from Haifa to Alexandria on 15 Jan. 1915.*

middle of the year The defection of Dr Amín Faríd, 'Abdu'l-Bahá's translator while in America, becomes publicly known. [AB407]

- For his activities against 'Abdu'l-Bahá see AB230, 402, 407–9.

28 Jul Austria declares war on Serbia.

4 Aug England declares war on Germany.

27 Aug Áqá Mírzá Yúsif-i-Qá'iní is killed in Mashhad. [BW18:387]

1 Nov Turkey enters the war on the side of the Central Powers.

- Palestine is blockaded and Haifa is bombarded. [GPB304]

- 'Abdu'l-Bahá sends the Bahá'ís to the Druze village of Abú-Sinán for asylum. [AB411; DH124; GPB304]

- For 'Abdu'l-Bahá in war time see CH188–228.

- 'Abdu'l-Bahá had grown and stored corn in the years leading up to the war and was now able to feed not only local people but the British army. [AB415, 418; CH210; GPB304, 306]

- See CH209–10 for other villages inhabited by Bahá'ís.

6 Nov Agnes Alexander arrives in Japan. [TR30]

- She lives there for a total of thirty-two years. [PH32]

See also TR26–30.

1915

In the year Jamál Pá<u>sh</u>á, Commander of the 4th Army Corps of the Turkish army, is put in military control of Syria, including the Holy Land. [AB412]

- For an account of his relationship with 'Abdu'l-Bahá see AB412–14.

- He threatens to crucify 'Abdu'l-Bahá and to destroy the Shrine of Bahá'u'lláh. [AB414; GPB304, 317]

A plan to fund part-time travelling Bahá'í teachers is approved. [BBRSM:105, 219]

Mírzá Ḥusayn-i-Hudá is martyred in Urúmiyyih. [BW18:387]

14 Mar <u>Sh</u>ay<u>kh</u> 'Alí Akbar-i-Qú<u>ch</u>ání is shot to death in Ma<u>sh</u>had. Considerable anti-Bahá'í agitation follows and many Bahá'ís are forced to seek sanctuary. Three hundred people are arrested. [BBRXXX; BW18:387; GPB298–9]

19–25 Apr The first International Bahá'í Congress is held in San Francisco. [BW8:797–808]

- It is held under the auspices of the Panama-Pacific International Exposition. [BW8:797]

May The Bahá'ís of Haifa and 'Akká return to their homes from the village of Abú-Sinán. [DH147]

1915

16 Jun Miss Margaret Green of Washington DC arrives in Alaska, the first known resident Bahá'í.

latter half 'Abdu'l-Bahá's *Memorials of the Faithful* takes shape. [AB417; MFXII]

- 'Abdu'l-Bahá tells stories of Bahá'í heros and heroines to the weekly gatherings of Bahá'ís in Haifa. These are compiled and published as a book. [AB417]

- The book is not published until 1924. [AB417; MFXII]

11 Oct Arthur Pillsbury Dodge, Disciple of 'Abdu'l-Bahá, dies in Freeport, New York. [SBR15]

Arthur Pillsbury Dodge

- For biographies see BFA1:116–17, SBR1–16 and SW6,13:100–1.

- For his obituary see SW6,19: 161–7.

- His books include *The Truth of It* (1901) and *Whence? Why? Wither?* (1907). [SW6,13:101]

1916

The United States census shows 2,884 Bahá'ís. [BBRSM:105; SBBH1:117]

Anthony Yuen Seto and his wife Mamie Loretta O'Connor become Bahá'ís in Hawaii. Mr Seto is the first Chinese Bahá'í in the Hawaiian Islands and the first Chinese-American Bahá'í in the United States. [PH30]

22 Feb In Sulṭánábád Mírzá 'Alí-Akbar, his wife, his sister-in-law (aged 12) and their four children (aged from 46 days to 11 years) are killed by having their throats cut. [BW18:387; GPB299]

- See DB610 for picture.

26 Mar – 22 Apr 'Abdu'l-Bahá reveals eight of the Tablets of the Divine Plan. [AB420; BBD219; BBRSM:157; SBBH132–3; TDPX]

- For the order and place of their revelation see AB420–2 and TDP.
- For a description of their content see AB422–3.
- Shoghi Effendi characterizes them as a 'mandate' and a 'supreme charter for teaching'. [GPB255; TDPVII]

Apr or May The first Chinese Bahá'í in China, Chen Hai An (Harold A. Chen), becomes a Bahá'í in Chicago through the efforts of Dr Zia Baghdádí. [PH29–30]

Notes PH30 *says this was 1919 but this is clearly a typographical error.*

- He returns to China in December 1916.

1 May Lua Getsinger, Disciple of 'Abdu'l-Bahá, dies of heart failure in Cairo. [BBD87; SW7,4:29]

- For an her obituary see SW7,4:29–30.
- She is buried in the Protestant Cemetery in Cairo. In 1940 a court ruling enables the Bahá'ís to reinter her in the first Bahá'í cemetery established in Egypt. Her grave is now beside that of Mírzá Abu'l-Faḍl. [GPB344]

1916–1917

See also *Sears and Quigley,* THE FLAME.

summer Mr Vasily Eroshenko, a young blind Russian, visits Thailand, the first Bahá'í to do so.

28 Jul Mullá Naṣru'lláh-i-Shahmírzádí is martyred at Sangsar, Khurásán. [BW18:387]

8 Sep The first five Tablets of the Tablets of the Divine Plan are published in *Star of the West.* [BBD219; SW7, 10:87–91]

- For editorial comment see SW7, 10:86.
- After this, communication is cut off with the Holy Land. [BBD219]

1917

In the year By this year at least a hundred Bahá'í books and pamphlets have been produced in English. [BBRSM:103–4]

Foreign troops occupy nearly all of neutral Iran. [AB416; BBRSM:87]

Ibn-i-Abhar (Mullá Muḥammad Taqí), Hand of the Cause of God, dies. [BBD114; EB268]

The Nownahalan (literally 'saplings') Company is founded as a thrift club for Bahá'í children in Iran. [BI13]

- See BI13 for its non-profit and charitable activities.

2 Feb – 8 Mar 'Abdu'l-Bahá reveals six Tablets of the Divine Plan. [AB422; BBD219]

- As there is no communication with America at this time, the Tablets are stored in a vault under the Shrine of the Báb. [BBD219]

17 Feb A mob in Najafábád disinters the bodies from two Bahá'í graves. A general agitation against Bahá'ís follows. The Bahá'ís are boycotted in the bazaar and public baths and 32 are arrested. [BW18:387]

6 Apr The United States enters World War I.

- See CF36 for Shoghi Effendi's opinion of its participation in the war.

2 May The martyrdom of Mírzá Muḥammad-i-Bulúr-Furúsh in Yazd. [BBRXXX, BBR443]

Nov 'Abdu'l-Bahá sends a message to the Bahá'ís of the world assuring them of His safety. [AB412]

- The Tablet is carried by an aged Arab Bahá'í, Ḥájí Ramaḍán. It takes him 45 days to walk from 'Akká to Ṭihrán. On his return trip he brings gold and messages. [AB412; CH206–7]
- For text of the Tablet see CH207–8.

9 Dec General Allenby enters Jerusalem. [AB425]

- Major Wellesley Tudor Pole risks court martial to alert the British Cabinet of the danger to 'Abdu'l-Bahá. [ER169]

Major Wellesley Tudor Pole

1918

In the year Shoghi Effendi finishes his education in Arts and Sciences at the American University at Beirut. [DH148; GBF9]

- He receives a Bachelor of Arts degree. [GBF:9]
- He serves as 'Abdu'l-Bahá's secretary for two years before resuming his education in England. [DH148; GBF9; PP26–7]
- For a picture of Shoghi Effendi at this time see BW13:131, GBF50–1 and PP88–9.

Shaykh Káẓim-i-Samandar, Apostle of Bahá'u'lláh, dies early in the year.

- For the story of his life see EB191–215.

Centre front, Shaykh Káẓim-i-Samandar, with Bahá'ís in Qazvín

Jan The British Bahá'ís alert the Foreign Office about the importance of ensuring 'Abdu'l-Bahá's safety in Haifa. [BBR332–5; CH219; GPB305–6]

Notes CH219 *says this was spring but letters to the Foreign Office are dated Jan. 1918.*

- For the actions of Lady Blomfield see BBR333, CH219–20 and ER 169.

- For the role of Major Wellesley Tudor Pole see BBR332–3; CH222–5; and ER168–70.

Mar The British Military Administration of Palestine begins. [BBR488]

15 Mar Áqá Mírzá Javád, I'tmádu't-Tujjár, is shot in Bandar Jaz and the houses of the Bahá'ís are looted, causing the death of Javád's 14-year-old nephew. [BW18:387]

18 Sep Allenby begins his last offensive against Haifa. [BBR335]

23 Sep The British army takes Haifa. [BBR335; DH148]

- For details of the battle see BBR335–6.
- For letters from the British authorities stating that 'Abdu'l-Bahá is safe see BBR336–7.

1919

In the year Amelia Collins, Hand of the Cause, becomes a Bahá'í in Pasadena, California. [PSBW74]

Ibrahim Kheiralla dies, having been abandoned by all of his followers. [CB252]

The first Norwegian to accept the Faith, Johanna Christensen-Schubarth, 'the mother of the Norwegian Bahá'í Community', becomes a Bahá'í in the United States. [BW12:694–6].

13 Apr Phoebe Apperson Hearst dies.

26 Apr – 1 May The 14 Tablets of the Divine Plan are unveiled in a dramatic ceremony at the Hotel McAlpin in New York, during the 'Convention of the Covenant'. [BBD219; PP437; SBBH1:134; SBBH2:135; SBR86; TDPXI]

- For details of the convention programme, Tablets and talks given see SW10, 4:54–72; SW10, 5:83–94; SW10, 6:99–103, 111–12; SW10, 7:122–7, 138; SW10, 10:197–203; and SW10, 12:227–9.
- Mary Maxwell (Rúḥíyyih Khánum) is among the young people who unveil the Tablets. [PP437]

Amelia Collins

- Agnes Parsons arrives from her pilgrimage just before the close of the convention and is able to convey the instructions from 'Abdu'l-Bahá to arrange a Convention for 'the unity of the coloured and white races'. [BW5:413; SBR87]

- Hyde and Clara Dunn and Martha Root respond immediately to the appeal, the Dunns going to Australia where they open 700 towns to the Faith, and Martha Root embarking on the first of her journeys which are to extend over 20 years. [GPB308; MR88]

See also CT138–9.

28 Jun The Treaty of Versailles is concluded.

22 Jul Martha Root leaves New York on the first of her teaching journeys for the Bahá'í Faith. [MR90]

c. 4 Aug Martha Root sets foot in South America for the first time, at Para (Belém), Brazil. [MR 93; MRHK 44]

- See MR93–100 and MRHK44–59 for her teaching work in Brazil.

13 Aug Adíb, Mírzá Ḥasan Ṭáliqání, Hand of the Cause of God, dies in Ṭihrán. [BBD98]

Notes EB273 *says he died on 2 September.*

- For a brief history of his life see EB272–3.

19 Sep Martha Root arrives in Montevideo, Uruguay, the first Bahá'í to visit the country.

- She spends 12 hours in the city, gives books to two libraries and places an article about the Faith in the newspaper *El Dia*.

20 Sep Martha Root arrives in Argentina, the first recorded visit of a Bahá'í to this country. [MR101]

- She remains in Buenos Aires until 4 October. [MR101]

- See MR101–2 and MRHK 61–5 for her teaching work in Argentina.

Above: Agnes Parsons with 'Abdu'l-Bahá

Below: Martha Root

Adíb

- See MR103–6 and MRHK66–9 for her journey over the Andes on a mule.

Oct Martha Root visits Chile, the first Bahá'í to do so.

- During her four-hour stay in Valparaiso she meets with the Theosophical Society to speak about the Bahá'í Faith.

25 Oct Martha Root arrives in Panama, the first Bahá'í to visit the country. She spends one week there.

Nov William Harry Randall, an American, asks 'Abdu'l-Bahá if he might contribute to the building of the Western Pilgrim House. [DH179]

• Plans are drawn up and work begun but the funds available are insufficient to continue the work until 1923, when money is contributed by Amelia Collins. [BBD178; DH180; GPB307]

17 Dec 'Abdu'l-Bahá sends His 'Tablet to the Central Organization for a Durable Peace at the Hague' in response to a communication addressed to Him by the executive committee. [AB438; BBD115; GPB 308]

• It is delivered in person by Ibn-i-Aṣdaq. [EB176]

• It defines the Bahá'í peace programme. [BW3:12]

• For the text of the Tablet see AB438–9.

late Martha Root visits Cuba for one day, the first Bahá'í to do so, and lectures on the Bahá'í Faith.

1920

In the year The British Mandate for Palestine begins. [BBR488]

• For 'Abdu'l-Bahá's attitude to the administration see BBR339.

• For British accounts of 'Abdu'l-Bahá and the Bahá'ís in this period see BBR339–43 and CH225–8.

The House of Bahá'u'lláh in Bag<u>h</u>dád is seized by <u>Sh</u>í'ís. [BBD109; GBF33; GPB356–7]

• For details see SA140–3.

Mírzá Ibráhím <u>Kh</u>án, Ibtiháju'l-Mulk, is martyred in Ra<u>sh</u>t at the hands of the Jangalís. [BW18:387]

Hyde and Clara Dunn arrive in Samoa, the first Bahá'ís to visit the islands.

John and Louise Bosch visit Tahiti for five months, the first Bahá'ís to travel to the island.

George Townshend becomes a Bahá'í, sending a letter of acceptance of the Faith to 'Abdu'l-Bahá. [GT49]

George Townshend

Fanny Knobloch arrives in Mozambique, the first Bahá'í to visit this country. She gives some 'drawingroom talks' at the mansion of the Portuguese Governor-General and speaks at various clubs.

Jan Abdu'l-Bahá writes a Tablet to a group in Chile. [SWAB:246–50]

Apr Mírzá Asadu'lláh Fáḍil-i-Mázandarání arrives in North America with Manúchir Khán in time to speak at the national convention. [AB443; SBR88]

- His purpose is to assist and stimulate the Bahá'í communities. [AB443]

- He stays for one year. [AB443]

10 Apr Clara and Hyde Dunn arrive in Sydney, Australia. [AB445]

Notes SBR158 *says this was 18 Apr 1919.*

The Dunns

27 Apr 'Abdu'l-Bahá is invested in Haifa with the insignia of the Knighthood of the British Empire. [AB443; BBRXXX, 343–5; CH214; DH 149; GPB306]

- For the document recommending 'Abdu'l-Bahá for knighthood, see BBR344.

- The knighthood is in recognition of 'Abdu'l-Bahá's humanitarian work during the war for famine relief. [AB443]

- He accepts the honour as a gift from a 'just king'. [AB443]

- He does not use the title. [AB443]

'Abdu'l-Bahá is knighted

• For Lady Blomfield's account see AB443–4 and CH214–15.

Louis Bourgeois is selected as the architect for the Chicago House of Worship. [DP94; GPB303; SBBH1:145]

• For details of the designs and selection process see DP76–100.

Charles Greenleaf

21 May The execution at Sulṭánábád of Ḥájí 'Arab by hanging. [BBRXXX, 444–6; BW18:387]

24 May Charles Greenleaf, Disciple of 'Abdu'l-Bahá, dies at the home of William Harry Randall in Chicago. [SBR105]

- For details of his life see SBR97–105.
- For his obituary see SW11, 19:321–2.

Jul-Aug Fanny Knobloch, the first Bahá'í teacher in South Africa, arrives in Cape Town. [BW2:40].

- In her first week she meets Miss Busby who within a very short time is the first person to become a Bahá'í in South Africa.

8 Jul August Rudd, a Swede who became a Bahá'í in America, returns to his native country, becoming the first Bahá'í in Sweden. [BW18:980–2].

after Jul The first Argentineans to become Bahá'ís, Hermann Grossman and his sister Elsa Grossman, accept the Faith in Leipzig in 1920.

- They were born in Argentina and emigrated to Germany in 1909.
- Dr Grossman hears of the Faith at a public meeting given by Harlan and Grace Ober at the Theosophical Society. [BW13:869]

Sep The tombs of the King of Martyrs and the Beloved of Martyrs in Iṣfahán are demolished by a mob. [BBR437]

- For Western responses see BBR437–9.

24 Sep Boring begins at the site of the Ma<u>sh</u>riqu'l-A<u>dh</u>kár in Wilmette to determine the depth of the bedrock. [DP104]

- Soon afterwards construction begins. [DP108]

Oct Shoghi Effendi enters Balliol College, Oxford University. [CB284; DH149; GBF11–12]

- For his purpose in going to Oxford see GBF12.
- For his time in Oxford see PP34–8.

1920–1921

Mírzá Muṣṭafá is killed at Farúgh, Fárs, and other Bahá'ís are imprisoned. [BW18:387]

1 Dec Lillian Kappes dies of typhus fever in Ṭihrán. [BFA2:361; SW11,19:324–5]

- She had gone to Ṭihrán nine years previously to help set up the Tarbíyat School for Girls. [SW11, 19:324]

27 Dec Ḥájí Mírzá Ḥaydar-'Alí, the 'Angel of Carmel' dies in Haifa. [BBD98; EB250]

- For his biography see EB237–50.

27–9 Dec The first All-India Bahá'í Convention is held in Bombay with 175 in attendance. [AB446; BBRSM194; 115]

1921

In the year Eduardo Duarte Vieira, the first African Bahá'í martyr, is born in Portuguese Guinea.

Agnes Alexander takes the Bahá'í teachings to Korea. [BW2:44]

Reza Khán, a Cossack officer, marches on Ṭihrán, effecting a coup d'état, with the support of certain Persian politicians and the British government. [BBRSM87]

- He declares himself prime minister.

23 Jan Mírzá Ya'qúb-i-Muttaḥidih is assassinated in Kirmánsháh. [BBR XXX, 446–50; BW18:387; GPB299]

- He is the last to lay down his life in the ministry of 'Abdu'l-Bahá. [GPB299]

1 Feb Leonora Holsapple Armstrong, the first Bahá'í pioneer in Latin America, arrives in Rio de Janeiro.

21 Mar Construction begins on the Mashriqu'l-Adhkár in Wilmette. [DP108]

• See DP107 for a picture of Bahá'ís inaugurating the construction of Foundation Hall.

19–21 May The first Race Amity Conference is held in Washington DC. [BW2:281]

• For details of the conference see BW2:281–2.

29 May Alessandro Bausani, the Italian Bahá'í who was an Islamic scholar, linguist and historian of comparative religions, is born in Rome.

spring Dr Genevieve Coy is chosen as the director of the Tarbíyat School for Girls in Ṭihrán to replace Lillian Kappes. [SBR203]

summer Siegfried Schopflocher, Hand of the Cause of God, becomes a Bahá'í.

Genevieve Coy

9 Jul Fáḍil-i-Mázandarání leaves the United States for the Holy Land. [AB443]

Jul–Aug Bahá'ís of Zoroastrian background are harassed by the Zoroastrian agent in Qum. [BW18:388]

20 Aug–19 Sep Agnes Alexander visits Korea, the first Bahá'í to do so.

20 Oct Áqá Siyyid Muṣṭafá Ṭabáṭabá'í is poisoned in Sangsar. Continual agitation prevents the burial of the body for several days. [BW18:388]

28 Nov **The Ascension of 'Abdu'l-Bahá**

'Abdu'l-Bahá dies at about 1:00 a.m., in Haifa. [AB452; BBD4; BBR347; GPB311; UD170]

Siefgried Schopflocher

- For details of His passing see AB452, BW1:19–23; BW15:113–15 and GPB310–11.

- This marks the end of the Apostolic, Heroic or Primitive Age of the Bahá'í Faith and the beginning of the Transitional, Formative or Iron Age. [BBD35–6]

- For a photograph of the cable sent announcing His passing see SW12, 15:245.

See also AB452–83; HLS93–100.

29 Nov The funeral of 'Abdu'l-Bahá. [BW15:115]

- For details of the funeral see AB464–74; BW1:23–6; BW15:115–19; GPB312–14; and SW12,17:259–67.

'Abdu'l-Bahá

- For Western and newspaper accounts see AB474–80; BBR347–9; BW1:26–8; and BW15:119–20.

- For eulogies to 'Abdu'l-Bahá see AB481–2, BW1:28–9 and BW15:120–1.

'Abdu'l-Bahá's funeral procession

- Ten thousand people attend 'Abdu'l-Bahá's funeral. [V7]

- For a number of pictures of the funeral procession see SW12, 91:290, 292–8.

- Bahíyyih Khánum looks for instructions on where to bury 'Abdu'l-Bahá and, finding none, emtombs Him in a vault next to the one where the remains of the Báb lie. [AB464; GBF14]

- The Faith has spread to 35 countries. [MBW61; PP391]

- The Bahá'í property at Bahjí does not exceed a thousand square metres; the Bahá'í property on Mount Carmel is about ten thousand square metres. [PP267]

See also *Balyuzi,* 'ABDU'L-BAHÁ; *Blomfield,* THE CHOSEN HIGHWAY; *Honnold,* VIGNETTES FROM THE LIFE OF 'ABDU'L-BAHÁ; SW12,15:245 *and several following issues.*

A cable is sent to London with news of 'Abdu'l-Bahá's death. Shoghi Effendi learns of his grandfather's passing about noon. [GBF13]

- See GBF13 and PP39–40 for Shoghi Effendi's reaction.

2 Dec Ethel Rosenberg arrives in the Holy Land, having learned on the train from Port Said of the passing of 'Abdu'l-Bahá. [ER181–2]

4 Dec On the seventh day after the passing of 'Abdu'l-Bahá corn is distributed in His name to about a thousand of the poor of Haifa. [BW15:121–2]

- Up to this day 50 to 100 poor are fed daily at the Master's House. [BW15:122]

following 'Abdu'l-Bahá's death Mírzá Muḥammad-'Alí publishes far and wide that he is the successor to 'Abdu'l-Bahá. [CB277]

- The Egyptian Bahá'ís respond to this by publishing a refutation of his claims. [CB276; SW12,19:294–5]

5–6 Dec The second Convention for Amity between the White and Coloured Races is held in Springfield, Massachusetts. [BW2:282; SBR92]

- Over a thousand people attend. [SW13, 3:51]

- For a report of the convention see SW13,3:51–5, 60–1.

- For a photograph see SW13,3:50.

16 Dec Shoghi Effendi leaves England for Haifa in the company of Lady Blomfield and his sister Rouhangeze. [GBF13–14; PP42; SBR66]

- Owing to passport difficulties Shoghi Effendi cannot leave sooner. [GBF13; PP42; SBR66]

29 Dec Shoghi Effendi arrives in the Holy Land from England by train from Egypt. [GBF14; PP42]

- He is so worn and grief-stricken that he has to be assisted up the stairs and is confined to bed for a number of days. [CB285]

late in the year Mírzá Ḥusayn Tútí arrives in the Philippines, the earliest known visit by a Bahá'í to this country. He stays for four months.

1922

In the year Oswald Whitaker, a Sydney optometrist, and Euphemia Eleanor 'Effie' Baker, a photographer, become Bahá'ís, the first Australians to accept the Faith. [BW14:320; SBR160–1]

- For Effie Baker's obituary see BW14:320–1.

Effie Baker

- In the 1930s Effie Baker travelled to Persia to take photographs of historical sites. [BW14:320]

The first local assembly of Montreal is formed. [BW8:639]

3 Jan The Will and Testament of 'Abdu'l-Bahá is read aloud for the first time, to a group of nine men, mainly senior members of 'Abdu'l-Bahá's family. [BBRSM115; CB286; ER194; GBF14; PP45]

- Shoghi Effendi is not present at the reading. [CB286; ER194]

- Shoghi Effendi is appointed Guardian of the Bahá'í Faith. [WT11]

- Shoghi Effendi had no fore-knowledge of the institution of the Guardianship nor that he would be appointed Guardian. [CB285; PP42–3]

6 Jan A memorial feast for 600 people of Haifa, 'Akká and the surrounding area is held 40 days after the passing of 'Abdu'l-Bahá. [BW15:122; ER195]

Shoghi Effendi

• More than a hundred poor are also fed. [BW15:122; ER195–6]

• For details of the memorial service see ER195–9 and SW13,2:40–4.

7 Jan The Will and Testament of 'Abdu'l-Bahá is read publicly to an assembled gathering of Bahá'ís from many countries. [ER199–200]

• Shoghi Effendi is again absent. [ER200]

The Greatest Holy Leaf sends two cables to Persia, informing the Bahá'ís that Shoghi Effendi has been appointed Guardian and instructing them to hold memorial services for 'Abdu'l-Bahá. [PP47]

9 Jan William H. Hoar, Disciple of 'Abdu'l-Bahá, dies in Fanwood, New Jersey. [SW12,19:310]

- For his obituary see SW12,19:310–12.

16 Jan The Greatest Holy Leaf cables the United States that Shoghi Effendi has been appointed Guardian. [PP48]

21 Jan Shoghi Effendi writes to the two major communities of the Faith, Persia and America, urging the believers to arise in service for the triumph of the Cause. [BA15–17; CB298–300; CT154]

24 Jan Dr Sarah A. Clock dies in Ṭihrán. She had gone there in 1911 to assist Dr Moody at the Tarbíyat School. [BFA2:361; SW12,19:309]

30 Jan Mírzá Muḥammad-'Alí and Badí'u'lláh seize the keys to the Shrine of Bahá'u'lláh. [BBR456–7; CB288–9, 333; ER205; GBF18; PP53]

- The governor of 'Akká orders that the keys be handed over to the authorities and posts a guard at the Shrine. [BBR457; PP53–4]

- For Western accounts of the episode see BBR456–7.

Helen Goodall

19 Feb Helen Goodall, Disciple of 'Abdu'l-Bahá, dies in San Francisco. [SEBW33]

• See SEBW21–33 for details of her life.

22 Feb King Feisal of Iraq orders the Bahá'ís to be turned out of the Most Great House in Baghdád to keep the peace. [BW354; GPB343; PP54]

Feb–Mar Shoghi Effendi calls together a group of well-known Bahá'ís to discuss the future development of the Faith and the possible election of the Universal House of Justice. [BBRSM:120, 126; ER207; PP247–8]

• See ER207–8 and PP55 for those attending.

• It seems he decided that a firm base of local and national institutions to support the House of Justice would be required first. [PP248; SBR66]

5 Mar Shoghi Effendi writes to the Bahá'ís calling for the establishment of local assemblies wherever nine or more believers reside and directing that all activities be placed under the authority of the local and national assemblies. [BA17–25 BBRSM120–1; CB300]

Apr Shoghi Effendi sends verbal messages through Consul Schwarz to Germany and Ethel Rosenberg to Britain to form local spiritual assemblies and to arrange for the election of a national spiritual assembly in each country. [CB293; ER209, 211–12; PP56]

To the United States and Canada he sends a message to transform the 'Executive Board' into a legislative institution. [CB293; CT160; ER211–12; PP56]

c. Apr Shoghi Effendi appoints a body of nine people to act tentatively as an assembly in the Holy Land while he is away and entrusts the affairs of the Faith to the Greatest Holy Leaf. [GBF19; PP57, 276]

5 Apr Shoghi Effendi leaves the Holy Land for Europe, accompanied by his eldest cousin. [PP57]

9 Apr Work commences on the Western Pilgrim House. [PP69]

21 Apr The Shrines of Bahá'u'lláh and the Báb are electrically illuminated for the first time. [PP69]

• For the story of this see HLS.

25 Apr A National Spiritual Assembly was elected in the United States to replace the Executive Board of the Bahá'í Temple Unity. [SBR94]

• The difference between this body and its forerunner is little more than a change in name. [DP122]

• The conversion of the Bahá'í Temple Unity into the National Spiritual Assembly took four years; it was not until 1925 that Shoghi Effendi recognized the American national body as a National Spiritual Assembly. [CT161; DP121–2; GPB333]

• The election procedure followed that used in the United States: there was electioneering and canditates were nominated, with a straw poll taken to trim the number of eligible canditates. [CT160; DP122]

late May The communities of London, Manchester and Bournemouth elect a Bahá'í Spiritual Assembly for England. [ER213; SBR28, 67]

• This is also known as the Spiritual Assembly for London and the All-England Bahá'í Council. [ER213; SBR67]

• See ER213 and SBR28 for membership.

6 Jun The All-England Bahá'í Council meets for the first time. [SBR28; UD9, 468]

Notes ER213 *says it first met 17 June.*

• The meeting is held in the home of Mrs Thornburgh-Cropper. [SBR28, 67]

9 Jul Bahá'ís gather in the Foundation Hall of the Chicago House of Worship for the first time, to commemorate the martyrdom of the Báb. [CT158–9; SW13,6:132]

• Regular meetings are not held here until 1927. [CT158–9]

autumn The Greatest Holy Leaf sends Shoghi Effendi's mother and other family members to Switzerland to ask him to return to the Holy Land. [PP63]

15 Dec Shoghi Effendi returns to the Holy Land to take up his duties as Guardian. [PP63–4]

1923

In the year Charles Mason Remey makes preliminary plans for a monumental domed superstructure for the Shrine of the Báb. [BW6:723]

Bahai Scriptures, edited by Horace Holley, is published. [SBR231]

- It is the first comprehensive collection of Bahá'í writings made thus far in English. [SBR231]

Amelia Collins contributes the funds necessary to complete the Western Pilgrim House. [DH180; PSBW76]

Jan The Guardian sends 'Abdu'l-Ḥusayn, Ávárih, to Europe to deepen the believers. [CB335, SBR68]

- For his life and eventual Covenant-breaking see CB334–42 and PP120.

Feb Shoghi Effendi sends his early translation of the *Hidden Words* to America. [PP205]

8 Feb The keys to the Shrine of Bahá'u'lláh are returned to Shoghi Effendi. [GBF23; PP71]

Mar An article entitled 'Bahai Organization: Its Basis in the Revealed Word' appears in *Star of the West*. [SW13,12:323–8]

- The purpose of the article is to convince those who are opposed to a structured form of Bahá'í administration. [BBRSM123]

12 Mar Shoghi Effendi writes to Bahá'ís in America, Great Britain, Germany, France, Switzerland, Italy, Japan and Australasia about Bahá'í administration, outlining the process for annual elections of assemblies and calling for the establishment of local and national funds. [BA34–43; PP330]

- See ER223–4 for the response of the British Bahá'ís.

1923

Apr National Spiritual Assemblies are elected in the British Isles, India and Germany. [GPB333]

- The election of the British National Spiritual Assembly is by postal ballot. [ER228]
- For membership of the British National Spiritual Assembly see ER228 and SBR71.

See also ER223–31 *for the election and functioning of the British National Spiritual Assembly.*

25 Apr Martha Root leaves Osaka for northern China. [PH31]

- It is her second visit to China and lasts until March 1924. [PH31–2]

Jun Shoghi Effendi leaves Haifa for Switzerland. [PP72; BBRSM116]

- He returns to Haifa in November 1923. [BRRSM116]

early Sep J. E. Esslemont's *Bahá'u'lláh and the New Era* is published in Britain by George Allen and Unwin. [DJEE28; RG77]

- Shoghi Effendi views this as a landmark in British Bahá'í history. [UD97]
- Over the years he encourages its translation into dozens of languages. [RG77]
- See DJEE37–8 for the importance of this work.

13 Oct The National Spiritual Assembly of the British Isles meets for the first time, at the home of Ethel Rosenberg. [ER228; UD13, 163]

Nov (sometime before 14 Nov) Shoghi Effendi returns from Switzerland. [PP73]

4 Nov The first recorded Bahá'í Feast in China is held in Beijing. [PH33]

- Martha Root and Agnes Alexander are present. [PH33]

Dec The first local spiritual assembly in Australia is formed in Melbourne.

1924

In the year	Miss Nora Lee, who became a Bahá'í in New Zealand, is the first Bahá'í to travel to Fiji, working as a nanny in Labasa from 1924 to about 1930.
	Memorials of the Faithful is published under the auspices of the Haifa Bahá'í Assembly. [MFXII]
	Gretta Lamprill becomes the first Bahá'í in Tasmania in the latter part of the year. [SBR162]
	Amelia Collins visits Iceland for two days, meeting Hómfrídur Arnadóttir, who later becomes the first Icelandic Bahá'í. [BW13:836; PSBW78]
28 Jan	Isabella Brittingham, Disciple of 'Abdu'l-Bahá, dies at the Revell home in Philadelphia. [SEBW138]
	• For her life see SEBW131–8.
9 Mar	Two Bahá'ís are imprisoned for several months in Marághih, Iran, after two mullás stir up trouble against the Bahá'ís. [BW18:388]
21–8 Mar	Daily attacks on Bahá'ís and their shops in Mashhad culminate in the expulsion from the town of Áqá Gulkání and other Bahá'ís. [BW13:388]
28–30 Mar	The third Convention for Race Unity is held in New York City. [BW2:282–3; SBR93; TMW146–7]
2 Apr	Bahá'ís in Turbat-i-Ḥaydarí, Iran, are attacked; some are arrested and imprisoned and others are forced to leave the town permanently. [BW18:388]
5 Apr	Shaykh 'Abdu'l-Majíd is beaten to death in Turshíz, Khurásán, Iran. [BW18:388]
22 Jun	Áqá Ḥusayn-'Alí is martyred in Firúzábád, Fárs, Iran. [BW18:388]
Jul	The second local spiritual assembly in Australia is formed in Perth.
18 Jul	American Vice-Consul Major Robert Imbrie is murdered in Ṭihrán

for being a Bahá'í, which he is not, straining relations between the Persian and American governments. [BBR462–5; BW18:388]

- For a picture of the floral tribute sent to his funeral by the Bahá'ís of Persia and America see BW1:100.

Sep Shoghi Effendi returns to the Holy Land after an absence of some six months. [BA65–7; BBRSM117; UD27–9]

22 Sep–3 Oct The conference 'Some Living Religions within the British Empire' is held in London. [BW2:225; ER233; GPB342]

- For details of the planning of the conference and its outcome see ER231–5.

- For Shoghi Effendi's attitude to the conference see UD17, 19, 21–2, 24–5.

- Two papers about the Bahá'í Faith are read at the conference, one by Horace Holley read by Mountfort Mills and the other by Ruhi Afnan. [BW2:225; ER232–3; SBR73]

- For texts of the papers see BW2:227–42.

Nov The Supreme Court of Iraq decides against the Bahá'ís in the dispute over the House of Bahá'u'lláh in Baghdád. [UD37–8]

21 Nov Dr John E. Esslemont arrives in Haifa to help Shoghi Effendi with his work. [DJEE31; SBR233]

Dec The National Spiritual Assembly of Egypt and the Sudan is formed, the first national body in Africa. [BBRSM121; GPB333]

Martha Root gives the first African radio broadcast about the Bahá'í Faith, in Cape Town.

24 Dec The first *Bahá'í News Letter*, forerunner of *Bahá'í News*, is published in New York by the National Assembly of the United States and Canada with Horace Holly as the editor. [BBRSM122; BW10:180; BW13:856; SBR232]

1925

c. 1925 Fanny Knobloch and her sister Pauline Hannen are the first Bahá'ís to visit Southern Rhodesia.

Louisa Gregory is the first Bahá'í to visit Romania.

In the year There are 43 local spiritual assemblies in North America by this date. [BBRSM121]

Of the 38 localities in Europe in which Bahá'ís reside by this year, 26 are in Germany. [BBRSM182]

The Bahá'í Esperanto magazine *La Nova Tago* (The New Day) is first published. [BBRSM150]

- It continues publication until 1937. [BBRSM150]

early in the year Johanne Sorensen becomes a Bahá'í in Hawaii, the first Dane to accept the Faith. She returns to Denmark soon afterwards and remains the only Bahá'í there for 21 years.

Jan The American Bahá'ís publish Shoghi Effendi's revised *Hidden Words*. [ER255]

- A final translation is made in 1926–7. [ER254; GT55–8]

The Spiritual Assembly of Alexandria is established, the second assembly to be formed in Africa.

spring The International Bahá'í Bureau is established in Geneva by Jean Stannard under the direction of Shoghi Effendi. [BW4:257]

- For the history and work of the Bureau see BW4:257–61, BW6: 130–5, BW7:108–13, BW11:507–8.
- Its function is to act as intermediary between Haifa and other Bahá'í centres. [BBD118; BW4:261]

10 Apr Shoghi Effendi writes to the American National Spiritual Assembly indicating that the word 'assembly' is to apply only to the elected body of nine believers in each locality or to the national assembly, not to the believers as a whole. [BA83; SBBH258]

1925

10 May A Muslim Court in Egypt pronounces the Faith to be an independent religion. [BBRSM173; BW2:31; BW3:49]

- For text of the judgement see BW3:48–50.
- This was 'the first charter of liberty emancipating the Bahá'í Faith from the fetters of orthodox Islam'. [BA122; BW3:110–11; GPBXII, 302, 365; CB306; PP319–20; UD65; WOB99]

4–9 Jul The Seventeenth Annual Convention of the Bahá'ís of the United States and Canada is held at Green Acre. [GAP117; SBR94]

The National Spiritual Assembly of the Bahá'ís of the United States and Canada is elected for the first time. [GPB333]

- Horace Holley becomes its first full-time secretary. [BW13:852; SBR233]

Sep Bertram Dewing begins publication of the Bahá'í magazine *Herald of the South* in Auckland. [BEL174; SBR163]

31 Oct Aḥmad Sháh is deposed and the Qájár dynasty terminated. [BBD190; BBR482; BBRSM87]

John Esslemont

22 Nov John Esslemont, Hand of the Cause of God, Disciple of 'Abdu'l-Bahá, dies in Haifa. [BBD81]

- For letters of Shoghi Effendi announcing his death and giving details of his life and funeral see BA97–8 and UD40–3.

- For an obituary see BW1:133–6 and BW8:929–35.

- He is buried next to the grave of Vakílu'd-Dawlih, the chief builder of the House of Worship at 'Ishqábád. [DJEE37]

Shoghi Effendi elevates him to the station of Hand of the Cause of God on his death. [BA98; BW13:333; DJEE40; PP92; UD40–3]

See also *Momen,* DR JOHN E. ESSLEMONT.

Dec 13 The keys to Bahá'u'lláh's house in Baghdád are given to the Shí'ís. [UD45]

Riḍá Sháh accedes to the throne of Iran. The Pahlaví dynasty commences. [BBR482]

1926

c. 1926 Shoghi Effendi visits Finland.

In the year *The Bahá'í World* is first published. [BW1:4; GT77; PP209; SBR232]

- The first edition, April 1925 to April 1926, is called *The Bahá'í Yearbook.*

- For Shoghi Effendi's impression of it see UD82–4.

The first local spiritual assembly of Vienna is formed.

Green Acre comes under the direct supervision of the National Spiritual Assembly of the United States and Canada. [GAP118]

Opposition to the Faith begins in Russia. [BW3:35; BBR473]

- For details see BW3:34–43.

For most of the year severe restrictions are placed on the Bahá'ís of Marághih in Ádharbáyján, the governor of the district effectively suspending all constitutional and civil rights of the Bahá'í community. [BBR472; BW18:388]

• For a list of deprivations see BBR473.

28 Jan Martha Root sends a note and a copy of *Bahá'u'lláh and the New Era* to Queen Marie of Romania. [GBF42; GPB390; MR242]

30 Jan Martha Root meets with Queen Marie of Romania for the first time. [BBR59; GBF42; GPB390; PP107]

Queen Marie of Romania

• For the details of the meeting and the acceptance of the Faith by Queen Marie see GBP389–96 and MR240–6.

• This was the first of eight meetings between Martha Root and Queen Marie.

first week in Feb Martha Root arrives in Bulgaria, the earliest documented visit to that country by a Bahá'í. [MR247]

• She stays 12 days. [MR247]

• Bahá'ís had passed through Bulgaria on their way to Turkey, but Martha Root's visit is the first one documented.

Feb–Mar Shoghi Effendi leaves Haifa for a rest. [PP97]

c. Apr Lidia Zamenhof, a daughter of the founder of Esperanto Ludwik Zamenhof, becomes a Bahá'í, the first Pole to accept the Faith. [L71]

7 Apr Eight Bahá'ís are beaten to death in Jahrum, Fárs, Iran. [BW18:388]

Notes *It is first reported that 12 Bahá'ís are killed.* [PP98]

- For the response of Shoghi Effendi see BA104–6, 106–8; GBF36–7; PP98–9; and UD48–53.
- For Western accounts and responses see BBR465–72.

4 May Queen Marie of Romania writes three articles as a testimonial to the Bahá'í Faith for a syndicated series entitled 'Queen's Counsel', which appears in over 200 newspapers in the United States and Canada. [BBR61]

- For text of the articles see BBR60–1.
- For Shoghi Effendi's response see BA110–13 and UD56–8.

24 Jun Enoch Olinga, Hand of the Cause of God, is born in Abaango, Uganda.

29 Jun Three Bahá'ís are martyred in Zavárih, near Iṣfahán. [BW18:388]

16 Jul The National Spiritual Assembly of the Bahá'ís of the United States and Canada makes representations to the Iranian government concerning the martyrdoms in Jahrum and asking the Sháh to intervene on behalf of the oppressed Bahá'ís. [BBR469; BW2:287]

- For text of the petition see BW2:287–300.

2 and 4 Aug Two Bahá'í Esperanto conventions are held in conjunction with the Eighteenth Universal Esperanto Congress in Scotland. [BW2:266]

26 Dec Howard MacNutt, Disciple of Bahá'u'lláh, dies in Florida in a road accident. [SEBW42]

- For details of his life see SEBW35–42.

Above: Howard McNutt.
Right: Mountfort Mills

1927

c. 1927 Sadie Oglesby and her daughter Bertha Parvine go to Haifa, the first black American women to make the pilgrimage. [TMW173, 206]

In the year The National Spiritual Assembly of the Bahá'ís of the United States and Canada draws up and publishes a 'Declaration of Trust' and 'By-laws of the National Spiritual Assembly'. [BW2:89]

- For text see BW2:90–8.
- The Guardian describes it as the Bahá'í 'national constitution' heralding 'the formation of the constitution of the future Bahá'í World Community'. [GPB335; PP302–3]
- The drafting is largely the work of Horace Holley with assistance from the lawyer Mountfort Mills. [SBR234]

Shoghi Effendi retranslates the *Hidden Words.*

- He is assisted by George Townshend and Ethel Rosenberg, the 'English friends' mentioned on the title page. [ER246–7, 253–6; GT109]

8 Jan The National Spiritual Assembly of the United States and Canada appoints seven people to a National Race Unity Committee. [SBR94; TMW166]

- For the functions and challenges faced by the committee see TMW165–72.

13–16 Jan A World Unity Conference is held in Dayton, Ohio, one of many such conferences to be held in the year in major cities of the United States. [TMW159, 165]

25 Mar Áqá 'Abdu'l-'A'ẓím, Amínu'l-'Ulamá' is martyred in Ardibíl, Iran, by the order of the mujtahid. [BW18:388]

Apr–May Martha Root journeys through the Baltic States, becoming the first Bahá'í to visit Latvia, Lithuania and Estonia (2 May). [MR272–4]

Apr The American National convention is held in Montreal, a major subject of which is race relations. [TMW178]

- Edwina Powell speaks on the subject, as she had been asked by Shoghi Effendi. [TMW178]
- In her address, Sadie Oglesby recalls her conversations with Shoghi Effendi on the subject of race. [TMW178–80]

4 Apr The National Spiritual Assembly of the United States and Canada adopts its Declaration of Trust. [BW10:180]

29 Apr The British National Spiritual Assembly elects ten members as there is an equal number of votes for ninth and tenth places. [ER253; UD70–1]

- One of the members is a Rev. Biggs. [ER253; UD71]
- Shoghi Effendi writes on 13 May recommending that next year the number of members be strictly confined to nine. [ER253; UD70]

19 Jun Karbalá'í Asadu'lláh-i-Saqaṭ-furúsh is martyred in Kirmán, Iran. [BW18:388]

1 Aug Geyserville Bahá'í Summer School, the first American Bahá'í summer school, is established on property in California donated by John Bosch. [BBD87; BW10:180; GPB340]

Notes BW5:28–9 *says this was the second Bahá'í summer school in America but Shoghi Effendi indicates in* GPB340 *that Green Acre is formally established as a Bahá'í summer school in 1929.*

The big tree at Geyserville

9 Sep–2 Dec Leonora Holsapple (later Armstrong) makes a teaching trip through Latin America and the Caribbean, becoming the first Bahá'í to visit Venezuela, Colombia, Haiti, Curaçao, Trinidad (2–12 Oct), the Guianas (29 Oct), Barbados (Dec) and several islands in the Antilles group.

14 Sep Dr George Augur, Disciple of 'Abdu'l-Bahá, dies in Hawaii. [SBR198]

- For the story of his life see SBR187–98.

1928

Ibn-i-Aṣdaq

In the year In this year there are 579 localities in the world in which Bahá'ís live, 102 local spiritual assemblies, nine national spiritual assemblies, and about eight languages into which Bahá'í literature is translated. [BBRSM160–1]

Louisa Mathew Gregory moves to Varna, the first Bahá'í to settle in Bulgaria.

Ibn-i-Aṣdaq, Mírzá 'Alí-Muḥammad, Hand of the Cause of God, Apostle of Bahá'u'lláh, dies in Ṭihrán. [BBD115; EM176]

• For details of his life see EB171–6.

The first local assembly of Shanghai is formed. [PH28]

spring Ḥájí Amín, Abu'l-Ḥasan-i-Ardikání, Hand of the Cause of God and Apostle of Bahá'u'lláh, dies in Ṭihrán. [BBD7; EB263]

• For his biography see EB263.

• He is named a Hand of the Cause of God posthumously by Shoghi Effendi. [BBD7; EB263]

• See BBD7 for a picture and an account of his life.

Ḥájí Amín

Apr The Soviet authorities abrogate the constitution of the Spiritual Assembly of 'Ishqábád and the assembly is dissolved. [BW3:37]

• Bahá'í schools and libraries are closed. [BBRSM173]

• Not long after, the government orders that all religious buildings in the Soviet Union are the property of the government and the Mashriqu'l-Adhkár is expropriated and leased back to the Bahá'ís. [BBD122; BBR473; BBRSM161; BW3:37]

• For the history of the persecution of the Bahá'ís in the Soviet Union see BBR473 and BW3:34–43.

Notes PP364–5 *says it was 1929.*

26–30 Apr The National Convention of the Bahá'ís of the United States and Canada is held in the Foundation Hall of the House of Worship for the first time. [BW2:180; CT167]

• See BW2:180 for a picture.

Jul The first International Religious Congress for World Peace was held at The Hague. It was attended by Martha Root. [BW3:45]

7 Aug The word 'Bahá'í' is registered with the United States Patent Office as a trademark. [BW6:348]

11 Sep The National Spiritual Assembly of the Bahá'ís of Iraq submits a petition to the Permanent Mandates Commission of the League of Nations for the return of the House of Bahá'u'lláh in Baghdád. [BW3:198–206]

Oct A newspaper campaign of opposition to the Bahá'ís begins in Turkey. [BBR474]

- Several Bahá'ís are arrested as a result and a close investigation of Bahá'í affairs in Turkey is made by the judiciary and the police. [BBR474]

26 Oct–13 Nov The case of the House of Bahá'u'lláh in Baghdád is taken before the fourteenth session of the Permanent Mandates Commission of the League of Nations. [BW3:207]

- The right of the Bahá'ís to the House is upheld and the government of Iraq is strongly pressed to find a solution but the House is not returned to the Bahá'ís. [BW3:207–9; GBF35; PP96–7]

- For Shoghi Effendi's comment on these developments see BW3:206–9.

- The Shí'is turn the House into a Ḥusayníyyih, where the death of the Imám Ḥusayn is mourned. [BBD113–14]

13 Dec The case arising out of the newspaper persecution of the Bahá'ís of Turkey is brought before a criminal tribunal. [PP316]

- The Bahá'ís are able to make known the history and tenets of the Faith. [PP316–17; UD78–9]

20 Dec Hippolyte Dreyfus-Barney, Disciple of 'Abdu'l-Bahá, dies in Paris. [UD84–5]

- For Shoghi Effendi's eulogy of him see BW3:210–14 and UD84–5.

1929

In the year Work begins on the three additional chambers of the Shrine of the Báb. [DH154]

- These rooms, when completed, are used as the International Bahá'í Archives. [GPB347]

11 Feb William 'Harry' Randall, Disciple of 'Abdu'l-Bahá, dies.

- For Shoghi Effendi's obituary of him see BW3:213.

Mar The Council of the League of Nations adopts the conclusion reached by the Mandates Commissions upholding the claim of the Bahá'í community to the House of Bahá'u'lláh in Baghdád. [BW3: 206–7]

- For Shoghi Effendi's response to this see BW3:206–9.

Apr The New History Society is founded in New York by 'Abdu'l-Bahá's former secretary and interpreter Ahmad Sohrab. [BBRSM124]

- It comes into conflict with the local Bahá'í Assembly, which sees the organization as a threat to the unity of the Bahá'í Faith. [BBRSM124]

May The American National Spiritual Assembly incorporates as a voluntary Trust. [BBRSM122; GPB335]

- This enables the National Spiritual Assembly to hold property, receive bequests and enter into contracts. [BBRSM122; GPB335–6]

4 May The Bahá'í Community of Haifa formally petitions the government that the Bahá'í laws on personal status be recognized in Israel. [BBR459; PP284]

- Recognition is granted later in the year. [BBR459; DH116; PP284]

summer Shoghi Effendi makes plans to hold an international conference to consider, among other things, how to establish national spiritual assemblies as a prelude to the Universal House of Justice. [PP250]

- He cancels the conference when he perceives that the Bahá'ís will find it a source of confusion and misunderstanding. [BBRSM126; PP250]

28 Jul Shoghi Effendi sails from England to Cape Town and proceeds overland to Cairo. [PP180–1]

12 Aug Green Acre becomes a fully fledged Bahá'í summer school when the National Spiritual Assembly of the Bahá'ís of the United States and Canada obtains legal title to the property. [BBD91; GAP118; GPB340; SBBH126]

end of Aug Martha Root arrives in Albania, the first Bahá'í to set foot in the country. [MR317]

- She obtains an audience with King Zog I and is warmly received by him. [MR319]
- For Martha Root's own account of her stay in Albania see MR319–20.

14 Sep The Green Acre Trustees are appointed by the National Spiritual Assembly of the United States and Canada. [GAP118]

19 Sep The British Bahá'ís open their new centre, at Walmar House, Upper Regent Street, London. [PSBW46–7]

6–26 Nov The case of the House of Bahá'u'lláh in Baghdád is taken before the sixteenth session of the Permanent Mandates Commission of the League of Nations. [BW4:237]

- The right of the Bahá'ís to the House is upheld and the government of Iraq is strongly pressed to find a solution but the House is not returned to the Bahá'ís. [BW4:237; GBF35; PP96–7]

27 Nov The Mansion at Bahjí is evacuated by the Covenant-breakers. [DH116; GPB355–6; PP231–2]

- For details of how the building is left see GBP356.
- For pictures of its neglected state see DH116.
- Covenant-breakers continue to occupy the adjacent house until June 1957. [PP233]

1930

In the year Leonora Holsapple Armstrong visits Gibraltar, the first Bahá'í to do so.

The first local assembly of Vienna is formed.

Mar The intended pilgrimage of Queen Marie of Romania to the Bahá'í Shrines is thwarted. [GBF49; GPBXVIII; PP114]

- For details of this episode see GBF49–50 and PP113–16.

Apr A ceremony is held at the American annual convention in dedication of the resumption of the building activities on the Wilmette Temple. [BBRSM183; BW3:47]

- Shoghi Effendi's gift to the Temple is 'the most valuable sacred possession in the Holy Land' a 'precious ornament of the Tomb of Bahá'u'lláh', an exquisite Persian carpet. [BA180–1; BW4:208–12]

Jul Shoghi Effendi completes his translation of *The Book of Certitude*, the first of his major translations of the writings of Bahá'u'lláh. [BBRSM63–4; GT60; PP214]

19 Aug Louis Jean-Baptiste Bourgeois, designer of the Mashriqu'l-Adhkár in Wilmette, dies. [DP145]

- For details of his life see DP76–86.

17 Nov Ethel Rosenberg, Disciple of 'Abdu'l-Bahá, 'England's outstanding Bahá'í pioneer worker', dies in London. [BW4:118–19; ER274–5]

- For her obituary see BW4:262–3.

See also *Weinberg,* ETHEL JENNER ROSENBERG *and* SEBW55–64.

Dec The first Asian Women's Conference is held in India. [BW17:180]

1931

In the year The first Chinese translation of *Bahá'u'lláh and the New Era* is published. [PH36]

The grave of Ethel Rosenberg

• The translation is made by Dr Tsao Yun-siang, President of the Xinhua University in Beijing. [PH36]

There are still only 30 Bahá'ís in Canada by this date. [BBRSM186]

The first German Bahá'í summer school is held, at Esslingen. [BBRSM182; BW5:44]

13 Jan Consul Albert Schwarz, Disciple of 'Abdu'l-Bahá, 'Germany's outstanding Bahá'í pioneer worker' dies. [BW4:118–19, 264]

• For his obituary see BW4:264–6.

Mar Marion Jack paints a view from the Mansion at Bahjí. The painting will eventually hang in the Mansion. [CT174]

Apr Marion Jack arrives in Sofia, Bulgaria, to begin her pioneering service.

28 Apr Mr Refo Capari (Chapary), the first Albanian Bahá'í, arrives in Tirana, Albania.

• He became a Bahá'í in America some time before 1931.

1 May The superstructure of the Wilmette House of Worship is completed and dedicated. [BW10:180; DP:156–7; SBBH1:145]

The National Spiritual Assembly of the Bahá'ís of Iraq is elected for the first time. [BBRSM:121]

May Lilian Barron McNeill, an English Bahá'í, and her husband, a retired British army officer, rent the house at Mazra'ih. [DH92]

- They restore the house, which has deteriorated, preserving those parts unchanged from the time of Bahá'u'lláh. [DH92–3]

Mazra'ih at the time the McNeills occupy it

A permanent summer school is established at Louhelen Ranch near Davison, Michigan. [BW10:181; GPB340]

27 Jul Swiss Bahá'í Auguste Forel, world-renowned psychiatrist, entomologist, anatomist, social reformer and peace worker, dies. [FGM2]

Nov The New York Bahá'í community drafts the by-laws of a Bahá'í local assembly. [GPB335]

- These become the pattern for all local Bahá'í constitutions throughout the world. [BBRSM122; GPB335; PP303]

Dr Auguste Forel

1932

In the year The Iranian government introduces measures against the Bahá'ís throughout Iran. Restrictions are placed on the import of Bahá'í books and periodicals by post and on the publication of Bahá'í literature. Bahá'í marriages are not recognized. [BW18:388]

Shoghi Effendi's translation of Nabíl's Narrative entitled *The Dawn-Breakers* is published. [GBF91; PP215]

- The work took him two years of research. [PP217]
- He sent Effie Baker to Iran to take photographs for the book. [PP217]
- For George Townshend's assistance to the project see GT59, 60, 64–9.
- For Shoghi Effendi's purpose in translating and editing the book see WOB123.

See also BBD64; GBF91–3; PP215–18.

Feb The Chicago Bahá'í Assembly incorporates, the first local spiritual assembly in the world to do so. [GPB336]

21 Mar The first Local Spiritual Assembly of Tokyo, consisting of journalists and other professional people, is formed.

- Owing to the situation in Japan, it is disbanded two years later.

Apr Pilgrims are able to stay overnight at Bahjí for the first time. [GBF101; PP232]

10 Jun The American National Spiritual Assembly addresses a petition to the Sháh of Iran requesting that the ban on Bahá'í literature be removed and asking that its representative, Mrs Keith Ransom-Kehler, be recognized to present in person the appeal. [BW5:390–1]

15 Jul The Greatest Holy Leaf, Bahíyyih Khánum, 'outstanding heroine of the Bahá'í Dispensation' dies in Haifa. [BW5:169; GPB108]

The Greatest Holy Leaf in her later years

- Her passing marks the end of the Heroic Age of the Faith. [BBD102; WOB98]
- She is comparable in rank to Sarah, Ásíyih, the Virgin Mary, Fáṭimih and Ṭáhirih. [GPB347]
- Shoghi Effendi is in Switzerland and immediately goes to Italy to commission a memorial for her grave. [DH156]

- For Tablets of Bahá'u'lláh and 'Abdu'l-Bahá revealed in her honour see BW5:171–3.

- For Shoghi Effendi's tribute to her see BW5:174–9.

- For Marjory Morten's obituary of her see BW5:181–5.

- The design of the monument for the resting place of the Greatest Holy Leaf is a symbol of the Bahá'í administrative order. [CB298]

Monument of the Greatest Holy Leaf

See also BAHÍYYIH KHÁNUM *and Gail,* KHÁNUM, THE GREATEST HOLY LEAF; BBD42; CB121–2, 305; DH156–61; GBF65–8; PP144–8.

15 Aug Keith Ransom-Kehler meets the Iranian Court Minister Taymur Tash. [BW5:392]

- She presents the American petition to him asking that the ban on Bahá'í literature in Iran be lifted and receives assurances from him that this will be effected. [BW5:392]

- For the history and unsuccessful outcome of this effort see BW5:391–8.

Nov A number of Bahá'ís are arrested in Adana, Turkey. [BBR474]

3 Nov–6 Dec Meeting of the 22nd Session of the Permanent Mandates Commission of the League of Nations in Geneva at which the Bahá'ís plead their case for the possession of the House of Bahá'u'lláh in Baghdád. [BW5:351–4]

23 Nov George Adam Benke dies in Sofia, Bulgaria.

- Shoghi Effendi calls him the first European martyr. [LDG1:263; MC359]
- For his obituary see BW5:416–18.

22 Dec By now there are 15 Bahá'ís under arrest in Adana, Turkey. [BBR474]

1933

In the year Bahá'ís in Gulpáygán, Iran, are refused admission to the public baths. Shaykh Ja'far Hidáyat is beaten and expelled from the town. [BW18:388]

The Tavakkul Bahá'í School in Qazvín, Iran, is closed. [BW18:388]

6 Feb By this date there are about 50 Bahá'ís under arrest in Adana, Turkey. [BBR475; PP317]

end Mar The 50 Bahá'ís imprisoned in Adana are released. [BBR475]

23 Oct Keith Ransom-Kehler dies of smallpox in Iṣfahán. [BW5:24, 398]

- For her obituary see BW5:389–410.
- She is buried near the grave of the King of Martyrs. [BW5:398]
- For a picture of her grave see BW5:399.
- Shoghi Effendi names her America's 'first and distinguished martyr'. [BW5:398]
- Shoghi Effendi elevates her to the rank of Hand of the Cause. [BW5:398]

Keith Ransom-Kehler

• For her mission in Iran see BW5:23–7.

See also PP306–7.

23 Oct–4 Nov The 24th session of the Permanent Mandates Commission of the League of Nations is held in Geneva at which the case of the possession of the House of Bahá'u'lláh in Ba<u>gh</u>dád is again raised. [BW5:354–5]

25 Nov The first Spiritual Assembly of Addis Ababa is formed. [BW6:70]

• The community is established by Sabri Elias, a pioneer from Egypt. [BW6:70]

• Ethiopia is the only independent Kingdom in Africa at this date. [BW6:70]

1934

In the year The government of Iran takes several measures against the Bahá'ís throughout the country. [BW18:389]

- Nineteen Bahá'í schools are closed in Káshán, Qazvín, Yazd, Najafabád, Ábádih and elsewhere.
- Bahá'í meetings are forbidden in many towns, including Ṭihrán, Mashhad, Sabzivár, Qazvín and Arák.
- Bahá'ís centres in Káshán, Hamadán and Záhidán are closed by the authorities.
- Some Bahá'í government employees are dismissed.
- Some Bahá'í military personnel are stripped of their rank and imprisoned.
- Bahá'ís in many places are harassed over the filling-in of marriage certificates, census forms and other legal documents.

The first Local Spiritual Assembly of Sofia, Bulgaria, is elected.

The first National Spiritual Assembly of Sudan is elected.

The first National Spiritual Assembly of Iran is elected. [BBRSM:121; BW6:268]

- For a picture see BW6:268.

23 Jan Shoghi Effendi gives Queen Marie of Romania the gift of a Tablet in the handwriting of Bahá'u'lláh. [GBF50; PP116]

Agnes S. Parsons dies after an automobile accident. [BW5:410; SBR96]

- She is primarily remembered for her contribution to the cause of race unity in North America. [BW5:413]
- For her obituary see BW5:410–14.

See also DIARY OF AGNES PARSONS; SBR76–96.

10 May Bahá'í properties on Mount Carmel are granted tax exemption. [GBF122; PP269]

- Shoghi Effendi states that this is tantamount to securing indirect recognition of the Faith. [GBF122; PP269]

15–18 May The first National Convention of the Bahá'ís of Australia and New Zealand is held in Sydney, with nine delegates in attendance. [SBR165]

- The first National Spiritual Assembly of Australia and New Zealand is elected with its seat in Sydney. [SBR165]

28 Aug Mis<u>h</u>kín-Qalam's calligraphic rendering of the Greatest Name is registered as a trade-mark with the United States patent office. [BW6:350]

23 Oct Dr Susan Moody dies in Iran. [BFA2:361]

- For her services in Iran and an obituary see BW6:483–6.
- She is buried near the graves of Lilian Kappes and Sarah Clock in the Ṭihrán Bahá'í cemetery. [BW6:486]

Dec The National Spiritual Assembly of Egypt and the Sudan incorporate. [GPB336]

- This is the first national assembly in an Islamic country to secure civil recognition and the status of an independent religion. [BW6:24]

6 Dec The Tarbíyat Bahá'í Schools in Ṭihrán are closed by the authorities when they fail to open on a holy day. [BBD221–2; BW18:389; CB312; GPB363; PP308]

- For Western accounts of the episode see BBR475–9.

1935

In the year The persecution against the Bahá'ís in Iran continues. [BW18:389]

- Meetings in the Bahá'í Centre in Ṭihrán are banned.

Tarbíyat School

• A number of Bahá'ís in Bandar Sháh are arrested and imprisoned.

• The secretary of the Local Spiritual Assembly of Arák is arrested.

• Bahá'ís in Qazvín are arrested and harassed.

• A Bahá'í in Záhidán is arrested.

Husayn Uskuli, a Bahá'í resident in Shanghai, travels to Taiwan, the first Bahá'í known to visit the island. [PH28]

Mar *World Order* magazine is founded. [SBR206, 236]

Jul Shoghi Effendi asks the Bahá'ís to withdraw from church membership. [BBRSM146, 221; BW6:198; SBBH1:201]

Oct Shoghi Effendi writes to the National Spiritual Assembly of the Bahá'ís of the United States and Canada stating that the laws of fasting, obligatory prayer, the consent of parents before marriage, the avoidance of alcoholic drinks and monogamy should he regarded as universally applicable and binding. [CB313]

1936

In the year The National Assembly of Australia and New Zealand first issues its news organ, the *Bahá'í Quarterly*.

Mr E. R. and Mrs Loulie Mathews arrive in Guatemala, the first Bahá'í teachers to visit the country.

1936

The first woman is elected to the National Spiritual Assembly of India, Shirin Fozdar.

Renée Szanto-Felbermann becomes a Bahá'í, the first to accept the Faith in Hungary. [BW19:633]

See also *Szanto-Felbermann,* REBIRTH: THE MEMOIRS OF RENÉE SZANTO-FELBERMANN.

Feb Martha Root meets with Queen Marie of Romania for the eighth and last time. [MRHK413]

summer Britain holds its first Bahá'í summer school. [GT137; UD109]

Jun The persecution of the Bahá'ís of Iran continues. [BW18:389]

- All Bahá'í meetings are banned throughout Iran.
- Several local Bahá'í centres are attacked or closed down.
- Bahá'ís in Bandar Sháh are interrogated by the police for closing their shops on Bahá'í holy days.

1 Jul The National Spiritual Assembly of the United States and Canada appoints the first Inter-America Committee, beginning an organized and coordinated effort to establish the Faith in the Republics of Central and South America. [BW10:181]

3–16 Jul The World Congress of Faiths is held in London under the auspices of the World Fellowship of Faiths. [GPB342; GT123]

- Shoghi Effendi is asked in a personal letter from the chairman of the Congress, Sir Francis Younghusband, to contribute a paper, a task Shoghi Effendi delegates to George Townshend. [GT123; UD104]
- George Townshend reads the paper 'Bahá'u'lláh's Ground Plan of World Fellowship', which has been approved by Shoghi Effendi. [BW7:635; GT132–3]
- For text of the paper see BW6:614–19.
- For the conference programme see BW7:634–45.

31 Dec   Khusraw Bimán (<u>Th</u>ábit) dies in Bombay at the age of 103 or 104. [1:56]

• He is the first Zoroastrian to accept the Faith in India. [1:44–6]

• For the story of his life see 1:39–60.

1937

In the year   The persecution of the Bahá'ís in Iran continues throughout the country. [BW18:389]

• Many Bahá'ís employed in the police force, army and government departments are dismissed.

• Six members of the Local Spiritual Assembly of Ahváz are arrested.

• Bahá'ís closing their shops on Bahá'í holy days in Bandar <u>Sh</u>áh are arrested.

• All Bahá'í meetings in Kirmán<u>sh</u>áh, Bírjand, Arák and other towns are prohibited by police order.

• Five Bahá'í families are attacked in their homes in <u>Ch</u>am-tang, near Hindíyán. They are severely beaten and forced to leave the village.

The British Bahá'í Publishing Trust is founded. [BBRSM184; BW9:32; GT138–42]

25 Mar   Shoghi Effendi marries Mary Maxwell, Amatu'l-Bahá Rúḥíyyih <u>Kh</u>ánum. [PP151; UD115]

• For a description of the simple wedding see GBF68–9 and PP151–2.

• Shoghi Effendi stresses that the marriage draws the Occident and the Orient closer together. [GBF69–70; PP153]

• The American Bahá'í community sends $19 from each of its 71 Assemblies as a wedding gift. [GBF70; PP153]

• An extension is built onto Shoghi Effendi's apartment on the roof of 'Abdu'l-Bahá's house in Haifa to accommodate the couple. [BBD107; DH152]

See also MA8–9.

May Several prominent Bahá'ís are arrested in Yazd. [BW18:389]

• They are imprisoned in Ṭihrán for four years; one dies in prison. [BW18:389]

All Bahá'í activities and institutions are banned in Germany by order of the Gestapo owing to the Faith's 'international and pacifist teachings'. [BBRSM185]

Notes PP305 *says this was June.*

• Bahá'í books, archives and records are confiscated and a number of Bahá'ís are later tried and imprisoned. [BBRSM185]

The First Seven Year Plan is launched in North America. [BBD180; BBRSM158; BW7:17–18; MA9]

• For the role of individuals, local spiritual assemblies and the National Spiritual Assembly see MA11–12.

• The Plan calls for :

  • the completion of the exterior of the Wilmette Temple. [BW7:17–18; PP385]

  • the establishment of a local spiritual assembly in each state and province of the United States and Canada. [PP385]

  • the establishment of a centre in each of the republics of Latin America. [PP385]

2 May The Yerrinbool Bahá'í School (originally known as 'Bolton Place') is officially opened in Australia.

Jul Nine Bahá'ís are imprisoned in Sangsar, Khurásán, Iran, for closing their shops on Bahá'í holy days. [BW18:389]

• They are imprisoned for two months. [BW18:389]

20 Dec Muḥammad-'Alí, half-brother of 'Abdu'l-Bahá and Arch-breaker of the Covenant of Bahá'u'lláh, dies. [CB355; GPB320; MA11]

• For details of his death and funeral see DH117 and GPB320.

1938

In the year Persecution of the Bahá'ís of Iran continues throughout the country. [BW18:389]

• Bahá'ís marrying without a Muslim ceremony are investigated, including several hundred in Ṭihrán alone. Most are imprisoned pending trial and are imprisoned for six to eight months afterwards and fined.

• Bahá'í meetings in Kirmánsháh, Záhidán, Mashhad and other towns are harassed by the police.

The first Bahá'í visits the Dominican Republic, William DeForge, who comes on a one-day trip from Puerto Rico.

The Bahá'ís of India, Pakistan and Burma institute a Six Year teaching plan. [BBRSM158]

• Lack of funds prevent the plan from being implemented until 1940. [SBBH2:160]

The first native person to become a Bahá'í in Canada, Melba Loft (née Whetung), a Chippewa, accepts the Faith.

The first Bahá'í to be resident in Finland, Aminda Josephine Kruka, an American nurse, arrives in the country.

Shoghi Effendi remains in Europe for the year owing to terrorist activities in Palestine. [PP219]

Feb Felix Ricardo Maddela, a school teacher and draftsman from Solano, Philippines, and the first Filipino Bahá'í, accepts the Faith in Manila.

1938

5 Feb Bahá'ís in the Soviet Union are persecuted by the authorities. [BBR473; BW8:87–90, 179–81]

- Five hundred Bahá'í men are imprisoned in Turkistan. [BW8:89]
- Many Iranian Bahá'ís living in various cities of the Soviet Union are arrested; some are sent to Siberia, others to Pavladar in northern Kazakhstan and others to Iran. [BW8:87, 179, 184]
- Six hundred refugee Bahá'ís – women, girls, children and a few old men – go to Iran, mostly to Mashhad. [BW8:89]
- The Bahá'í Temple in 'Ishqábád is confiscated and turned into an art gallery. [BDD122; BW8:89]
- The Bahá'í schools are ordered closed. [BW8:89]
- Spiritual Assemblies and all administrative institutions in the Caucasus are dissolved. [BW8:89]

15 Mar Mary Virginia Thornburgh-Cropper (Maryam Khánum), the first Bahá'í of the British Isles, dies in Kensington, London. [SBR30]

- For details of her life see BSR17–30.
- For her obituary see BW8:649–51.

Notes *It is possibly she, rather than her mother, Mrs Thornburgh, who is referred to as a Disciple of 'Abdu'l-Bahá in* BW3:84–5. *The picture is not that of Mrs Thornburgh-Cropper.*

Apr The first local spiritual assembly in the whole of Latin America is formed in Mexico City.

30 Apr Munírih Khánum, the Holy Mother, wife of 'Abdu'l-Bahá, dies. [BBD166; BW8:260; CB358; DH161]

Notes UD119 *say this was 28 April.*

- Shoghi Effendi inters her body just west of the Shrine of Bahíyyih Khánum and erects a simple monument over her grave. [DH161]
- For excerpts from her autobiography see BW8:259–63.

Monument to the Holy Mother

• For tributes to her see BW8:263–7.

Jul The first Finnish Bahá'í, Pastor Väinö Rissanen, accepts the Faith. [BW8:935; BW17:129]

• For a letter from him about Finland see BW8:936.

25 Jul Queen Marie of Romania dies. [BBD144; GPB395]

• For her services to the Bahá'í Faith see GPB389–96.

• For tributes paid by her to the Bahá'í Faith see BW8:269–71.

• For her relationship with the Bahá'í Faith see BW8:271–6.

• For tributes to her see BW8:276–82.

Sep The first Bahá'í summer school to be held in India takes place in Simla. [BBRSM194; BW8:199]

27 Nov In a letter to the National Spiritual Assembly of the Bahá'ís of the British Isles, Shoghi Effendi outlines the attitudes and obligations of Bahá'ís regarding military service. [BW17:384–5; UD122–3, 128–9, 134]

25 Dec Shoghi Effendi addresses *The Advent of Divine Justice*, a book-length letter, to the Bahá'ís of the United States and Canada. [ADJ]

1938–9 Shoghi Effendi disbands the Haifa Spiritual Assembly and sends the local community away. [PP348]

1939

In the year Shoghi Effendi orders from Italy twin monuments similar in style to that of the Greatest Holy Leaf and seeks permission from the British authorities to reinter the remains of Navváb and the Purest Branch on Mount Carmel near those of Bahíyyih Khánum and the Holy Mother. [DH162; PP259]

The first Bahá'í of Paraguay, Maria Casati, of Formosa, Paraguay, becomes a Bahá'í in Buenos Aires.

Emeric and Rosemary Sala of Canada arrive in Venezuela, the first pioneers to that country.

Feb A.-L.-M. Nicolas, the French consular official and orientalist who made a study of the Bábí Faith, dies in Paris.

• His important collection of manuscripts is auctioned and the items relevant to the Bahá'í and Bábí Faiths are purchased by the Bahá'í World Centre.

Apr The National Spiritual Assembly of the Bahá'ís of the British Isles incorporates after a long and difficult struggle. [BW8:161–2; UD127]

8 May Philip and Laili June Marangella arrive in Cuba, the first Bahá'í pioneers to the country.

27 Aug The first Bahá'í resident in Guatemala, Gerrard Sluter, arrives in the country.

3 Sep World War II begins with Britain and France declaring war on Germany after Germany invades Poland.

18 Sep John and Rosa Shaw arrive in Kingston, Jamaica, from San Francisco, the first Bahá'ís to visit the country.

22 Sep The State of Illinois issues the first Bahá'í marriage licence, authorizing the Spiritual Assembly of Chicago to solemnize Bahá'í marriages and issue Bahá'í marriage certificates. [GPB373]

28 Sep Martha Root, 'foremost Hand raised by Bahá'u'lláh', dies in Honolulu. [BBD198–9; GPB388; MRHK486; PP105]

- For Shoghi Effendi's tribute to her see GPB386–9.
- Shoghi Effendi calls her the 'archetype of Bahá'í itinerant teachers', the 'foremost Hand raised by Bahá'u'lláh since 'Abdu'l-Bahá's passing', 'Leading ambassadress of His Faith' and 'Pride of Bahá'í teachers'. [GPB386]
- For her obituary see BW8:643–8.
- She is buried in the Nuuanu Cemetery, Honolulu.

See also *Garis,* MARTHA ROOT: LIONESS AT THE THRESHOLD *and* MARTHA ROOT: HERALD OF THE KINGDOM.

Oct Antonio Roca, the first Bahá'í in Honduras, enters the country.

1 Oct The national Bahá'í office of the United States is established at 536 Sheridan Road, Wilmette, Illinois. [BW10:181]

Horace Holley

Horace Holley, the full-time secretary of the National Spiritual Assembly of the Bahá'ís of the United States and Canada, transfers his office from New York to the Ḥaẓíratu'l-Quds in Wilmette. [SBR238]

25 Oct John Eichenauer, the first pioneer to El Salvador, arrives in San Salvador from Phoenix, Arizona.

- He is 17 years old, the youngest pioneer sent out in the First Seven Year Plan.

late in the year Sr. Perfecto Pérez Toledo, the first Cuban Bahá'í, accepts the Faith.

Nov F. Ferrari becomes a Bahá'í, the first to accept the Faith in Honduras.

1 Nov Mathew Kaszab, arrives in Nicaragua, the first Bahá'í pioneer to that country.

- In March 1942 he is arrested and imprisoned for 23 days; he is again arrested in September 1942; he is sent back to the United States very ill, where he dies in January 1943 from the effects of his imprisonment. [BW9:614–16]

2 Nov The first people to become Bahá'ís in El Salvador, Luis O. Pérez, Emilio Bermudez and José Manuel Vela, accept the Faith in San Salvador.

4 Nov The first Nineteen Day Feast is held in San Salvador with four Bahá'ís.

3 Dec Shoghi Effendi obtains permission from the British authorities in Palestine to reinter the bodies of Navváb and the Purest Branch on Mount Carmel. [DH162; PP260]

- For the report of the Haifa District Commissioner see BBR460–1.

5 Dec Shoghi Effendi disinters the remains of Navváb and the Purest Branch. [DH162; PP260]

- He goes at daybreak to 'Akká cemetery and removes the remains of Navváb to a new coffin. [DH162; PP260]
- He then goes to the Nabí Ṣáliḥ cemetery and transfers the remains of the Purest Branch to a second new coffin. [DH162; PP260]

- He transports them to Mount Carmel, near the grave of the Greatest Holy Leaf. [DH162; PP260]

- For his cable announcing this to the Bahá'í world see BW8:245 and DH162 and PP261.

8 Dec Margaret Lentz, a German stenographer, arrives in the Dominican Republic from Geneva, the first Bahá'í to settle in that country.

12 Dec The Bahá'ís of Caracas, Venezuela, hold their first Nineteen Day Feast and afterwards elect a 'Provisional Assembly'.

24 Dec Shoghi Effendi reinters the remains of Navváb and the Purest Branch. [DH162; GBF116; GPB347–8]

- Two vaults are cut into the solid rock in the garden area near the monument of the Greatest Holy Leaf. [DH162]

- For Shoghi Effendi's cable announcing this see DH162 and PP262.

- For Shoghi Effendi's letters and cables concerning this see BW8:245–53.

- For a description of the reinterment see BW8:253–8.

The Monuments to Navváb and the Purest Branch

• For the prayer of visitation to the resting place of Navváb see BW8:251 and DH166.

31 Dec Lady Blomfield, entitled Sitárih Khánum, dies in London. [BW8:651; SEBW109]

• For details of her life see SEBW101–10.

• For her obituary see BW8:651–6.

1940

In the decade By the mid-1940s Corporal Thomas Bereford Macauley becomes a Bahá'í in Nigeria, the first Bahá'í in the country.

The first Bahá'ís reside in the Belgian Congo (Zaire), Mr Rajah Ali Vahdat and Mme Marthe Molitor.

The first Egyptian Bahá'í summer school is held in the mid-1940s.

Bahá'ís in Argentina face opposition throughout the decade with both the police and nationalists intimidating them.

In the year Eleanor Smith Adler, a new Bahá'í from Los Angeles, settles in La Paz, the first pioneer to Bolivia.

Marcia Atwater, from the United States, arrives in Santiago, Chile, as the first long-term pioneer.

Narayenrao Rangnath Shethji, a Bahá'í from India surnamed Vakíl, visits Nepal, the first Bahá'í to do so.

The Grand Mufti of Egypt states that Bahá'ís cannot be buried in Muslim cemeteries, forcing the authorities to allow the Bahá'ís to have their own.

• The graves of Mírzá Abu'l-Faḍl Gulpáygání and Lua Getsinger are transferred to the cemetery near Cairo.

A Bahá'í centre is opened in Havana, Cuba, and an organized group is formed.

The Canadian Department of National Defence exempts Bahá'ís from combatant military duty.

The first local spiritual assembly in Brazil is established in Bahia, with the assistance of Leonora Holsapple Armstrong.

13 Jan María Teressa Martín de López (Irizarry), from Puerto Rico, becomes a Bahá'í in the Dominican Republic while on a visit. She is the first Puerto Rican Bahá'í and the first person to become a Bahá'í in the Dominican Republic.

- For the story of her life see BW17:437–8.

9 Feb The monuments of Navváb and the Purest Branch are dedicated at a ceremony in Haifa. [ZK293]

- For details of the ceremony, see ZK293–6.

1 Mar May Bolles Maxwell dies in Buenos Aires. [BBD153; BW8:631]

- Shoghi Effendi awards her the honour of a 'martyr's death'. [BW8:631; MA38]

May and Sutherland Maxwell

- For the story of her life see BW8:631–42.

- Shoghi Effendi asks her husband, Sutherland Maxwell, to design her tomb, which is to be a 'historic centre' for 'pioneer Bahá'í activity'. [BW8:642]

• For an account of the erection of the monument to her see PSBW83–6.

Monument of May Maxwell in Buenos Aires

Apr The first local spiritual assembly of Argentina is established in Buenos Aires.

15 May Shoghi Effendi determines to go to England; Shoghi Effendi and Rúḥíyyih Khánum leave Haifa for Italy en route to London. [PP178]

• For the difficulties and dangers of this journey see PP178–80.

25 May Shoghi Effendi and Rúḥíyyih Khánum leave for England via Menton and Marseilles after having obtained a visa for Britain in Rome. A few days later the Italians enter the war against the Allies. [PP179]

2 Jun Shoghi Effendi and Rúḥíyyih Khánum leave St Malo, France, for England one day before the city is occupied by the Nazis. [PP179–80]

30 Jun George Townshend preaches a sermon in St Patrick's Cathedral, Dublin, proclaiming the Bahá'í Faith to the congregation. [GT171]

Jul Gerrard Sluter, a German with Canadian citizenship and previously a pioneer in Guatemala, arrives in Colombia, the first Bahá'í to settle in the country.

- He later becomes a Covenant-breaker and causes much difficulty to the Bahá'ís in many South American countries.

28 Jul Shoghi Effendi, Rúḥíyyih Khánum and Sutherland Maxwell leave England for South Africa. [PP180]

- This is the only route open back to Palestine, as Italy's entrance into the war has closed the Mediterranean to Allied ships. [PP180]

- The trip across Africa takes them to Stanleyville, Congo; Juba in the Sudan; down the Nile to Khartoum and back to Palestine through Cairo. [PP180–1]

1 Aug The first four people to become Bahá'ís in Costa Rica accept the Faith after Gayle Woolson and Amelia Ford from the United States arrive in Puerto Limón on 29 March 1940.

William Sears

- The first to enrol is Raul Contreras, followed by his cousin Guido Contreras, and by José Joaquin Ulloa and Felipe Madrigal.

Sep William Sears, Hand of the Cause of God, becomes a Bahá'í in Salt Lake City, Utah.

20 Oct Ralph Laltoo, the first Trinidadian to become a Bahá'í, accepts the Faith in Halifax, Nova Scotia.

Dec Gerald and Vivian MacBeans, a Jamaican couple, and their niece, Miss May Johnson, become the first people to accept the Faith in Haiti.

Luis Carlo Nieto becomes the first Bahá'í in Colombia.

- He soon leaves the Faith and Aura Sanchez, who becomes a Bahá'í in 1941, is considered the first Colombian believer.

Eduardo Gonzales, a university student, accepts the Faith, becoming the first native Bahá'í of Ecuador.

- He is not formally registered until his twenty-first birthday on 15 October 1941.

27 Dec Shoghi Effendi and Rúḥíyyih Khánum are back in Haifa. [PP181]

Elizabeth Cheney, the 'spiritual mother of Paraguay', arrives in Paraguay, the first pioneer to the country.

1941

In the year Shaykh Káẓim is martyred in Bunáb, Ádharbáyján. [BW18:389]

John Ferraby, Hand of the Cause of God, hears about the Bahá'í Faith from Victor Cofman, a non-Bahá'í.

Aura Sanchez becomes a Bahá'í in Colombia, considered the first Bahá'í of the country.

Jan Nine Bahá'ís are arrested in Sangsar, Khurásán, Iran, and banished to other towns for closing their shops on Bahá'í holy days. [BW18:389]

17 Feb John Henry Hyde Dunn, Hand of the Cause of God, dies in Sydney. [BW9:595; SBR166]

- For the story of his life see SBR153–68.

- For his obituary see BW9:593–7.

18 May Yvonne Cuellar, a Frenchwoman, becomes a Bahá'í in Bolivia.

- Although Marina del Prado was the first to become a Bahá'í, on 2 February 1941, she did not remain active, so Yvonne Cuellar is recognized as the first Bahá'í in Bolivia. She was called by Shoghi Effendi 'Mother of Bolivia'.

- For the story of her life see BW19:619–22.

Jun Eve Nicklin arrives in Peru from the United States and becomes the first resident pioneer to settle in Lima.

summer The first Canadian Bahá'í summer school is held, in Montreal. [BW9:28]

16 Sep In Iran, Riḍá Sháh abdicates and Muḥammad-Riḍá Sháh accedes to the throne. [BBR482]

- Riḍá Sháh is overthrown by the British and Russians. [BBRSM173]

18 Oct Four members of a Bahá'í family are killed and several other family members severely beaten in an attack on their home by an armed mob in Panbih-Chúlih, near Sárí, Iran. [BW18:389]

1942

In the year The House of the Báb in Shíráz is attacked and damaged by fire. [BBD108; BW18:389]

Lidia Zamenhof is killed in the gas chambers at Treblinka.

- For her obituary see BW10:533–8.

See also *Heller,* LIDIA.

13 Feb Ustád Ḥabíbu'lláh Mu'ammarí is martyred in Nayríz, Iran. [BW18:389]

Apr The first local spiritual assembly in Haiti is established in Port-au-Prince.

The first local spiritual assembly in Cuba is established in Havana.

• A loose organization had been formed in 1940.

21 Apr The first local assembly in El Salvador is established in San Salvador.

25 May 'Abdu'l-Jalíl Bey Sa'ad dies and is named a Hand of the Cause of God posthumously. [BW9:597]

• For his obituary see BW9:597–9.

Jun The Spiritual Assembly of San José, Costa Rica, is legally registered with the government, the first local assembly to be incorporated in Latin America. [BW11:46]

26 Oct Marion Lord Maxwell ('Miss Mac') becomes a Bahá'í, the first Jamaican to accept the Faith. [BW17:429]

• For the story of her life see BW17:429–30.

16 Nov Manuel Bergés Chupani, of Sánchez, Dominican Republic, becomes a Bahá'í, perhaps the first native Dominican person to accept the Faith.

late in the year Shoghi Effendi asks Sutherland Maxwell to design the superstructure of the Shrine of the Báb. [BBD210; DH140; GBF103–5]

1943

Margot Vandenbroeck-Levy (Galler) becomes a Bahá'í in Chicago, the first native Luxembourger to accept the Faith.

• She returns to Luxembourg in 1948.

The first Bahá'í group is formed in Bogotá, Colombia, with the celebration of a Unity Feast.

8 Jan The exterior ornamentation of the Wilmette Temple is completed. [BW10:181; UD155–6]

- The cost of the building is $1.3 million. [UD165]

2 May Narayenrao Sethji, Vakíl, the first Hindu believer, dies in Poona. [BW9:638]

- For the story of his life see PH17–25.

23 May Melba M King (née Call) becomes a Bahá'í in Albuquerque, New Mexico, the first full-blooded Eskimo, a Yup'ik, to accept the Faith. [BW18:687–8]

4 Sep The first local spiritual assembly in Alaska is established at Anchorage.

1944

The first Bahá'ís arrive in the Mariana Islands.

- Joseph F. Peter and Joseph Tierno, United States servicemen, are based on Saipan, 1944–5.

Hand of the Cause Collis Featherstone and his wife, Madge, are introduced to the Bahá'í Faith by Bertha and Joe Dobbins in Adelaide, Australia. They become Bahá'ís later in the year.

A Bahá'í committee in Ṭihrán identifies the House of Bahá'u'lláh in the city and purchases it.

The National Spiritual Assembly of Australia incorporates.

Apr The first Bahá'í shortwave radio broadcast is beamed from New York towards South America. [BW9:44–5]

Notes VV76 *says this was 1943.*

21 Apr The first local spiritual assembly in Peru is established in Lima.

The first local spiritual assembly in Jamaica is established in Kingston.

1944

The first local spiritual assembly in Puerto Rico is established in San Juan.

The first local spiritual assembly in Colombia is established in Bogotá.

The first local Assembly of Bogotá with Dorothy Baker, seated second from right

The first local spiritual assembly in Honduras is established in Tegucigalpa.

May The British at national convention decide to ask the Guardian for their own Six Year Plan. [UDXVI]

- He responds immediately by setting them the task of forming 19 assemblies spread over England, Wales, Scotland, Northern Ireland and Eire. [UD173]
- Shoghi Effendi describes this as 'their first collective enterprise'. [UDXVI, 173–4]

See also BBRSM158, 185

The first All-American Bahá'í Convention is held.

- For the first time the delegates have been selected at state and provincial conventions by votes from all believers rather than by communities with local assemblies. [BW9:44; PP390]

12 May Bahá'ís are persecuted at Ábádih, Iran. The Bahá'í centre is attacked by a mob of four thousand, the building is looted and destroyed and several Bahá'ís badly beaten. [BW18:389]

- For Western accounts see BBR479.

19–25 May An international celebration of the Centenary of the founding of the Faith is held at the House of Worship in Wilmette.

- For a description of this event see BW10:158–61.
- For the programme see BW10:162–70.
- For a list of the countries participating in the conference see BW10:168.

22 May Centenary of the Declaration of the Báb.

- For a survey of the growth and development of the Bahá'í Faith in the hundred years since its inception see BW10:142–9.
- Celebrations are held in many parts of the world:

  Britain [BW10:188–201]
  India [BW10:202–8]
  Egypt [BW10:208–17]
  Iraq [BW10:217–22]
  Australia [BW10:222–8]
  Latin America [BW10:228–33]

- The end of the celebrations marking this occasion signal the end of the First Epoch of the Formative Age. [BBD79; CF5; PP390]

The Centenary of the Declaration of the Báb is celebrated at the House of the Báb in Shíráz. [BW10:181]

- Ninety delegates to the national convention and members of the National Spiritual Assembly of Iran assemble discreetly for the occasion.
- For details of this event and the caution with which the arrangements for it are made see BW10:181–3.

• The Guardian sends the Persian Bahá'ís a lengthy letter detailing how the observance and the week-long festivities to follow are to be made. [BW10:183]

• For details of the events see BW10:183–8.

22–3 May The Centenary of the Declaration of the Báb is commemorated in the Holy Land. [BW10:150]

• For a description of this event by Rúḥíyyih Khánum see BW10: 150–7.

• For press accounts see BW10:156–7.

23 May Shoghi Effendi unveils the model of the Shrine of the Báb at the centenary celebration of the Declaration of the Báb in Haifa. [BBD210; BW10:154, 157; DH140; GBF104; PP239–40; UD166]

Notes BW10:157 *suggests this was 24 May.*

8 Aug Three Bahá'ís are murdered in Sháhrúd, Iran, after three weeks of anti-Bahá'í agitation. Many Bahá'í houses are attacked and looted. [BW18:389]

• The murderers confess, are put on trial and are acquitted. [BW18:389]

after Aug Following the murder of Bahá'ís at Sháhrúd, Iran, and the widespread publicity on the outcome of the trial, there is an upsurge in persecution of Bahá'ís throughout Iran. [BW18:389]

• At Ábádih Bahá'ís are beaten and their houses sacked. [BW18:389]

• The Bahá'í centre at Bandar Jaz is attacked. [BW18:389]

• Two Bahá'ís are knifed at Bandar Sháh. The attackers are set free and attack a further three Bahá'ís, leaving one an invalid. [BW18:390]

• Bahá'ís, including women and children, are attacked and beaten at Bushrúyyih, their homes and shops looted and burned and the Bahá'í cemetery desecrated. [BW18:390]

• Bahá'í houses are attacked and looted at Fárán, Káshán and Ná'in. [BW13:390]

• Bahá'í houses are set on fire in Gulpáygán and Zábul. [BW18:390]

• Bahá'ís are driven from town in Bujnúrd, Gunábád and Ṭabas. [BW18:390]

• The Bahá'í cemetery at Maḥmúdábád is desecrated.

• Bahá'ís are beaten at Miyán-du-áb, Rafsanján, Sangsar and Sírján. [BW18:390]

• Bahá'ís are stoned at Qaṣr-i-Shírín. [BW18:390]

Nov The Local Spiritual Assembly of Bogotá, Colombia, is disbanded.

• It is not reformed until April 1946.

Nov (mid) *God Passes By*, a history of the first century of the Bábí and Bahá'í Faiths and the only full-sized book by Shoghi Effendi, is published. [BBRSM137; CB308–9; GPBXI]

• Shoghi Effendi intended the book to be a gift to the Bahá'ís of the West on the occasion of the hundredth anniversary of the Declaration of the Báb but conditions in the United States delayed its publication. [GT79–80; PP224]

• For how Shoghi Effendi wrote the book see GBF95–6 and PP222–4.

1945

See BBRSM166–7 for a chart showing the distribution of the Bahá'í Assemblies and localities in this year.

In the year Bahá'ís throughout Iran are dismissed from National Teacher Training Colleges by the National Board of Education. [BW18:390]

The World Forestry Charter Gathering is founded in Britain by Richard St Barbe Baker. [VV106; WH75]

13 Mar Siyyid Muṣṭafá Rúmí dies at the age of 99, in Burma. [BW10:519; PH23]

• He is named a Hand of the Cause of God posthumously. [BW10:519]

Right: Richard St Barbe Baker in 1944

Far right: Siyyid Muṣṭafá Rúmí

• For his obituary see BW10:517–20.

• For Shoghi Effendi's tribute see BW10:519–20 and DND215.

Apr The first local spiritual assembly in Ecuador is established in Guayaquil.

The first local spiritual assembly in the Dominican Republic is established in Santo Domingo.

• There are nine indigenous believers in the city.

The first local spiritual assembly of Bolivia is established in La Paz.

The first local spiritual assembly of Venezuela is established in Caracas.

25 Apr The United Nations convenes in San Francisco.

• For the Bahá'í response see BW17:81.

8 May The war in Europe ends.

• For Shoghi Effendi's response see MA80–1, PP185 and UD175.

• For the war's effect on the Bahá'í community worldwide see BW17:80.

• See CF36 for Shoghi Effendi's opinion of the significance of the role of the United States in the war.

Jun The 20 Bahá'ís in Port-au-Prince, Haiti, are a sufficient number for the local spiritual assembly to gain legal recognition for the Bahá'í Faith as a religion.

• It is registered as a cultural, religious and social organization on 5 August 1946.

Aug Marguerite Wellby Preston, an English Bahá'í married to a Kenyan tea grower, settles in Sotik, Kenya, becoming the first Bahá'í in the country. [UD484]

• Until the 1950s she is the only Bahá'í in East Africa. [UD484]

1 Aug A children's hostel is founded in Panchgani, Maharashtra state, India. [BBD171; BBRSM153; BW16:320]

• It expands into the New Era High School.

• For the history of the school see BW16:320–6.

14 Aug The German Bahá'ís, 80 per cent of whom live in the American sector of occupied Germany, obtain permission to re-organize. [BBRSM185]

2 Sep The war in Japan ends.

24 Oct The United Nations is formally established.

• For the relationship of the Bahá'í Faith to the United Nations see BW16:327–52.

1946

In the year Between 1946 and 1951, Johanne Sorensen (later Hoeg), the first Danish Bahá'í, sends letters and Bahá'í literature to 93 towns, villages, settlements, and radio stations throughout Greenland.

• Hendrik Olsen, the first Bahá'í indigenous to Greenland, enrols in 1965 after receiving a Bahá'í book from Miss Sorensen in 1946 and maintaining a 17-year correspondence with her.

The restoration of the House of Bahá'u'lláh in Ṭihrán is completed.

The first Bahá'í summer school in Argentina is held in Ezeiza. [BW11:45]

Apr The National Spiritual Assembly of Germany and Austria is re-established. [BBRSM185]

- It is elected for the first time since 1937.
- Three American soldiers are members. [BBRSM185]

11 Apr Shoghi Effendi instructs Sutherland Maxwell to set plans in motion for the first stages of the building of the superstructure of the Shrine of the Báb. [GBF104–5]

21 Apr The first local spiritual assembly in Brazil is established in Rio de Janeiro.

The first local spiritual assembly in Panama is established in Panama City.

Apr–May A 45-month teaching plan (1946–53) for Iran is launched. [BBRSM158; CB316]

The Second Seven Year Plan of the United States and Canada is launched. [BBR180; BBRSM158, 185; MA87–9]

- This marks the beginning of the second epoch of the Formative Age. [CB316; CF5–6]
- For details of the plan see BW16:81–2.

Jun Rita Marshall, the first person native to St Vincent in the Caribbean to become a Bahá'í, accepts the Faith while in Halifax, Nova Scotia.

- Her husband, Ernest Marshall, becomes a Bahá'í in November 1946.

5 Aug The Bahá'í Faith is registered as a cultural, religious and social organization in Haiti.

Oct A four-and-a-half year teaching plan for India, Pakistan and Burma (1946–50) is launched. [BBRSM158; CB316]

Nov The first teaching conference in Latin America is held in Buenos Aires on the instructions of Shoghi Effendi.

- Twenty-five delegates from ten South American countries attend. [BW11:46]

22 Nov Amelia Collins is appointed a Hand of the Cause of God by Shoghi Effendi. [PP258; PSBW87–8]

- He does not make this appointment public until 1951.

13 Dec Muḥammad Taqíy-i-Iṣfahání dies in Egypt. He was born in Iran. [BW11:500]

- Shoghi Effendi names him a Hand of the Cause of God posthumously. [BW11:502]
- For his obituary see BW11:500–2.

23 Dec Virginia Orbison, from the United States, leaves Brazil for a pioneer post in Madrid.

- The airplane she travels in is named 'O bandeirante' ('The Pioneer').

1947

In the year The first summer school in Chile takes place in Loncoche on property donated by Mrs Fabienne Guillon.

The first Chilean Teaching Conference is held in Santiago.

Gladys Anderson Weeden arrives at the World Centre to assist Shoghi Effendi, taking responsibility for liaising with government and other officials. [BW18:694]

- She marries Ben Weeden on 20 March 1948 in Jerusalem; he assists with building projects at the World Centre. [BW15:478; BW18:694]

The Ḥaẓíratu'l-Quds of Ṭihrán is completed. [BW11:588]

The Iraqi teaching plan (1947–50), comprising internal goals only, is launched. [BBRSM158]

The Australian–New Zealand teaching plan (1947–53), comprising internal goals only, is launched. [BBRSM158]

7 Feb Honor Kempton arrives in Luxembourg, the first pioneer to the country.

Apr The Tokyo Spiritual Assembly, suspended during the war, is established.

The National Spiritual Assembly of India and Burma is established.

spring The National Spiritual Assembly of the Bahá'ís of the United States and Canada is accredited by the United Nations as a non-governmental organization. [BW12:597; PP303]

May Clarence Iverson visits the Bahamas, the first recorded visit to the islands by a Bahá'í.

20 Jun George Townshend sends a letter of resignation from the Church of Ireland to the Bishop of Killaloe, naming 30 September for its coming into effect. [GT195]

4 Jul 'Abbás Sháhídzádih is martyred in Sháhí, Mázandarán, Iran. [BW18:390]

5 Jul Manuel Garcia Vásquez becomes a Bahá'í in Spain, the first new believer in the country.

9 Jul Shoghi Effendi receives a letter from the chairman of the United Nations Special Committee on Palestine requesting a statement on the relationship the Bahá'í Faith has to Palestine and the Bahá'í attitude to any future changes in the status of the country. [BW11:43]

- Shoghi Effendi replies on 14 July setting out the non-political character of the Bahá'í Faith and explaining that Palestine is both the administrative and the spiritual headquarters of the religion. [BW11:43–4]

- He also includes a statement of the history, aims and significance of the Bahá'í Faith, later published by the American National Spiritual Assembly in pamphlet form. [BW11:44; PP351]

• For the text of this latter statement see GTT1–10.

Sep Léa Nys becomes a Bahá'í in Belgium, the first Belgian to accept the Faith after World War Two.

• She is considered the first Belgian Bahá'í.

30 Sep George Townshend, at the age of 71 years, resigns his position with the Church of Ireland. [GT195]

• He is the first ordained priest of a Christian Protestant church to renounce his Orders and to become a fully accredited member of the Bahá'í community. [GT183]

• For the story of his resignation and transition to a lay life see GT199–200, 202.

Palle Bischoff, with his wife Ingegerd

17 Nov The first two Danes accept the Bahá'í Faith, May Marit Vestby and Palle Benemann Bischoff.

12 Dec The first pioneer to Portugal, Valeria Lamb Nicols, arrives from a pioneer post in Denmark.

31 Dec Suzette Hipp becomes a Bahá'í in Luxembourg, the second Luxembourger to accept the Faith and the first to do so in Luxembourg.

1948

In the year Douglas P. Hillhouse, a Captain in the United States military, is stationed on St Thomas until 1951, the first Bahá'í to reside on the island.

The first Bahá'í school in Haiti is inaugurated in Carrefour, a suburb of Port-au-Prince.

Pauline Campbell arrives in Bermuda, where her husband is stationed at the United States Air Force Base. She is the only Bahá'í in Bermuda until 1951.

The Canadian teaching plan (1948–53) is launched, the objective being to expand the Faith into Newfoundland and Greenland. [BBRSM158]

The Germano-Austrian teaching plan (1948–53), comprising internal goals only, is launched. [BBRSM158]

The Bahá'í centre in Ṭihrán is attacked by a mob incited by Áyatu-'lláh Ká<u>sh</u>ání. [BW18:390]

The Bahá'í centre in Yazd, Iran, is attacked by a mob incited by <u>Sh</u>ay<u>kh</u> Khálişízádih. [BW18:390]

A Bahá'í is killed after an attack on his home at <u>Ch</u>álih-Zamín, Iran. [BW18:390]

The Bahá'í Temple in 'I<u>sh</u>qábád is damaged by an earthquake. [BBD122; BW14:480]

War breaks out in Palestine.

• See DH118 for the effect on the Bahá'ís.

The owners of a house near the Shrine of Bahá'u'lláh flee and the house becomes government property. [DH226]

• Shoghi Effendi restores the house and makes it a pilgrim house. [DH226]

• He acquires the title in about 1956 as part of the exchange of the Ein Gev properties. [DH226]

11 Jan Ḥabíbu'lláh Hú<u>sh</u>mand is martyred in Sarvistán, Iran. [BW18:390]

Mar The name 'Bahá'í International Community' is first used to refer to the eight existing National Spiritual Assemblies recognized collectively as a non-governmental organization. [BBRSM149; BW11:43; BW12:597]

- Mildred Mottahedeh is appointed to serve as the accredited Bahá'í International Observer, a post she holds as a volunteer for almost 20 years. [BW12:601]

Apr Contracts are placed in Italy for the rose Baveno granite columns for the Shrine of the Báb. [BBD210; DH140]

- The first shipment of stone reaches Haifa on 23 November 1948.
- For details of securing the contract and cutting the stone see SE68–83.

19 Apr The Havana Bahá'ís incorporate as an 'assembly', meaning 'group'.

- It is incorporated as a local spiritual assembly in 1949.

20 Apr The first local spiritual assembly in Spain is established in Madrid.

21 Apr The first All-Native Bahá'í Assembly is established in Macy, Nebraska. [BW13:837; CF72]

- See BW11:536 for a picture.
- For the role of Amelia Collins in establishing this Assembly see PSBW88.

The first local spiritual assembly in Sweden is established at Stockholm. [BW11:689]

- For picture see BW11:689.

The first local spiritual assembly of the Netherlands is established in Amsterdam.

The first local spiritual assembly in Belgium is established in Brussels.

The first local spiritual assembly in Afghanistan is established in Kabul.

The first local spiritual assembly in Ireland is established in Dublin.

The National Spiritual Assembly of the Dominion of Canada is established. [BBRSM:186; BW13:856; MBW143; PP397]

• See BW11:160, 184 for pictures.

May The Bahá'í International Community takes part in its first United Nations conference, on human rights. [BW11:43]

14 May The British Mandate in Palestine ends and the state of Israel is proclaimed.

22–6 May The first Bahá'í European Conference is held in Geneva. [BW11:51]

• For details of the conference see BW11:51–2.

Dec Amjad Ali arrives in East Pakistan, from Chapra in Bihar, northern India, the first pioneer to the country.

1949

In the year Agnes Harrison (née Parent), an Athabascan, becomes a Bahá'í in Alaska, the first Native Alaskan to accept the Faith in the country.

An Egyptian teaching plan (1949–53) is launched. [BBRSM158]

Construction begins on the superstructure of the Shrine of the Báb. [BBD210]

A Bahá'í in Kamshatti, near Culcutta, is martyred by a religious fanatic. [BW11:34]

21 Jan Shoghi Effendi has a private interview with Prime Minister Ben Gurion of Israel. [GBF136; PP174–5, 289]

15 Apr Dr M. E. Lukmani, a homeopathic physician from India, arrives in Colombo, the first Bahá'í to settle in Ceylon (Sri Lanka).

20 Apr The first local spiritual assembly in Portugal is established in Lisbon.

21 Apr The first local spiritual assembly of Denmark is established in Copenhagen.

5–7 Aug The second European Teaching Conference is held in Brussels. [BW11:52]

1950

In the decade In Iran, the Ḥujjatiyya Society is started by Shaykh Maḥmúd Ḥalabí to persecute and harass the Bahá'ís. [SI296]

- During the Pahlaví era it confined itself to this end and was called the Anti-Bahá'í Society. [SI296]

John Z. T. Chang arrives in Hainan Island and is named a Knight of Bahá'u'lláh. [BW13:452]

'Abdu'l-Raḥmán arrives in the Seychelles and is named a Knight of Bahá'u'lláh. [BW13:455]

Clifford and Catherine Huxtable arrive in the Gulf Islands and are named Knights of Bahá'u'lláh. [BW13:457]

In the year By this year the Bahá'í population of Black Africa is probably no more than 12. [BBRSM190–1]

The Court of the First Instance in Karkúk, Iraq, registers a Bahá'í marriage certificate. [MBW4; UD248]

- This is the first time in the East, outside Israel, that a Bahá'í marriage is recognized as being legal, an important precedent for other Oriental countries. [MBW4; UD248]

Jan World Religion Day is first observed in the United States. [BBD242]

- Its purpose is to associate the term 'world religion' with the Bahá'í Faith. [BBD242]

3 Feb Dr Sulaymán Birgís is martyred in Káshán, Iran. [BW18:390]

- For his obituary see BW12:684–5.

Apr Shoghi Effendi announces the Africa Campaign in a cable to the British national convention. [BW12:52; UD245–6]

- The British community is to lead the campaign supported by the Bahá'ís of the United States and Egypt. [UD245]

- For the objectives of the campaign see UD245–6.

- For the importance of the enterprise see UD260–3.

- The plan is to be launched after a year's respite but the British Bahá'ís begin to implement the plan immediately. [CB317]

The British Africa Committee, shown here in 1952

25 Apr Shoghi Effendi cables the Bahá'í world with the successes of the Bahá'í work in the past year. [MBW3]

- The number of sovereign states and dependencies where the Faith is established reaches 100, an increase of 22 countries since 1944.

25 May Dr Khodadad M. Fozdar, a medical officer of the State Railways in India, arrives in Singapore, the first pioneer to the country. [BW13:393]

- His wife, Shirin Fozdar, joins him in September 1950.

Jul The British Six Year Plan is successfully completed. [BW11:25; MBW4]

9 Jul The Centenary of the Martyrdom of the Báb is commemorated.

- For Shoghi Effendi's message to the Bahá'ís on this occasion see BW12:191–3.

- For accounts of commemorations around the world see BW12:205–8.

- A small group of Bahá'í pilgrims visit the site of the Báb's martyr-

The commemoration in Tabríz of the Centenary of the Martyrdom of the Báb

dom and other places associated with His life. [BW12:217–26]

- The columned arcade and parapet of the Shrine of the Báb are completed. [ZK284–5]

24–30 Jul The third European Teaching Conference is held in Copenhagen. [BW12:49]

The Third European Teaching Conference, Copenhagen

- 177 Bahá'ís from 22 countries attend.

Sep–Oct Four Bahá'ís in Iran are arrested on trumped-up charges. The trial lasts until 1954, when the accused are given prison sentences. [BW18:390]

23 Oct Nur Ali, a well-known and respected public servant in Suva, becomes a Bahá'í, the first to accept the Faith in Fiji.

Nov Mírzá Badí'u'lláh, the youngest son of Bahá'u'lláh, described by Shoghi Effendi as the 'chief lieutenant' of the 'archbreaker' of the 'divine Covenant' dies. [CB340, 355–6; CF89]

Brian Burland, the first Bermudian to become a Bahá'í, accepts the Faith in Canada.

From Switzerland, Shoghi Effendi invites five Bahá'ís – Lotfullah Hakim, Jessie and Ethel Revell, Amelia Collins and Mason Remey – to Haifa. [PP251]

- They, together with Ben and Gladys Weeden who are already there, are told that they will constitute the International Bahá'í Council. [PP251–2]

Dec Jalál Nakhjavání arrives in Tanganyika, the first Bahá'í pioneer to the country. [BW18:79]

16 Dec Shoghi Effendi leases Mazra'ih after a protracted struggle to obtain the property. [CB331; MBW7]

- The property is a Muslim religious endowment and Shoghi Effendi's attempts to procure it have long been thwarted. [GBF137; PP290]
- The Guardian appeals directly to Israel's Prime Minister David Ben-Gurion to recognize the interest of the Bahá'í community in the property as a holy place. [DH93]

1951

In the year By this year the first Canadian Inuit has become a Bahá'í.

Portuguese Bahá'ís Mr António and Mrs Ema Rocha, Mrs Guedes DeMelo Rocha and Mrs D. Laura Rodriquez, the first pioneers to Angola, take up residence in Luanda.

Palle Benemann Bischoff, the first to become a Bahá'í in Denmark, settles in Aasiaat, becoming the first Bahá'í to live in Greenland. [MC22]

- He is best known for being the first person to teach the Greenlanders to ski and for having organized the first ski competition in West Greenland.

Shoghi Effendi receives the original manuscript of the Kitáb-i-Íqán, in the handwriting of 'Abdu'l-Bahá with some marginal additions by Bahá'u'lláh, and places it in the International Bahá'í Archives.

Throughout Iran, the government introduces repressive measures against Bahá'ís. [BW18:390]

- Bahá'ís are dismissed from government positions. [BW18:390]

- Fifty Bahá'í employees of the public hospital in Mas͟hhad are dismissed. [BW18:390]

Bahá'ís in Árán, Ká<u>sh</u>án, Iran, are attacked, and one dies. [BW18:390]

The Nineteen-Month Teaching Plan (1951–3) for India, Pakistan and Burma is launched. [BBRSM158; DND148–50]

Bahá'í women in Egypt are extended the right of membership on local spiritual assemblies. [MBW12]

- Shoghi Effendi calls this 'a notable step in the progress of Bahá'í women of the Middle East'. [MBW12]

9 Jan Shoghi Effendi announces the establishment of the International Bahá'í Council. [BBD118; BBRSM127; GBF109; MBW7–8; PP252]

- It is a forerunner to the Universal House of Justice. [BBD118]

- For its functions see MBW7–8.

- Its seat is the Western Pilgrim House. [BBD178]

- For the stages of its evolution see CB324.

25 Jan Claire Gung arrives in Tanganyika, the second Bahá'í pioneer to the country.

Mar The Bahá'ís of El Salvador call on the president of the republic to dispel any suspicions that the Bahá'í community is linked to communism.

2 Mar Shoghi Effendi announces the completion of the restoration of the House of 'Abbúd. [MBW8]

12 Mar Bahá'ís in Taft, Iran, are attacked and one dies. [BW18:390]

Apr The Africa Campaign is officially launched. [BBRSM158]

22–4 Apr The National Spiritual Assembly of South America is elected at a convention in Lima, Peru. [BW12:60]

- 18 of the 27 delegates are present at the convention. [BW12:60]

The National Spiritual Assembly of the Bahá'ís of Central America is elected at a convention in Panama City. [BW12:60]

- 25 delegates representing 12 countries are present at the convention. [BW12:60]

25 Apr Shoghi Effendi cables the Bahá'í world with the successes of the Bahá'í work in the past year. [MBW11–13]

- The number of sovereign states and dependencies open to the Faith is 106, while some of the writings have been translated into more than 80 languages. [MBW11]

The Bahá'í International Fund is established. [MBW13–14]

23 May Jamshed and Parvati Fozdar arrive in Kuching with their son, Vijay, the first Bahá'ís to settle in Sarawak.

Jun Bahá'ís in Fárán, Iran, are attacked and several houses burned. [BW18:390]

Jul Mr P. K. Gopalakrishnan Nayer, an Indian, becomes a Bahá'í in Dar-es-Salaam, the first person to accept the Faith in Tanganyika. [BW12:53]

30 Jul Louis Gregory, Hand of the Cause of God, dies in Eliot, Maine. [BW12:666; TMW310]

- On his passing he is designated by Shoghi Effendi the first Hand of the Cause of his race. [BBD91; BW12:666]

- For his obituary see BW12:666–70.

See also *Morrison*, TO MOVE THE WORLD.

2 Aug Músá and Samí'ih Banání; their daughter, Violette and her husband, 'Alí Nakhjavání; their baby daughter, Bahiyyih; and Philip Hainsworth from England arrive in Kampala, the first pioneers to Uganda.

'Alí and Violette Nakhjavání

Oct Marthe Jeanne Molitor, the first Belgian Bahá'í to settle in another country, leaves for the Belgian Congo (Zaire) one day after becoming a Bahá'í.

11 Oct Edmund (Ted) Cardell, arrives in Kenya, the first Bahá'í pioneer to the country in the Africa Campaign. [UD488]

- Marguerite Preston, the wife of a tea grower, has been living in Kenya since August 1945. She is killed in an air crash in February 1952.

22 Oct Ethel Stephens, the first black American pioneer to Africa, arrives in Accra, the first Bahá'í pioneer to Ghana.

30 Nov Shoghi Effendi announces plans for the Great Jubilee commemorating the centenary of the birth of the Revelation of Bahá'u'lláh in the Síyáh-Chál. [BW12:24–6, 115–16; MBW16–18]

Dec Brothers-in-law Fred Bigabwa, a Mutoro, and Crispin Kajubi, a Muganda, become Bahá'ís in Uganda, the first to accept the Faith in that country.

20 Dec Roy C. Wilhelm, Hand of the Cause of God, dies in Lovel, Maine. [BW12:662]

- On his passing Shoghi Effendi designates him a Hand of the Cause of God. [BW12:662]
- For his obituary see BW12:662–4.

Roy Wilhelm

24 Dec Shoghi Effendi appoints 12 Hands of the Cause of God, the first contingent of Hands to be appointed. [BBRSM127; BW12:38–40, 374–5; BW13:333–4; MBW 20]

- They are Sutherland Maxwell, Mason Remey, Amelia Collins (she had been appointed in 1946, but her appointment had not been made public), Valíyu'lláh Varqá, Ṭarázu'lláh Samandarí, 'Alí-Akbar Furútan, Horace Holley, Dorothy Baker, Leroy Ioas, George Townshend, Herman Grossmann and Ugo Giachery. [GBF110–11; MBW20; PP253–4]

1952

In the year Walli Khan, a Fiji Indian, becomes a Bahá'í, the first person in Fiji to accept the Faith.

Below left: Ṭarazu'lláh Samandarí; *right:* Ali-Akbar Furútan

Eric Manton and his son Terry arrive in Northern Rhodesia (Zambia), the first Bahá'ís to settle in the country.

Enoch Olinga

Mr Narain Das, a textile salesman from India working in Singapore, becomes a Bahá'í, the first person in the country to accept the Faith. A few months later Mr Teo Geok Leng, a Chinese Singaporean, becomes a Bahá'í, the first native of Singapore to accept the Faith.

Bahá'ís and their homes are attacked in Najafábád, Iran, and several houses are set on fire. [BW18:390]

Dudley Smith Kutendere from Zomba in the south of Malawi becomes a Bahá'í in Dar-es-Salaam, the first African to become a Bahá'í in Tanganyika and the first in all of Central and East Africa.

Feb Enoch Olinga becomes a Bahá'í, the third Ugandan and the first of the Iteso tribe to accept the Faith.

29 Feb Shoghi Effendi appoints the second contingent of Hands of the Cause of God. [BW12:375–6; CT202–3; MBW20–1; PP254; ZK47]

Below left: Corinne True; *centre:* Shu'á'u'lláh 'Alá'í; *right:* Músá Banání

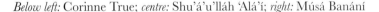

- They are Fred Schopflocher, Corinne True, <u>Dh</u>ikru'lláh <u>Kh</u>ádem, Shu'á'u'lláh 'Alá'í, Adelbert Mühlschlegel, Músá Banání and Clara Dunn. [BW12:375–6; MWB19–20]

- Shoghi Effendi describes their two-fold function: propagation of the Faith and preservation of its unity. [BW12:376; MBW21]

Mar Mariette Bolton of Australia visits New Caledonia, the first Bahá'í to visit the islands.

- During her visit Mlle Françoise Feminier becomes a Bahá'í, the first person in New Caledonia to accept the Faith.

The octagonal second component of the Shrine of the Báb is completed.

4 Mar Shoghi Effendi describes plans for a marble colonnade to encircle the Shrine of the Báb as an intermediate step to building a superstructure for the Shrine and sends his ideas to Italy for scale drawings and estimate. [SE133–4]

The Shrine of the Báb in 1952

8 Mar Shoghi Effendi announces the enlargement of the International Bahá'í Council to eight members. [MBW22; PP252–3]

- Its members are Amatu'l-Bahá Rúḥíyyih <u>Kh</u>ánum, Mason Remey, Amelia Collins, Ugo Giachery, Leroy Ioas, Jessie Revell, Ethel Revell and Lotfullah Hakim. [BW12:379; MBW22]

26 Mar Sutherland Maxwell, Hand of the Cause of God, dies in Montreal. [DH143; MBW132; PP246]

- For his obituary see BW12:657–62.

- For his relationship with Shoghi Effendi and work on the superstructure of the Shrine of the Báb see PP236–43.

Left to right: Mary, Ethel and Jessie Revell

• Shoghi Effendi names the southern door of the Báb's tomb after him in memory of his services.

Amatu'l-Bahá Rúḥíyyih Khánum is appointed Hand of the Cause of God to replace her father. [GBF111; MBW132–3]

Apr The first local spiritual assembly in Tanganyika is established in Dar-es-Salaam.

The first local spiritual assembly of Singapore City is established. [BW12:573; PH58. 67]

21 Apr The first local spiritual assembly of Uganda is established in Kampala.

• Enoch Olinga is a member.

27 Apr Hyde Dunn is posthumously appointed a Hand of the Cause of God in a cable sent to the National Spiritual Assembly of Australia and New Zealand. [BW13:861; SBR169]

18 May The case brought against Shoghi Effendi by the Covenant-breakers in connection with the demolition of a house adjoining the Shrine and Mansion of Bahá'u'lláh at Bahjí is removed from the civil courts by the government of Israel. [CB330; GBF138–9; PP233–4, 290]

• For the history of this case and the outcome see BW12:384–7.

1952

Jun Aaron ('Arthur') B. Wellesley Cole, a Sierra Leonean barrister, returns to Sierra Leone from England, the first Bahá'í to enter the country.

c. Jun Dudley Smith Kutendere returns to his home in Nyasaland, becoming the first Bahá'í in the country.

- He teaches the Bahá'í Faith to his brother, who becomes the first person to accept the Faith in Nyasaland.

Jun or Jul Mr C. C. Cheng, a newspaper reporter; Professor L. S. Tso, a professor of engineering; and Miss Rosie Du (Ruthy Tu) become Bahá'ís in Taiwan, the first people to accept the Faith in the country.

8 Oct Holy Year, October 1952 to October 1953, is inaugurated. [BW12:116; DG84; PP409–10; SBR170–1]

- Centenary celebrations of the birth of Bahá'u'lláh's mission are initiated. [MBW16–18]

Shoghi Effendi announces his decision to launch 'the fate-laden, soul-stirring, decade-long world-embracing Spiritual Crusade' in the coming year. [BW12:253–5; MBW41]

- For the objectives of the Crusade see BW12:256–74.
- Among the goals to be achieved is the construction of the International Bahá'í Archives building. [BBD22; DH168; MBW43]
- He calls upon the Hands of the Cause to appoint during Riḍván 1954 five auxiliary boards to act as their adjuncts or deputies to work with the national spiritual assemblies to execute the projected national plans. [MBW44]

12 Nov Dagmar Dole, pioneer to Alaska and Denmark, dies in Glion, Switzerland.

- Shoghi Effendi says she is the 'first to give her life for the Cause in the European project'. [BW12:702; ZK66–7]
- For her obituary see BW12:701–2.

The government of Israel exchanges 145,000 square metres of land

Dagmar Dole

surrounding Bahjí for property at Ein Gev on the eastern side of the Sea of Galilee belonging to the descendants of Bahá'u'lláh's brother Mírzá Muḥammad-Qulí and given to the Faith for this purpose. [DH118, 208; PP233]

- Bahá'í holdings at Bahjí up to now amount to only 4,000 square metres.

1953

In the year Grant Mensah, a Ghanaian, becomes a Bahá'í in Ruanda-Urundi, the first person to accept the Faith in that country.

Bahá'ís and their houses are attacked in Bus͟hrúyyih and Fárán, Iran. [BW18:390]

Áqá Raḥmán Kulayní-Mamaqání is martyred in Durúd, Iran. [BW18:390]

Katharine Meyer arrives on Margarita Island and is named a Knight of Bahá'u'lláh. [BW13:454]

Alfred Amisi (Maragoli), Jacob Kisombe (Mtaita), Laurence Ouna (Mluhya), Labi Mathew (Zulu), and Zablon Bolo (Luo) are among the first Kenyans to become Bahá'ís.

12–18 Feb The first Intercontinental Teaching Conference is convened by the

British National Spiritual Assembly in Kampala, Uganda. [BW12:121]

- For Shoghi Effendi's message to the conference see BW12:121–4.
- For a report of the conference see BW12:124–30.
- It is attended by ten Hands of the Cause, Bahá'ís from 19 countries and representatives of over 30 tribes. [PP413]
- Over a hundred new African believers attend as personal guests of the Guardian. [PP413]

Hand of the Cause Leroy Ioas greeting some of the hundred new African believers at the African Teaching Conference

- With this conference the Ten Year World Crusade is launched. [BBRSM158–9; BW12:253; MBW41]

19 Mar Suhayl Samandarí arrives in Mogadishu and is named a Knight of Bahá'u'lláh for Italian Somaliland. [BW13:452]

- Within a short time, Sa'íd 'Alí Masqatí, a Somali from the port of Baraawe, becomes a Bahá'í, the first person to accept the Faith in Somalia.

Four of the first African pioneers

Some of the first pioneers to Africa

25 Mar Enayat Sohaili, an Iranian, arrives in Mozambique from India, the first Bahá'í pioneer to the country. [BW13:290]

- He is imprisoned and deported in June 1953. [BW13:290]

Apr The first local spiritual assembly in Finland is established in Helsinki.

19 Apr Shoghi Effendi announces plans to build a House of Worship in Frankfurt. [BW13:733; LDG191–2]

• For the difficulties in pursuing the project see BW13:733–7.

21 Apr Bahjí is lit for the first time by 99 four-branched wrought iron lamp posts. [GBF32; PP89–90]

The first local spiritual assembly of the whole of Malaysia is established in Kuching.

Meherangiz Munsiff, the wife of an Indian diplomat in London, arrives in Madagascar and is acknowledged as the first Bahá'í in the country.

Meherangiz Munsiff

Some of the participants at the first Italo-Swiss Bahá'í Convention, 23–7 April 1953

• There was one other Bahá'í in Madagascar before Mrs Munsiff but he was not a Bahá'í in good standing.

The first local spiritual assembly in Kenya is established in Nairobi.

The National Spiritual Assembly of Italy and Switzerland is established.

29 Apr In a moving ceremony, Shoghi Effendi places a silver box containing a fragment of plaster from the ceiling of the Báb's cell in Máh-Kú under a tile in the golden dome of the Shrine of the Báb. [BW12:239; ZK285]

29 Apr–2 May The All-American Jubilee celebrations begin. [BW12:149]

May Mary and Reginald (Rex) Collison, an elderly Canadian-American couple, arrive in Ruanda-Urundi (Burundi) from Uganda and are named Knights of Bahá'u'lláh. [BW13:455]

- For the story of Mary Collison's life see BW15:486–8.

1 May The House of Worship in Wilmette is consecrated in a simple ceremony for Bahá'ís only. [BW12:143, 152; ZK93]

- For details of the dedication see BW12:152–4.

2 May The House of Worship in Wilmette is dedicated in a public ceremony. [BW12:142]

- For the text of the Guardian's message of dedication see BW12:141–2.

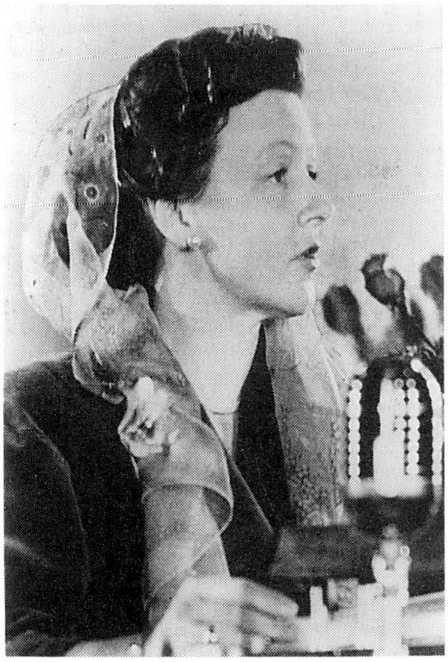

Rúḥíyyih Khánum reading the message of Shoghi Effendi at the dedication of the Wilmette Temple

- For an account of the event see BW12:154–63.

3–6 May The All-America Intercontinental Teaching Conference is held in Chicago. [BW12:133]

• For the texts of Shoghi Effendi's messages to the conference see BW12:133–41 and MBW142–6.

• Twelve Hands of the Cause are present. [BW12:143]

• At the conference, five members of the National Spiritual Assembly of the United States resign from that body in order to go pioneering: Elsie Austin, Dorothy Baker, Matthew Bullock, Mamie Seto and Dr William Kenneth Christian. [ZK102]

National Spiritual Assembly of the Bahá'ís of the United States 1953. Left to right: H. Borrah Kavelin, Mamie Seto, W. Kenneth Christian, Elsie Austin, Paul Haney, Edna True, Horace Holley, Dorothy Baker, Matthew Bullock.

Jun Dunduzu Chisiza, a Nyasaland student who has recently become a Bahá'í in Uganda, arrives in Ruanda-Urundi [Burundi] and is named a Knight of Bahá'u'lláh. [BW13:455]

Ghulám 'Alí Kurlawala arrives in Daman and is named a Knight of Bahá'u'lláh. [BW13:451]

6 Jun 'Izzatu'lláh Zahrá'í (Ezzat Zahrai) arrives in Southern Rhodesia (Zimbabwe) and is named a Knight of Bahá'u'lláh. [BW13:456]

Ezzat Zahrai

Jul Rawshan Áftábí and Fírúzih Yigánigi arrive in Goa and are named Knights of Bahá'u'lláh. [BW13:452]

Arthur and Ethel Crane arrive in Key West and are named Knights of Bahá'u'lláh. [BW16:453]

Sa'id Nahví arrives in Pondicherry and is named a Knight of Bahá'u'lláh. [BW13:455]

Jack Huffman and Rose Perkal arrive on the Kodiak Islands and are named Knights of Bahá'u'lláh. [BW13:453]

Jenabe and Elaine Caldwell arrive in the Aleutian Islands and are named Knights of Bahá'u'lláh. [BW13:449]

21–6 Jul The European Intercontinental Teaching Conference is held in Stockholm. [BW12:167]

Hands of the Cause attending the Stockholm Teaching Conference

- For Shoghi Effendi's message to the conference see BW12:167–71.

- For a report of the conference see BW12:171–8.

- Fourteen Hands of the Cause are present. [BW12:171]

- 374 Bahá'ís from 30 countries attend, of these 110 come from the ten goal countries. [BW12:171]

27 Jul Siegfried Schopflocher, Hand of the Cause of God, dies in Montreal. He was born in Germany in 1877. [BW12:666]

- For his obituary see BW12:664–6.

Aug 'Abbás Vakíl arrives in Cyprus and is named a Knight of Bahá'u'lláh. [BW13:450]

Shiyam Behari arrives in Pondicherry and is named a Knight of Bahá'u'lláh. [BW13:455]

Amír Húshmand Manúchihrí arrives in Liechtenstein and is named a Knight of Bahá'u'lláh. [BW13:453]

Salísa Kirmání and Shírín Núrání arrive in Karikal and are named Knights of Bahá'u'lláh. [BW13:452]

Amín and Sheila Banání, a Persian-American couple, settle in Athens-Kifissia in August 1953 and are named Knights of Bahá'u'lláh for Greece. [BW452]

Eskil Ljungberg of Sweden, aged 67, arrives in the Faroe Islands and is named a Knight of Bahá'u'lláh. [BW13:451]

- He is the only Bahá'í on the islands for over a decade.

- For the story of his life see BW19:658–61.

Eskil Ljungberg

Edythe MacArthur arrives in the Queen Charlotte Islands and is named a Knight of Bahá'u'lláh. [BW13:455]

Udai Narain Singh arrives in Sikkim and is named a Knight of Bahá'u'lláh. [BW13:455; PH63]

2 Aug Fred Schechter, an American, arrives in Djibouti and is named a Knight of Bahá'u'lláh for French Somaliland. [BW13:451]

Above: Fred Schechter

Below: Virginia Orbison

11 Aug Virginia Orbison arrives in the Balearic Islands from a pioneer post in Spain and is named a Knight of Bahá'u'lláh for the Balearic Islands. [BW13:449]

26 Aug Ella Bailey dies in Tripoli. [BW12: 687]

- She is 88 years old.
- She is elevated to the rank of the martyrs. [MBW170]

Below: Ella Bailey

• For the story of her life see PSBW131–42.

• For her obituary see BW12:685–8.

28 Aug Mildred Clark, a pioneer in Norway, and Loyce Lawrence (née Drugan), a nurse and hospital matron, arrive in the Lofoten Islands and are named Knights of Bahá'u'lláh. [BW13:453]

• Mrs Lawrence begins teaching the Saami.

Sep Brigitte Hasselblatt arrives in Shetland and is named a Knight of Bahá'u'lláh. [BW13:455]

Ada Schott, Elizabeth Hopper, Sara Kenny and Ella Duffield arrive in the Madeira Islands and are named Knights of Bahá'u'lláh. [BW13:453]

Kathleen Weston arrives in the Magdalen Islands and is named a Knight of Bahá'u'lláh. [BW13:453]

Nellie French arrives in Monaco and is named a Knight of Bahá'u'lláh. [BW13:454]

Julius Edwards arrives in the Northern Territories Protectorate and is named a Knight of Bahá'u'lláh. [BW13:455]

Doris Richardson arrives on Grand Manan Island and is named a Knight of Bahá'u'lláh. [BW13:452]

Howard Snider arrives in Key West and is named a Knight of Bahá'u'lláh. [BW13:453]

Elsa Grossman arrives in the Frisian Islands and is named a Knight of Bahá'u'lláh. [BW13:452]

Hugh McKinley and his mother, Violet, arrive in Cyprus and are named Knights of Bahá'u'lláh. [BW13:450]

Dick Stanton arrives in Keewatin and is named a Knight of Bahá'u'lláh. [BW13:453]

Jameson and Gale Bond arrive in Franklin and are named Knights of Bahá'u'lláh. [BW13:451]

Ḍiá'i'lláh Aṣgharzádih and Evelyn Baxter arrive in the Channel Islands and are named Knights of Bahá'u'lláh. [BW13:450]

Helen Robinson arrives on Baranof Island and is named a Knight of Bahá'u'lláh. [BW13:449]

Cora Oliver arrives in British Honduras (Belize) and is named a Knight of Bahá'u'lláh. [BW13:449]

9 Sep José (d.1985) and Hilda (née Summers) Xavier Rodrigues, a Portuguese–English couple, arrive in Bissau from Portugal as the first Bahá'í pioneers to Portuguese Guinea (Guinea Bissau) and are named Knights of Bahá'u'lláh. [BW13:455]

18 Sep Dwight and Carole Allen arrive in Athens and are named Knights of Bahá'u'lláh for Greece. [BW13:452]

23 Sep Ted and Joan Anderson arrive in Whitehorse, Canada, and are named Knights of Bahá'u'lláh for the Yukon. [BW13:457]

27 Sep Tábandih Paymán arrives in San Marino and is named a Knight of Bahá'u'lláh in November. [BW13:455]

30 Sep Manúchihr Ḥizárí and Hurmuz Zindih arrive in Tangier and are named Knights of Bahá'u'lláh for Morocco (International Zone). [BW13:454]

Oct Charles Dunning arrives in the Orkney Islands and is named a Knight of Bahá'u'lláh. [BW13:455]

Emma Rice and Stanley and Florence Bagley arrive in Sicily and are named Knights of Bahá'u'lláh. [BW13:455]

Lionel Peraji arrives in Mahé and is named a Knight of Bahá'u'lláh. [BW13:454]

Geraldine Craney arrives in the Hebrides and is named a Knight of Bahá'u'lláh. [BW13:452]

Marie Ciocca arrives on Sardinia and is named a Knight of Bahá'u'lláh. [BW13:455]

Earle Render arrives in the Leeward Islands and is named a Knight of Bahá'u'lláh. [BW13:453]

Salvador and Adela Tormo arrive on the Juan Fernandez Islands and are named Knights of Bahá'u'lláh. [BW13:452]

Zunilda de Palacios arrives on Chiloé Island and is named a Knight of Bahá'u'lláh. [BW13:450]

Elly Becking arrives in Dutch New Guinea and is named a Knight of Bahá'u'lláh. [BW13:451]

Gertrud Ankersmidt and Ursula von Brunn arrive in the Frisian Islands and are named Knights of Bahá'u'lláh. [BW13:452]

Frederick and Jean Allen and Irving and Grace Geary arrive on Cape Breton Island and are named Knights of Bahá'u'lláh. [BW13:450]

Richard and Lois Nolen arrive in the Azores and are named Knights of Bahá'u'lláh. [BW13:449]

Shirley Warde arrives in British Honduras (Belize) and is named a Knight of Bahá'u'lláh. [BW13:449]

Dr Malcolm King, an American pioneer in Jamaica, arrives in British Guiana and is named a Knight of Bahá'u'lláh. [BW13:449]

Rolf Haug settles in Crete and is named a Knight of Bahá'u'lláh for that island. [BW13:450]

Albert Nyarko Buapiah becomes a Bahá'í in Ghana, the first Ghanaian to become a Bahá'í in the country.

Muḥammad Muṣṭafá Sulaymán, an Egyptian, arrives in Spanish Sahara (Western Sahara) and is named a Knight of Bahá'u'lláh. [BW13:456]

- For the story of his life see BW18:768–71.

'Amín Baṭṭáḥ, an Egyptian, arrives in Río de Oro (Western Sahara) and is named a Knight of Bahá'u'lláh. [BW13:455]

Una Townshend arrives in Malta and is named a Knight of Bahá'u'lláh. [BW13:454]

Max Kanyerezi, a Ugandan, is brought to Brazzaville by Violette and Ali Nakhjavani and is named a Knight of Bahá'u'lláh for French Equatorial Africa. [BW13:451]

Bertha Dobbins arrives in Port Vila on the island of Efate from Adelaide, Australia, and is named a Knight of Bahá'u'lláh for the New Hebrides Islands (Vanuatu). [BW13:454]

Mrs (Alexandra) Ola Pawlowska arrives in St Pierre and is named a Knight of Bahá'u'lláh for Miquelon Island and St Pierre Island. [BW13:454]

Gail and Gerald Curwin and Maurice and Ethel Holmes arrive in Nassau and are named Knights of Bahá'u'lláh for the Bahama Islands. [BW13:449]

Jean and Tove Deleuran arrive in the Balearic Islands and are named Knights of Bahá'u'lláh in December. [BW13:449]

Claire Gung arrives in Southern Rhodesia (Zimbabwe) and is named a Knight of Bahá'u'lláh.

Edmund ('Ted') Cardell arrives in Windhoek and is named a Knight of Bahá'u'lláh for South West Africa (Namibia). [BW13:456]

- He is later joined by his wife Alicia and the first German Bahá'ís to pioneer to Africa, Martin and Gerda Aiff and their children.

Enoch Olinga arrives in Victoria (Limbé) and is named a Knight of Bahá'u'lláh for the British Cameroons. [BW13:449]

- The first Cameroonian to become a Bahá'í in British Cameroon is a youth, Jacob Tabot Awo.

- The first Cameroonian adult to become a Bahá'í is Enoch Ngompek of the Bassa tribe.

- The first Cameroonian woman to become a Bahá'í is Esther Obeu, the wife of David Tanyi.

The superstructure of the Shrine of the Báb is completed. [BBD210; CB324–5; PP235; ZK85–6]

The Shrine of the Báb

7 Oct William Danjon Dieudonné arrives in Andorra and is named a Knight of Bahá'u'lláh. [BW12:449]

- He continues to live in the country.

7–15 Oct The Asian Intercontinental Teaching Conference is held in New Delhi. [BW12:178]

- For Shoghi Effendi's message to the conference see BW12:178–81.
- For a report of the conference see BW12:181–8.
- This is the first international Bahá'í gathering ever to be held in the East. [BW12:181; SBR171]
- It is attended by 489 Bahá'ís representing 31 countries. [BW12:181]
- The design for the International Bahá'í Archives is revealed to the Bahá'ís of the world for the first time at this conference. [DH168]

11 Oct Fawzí Zaynu'l-'Ábidín and his wife, Bahiyyih 'Alí Sa'di'd-Dín, and their sons Kamál and Sharíf arrive in Tetuán from Egypt and are named Knights of Bahá'u'lláh for Spanish Morocco. [BW13:456]

• For the story of Fawzí Zaynu'l-'Ábidín's life see BW16:544–6.

13 Oct Frederick and Elizabeth Laws arrive in Basutoland (Lesotho) and are named Knights of Bahá'u'lláh. [BW13:449]

• For the story of the life of Elizabeth Laws see BW17:459–60.

Esther Evans and Lillian Middlemast arrive in Castries, St Lucia, and are named Knights of Bahá'u'lláh for the Windward Islands. [BW13:457]

14 Oct Shoghi Effendi announces the settling of 13 further Knights of Bahá'u'lláh, with 178 territories now open to the Faith. [MBW173]

Edith M. Danielsen arrives on Aitutaki Island, 150 miles north of Rarotonga, before leaving for Avarua, Rarotonga, five days later and is named a Knight of Bahá'u'lláh for the Cook Islands. [BW13:450]

• For the story of her life see BW19:625–6.

Gertrude Eisenberg arrives in Las Palmas and is named a Knight of Bahá'u'lláh for the Canary Islands. [BW13:450]

Robert and Elinor Wolff arrive in Dutch Guiana and are named Knights of Bahá'u'lláh. [BW13:451]

15 Oct Eberhard Friedland arrives in French Guiana from the United States and is named a Knight of Bahá'u'lláh. [BW13:451]

Enoch Olinga arrives in Mamfé and is named a Knight of Bahá'u'lláh for British Cameroons. [BW13:449]

16 Oct Benjamin Dunham Weeden and his wife Gladys (née Anderson) arrive in Antigua and are named Knights of Bahá'u'lláh for the Leeward Islands. [BW13:453]

• For the story of Ben Weeden's life see BW15:478–9.

• For the story of Gladys Weeden's life see BW18:692–6.

18 Oct George and Marguerite (Peggy) True arrive on Tenerif with their 12-year-old son Barry and are named Knights of Bahá'u'lláh for the Canary Islands. [BW13:450]

20 Oct Frances Heller arrives in Macau and is named a Knight of Bahá'u-'lláh for the island. [BW13:453; PH73]

• She is the first Knight of Bahá'u'lláh to settle in Chinese territory.

24 Oct Luella McKay, John and Erleta Fleming, and Alyce Janssen arrive in Spanish Morocco and are named Knights of Bahá'u'lláh. [BW13:456]

Elsie Austin arrives in Tangier from the United States and Muḥammad-'Alí Jalálí, an Iranian, also arrives. They are both named Knights of Bahá'u'lláh for Morocco (International Zone). [BW13:454]

Elsie Austin meeting African believers

29 Oct Gladys ('Glad') Irene Parke and Gretta Stevens Lamprill arrive in Papeete from Australia and are named Knights of Bahá'u'lláh for the Society Islands, French Polynesia. [BW13:455]

• For the story of Gladys Parke's life see BW15:457–8.

• For the story of Gretta Lamprill's life see BW15:534–5.

Opal Jensen arrives on Réunion Island from the United States and is named a Knight of Bahá'u'lláh. [BW13:455]

• She is later declared a Covenant-breaker.

Nov Samíra Vakíl arrives in Cyprus and is named a Knight of Bahá'u-'lláh. [BW13:450]

Mary Olga Katherine Mills (née Bieymann) arrives in Malta and is named a Knight of Bahá'u'lláh. [BW13:454]

Dr Mihdi Samandari arrives in Italian Somaliland and is named a Knight of Bahá'u'lláh. [BW13:452]

• His wife Ursula (née Newman) arrives in 1954 and is also named a Knight of Bahá'u'lláh.

Ursula Samandari

Labíb Iṣfahání arrives in Dakar from Egypt and is named a Knight of Bahá'u'lláh for French West Africa. [BW13:452]

Dr Khodadad M. Fozdar, an Indian of Parsi background, arrives in the Andaman Islands and is named a Knight of Bahá'u'lláh. [BW13:449]

• For the story of his life see BW13:892–3.

Ḥusayn Rawḥání Ardikání and his wife, Nuṣrat, arrive in Tangier with their daughter, Shahlá, and are named Knights of Bahá'u'lláh for Morocco (International Zone). [BW13:454]

'Alí Akbar Rafí'í (Rafsanjání) and his wife, Sháyistih, and their 19-year-old son, 'Abbás, arrive in Tangier and all are named Knights of Bahá'u'lláh for Morocco (International Zone). [BW13:454]

Matthew W. Bullock of Boston, Massachusetts, arrives in the Dutch West Indies and is named a Knight of Bahá'u'lláh. [BW13:451]

11 Nov Shoghi Effendi announces the settling of a further contingent of Knights of Bahá'u'lláh in 21 virgin areas, bringing the number of territories open to the Faith to 200. [MBW52–3]

Ottilie Rhein, an American of German origin, arrives in Mauritius and is named a Knight of Bahá'u'lláh for the island. [BW13:454]

• For the story of her life see BW18:703–5.

13 Nov Kámil 'Abbás arrives in the Seychelles from Iraq and is named a Knight of Bahá'u'lláh. [BW13:455]

• For the story of his life see BW18:722–3.

Dec Adíb Baghdádí arrives in Hadhramaut and is named a Knight of Bahá'u'lláh. [BW13:452]

Kaykhusraw Dahamobedi, Bahíyyih Rawḥání and Gulbár Áftábí arrive on Diu Island and are named Knights of Bahá'u'lláh. [BW13:451]

7 Dec Jalál Kházeh is appointed a Hand of the Cause of God after the passing of Hand of the Cause of God Siegfried Schopflocher. [GBF111–12; MBW55]

8 Dec Loretta and Carl Scherer arrive in Macau from Milwaukee and are named Knights of Bahá'u'lláh for that island. [BW13:453; PH73]

• For the stories of their lives see BW18:738–40.

13 Dec A separate department for the Bahá'í Faith is established by the Israeli Ministry of Religious Affairs. [GBF137; PP291; PP320]

19 Dec Yan Kee Leong becomes a Bahá'í, the first person to accept the Faith in Malaya.

27 Dec Gilbert and Daisy Robert, a French couple, become Bahá'ís in Madagascar, the first people to accept the Faith in the country.

late in the year 'Abdu'l-Karím Amín Khawja becomes a Bahá'í in Algeria, the first person to accept the Faith in that country.

1954

c. 1954 Khodadad Irani settles in Zanzibar, the first Bahá'í to do so.

In the year The first native Fijian, the first Pygmy, the first Berber and the first Greenlander to accept the Bahá'í Faith enrol. [MBW262]

The first Tlinget from Alaska to become a Bahá'í, Eugene King, enrols.

The first person to become a Bahá'í in the Balearic Islands, C. Miguel, enrols.

'Aynu'd-Dín and Ṭáhirih 'Alá'í arrive in Southern Rhodesia and are named Knights of Bahá'u'lláh. [BW13:456]

Grace Bahovec arrives in the Baranof Islands and is named a Knight of Bahá'u'lláh. [BW13:449]

Mr and Mrs Sandikonda, Eliam Chisengalumbwe, Mr Musonda, Peter Chitindi and Elias Kanayenda become Bahá'ís, the first African Bahá'ís to enrol in Northern Rhodesia (now Zambia). [BANANI BULLETIN, 1 AUG 1954]

José Mingorance Fernandez and his wife, Carmen Tost, a Spanish couple, accept the Bahá'í Faith, the first to enrol in Andorra.

Mehraban Isfandiar Sohaili arrives on Mayotte and stays for two months, the first Bahá'í to visit the island.

The purchase of the House of Bahá'u'lláh in Istanbul is concluded. [SS38]

Jan Jean Sevin arrives in Tuamotu Archipelago and is named a Knight of Bahá'u'lláh. [BW13:457]

Charles M. Ioas arrives in the Balearic Islands and is named a Knight of Bahá'u'lláh. [BW13:449]

Munír Vakíl, a former general in the Iraqi army, settles on one of the Kuria-Muria Islands in the Arabian Sea and is named a Knight of Bahá'u'lláh. [BW13:453]

• For the story of the hardships of his pioneering post see ZK99–101.

Munír Vakíl

Elizabeth Bevan (later Mrs Golmohammed) arrives in Rhodes and is named a Knight of Bahá'u'lláh. [BW13:455]

Virginia Breaks arrives on the island of Truk and is named a Knight of Bahá'u'lláh for the Caroline Islands. [BW13:450; MBW57]

Kenneth and Roberta Christian arrive in Southern Rhodesia (Zimbabwe) and are named Knights of Bahá'u'lláh. [BW13:456]

Andrew and Nina Matthisen arrive in the Bahamas and are named Knights of Bahá'u'lláh. [BW13:449]

3 Jan Howard and Joanne Menking arrive in the Cape Verde Islands and are named Knights of Bahá'u'lláh. [BW13:450]

10 Jan Dorothy Baker, Hand of the Cause of God, dies in a plane crash in the Mediterranean Sea, near the island of Elba. [BW12:670]

- For the Guardian's cable see BW12:670, CF161.

- For her obituary see BW12:670–4.

See also *Freeman*, FROM COPPER TO GOLD.

14 Jan Lilian E. Wyss arrives in Apia from Australia and is named a Knight of Bahá'u'lláh for the Samoa Islands. [BW13:455]

15 Jan 'Abdu'l-Raḥmán Zarqání, from India, arrives in the Seychelles and is named a Knight of Bahá'u'lláh. [BW13:455]

18 Jan Mrs Dulcie Burns Dive arrives in the Cook Islands from Australia and is named a Knight of Bahá'u'lláh. [BW13:450, 925]

25 Jan Stanley P. Bolton, Jr. arrives in Nuku'alofa, on Tongatapu Island, from Australia and is named a Knight of Bahá'u'lláh for Tonga Islands. [BW13:456]

Feb Raḥmat'u'lláh and Írán Muhájir arrive in Mentawai Islands and are named Knights of Bahá'u'lláh. [BW13:454]

- For the story of their pioneering activity see Muhájir, *Dr Muhajir, Hand of the Cause of God, Knight of Bahá'u'lláh.*

'Azízu'lláh and Shamsí Navídí arrive in Monaco and are named Knights of Bahá'u'lláh. [BW13:455]

Joan Powis arrives in Southern Rhodesia (Zimbabwe) and is named a Knight of Bahá'u'lláh. [BW13:456]

Bernard H. Guhrke arrives on the Kodiak Islands and is named a Knight of Bahá'u'lláh. [BW13:453]

Gail Avery arrives in the Baranof Islands and is named a Knight of Bahá'u'lláh. [BW13:449]

John and Audrey Robarts and their son Patrick arrive in Mafikeng and are named Knights of Bahá'u'lláh for Bechuanaland (Botswana). [BW13:449]

David Schreiber, an American, arrives in Antigua and is named a Knight of Bahá'u'lláh for the Leeward Islands. [BW13:453]

Faríburz Rúzbihyán (Feriborz Roozbehyan) arrives in The Gambia and is named a Knight of Bahá'u'lláh. [BW13:452]

Elise Schreiber (later Lynelle) arrives on St Thomas Island and is named a Knight of Bahá'u'lláh. [BW13:456]

Shirin Fozdar arrives in Saigon, the first pioneer to Vietnam.

Husayn Halabi arrives in Hadhramaut and is named a Knight of Bahá'u'lláh. [BW13:452]

10 Feb John Leonard arrives in the Falkland Islands and is named a Knight of Bahá'u'lláh. [BW13:451]

15 Feb Charles Duncan (a musician) and Harry Clark, both Americans, arrive in Brunei from Kota Kinabalu (Jesselton) in Sabah, where they have been waiting for several weeks, and are named Knights of Bahá'u'lláh. [BW13:451; PH63]

21 Feb Charles ('Chuck') and Mary Dayton from the United States, settle in Charlotte Amalie, on St Thomas, and are named Knights of Bahá'u'lláh for the Leeward Islands. [BW13:453]

Mar Qudratu'lláh Rawḥání and Khudáraḥm Muzhgání arrive in Mahé and are named Knights of Bahá'u'lláh. [BW13:454]

Olivia Kelsey and Florence Ullrich arrive in Monaco and are named Knights of Bahá'u'lláh. [BW13:454]

1 Mar Shirin Fozdar visits Cambodia to receive the first medallion and Certificate of Satrei Vatthana (Champion of Women) from His Majesty King Norodom Sihanouk. She is the first Bahá'í to enter the country.

- She is not able to teach the Faith openly but she does speak about it to the king's parents.

Alvin J. Blum and his wife, Gertrude (née Gewertz), arrive in Honiara and are named Knights of Bahá'u'lláh for the Solomon Islands. They are accompanied by their eight-year-old daughter Keithie. [BW13:456]

5 Mar Roy and Elena Maria Marsella Fernie arrive in Buota on Abaiang Island and are named Knights of Bahá'u'lláh for the Gilbert and Ellice Islands. [BW13:452]

19 Mar Paul Haney is appointed Hand of the Cause of God following the death of Hand of the Cause of God Dorothy Baker. [GBF111; MBW57]

Hand of the Cause Paul Haney

1954

21 Mar Shoghi Effendi announces that there are Bahá'ís in 219 countries. [MBW57]

25 Mar Leland Jensen arrives on Réunion Island from the United States and is named a Knight of Bahá'u'lláh. [BW13:455]

- He is later declared a Covenant-breaker.

Marion Jack dies in Sofia, Bulgaria. [BW12:674; CF163]

- Shoghi Effendi calls her 'a shining example to pioneers of present and future generations of East and West'. [CF163]

- For her obituary see BW12:674–7.

See also BFA2:155; MC359.

28 Mar Suhráb Paymán, together with his five-year old-daughter Ghitty, arrives in San Marino from Ṭihrán to join his wife. He is named a Knight of Bahá'u'lláh in April. [BW13:455]

spring The Síyáh-Chál is acquired by the Bahá'ís. [BW12:64–5; SE153; SS45]

- The purchase cost is $400,000. [BW12:65]

Apr Bahá'í women in Iran are accorded full rights to participate in membership of both national and local Bahá'í assemblies. [MBW65]

- This removes the 'last remaining obstacle to the enjoyment of complete equality of rights in the conduct of the administrative affairs of the Persian Bahá'í Community'. [MBW65]

Dr John Fozdar arrives in Brunei in April 1954 and is named a Knight of Bahá'u'lláh. [BW13:450]

Samuel Njiki, the first Bahá'í of the Bamiliki tribe, arrives in French Cameroons from British Cameroons and is named a Knight of Bahá'u'lláh. Mehrangiz Munsiff arrives in French Cameroons and is named a Knight of Bahá'u'lláh. [BW13:451]

Edward Tabe and Albert Buapiah arrive in British Togoland and are named Knights of Bahá'u'lláh. [BW13:450]

Benedict Eballa arrives in Ashanti Protectorate and is named a Knight of Bahá'u'lláh. [BW13:449]

Martin Manga arrives in the Northern Territories Protectorate, Australia, and is named a Knight of Bahá'u'lláh. [BW13:455]

Ḥabíb Iṣfahání arrives in Dakar and is named a Knight of Bahá'u-'lláh for French West Africa. [BW13:452]

Gayle Woolson arrives in the Galápagos Islands and is named a Knight of Bahá'u'lláh. [BW13:452]

Kay Zinky arrives in the Magdalen Islands and is named a Knight of Bahá'u'lláh. [BW13:453]

Howard Gilliland arrives in Labrador and is named a Knight of Bahá'u'lláh. [BW13:453]

Corporal Richard Walters and his wife, Evelyn, and Richard and Mary L. Suhm arrive in Tangier from the United States and are all named Knights of Bahá'u'lláh for Morocco (International Zone). [BW13:454]

John and Marjorie Kellberg of Oak Park, Illinois, arrive in the Dutch West Indies and are named Knights of Bahá'u'lláh. [BW13:451]

Robert B. Powers, Jr, a member of the U.S. armed forces at the Navy Air Station, arrives in Guam and is named a Knight of Bahá'u'lláh for the Mariana Islands. [BW13:454]

The site for the first Mashriqu'l-Adhkár of the Holy Land is selected. [DH175; MBW63]

Shoghi Effendi announces that plans for the International Bahá'í Archives have been completed and that steps have been taken to begin its construction. [BBD22–3; DH169; GBF117–8; MBW64]

Shoghi Effendi announces that there are Bahá'ís in 228 countries and that Bahá'í literature has been translated into 130 languages. [MBW61–2]

6 Apr Shoghi Effendi announces the creation of five Auxiliary Boards with the following number of members: Asia 7; America 9; Europe 9; Africa 9; Australia 2. [MBW59]

- Their function is to 'act as deputies of the Hands in their respective continents', to 'aid and advise them in the effective prosecution of the Ten-Year Plan' and to assist them 'in the discharge of their dual and sacred task of safe-guarding the Faith and of promoting its teaching activities'. [MBW63]

See also BBD26; BBRSM127; MC3.

Five Continental Bahá'í Funds are inaugurated by Shoghi Effendi. [MBW59]

11 Apr Bula Mott Stewart arrives in Swaziland and is named a Knight of Bahá'u'lláh. [BW13:456]

13 Apr David Tanyi, a tailor, arrives in French Togoland from British Cameroons and is named a Knight of Bahá'u'lláh. [BW13:451]

18 Apr John and Valera Allen arrive in Swaziland and are named Knights of Bahá'u'lláh. [BW13:456]

21 Apr Bruce Matthew arrives at Goose Bay and is named a Knight of Bahá'u'lláh for Labrador. [BW13:453]

Adelaide Sharp, who had been in Iran since 1929, is elected to the National Spiritual Assembly of Iran, the first woman elected to that body. [BFA2:361]

The first local spiritual assembly in the Malay Peninsula is established in Seremban.

The first all African local spiritual assembly in Tanganyika is formed in Bukoba.

The first local spiritual assembly is formed in British Cameroons.

The first local spiritual assembly is formed in Ruanda-Urundi.

The first local spiritual assembly in Algeria is formed in Algiers.

26 Apr President of Israel Ben Zvi and his wife visit the Shrines on Mount

Carmel, the first official visit paid by a head of a sovereign state to the Shrines of the Báb and 'Abdu'l-Bahá. [GBF139–140; MBW68; PP292–3]

May Elinore Putney arrives in the Aleutian Islands and is named a Knight of Bahá'u'lláh. [BW13:449]

Elise Schreiber (later Lynelle) arrives in Bata, the capital of Rio Muni, and is named a Knight of Bahá'u'lláh for a second time, this time for Spanish Guinea. [BW13:456]

Haig Kevorkian arrives in the Galápagos Islands and is named a Knight of Bahá'u'lláh. [BW13:452]

2 May Mavis Nymon and Vivian Wesson, both Americans, arrive in French Togoland and are named Knights of Bahá'u'lláh. [BW13:451]

Cynthia R. Olson of Wilmington, Delaware, settles in Barrigada, the largest village in Guam, and is named a Knight of Bahá'u'lláh for the Mariana Islands. [BW13:454]

Haig Kevorkian

4 May Shoghi Effendi closes the Roll of Honour, except for those pioneers who have already left for their posts and those first arriving in the remaining virgin territories inside and outside the Soviet Republics and satellites. [MBW69]

Elizabeth Stamp, an Irish-American widow from New York City, arrives in St Helena and is named a Knight of Bahá'u'lláh. [BW13:456]

5 May Ṣabrí and Fahima (Ra'isa) Elias, an Egyptian couple with four children, arrive in Djibouti and are named Knights of Bahá'u'lláh for French Somaliland. [BW13:451]

26 May Shoghi Effendi, Rúḥíyyih Khánum and Leroy Ioas return the visit of President Ben Zvi by visiting him in Jerusalem. [GBF 140; PP293–4]

Elizabeth Stamp

Jun Shawqí Riyáḍ Rawḥaní (Shoghi Riaz Rouhani), an Iranian from Egypt, arrives in Las Palmas and is named a Knight of Bahá'u'lláh for the Canary Islands. [BW13: 450]

Harold and Florence Fitzner arrive in Portuguese Timor and are named Knights of Bahá'u'lláh. [BW13:455]

Louise Groger arrives on Chiloé Island and is named a Knight of Bahá'u'lláh. [BW13:450]

18 Jun The first islander to become a Bahá'í in the Seychelles, Marshall Delcy, a local school teacher, enrols.

19 Jun The first Canary Islander to become a Bahá'í, Sr. José Jacinto Castillo y Gonzalez, enrols.

24 Jun Sh͟ápúr Rawḥání and Ardis͟hír Furúdí, Iranian residents of India, arrive in Bhutan by foot and are named Knights of Bahá'u'lláh. [BW13:449]

- They are accompanied to the Bhutan border by the prime minister of Bhutan, Jigme Dorji.

second half of the year The first Somali to become a Bahá'í in Djibouti, 'Alí 'Abdu'lláh, a 21-year old employee of a commercial firm, enrols.

c. Jul The first person to become a Bahá'í in Brunei, Daphne Hassan, enrols.

Jul José Marques arrives in Portuguese Timor and is named a Knight of Bahá'u'lláh. [BW13:455]

Dr John George Mitchell, an English physician who became a

Bahá'í in 1950, arrives in Malta and is named a Knight of Bahá'u-'lláh. [BW13:454]

Reginald Stone and Allan Delph become Bahá'ís in British Guiana, the first two people to accept the Faith in that country.

5 Jul Violet Hoehnke, an Australian, arrives in Papua New Guinea and is named a Knight of Bahá'u'lláh for the Admiralty Islands. [BW13:449]

12 Jul Dudley Moore Blakely, an artist, sculptor and designer, and his wife, Elsa ('Judy'), British citizens living in Maine, arrive on Tongatapu and are named Knights of Bahá'u'lláh for Tonga Islands. [BW13:456]

15 Jul The first person to become a Bahá'í in Macau, Harry P. F. Yim (Yim Pui Foung), a 45-year-old small business proprietor born in Canton, China, enrols.

7 Aug Marcia Steward de Matamoros Atwater arrives in the Marshall Islands and is named a Knight of Bahá'u'lláh. [BW13:454]

28 Aug Mihribán Suhaylí (Mehraban Sohaili) arrives on the Comoro Islands and is named a Knight of Bahá'u'lláh. [BW13:450]

Sep Four people had become Bahá'ís in Zanzibar by this date.

6 Sep The first people to become Bahá'ís in Bechuanaland (Lesotho), Chadwick and 'Maselai (Mary) Mohapi, enrol. [BW17:449–52]

26 Sep The first native Greek to become a Bahá'í, Emmanuel Petrakis, enrols in Crete.

Oct The first person to become a Bahá'í in Nassau, Bahamas, Winfield Small, a young police officer from Barbados, enrols.

- Mr Small opened Barbados to the Faith.

1 Oct Shoghi Effendi announces that there are Bahá'ís in 235 countries and territories and over 3000 centres around the world. [MBW69–70]

Nov A plot of land of slightly less than half an acre owned by Farah Sprague, a Covenant-breaker, is purchased, overcoming the final obstacle to beginning the construction of the International Bahá'í Archives. [DH169; MBW73–4]

20 Nov The first person to become a Bahá'í in Tonga, Harry Terepo, born in Rarotonga, Cook Islands, enrols.

- He is a teacher, interpreter and guide living in Ohonua on the island of Eua.

27 Nov Shoghi Effendi describes the significance of the world administrative centre of the Faith and the 'structures, which will serve as the administrative seats of such divinely appointed institutions as the Guardianship, the Hands of the Cause, and the Universal House of Justice' to be ranged along a 'far-flung arc'. [MBW74]

8 Dec Bahá'ís in Ádharbáyján are dismissed from their employment in the Ministries of Health and Public Highways. [BW18:390]

1955

c. 1955 The first person to become a Bahá'í in Grenada, John Protain, a waiter at the Santa Maria Hotel, enrols.

The first person to become a Bahá'í in The Gambia, Mr Nichola Banna, a Lebanese merchant, enrols.

In the year The first indigenous Samoan to become a Bahá'í, Sa'ialala Tamasese, enrols.

- He is a member of one of the three royal families of Samoa. [BINS, NO.100, 1 MARCH 1979, P.1].

Labíb Iṣfahání arrives in Abidjan, French West Africa, from Dakar, the first Bahá'í to settle in what is now the Ivory Coast.

The first person to become a Bahá'í in Spanish Sahara, 'Abdu'l-Salam Salím Al-Sbintí, enrols.

Twenty-two African Bahá'ís are expelled from the Belgian Congo.

c. Jan The first Tswana Bahá'í, Stanlake Kukama, enrols in Mafikeng.

18–22 Jan Five Bahá'ís are arrested and beaten in Ḥiṣár, Khurásán, Iran; four of these are dragged around the town; Bahá'í houses are attacked, looted and set on fire. [BW18:390]

Feb The first local person to become a Bahá'í in Mauritius, Mr Yam-Lim, a Chinese Catholic, enrols.

4 Feb Bahá'í women in Ḥiṣár, Khurásán, Iran, are assaulted. [BW18:390]

8–15 Feb The first people to become Bahá'ís in Réunion, Paul and Françoise Tayllamin (8 Feb) and Jean Donat and Julien Araye (15 Feb), enrol.

Mar The first person to become a Bahá'í in the Solomon Islands, William Gina, a 43-year-old Solomon Islander from the Western Solomon Islands, enrols.

Kamálí Sarvístání arrives on Socotra Island and is named a Knight of Bahá'u'lláh. [BW13:456]

4 Mar The first Tongan to become a Bahá'í in Tonga, Tevita Ngalo'afe, enrols.

14 Mar The first person to become a Bahá'í in Guam, Charles T. Mackey, a United States civil service employee, enrols.

20 Mar Shoghi Effendi announces the commencement of the excavation for the foundations of the International Bahá'í Archives. [MBW75]

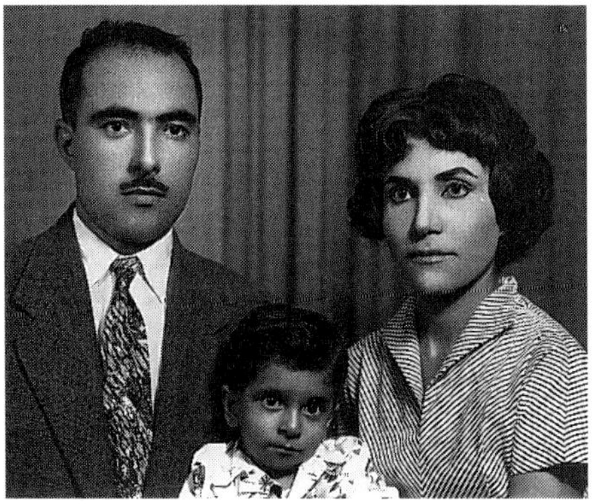

Kamálí Sarvístání, left, with his family

Apr Shoghi Effendi announces the acquisition of 36,000 square metres of land for the first Mashriqu'l-Adhkár of the Holy Land. [DH175; MBW78–9]

- The entire sum for the purchase was donated by Amelia Collins. [MBW79]

The first person to become a Bahá'í in the Bahamas, Molly Newbold, enrols.

• As she did not remain a Bahá'í, Arnold Wells, a tinsmith who became a Bahá'í on 20 April, is regarded as the first Bahá'í. Christine Thompson, who owned a small fruit and vegetable shop, and Frank Ferguson, who owned a gas station, also enrolled on 20 April.

Shoghi Effendi announces that the Bahá'í Faith is represented in 236 countries, in 3,200 locations, by over 40 ethnic groups. Bahá'í literature is translated into 176 languages. [MBW76–8]

Riḍván The first local spiritual assembly in the Bahamas is formed in Nassau.

The first local spiritual assembly in Zanzibar is formed.

The first local spiritual assembly in Réunion is formed.

The first five local assemblies in Bechuanaland (Lesotho) are formed in Seqonoka, Maseru, Mafeteng, Maphohloane and Sephapos' Gate.

The first four local spiritual assemblies in The Gambia are formed in Bathurst (Banjul), Serrekunda, Lamin and Brikama.

The first local spiritual assembly in Southern Rhodesia (Zimbabwe) is formed in Salisbury (Harare).

The first local spiritual assembly of French Togoland (Togo) is formed at Lomé.

The first local spiritual in Mozambique is established in Lourenço Marques. [BW13:290]

• The first native Mozambican Bahá'í, Festas Chambeni, takes the Bahá'í Faith to Angola. [BW13:290]

The first local spiritual assembly in Italian Somalia is formed in Mogadishu.

The first local spiritual assembly in Madagascar is formed in Tananarive (Antananarivo).

The first local spiritual assembly in the Seychelles is formed in Victoria.

The first local spiritual assembly in Vietnam is formed at Saigon-Cholon (Cholon is the Chinese section of Saigon).

- This body is also the first local assembly to be formed in Indochina.

23 Apr Ramaḍán begins. Shaykh Muḥammad-Taqí Falsafí makes an inflammatory speech against the Bahá'ís from a mosque in Ṭihrán. [BW18:390]

- This is broadcast on national radio and stirs up the people against the Bahá'ís. [BW18:390]

- Beatings, killings, looting and raping go on for several weeks, usually incited by the local 'ulamá. [BW18:390–1; MC16–17; ZK215–6]

- The House of the Báb in Shíráz is attacked and damaged by a mob led by Siyyid Núru'd-Dín, a mujtahid.

2 May The police lock the doors of the National Bahá'í Centre in Ṭihrán thus preventing the holding of the final day of the National Bahá'í Convention. [BW18:390]

4 May Sylvia Ioas is appointed to the International Bahá'í Council as its ninth member. [BW19:612; GBF110; MBW86; PP253]

7 May The Iranian army occupies the National Bahá'í Centre in Ṭihrán. [BW18:390]

8 May The Bahá'í centre at Rasht, Iran, is attacked and taken over. [BW18:390]

Bahá'ís are beaten at Dámghán, Khurásán, Iran. [BW18:390]

9 May The Bahá'í centre at Ahváz, Iran, is taken over. [BW18:390]

Bahá'í houses are attacked and looted at Shíráz, Iran. [BW18:390]

16 May The Bahá'í centre at Iṣfahán, Iran, is taken over. [BW18:390]

17 May The Iranian Minister of the Interior announces in parliament that the Government has issued orders for the suppression of the 'Bahá'í sect' and the liquidation of the Bahá'í centres. [BBRSM174; BW18:391]

22 May The dome of the National Bahá'í Centre in Ṭihrán is demolished with the personal participation of several high-ranking army officers. [BW18:391]

The dome of the National Bahá'í Centre in Ṭihran is demolished

- The publication of the pictures of this episode encourages a widespread outburst of persecution of Bahá'ís throughout Iran. [BW18:391]

- For pictures see BW13:293–4.

23 May The Bahá'í International Community submits its 'Proposals for Charter Revision' to the United Nations for the Conference for Revision of the UN Charter. [BW13:788, 795–802]

24 May The Bahá'í centre at Karaj, Iran, is taken over. [BW18:391]

27 May The Bahá'í centre at Máhfurúzak, Iran, is demolished. [BW18:391]

30 May Bahá'ís are attacked and wounded and their houses attacked at Ábádih, Iran. [BW18:391]

May–Jul Persecutions against the Bahá'ís continue throughout Iran. [BW18:391]

- Many Bahá'ís are beaten, including women and children.
- Bahá'í houses and shops are looted and burned.
- Bahá'ís employed in government service are dismissed.
- Bodies of dead Bahá'ís are disinterred and mutilated.
- Young Bahá'í women are abducted and forced to marry Muslims.
- Several Bahá'í women are publicly stripped and/or raped.
- Crops and orchards belonging to Bahá'ís are looted and destroyed.
- Bahá'í children are expelled from schools.
- The House of the Báb in Shíráz is damaged.

1 Jun The House of Bahá'u'lláh in Tákur, Mázandarán, Iran, is taken over. [BW18:391]

2 Jun The first pioneer to settle in Laos, Dr Heshmat Ta'eed, arrives in the country from Thailand.

4 Jun Frank Wyss of Australia arrives on Cocos and is named a Knight of Bahá'u'lláh. [BW13:450]

28 Jul Seven Bahá'ís are stabbed and beaten to death by a mob in Hurmuzak, Iran. [BW18:391]

• Several other Bahá'ís, including women, are beaten and injured; Bahá'í houses and property are damaged. [BW18:391]

See also *Labíb*, THE SEVEN MARTYRS OF HURMUZAK.

Aug Appeals are made by National Spiritual Assemblies around the world through the Bahá'í International Community to the UN Secretary-General Dag Hammarskjöld to ask the Iranian government to halt the attacks on the Bahá'ís. [BW13:789–91; BW16:329; MBW88–9; PP304, 311]

• The intervention of the Secretary-General of the UN, along with the efforts of the National Spiritual Assembly of the United States, bring an end to the physical persecution of the Bahá'ís, although their human rights are still denied. [BW13:790; BW16:329]

• This marks the first time the Faith is able to defend itself with its newly born administrative agencies. An "Aid the Persecuted Fund" was established.

23 Aug Shoghi Effendi announces plans to begin construction on the House of Worship in Kampala, Uganda. [MBW90; PP312]

Sep Fowzieh Sobhi arrives in British Somaliland from Egypt, the first Bahá'í to reside in the country.

Travelling by foot, Udai Narain Singh arrives in Tibet from Gangtok, Sikkim, and is named a Knight of Bahá'u'lláh, his second such distinction.

• He is named a Knight of Bahá'u'lláh in spring 1956. [BW13:456]

Sep–Oct Bahá'ís in Iran continue to be dismissed from their employment. Bahá'í students are expelled from Shíráz University. [BW18:391]

Oct Daniel Haumont arrives in the Loyalty Islands and is named a Knight of Bahá'u'lláh. [BW13:453]

12 Nov Hand of the Cause of God Valíyu'lláh Varqá dies in Stuttgart.

• For his obituary see BW13:831–4.

15 Nov 'Alí Muḥammad Varqá is appointed a Hand of the Cause to succeed his father. [GBF111; MBW91]

Dec The first Samoan woman to become a Bahá'í, Mrs Lotoa Refiti (later Lotoa Rock), enrols. [KOALA NEWS, NO. 22, FEBRUARY 1956]

1956

c. 1956 The first person in Tibet to become a Bahá'í, Chiten Tashi, a young businessman from the village of Chombethan, enrols.

Shoghi Effendi acquires the title to the Pilgrim House at Bahjí from the Israeli government as part of the exchange for the Bahá'í properties at Ein Gev. [BBD177; DH226]

In the year The first indigenous person to become a Bahá'í in Dutch Guiana (Suriname), George van Axel Dongen, enrols.

The first Tlinget to become a Bahá'í in Alaska, Joyce Anderson Combs, enrols.

Shoghi Effendi buys the ruined house known as the Master's Tea House.

The Tea House of 'Abdu'l-Bahá

The first people to become Bahá'ís in Cape Verde enrol.

The first indigenous person to become a Bahá'í in New Guinea,

Apelis Mazakmat, a school teacher and member of the local government council, enrols.

Kedar Pradhan, from neighbouring Sikkim, arrives in Nepal, the first pioneer to the country.

A Roman Catholic priest lodges a complaint against the Bahá'ís of Morocco with the Moroccan Security Service.

Jan The first Bahá'í pioneer in what is now the Central African Republic, Samson Nkeng, arrives in Bangui from the British Cameroons.

12 Feb The first four people to become Bahá'ís in Hong Kong, Nari Sherwani, Ng Ying Kay, Chan Lie Kun and Chan Lie Fun, enrol. [PH75]

25 Feb Husayn Uskuli, long-time pioneer to Shanghai from 'Ishqábad, dies in Shanghai at the age of 82 and is buried in the Kiangwan Cemetery in Shanghai. [PH29]

Apr Shoghi Effendi announces that the Bahá'í Faith is established in 247 countries, in 3,700 localities and that there are more than 900 local spiritual assemblies, of which 168 are incorporated. Bahá'í literature has been translated into 190 languages. [MBW92–3]

Shoghi Effendi announces the extension to Egyptian Bahá'í women of the right to be elected to the national spiritual assembly and to participate in the national convention. [MBW96–7]

7 Apr The first indigenous person to become a Bahá'í in Micronesia, 22-year-old Joe Erie Ilengelkei from Palau, Caroline Islands, enrols.

Riḍván The Regional Spiritual Assembly of South and West Africa is formed with its seat in Johannesburg, South Africa. [BW13:284]

- Its area of jurisdiction is the Union of South Africa, Basutoland, Zululand, Swaziland, Bechuanaland, South West Africa, Angola, Northern Rhodesia, Southern Rhodesia, Nyasaland, Mozambique, Madagascar, Réunion Island, Mauritius and St Helena Island.

The Regional Spiritual Assembly of Central and East Africa is formed with its seat in Kampala, Uganda. [BW13:284]

- Its area of jurisdiction is Uganda, Tanganyika, Kenya, Belgian Congo, Ruanda-Urundi, French Equatorial Africa, Zanzibar, Comoro Islands and Seychelles Islands.

The Regional Spiritual Assembly of North West Africa is formed with its seat in Tunis, Tunisia. [BW13:284]

- Its area of jurisdiction is Tunisia, Algeria, Morocco (International Zone), Spanish Morocco, French Morocco, Rio de Oro, Spanish Sahara, French West Africa, Gambia, Portuguese Guinea, Sierra Leone, Liberia, Gold Coast, Ashanti Protectorate, British Togoland, French Togoland, Nigeria, British Cameroons, French Cameroons, Spanish Guinea, St Thomas Island, Cape Verde Islands, Canary Islands and Madeira.

The Regional Spiritual Assembly of North East Africa is formed. [BW13:284]

- Its area of jurisdiction is Egypt, Libya, Sudan, Eritrea, French Somaliland, Italian Somaliland, Ethiopia and Socotra Island.

The first local spiritual assembly is formed in Morocco (International Zone).

The first local spiritual assembly in Taiwan is formed in T'ainan.

The first local spiritual assembly in Bermuda is formed.

The first local spiritual assembly of Bechuanaland is formed at Mafikeng.

The first local spiritual assemblies in Korea are formed at Seoul and at Kwangju.

With the enrolment of the first Micronesian Bahá'í, the first local spiritual assembly of Guam is formed.

The first local spiritual assembly of Hong Kong is formed.

The local spiritual assembly of Addis Ababa incorporates, the first one in Africa to do so. [BW13:287]

May Mary Zabolotny (later Mrs Ken McCulloch), of Polish background, arrives on Anticosti Island, Canada, and is named a Knight of Bahá'u'lláh. [BW13:449]

20 May Louisa Mathew Gregory, whose wedding to Hand of the Cause of God Louis Gregory in 1912 was the first interracial western Bahá'í marriage, dies in Eliot, Maine. [BW13:878]

- For her obituary see BW13:376–8.

9 Dec Juliet Thompson, who became a Bahá'í in Paris around the turn of the century, dies. [BW13:864]

- For her obituary see BW13:862–4.

1957

c. 1957 The first local person to become a Bahá'í in Cambodia, Mr Lim Incchin, a young Chinese, enrols.

In the year The first indigenous person to become a Bahá'í in the Dutch West Indies, Rhoma Matthew, enrols.

The first member of the Newari ethnic group of Nepal to become a Bahá'í, Rishi Prasad Joshi, enrols.

Charles Winfield Small, a native of Barbados and the first to become a Bahá'í in the Bahamas, returns to Barbados, the first Bahá'í to settle in the country.

The Berbers in Algeria are first contacted by the Bahá'ís and a number of Berber families enrol.

Bahá'í activity in Czechoslovakia is banned by the authorities, several members of the Prague community are arrested and Vuk Echtner is imprisoned for two years.

Nagoya, Japan, becomes the only spiritual assembly to be made up entirely of Japanese believers.

3 Feb Enoch Olinga arrives in the Holy Land, the first black African Bahá'í to go on pilgrimage.

25 Mar Hand of the Cause of God George Townshend dies in Dublin, Ireland. [BBD226]

• For his obituary see BW13:841–6.

See also *Hofman*, GEORGE TOWNSHEND.

27 Mar Agnes Alexander is appointed a Hand of the Cause of God on the passing of Hand of the Cause of God George Townshend. [GBF112; MBW174; PP255]

c. Apr 1957– Apr 1958 The first Tuareg to become a Bahá'í enrols in Rabat, Morocco.

Apr Shoghi Effendi announces that the Faith has been established in 251 countries, that there are more than a thousand local spiritual assemblies, that Bahá'ís live in more than 4,200 localities, and that every territory mentioned in the Tablets of the Divine Plan has been opened to the Faith. Bahá'í literature has been translated into 230 languages. [MBW105–6]

Shoghi Effendi announces that the Treasury Department of Israel has issued an expropriation order for the remaining property held by Covenant-breakers at Bahjí, mainly the dilapidated building north of the mansion. [MBW109]

Riḍván The Regional Spiritual Assembly of Scandinavia and Finland is formed with its seat in Stockholm, Sweden. [BW13:274]

The Regional Spiritual Assembly of the Benelux Countries is formed with its seat in Brussels, Belgium. [BW13:274]

• Its area of jurisdiction is Belgium, the Netherlands and Luxembourg.

The Regional Spiritual Assembly for the Iberian Peninsula is formed with its seat in Madrid, Spain. [BW13:274]

The Regional Spiritual Assembly of Mexico and the Republics of Central America is formed at Panama City, Panama. [BW13:257]

The Regional Spiritual Assembly of Argentina, Chile, Uruguay, Paraguay and Bolivia is formed at Buenos Aires, Argentina. [BW13:257]

The Regional Spiritual Assembly of Brazil, Peru, Colombia, Ecuador and Venezuela is formed at Lima, Peru. [BW13:257]

The Regional Spiritual Assembly of the Greater Antilles is formed with its seat in Kingston, Jamaica. [BW13:257]

The Regional Spiritual Assembly of North East Asia is formed with its seat in Tokyo, Japan. [BW13:304]

- Its area of jurisdiction is Japan, Korea, Formosa, Macau, Hong Kong, Hainan Island and Sakhalin Island.

The Regional Spiritual Assembly of South East Asia is formed with its seat in Djakarta. [BW13:302]

- Its area of jurisdiction is Borneo, Indo-China, Indonesia, Malaya, Sarawak, Siam, the Andaman and Nicobar Islands, Philippines, Dutch New Guinea, Mentawei Islands, Cocos Islands, Portuguese Timor and Brunei.

The National Spiritual Assembly of Pakistan is formed.

The National Spiritual Assembly of New Zealand is formed.

The National Spiritual Assembly of Alaska is formed and incorporated immediately upon formation.

- This is the first time a political entity (i.e. the United States) is subdivided to form a national spiritual assembly. [BW13:270]

The first local spiritual assembly in Laos has already been formed in Vientiane.

The first local spiritual assembly in Brunei has already been formed. [BW 13:302]

The first local spiritual assembly in Cape Verde is formed in Praia.

The first local spiritual assembly in Nyasaland is formed at Lilongwe.

The International Bahá'í Archives is completed. [DH169; GBF63–4; PP264–5]

• For details of its construction and photographs see BW13:403–33.

May Pouva Murday of Mauritius arrives in the Chagos Archipelago and is named a Knight of Bahá'u'lláh.

7 May Shoghi Effendi sends a fragment of the plaster from the room of the Báb in the Fortress of Máh-Kú to Australia to be set in the foundations of the Mashriqu'l-Adhkár. [LANZ134; SBR 172]

Pouva Murday

Jun The Covenant-breakers completely abandon Bahjí. [CB 367–9; DH215; MBW120–2; PP233–4]

4 Jun Shoghi Effendi adds protection of the Cause to the duties of the Hands of the Cause. [BBRSM127; CB380; MBW122–3]

8–21 Jun Hokkaido Island is opened to the Faith by Rouhollah Mumtazi and Gekie Nakajima with the enrolment of new believers Kinkichi Shimatani and Yoshiro Sasaki of Sapporo, Japan.

Jul Margaret Bates and her daughter Jean Frankel of the United States arrive in the Nicobar Islands and are named Knights of Bahá'u'lláh. [BW13:454; PH63]

6 Sep Shoghi Effendi announces 'the complete evacuation of the remnant of Covenant-breakers and the transfer of all their belongings from the precincts of the Most Holy Shrine'. [MBW124]

Oct The third contingent of Hands of the Cause of God is appointed: Enoch Olinga, William Sears, John Robarts, Hasan Balyuzi, John Ferraby, Collis Featherstone, Raḥmatu'lláh Muhájir and Abu'l-Qásim Faizí. [GBF111; MBW127; PP254, 442; SS47]

Shoghi Effendi designates the Hands of the Cause the 'Chief Stewards of Bahá'u'lláh's embryonic World commonwealth'. [MBW127]

Shoghi Effendi announces the appointment of a second Auxiliary

Board responsible for the protection of the Faith. [MBW127–8; PP442]

Shoghi Effendi calls for the convocation of a series of Intercontinental Conferences to be held successively in Kampala, Uganda; Sydney, Australia; Chicago, United States; Frankfurt, Germany; and Djakarta, Indonesia. [BW13:311–12; MBW125]

4 Nov Shoghi Effendi dies in London of coronary thrombosis after a bout of Asian influenza. [CB377; PP446]

- He was in London to purchase some furniture to complete the interior of the International Archives Building. [PP445]

- For a tribute to Shoghi Effendi written by Amatu'l-Bahá Rúḥíyyih Khánum see BW13:58–226.

See also *Rabbaní*, THE GUARDIAN OF THE BAHÁ'Í FAITH *and* THE PRICELESS PEARL.

9 Nov The funeral of Shoghi Effendi takes place in the Great Northern Centenary, London. [BW13:222; PP448]

- See BW13:222 for details of the funeral service.

- See BW13:222–5 and PP449–50 for a description of the funeral.

The Hands of the Cause of God and Bahá'ís from all over the world follow the hearse bearing the remains of Shoghi Effendi to his resting place

Above: The casket is carried to Shoghi Effendi's resting place

Below: The casket is interred in a flower-lined grave

Nov 1957– Apr 1963 The six year ministry of the Hands of the Cause residing in the Holy Land, or 'Custodians'. [BW16:90; WG45–6]

- This period is known as the 'interregnum'. [BBD120]

Thousands of flowers cover the grave of Shoghi Effendi

- See BW14:467 for a summary of the work of the Hands of the Cause during this period.

- The International Bahá'í Council continues to perform its duties at the World Centre under the direction of the Custodians. [BBD118]

See also THE MINISTRY OF THE CUSTODIANS 1957–1963.

15 Nov Hands of the Cause Rúḥíyyih Khánum, Mason Remey, Amelia Collins and Leroy Ioas, accompanied by Hand of the Cause Ugo Giachery, enter the apartment of Shoghi Effendi and seal with tape and wax the safe where his important documents were kept as well as the drawers to his desk. [BW13:341]

- The keys to the safe are placed in an envelope, which is sealed and signed by the five Hands and then placed in the safe of Leroy Ioas. [BW13:341]

18–25 Nov The first conclave of the Hands of the Cause of God is convened at Bahjí. [BBRSM128; DH215; MC8–11]

- This is the first meeting of the Hands of the Cause as a group.

- For a personal account of the Conclave by Hand of the Cause

Zikrullah Khadem see ZK119.

• For the nature of the six Conclaves see MC9–10, 12.

18 Nov The Hands of the Cause conduct a memorial meeting for Shoghi Effendi in the Ḥaram-i-Aqdas. [BW13:341; MC35]

19 Nov Nine Hands of the Cause are chosen by Rúḥíyyih Khánum to examine Shoghi Effendi's apartment. [BW13:341]

• These are the five members of the International Bahá'í Council (Rúḥíyyih Khánum, Mason Remey, Amelia Collins, Ugo Giachery and Leroy Ioas), an Afnán (Hasan Balyuzi), a representative of the Hands of the Western Hemisphere (Horace Holley), a representative of the Hands of the African continent (Músá Banání) and the Trustee of the Ḥuqúqu'lláh ('Alí Muḥammad Varqá). [BW13:341]

• After seeing that the seals are intact, the Hands examine the contents of Shoghi Effendi's safe and desk. [BW13:341]

• The nine Hands sign a document testifying that no Will or Testament of any nature executed by Shoghi Effendi has been found. This is reported to the entire body of Hands assembled in the Mansion of Bahjí. [BW13:341]

• See CB378–9 for an explanation of why Shoghi Effendi left no Will.

25 Nov Nine Hands are chosen to serve as Custodians of the Faith residing in the Holy Land. [BBD57; BW13:342; DH215]

• The Hands residing in the Holy Land are established as a legal body under the title 'The Custodians of the Bahá'í World Faith'.

• The Hands chosen as first Custodians are Rúḥíyyih Khánum, Mason Remey, Amelia Collins, Leroy Ioas, Hasan Balyuzi, 'Alí-Akbar Furútan, Jalál Kházeh, Paul Haney and Adelbert Mühlschlegel. [BW13:345–6; MC40–1]

A proclamation is issued stating that Shoghi Effendi left no heir and made no appointment of another Guardian. [BW13:341–5; MC25–30]

• See LOG310 for an explanation of the various meanings of the word 'Guardianship'.

- See CB388–9 for a discussion of the continuation of the institution of the Guardianship.

Dec The first summer school in Malaysia is held at Malacca.

2 Dec On the advice of their lawyer, Dr Abraham Weinshall, the Custodians ask each National and Regional Assembly to send a letter recognizing them as the supreme body in the Cause. [MC40–1]

25 Dec The Hands of the Cause announce the destruction of the long, two-storey house previously occupied by Covenant-breakers which was located near the garden wall of the Mansion of Bahá'u'lláh and of which Shoghi Effendi had acquired legal possession shortly before his passing. [MC11, 51]

- The rubble is used to complete the terraces begun by Shoghi Effendi north of the mansion and completing the northern gardens planned by him.

1958

In the year The first Aleut to become a Bahá'í, Vassa Lekanoff, enrols in Unalaska.

The first local spiritual assembly of Nepal is formed in Kathmandu.

23–8 Jan The first Intercontinental Conference held at the mid-point of the Crusade convenes in Kampala, Uganda. [BW13:317]

- Hand of the Cause Amatu'l-Bahá Rúḥíyyih Khánum, who had been designated by the Guardian as his representative, attends, accompanied by Dr Luṭfu'lláh Ḥakím.
- For the message of the Custodians to the conference see MC56–60.
- For a report of the conference see BW13:317.

26 Jan The foundation stone of the first Mashriqu'l-Adhkár of Africa is laid by Hands of the Cause Amatu'l-Bahá Rúḥíyyih Khánum and Músá Banání. [BW13:317]

21–4 Mar The second Intercontinental Conference held at the mid-point of the Crusade convenes in Sydney, Australia. [BW13:319]

- Hand of the Cause Charles Mason Remey, who had been designated by the Guardian as his representative and who is the architect of the Mother Temple of Australasia, attends, accompanied by four other Hands of the Cause. [BW13:317]

- For the message of the Custodians to the conference see MC72–5.

- For a report of the conference see BW13:319–21.

22 Mar The foundation stone of the first Mas͟hriqu'l-Ad͟hkár of the Antipodes is laid by Hands of the Cause Charles Mason Remey and Clara Dunn. [BW13:321]

Riḍván The first local spiritual assembly in the Kingdom of Tonga is formed at Nuku'alofa.

The first local spiritual assembly of Macau is formed.

21 Apr Mirza Ahmad (Esphahani) Sohrab, the Covenant-breaker who rebelled against Shoghi Effendi, dies. [MC90]

- For the story of his defection from the Faith see CB343–7.

26 Apr The National Spiritual Assembly of France is formed.

- For the message of the Custodians to the French National Convention see MC86–9.

May The first local spiritual assembly in Papua New Guinea is formed in Madina Village, in New Ireland.

- This is the first all-indigenous local spiritual assembly in the South Pacific.

2–4 May The third Intercontinental Conference held at the mid-point of the Crusade convenes in Wilmette, Illinois. [BW13:323]

- Hand of the Cause Dr Ugo Giachery, who had been designated by the Guardian as his representative, attends, accompanied by four other Hands of the Cause. [BW13:323]

- For the message of the Custodians to the conference see MC90–8.

• For a report of the conference see BW13:323–5.

12 Jun The Custodians release the 'Statement regarding the Guardianship', explaining that Shoghi Effendi had left no heir, that only he could appoint a second Guardian and that the Bahá'ís must dismiss all hopeful expectation that a Will appointing a second Guardian will be found. [MC100–2]

26 Jun Paul Adams, from Reading, England, having obtained permission to accompany Svalbard's chief hunter on a fishing tour in the summer and to spend the winter with him in Sassen Fjord, arrives in Spitzbergen and is named a Knight of Bahá'u'lláh. [BW13:456]

See also *Adams,* ARCTIC ISLAND HUNTER.

25–9 Jul The fourth Intercontinental Conference held at the mid-point of the Crusade convenes in Frankfurt, Germany. [BW13:327]

• Amelia Collins, who had been designated by the Guardian as his representative, attends, accompanied by ten other Hands of the Cause. [BW13:327]

• For the message of the Custodians to the conference see MC102–6.

• For a report of the conference see BW13:327–9.

c. 14 Sep A week before the fifth Intercontinental conference is due to convene in Djakarta, Indonesia, the government withdraws the permit to hold the conference. [BW13:331]

• For the story of why the permit was revoked see DM83–5.

• The cancellation of the conference in Djakarta begins a period of severe repression of the Faith in Indonesia which eventually leads to the Faith being banned in 1962. [DM85, 88]

21 Sep Hand of the Cause Leroy Ioas arrives in Indonesia and is plunged into negotiations regarding the holding of the conference. He meets with local Bahá'ís and anoints them with attar of roses as they pass to the room to view the portrait of Bahá'u'lláh. [BW13:331–2]

23 Sep Chartered planes take the conference delegates to Singapore.

27–9 Sep The fifth Intercontinental Conference held at the mid-point of the Crusade convenes in Singapore. [BW13:331]

- Hand of the Cause Leroy Ioas, who had been designated by the Guardian as his representative, attends, accompanied by eight other Hands of the Cause. [BW13:331–2]
- For the message of the Custodians to the conference see MC111–16.
- For a report of the conference see BW13:331–2.

1 Nov The monument marking Shoghi Effendi's resting place is completed. [MC117]

The Resting Place of Shoghi Effendi

- Dust from the Shrine of Bahá'u'lláh is placed in the foundations. [MC117]
- For a description of the resting place see BBD194–5 and MC135–6.
- The monument is paid for from a Memorial Fund established after Shoghi Effendi's passing. Money in excess of the amount required

is spent on the teaching work and on the construction of the Temples. [MC132]

21–8 Nov The Second Conclave of the Hands of the Cause convenes at Bahjí. [BW13:347–8; MC118]

- It is attended by 25 of the 27 Hands of the Cause. [BW13:347; MC118]

- The Hands of the Cause call for the election of the Universal House of Justice at the time of the Most Great Jubilee in 1963. [BBRSM129; BW13:351; MC122]

1959

In the year The House of 'Abbúd is renovated and restored. [MC219]

The mansion at Mazra'ih is renovated. [MC219]

The first Eskimo in Alaska to become a Bahá'í, William Wiloya, enrols in Nome.

The first contact is made with the aboriginal population of the Malayan peninsula, the Orang Asli, by Yan Kee Leong.

- His meeting with the Senoi tribe living in Kampong Jeram Mengkuang in Perak results in the enrolment of many members of the tribe including the village headman, Penghulu Salleh, and a local teacher, Deroah Leman.

Bahá'í communities in the United States begin the observation of World Peace Day to call attention to the need for world peace. [BBD175]

- This was replaced in 1985 by the observance of the UN International Day of Peace, which occurs on the third Tuesday in September. [BBD175]

1 Feb The 'first Dependency of the Mashriqu'l-Adhkár in Wilmette', the Bahá'í Home for the Aged, opens. [BW13:747]

- For the history of its building see BW13:743–8.

• For pictures see BW13:742, 744–7.

Mar A number of Bahá'ís, members of the local spiritual assembly, are arrested in Ankara, Turkey. [MC306]

• The incident receives wide coverage in the press and the Bahá'ís are eventually released from prison. [MC306]

• A court case is subsequently brought against the Bahá'ís by the public prosecutor, who claims that the Faith is a 'Tarighat', a sect forbidden by the law of the land, and lengthy litigation follows. [MC306–7]

10 Apr Representatives of the Bahá'í International Community present to the President of the Human Rights Commission, Ambassador Gunewardene of Ceylon, a statement endorsing the Genocide Convention. [BW13:791–4]

Riḍván The Custodians announce that the resting place of the remains of the father of Bahá'u'lláh has been identified. [MC144]

Separate national spiritual assemblies are formed for Germany and Austria. [BBRSM186]

• For the letter of the Custodians to the national convention of Austria see MC158–60.

Separate national spiritual assemblies are formed for India and Burma.

• For the letter of the Custodians to the national convention of Burma see MC155–7.

The National Spiritual Assembly of Turkey is formed.

• For the letter of the Custodians to the national convention see MC148–51.

The Regional Spiritual Assembly of the South Pacific Islands is formed with its seat in Suva, Fiji.

• Its area of jurisdiction comprises ten island groups: Samoa, Fiji, New Caledonia, New Hebrides, Loyalty Islands, Gilbert and Ellice

Islands, Marshall Islands, Cook Islands, Solomon Islands, and Tonga. [BW13:308]

- For the letter of the Custodians to the national convention see MC151–5.

The first local spiritual assembly in Grenada is formed in St George's Parish.

The first local spiritual assembly in Cambodia is formed in Phnom Penh.

The Custodians announce that the number of national and regional spiritual assemblies has risen to 31, the Faith is established in 255 countries, Bahá'ís live in over 5,200 localities and have formed nearly 1,275 local spiritual assemblies, and Bahá'í literature has been translated into 261 languages. [MC137–8]

2 Jun The first Greek woman to become a Bahá'í, Ketty Antoniou, enrols in Greece.

14 Jun The Hands of the Cause announce that the remains of the cousin of the Báb have been identified and have been transferred to a cemetery. [MC161]

18 Aug Cheong Siu Choi (John Z. T. Chang), the Chinese headmaster of the Leng Nam Middle School and a highly respected leader in Macau, arrives with his family on Hainan Island and is named a Knight of Bahá'u'lláh. [BW13:452]

Notes PH75 *says this was August 1958.*

19 Oct The Hands of the Cause announce that the remains of the father of Bahá'u'lláh, Mírzá Buzurg, have been reinterred in the Bahá'í burial ground in the vicinity of the Most Great House in Baghdád. [MC165]

23 Oct–1 Nov The third Conclave of the Hands of the Cause of God is convened at Bahjí. [BW13:351; MC161–2]

- For the agenda of the meeting see MC163–4.

- Charles Mason Remey unsuccessfully attempts to convince his fellow Hands that the Guardianship should continue. [BBRSM130; MC217]

4 Nov The Hands of the Cause issue a message from their third Conclave. [MC166–70]

- The date for the election of the Universal House of Justice is fixed at Riḍván 1963. [MC166]
- They call for the election at Riḍván 1961 of 21 national spiritual assemblies in Latin America. [MC167–8]
- They call for the election at Riḍván 1962 of 11 national spiritual assemblies in Europe. [MC168]
- They call for the election at Riḍván 1961 of the International Bahá'í Council by postal ballot of the members of the national and regional spiritual assemblies constituted at Riḍván 1960. [MC168]
- The name of Hand of the Cause Charles Mason Remey is missing from the list of signatories to this letter. [MC170]

1960

In the decade A number of Bahá'í primary schools are opened in Bolivia.

early 1960s The first woman Somali to become a Bahá'í, Fatumeh Jama, enrols.

Two Bahá'í primary schools open in Uganda.

In the year The first local spiritual assembly in the Cocos Islands is formed on West Island.

- For picture see BW13:1052.

The first Côte d'Ivorian to become a Bahá'í, Mr Uri Bodo, a Bété from the region of Gagnoa working as a policeman in Abidjan, enrols.

The first Maya-Quiche to become a Bahá'í in Guatemala, Filomena Cajas de Velasquez, a tourist guide, enrols.

• She is later the first Guatemalan woman to serve on the national spiritual assembly.

Bahá'ís in Angola are detained and questioned by officials.

• Joaquim Sampaio is carried off in the middle of the night and is never seen again. It is presumed that he was executed or died in a prison camp.

• One family is forced to leave the country.

c. Riḍván Hand of the Cause Charles Mason Remey claims he is the second, 'hereditary' Guardian of the Bahá'í Faith. [BW13:397; BW16:90; SS49]

• See MC205–6, 231–6 for details of Remey's claims.

See also BBRSM130–1, 138–9; CB386–91; MC196–217, 223–8; SBBH1:220, NOTE 207.

Riḍván The Custodians announce that the Bahá'í Faith is represented in over 256 territories and is established in over 5,800 localities; there are 31 national spiritual assemblies and nearly 1,500 local spiritual assemblies; and Bahá'í literature is in 268 languages. [MC183––96]

27 Apr The International Bahá'í Council by unanimous vote rejects the claim of Charles Mason Remey to be the second Guardian. [MC206–7]

28 Apr The Custodians call upon all believers to join the Hands in repudiation of the claims of Charles Mason Remey to be the second Guardian. [MC196–7]

30 Apr–10 May Twenty-four national spiritual assemblies and five national conventions send messages of support to the Custodians, repudiating the claim made by Charles Mason Remey to be the second Guardian. [MC199–202]

• The National Spiritual Assembly of France votes to recognize the claim. [MC203]

5 May Hand of the Cause Abu'l-Qásim Faizí is sent by the Custodians to France to meet with the National Spiritual Assembly and Bahá'ís of France. [MC197]

• After consultation, five members of the assembly continue to support Charles Mason Remey in his claim to be the second Guardian and resign from the assembly. The national assembly is dissolved. [MC203]

12–31 May Six national spiritual assemblies send messages of support to the Custodians, repudiating the claim made by Charles Mason Remey to be the second Guardian. [MC207–8]

13 May The International Bahá'í Council writes to the Custodians recording its decision taken on 27 April to reject the claims of Charles Mason Remey to be the second Guardian. [MC206–7]

17–18 May The Bahá'í International Community attends a meeting called by the United Nations Office of Public Information to discuss problems of cooperation 'with the United Nations family insofar as its programme affects the new nations'. The Bahá'í statement regarding this becomes part of the conference record. [BW13:792]

- For text of statement see BW13:792–4.

1 Jul Ben and Louise Whitecow (early Peigan believers) marry in Calgary, Alberta, the first Bahá'ís in Canada to have a legally recognized Bahá'í marriage. [BW13:687]

12 Jul Horace Holley, Hand of the Cause of God, dies in Haifa. [BW13:849]

- For his obituary see BW13:849–58.
- For cable from the Hands of the Cause see MC217–18.

See also SBR214–47.

26 Jul The Hands of the Cause of God declare Charles Mason Remey a Covenant-breaker. [BBRSM221; MC224–5]

Aug All Bahá'í activity in Egypt is prohibited by decree of the president of the United Arab Republic (Egypt and Syria). Bahá'ís are interrogated, arrested, fined and imprisoned and their property confiscated. [BBRSM174; MC228]

18–27 Oct The fourth Conclave of the Hands of the Cause of God is convened at Bahjí. [MC229]

2 Nov The Hands of the Cause issue a message from their fourth Conclave. [MC237–44]

- All the Hands of the Cause are henceforth to render their services on a global, rather than a regional, scale. [MC239]

18 Nov Clara Dunn, Hand of the Cause of God, dies in Sydney. [BW13:859; MC245]

- For her obituary see BW13:859–62.

- For cable from the Hands see MC245.

See also SBR153–75.

20 Nov The cornerstone of the fifth House of Worship is laid in Langenhain, Germany, by Hand of the Cause of God Amelia Collins. [BW13:739; MC238, 245, 249–50]

See also MC14–15, 236.

Dec Mr Yan Kee Leong of Malaysia takes the Bahá'í Faith to the remote Iban people of Brunei.

Philip Suning, the first member of the Iban tribe to become a Bahá'í, enrols.

late 1960 Eric Moyce and Gay Corker, both youth and the first two local people to become Bahá'ís in St Helena, enrol.

1961

In the year Knud Jensen (of mixed Danish, St Thomanian parentage), the first local person to become a Bahá'í in the Virgin Islands, enrols.

The military government in Indonesia issues instructions to local authorities to ban all Bahá'í activities and to confiscate all Bahá'í property. [MC329]

14 Jan The House of Worship in Kampala, the Mother Temple of Africa, is dedicated by Hand of the Cause Rúḥíyyih Khánum in a service for Bahá'ís only. [BW13:713–14]

• For details of the service and a picture see BW13:714.

The House of Worship in Kampala, Uganda

15 Jan The House of Worship in Kampala is officially opened by Hand of the Cause Rúḥíyyih Khánum in a public service attended by 1,500 people. [BW13:715–18; MC15]

• For message of the Custodians to the dedication service see MC250–3.

• For cable of the Custodians to the Bahá'ís of the world see MC253.

17 Jan Following the arrest of Bahá'ís in Turkey in March 1959 and the subsequent court case, the Turkish court receives the findings of three outstanding religious scholars that the Bahá'í Faith is an independent religion. [MC308]

• For details of the history of the case see MC306–8.

Jan–Feb Hand of the Cause of God Dr Raḥmatu'lláh Muhájir travels to India and demonstrates the principle of mass teaching. [DM172–84; SBBH2:165–7]

• Mass teaching begins in the rural area of Madhya Pradesh among the Hindu population. In 1961 there are 850 Bahá'ís; in 1963 87,000; by 1973 nearly 400,000; and by 1987 about two million. In 1983 45 per cent of all local spiritual assemblies are in India. [BBRSM195; BW13:299]

1961

21–5 Feb The first Indian congress of Bolivia is held in Oruro, with 116 Indians participating. [BW13:268]

Corinne True, Hand of the Cause of God, dies in Chicago. [BW13: 846]

- For her obituary see BW13:846–9.
- For cables from the Custodians see MC257.

See also *Rutstein,* CORINNE TRUE.

Riḍván The International Bahá'í Council is elected for the first time, by postal ballot of the members of the national spiritual assemblies. [BW13:397; MC282]

- The members are Jessie Revell, 'Alí Nakhjavání, Luṭfu'lláh Ḥakím, Ethel Revell, Charles Wolcott, Sylvia Ioas, Mildred Mottahedeh, Ian Semple and Borrah Kavelin. [MC282]
- See BW13:398 for picture.

See also BBD118; BBRSM131; BW16:90; CB324; MC168, 242.

The National Spiritual Assembly of Argentina is formed. [BW13:258]

The National Spiritual Assembly of Bolivia is formed. [BW13:258]

The National Spiritual Assembly of Brazil is formed. [BW13:258]

The National Spiritual Assembly of Chile is formed. [BW13:258]

- For picture see BW13:260.

The National Spiritual Assembly of Colombia is formed. [BW13:258]

The National Spiritual Assembly of Costa Rica is formed. [BW13:258]

- For picture see BW13:261.

The National Spiritual Assembly of Cuba is formed. [BW13:258]

The National Spiritual Assembly of Dominican Republic is formed. [BW13:258]

The National Spiritual Assembly of Ecuador is formed. [BW13:258]

The National Spiritual Assembly of El Salvador is formed. [BW13:258]

• For picture see BW13:263.

The National Spiritual Assembly of Guatemala is formed. [BW13:258]

The National Spiritual Assembly of Haiti is formed. [BW13:258]

The National Spiritual Assembly of Honduras is formed. [BW13:258]

• For picture see BW13:265.

The National Spiritual Assembly of Jamaica is formed. [BW13:258]

The National Spiritual Assembly of Mexico is formed. [BW13:258]

• For picture see BW13:266.

The National Spiritual Assembly of Nicaragua is formed. [BW13:258]

The National Spiritual Assembly of Panama is formed. [BW13:258]

The National Spiritual Assembly of Paraguay is formed. [BW13:258]

The National Spiritual Assembly of Peru is formed. [BW13:258]

The National Spiritual Assembly of Venezuela is formed. [BW13:258]

The National Spiritual Assembly of Uruguay is formed. [BW13:258]

• For picture see BW13:268.

1 May Kanichi (Moto) Yamamoto, the first Japanese Bahá'í, dies in Berkeley, California. [SBR185]

• For the story of his life see SBR176–86.

• For picture see SBR190.

23 Jun Fred Murray, the first full-blooded Aborigine and member of the Minen tribe to become a Bahá'í, enrols. [BW14:369]

25–6 Jun The newly-elected International Bahá'í Council meets for the first time. [BW13:397; MC285–6]

- For details of the meeting and excerpts from its minutes see MC285–91.

8 Jul The Custodians announce that mass conversion has begun in Ceylon, Central and East Africa, and Bolivia, while in Canada native peoples have begun to enter the Faith. [MC293]

Georges and Emma Wayenece, originally from Maré on the Loyalty Islands and the first Loyalty Islanders to become Bahá'ís, enrol in Nouméa. [BW17:415]

- Mrs Wayenece is the first Melanesian woman of the New Caledonia and Loyalty Islands area to become a Bahá'í. [BW17:415]

15 Jul The Turkish court declares the Bahá'í Faith to be a 'Tarighat', a sect forbidden by the law of the land.

- The Bahá'ís are 'forgiven', released and the case against them dropped. [MC308]

- The National Spiritual Assembly decides to appeal the decision to a higher court and national spiritual assemblies are asked to make representations to the Turkish ambassadors in their respective countries. [MC308]

16 Sep The House of Worship in Sydney, the Mother Temple of the Antipodes, is dedicated by Hand of the Cause Rúḥíyyih Khánum in a service for Bahá'ís only. [BW13:729; MC15]

- For details of the service and pictures see BW13:726–32.

17 Sep The House of Worship in Sydney is officially opened by Hand of the Cause Rúḥíyyih Khánum in two public services, each attended by 900 people. [BW13:732]

- For message of the Custodians to the dedication service see MC309–12.

- For cable of the Custodians to the Bahá'ís of the world see MC313.

The House of Worship in Sydney, Australia

Oct The first summer school to be held on Rarotonga Island takes place.

15 Oct–2 Nov The fifth Conclave of the Hands of the Cause of God is convened at Bahjí. [MC297]

- For the agenda see MC298.

5 Nov The Hands of the Cause issue a message from their fifth Conclave. [MC313–23]

- They call for the election of the Universal House of Justice at a convention to be held in the Holy Land on the first, second and third days of Riḍván 1963. [CB392; MC321]

- They ask the electors to leave the Hands free to 'discharge their duties'. [MC321]

- The celebration of the Most Great Jubilee, the Centenary of the Declaration of Bahá'u'lláh, is to be held in London rather than Bag͟hdád, owing to the situation in the Middle East. [MC322]

autumn/ winter The International Bahá'í Archives is opened to Bahá'í pilgrims. [BW13:429; MC20]

- For details of the Archives building and several pictures see BW13:403–34.

The International Bahá'í Archives

7 Dec An article appears in the nationally prominent Moroccan newspaper *Al Alam* lamenting the decline of Islam and attacking the Bahá'í Faith. [MC17]

• This gives rise to persecution of the Bahá'ís in ensuing months.

1962

In the year The administrative institutions of the Faith are banned in Indonesia by President Sukarno. [BW19:41]

Notes BW15:174 *says this was in 1964.*

Bahá'í homes in Morocco are searched by the police and Bahá'í literature seized. [MC17]

Thirty thousand new Bahá'ís enrol in India in six months. [VV9]

Jan A Bahá'í Professor of Fine Arts at the University of Tetuan, Morocco, is dismissed from his post and warned to have no association with other Bahá'ís. [MC17]

1 Jan Amelia Collins, Hand of the Cause of God, dies in Haifa. [BW13:399, 840; MC12]

• For her obituary see BW13:834–41.

• For the cable of the Hands of the Cause see MC333.

See also *Faizi,* MILLY *and* PSBW73–106.

Mar Aboubacar Kâ, a school teacher and the first Senegalese known to become a Bahá'í, enrols.

Apr Virginia Breaks, Knight of Bahá'u'lláh for the Caroline Islands, moves to Saipan, the first pioneer to the area.

12 Apr Four Bahá'ís are arrested in Nador, Morocco. [BW13:289; BW14:97]

• Eventually 14 Bahá'ís in total are arrested: 7 in Nador, 2 in Fez and 5 in Tetuan. [MC17]

• For an outline of the situation as it developed over 20 months see MC16–19.

Riḍván The National Spiritual Assembly of Belgium is formed. [BW13:283]

• For picture see BW13:275.

The National Spiritual Assembly of Denmark is formed. [BW13:283]

• For picture see BW13:276.

The National Spiritual Assembly of Finland is formed. [BW13:283]

• For picture see BW13:277.

The National Spiritual Assembly of Italy is formed. [BW13:283]

• For picture see BW13:278.

The National Spiritual Assembly of Luxembourg is formed. [BW13:283]

• For picture see BW13:279.

The National Spiritual Assembly of the Netherlands is formed. [BW13:283]

• For picture see BW13:279.

The National Spiritual Assembly of Norway is formed. [BW13:283]

• For picture see BW13:280.

The National Spiritual Assembly of Portugal is formed. [BW13:283]

• For picture see BW13:280.

The National Spiritual Assembly of Spain is formed. [BW13:283]

• For picture see BW13:281.

The National Spiritual Assembly of Sweden is formed. [BW13:283]

• For picture see BW13:281.

The National Spiritual Assembly of Switzerland is formed. [BW13:283]

• For picture see BW13:282.

The National Spiritual Assembly of Ceylon is formed in Colombo. [BW13:301]

The first local spiritual assembly of the Loyalty Islands is formed in Nouméa.

22 May The first Athabascan Indian north of the Arctic Circle to become a Bahá'í, Charley Roberts, enrols. [BW15:455]

28 Jun President Tubman of Liberia visits the Shrine of the Báb.

• This is the second official visit of a head of state and is notable in that Liberia is the first black republic on the continent of Africa. [BW13:400]

• See BW13:400 for picture.

22 Aug The Custodians ask the National Spiritual Assembly of the United States to make representations to the diplomatic missions of Morocco in Washington and at the United Nations concerning the

14 Bahá'ís imprisoned in Morocco. [MC368–9]

23 Sep The Custodians ask the National Spiritual Assembly of the United States to obtain an interview with the personal representative of the King of Morocco who heads that country's delegation to the United Nations General Assembly in New York in connection with the Bahá'ís imprisoned in Morocco. [MC373–4]

autumn A property is acquired outside of Gwalior, India, for a teaching institute. [DM192]

- The institute is later converted into a boarding hostel solely for Indian children and still later into the 'Rabbani School', now an accredited agricultural school. [DM192–3; VV82]

31 Oct The 14 Bahá'ís imprisoned in Morocco are arraigned before the Regional Court of Nador. [BW13:289; MC18]

- They are charged with rebellion and disorder, attacks on public security, constituting an association of criminals and attacks on religious faith. [BW13:289; BW14:97; MC18]

16 Nov The superstructure of the European House of Worship near Frankfurt is completed and the Temple is turned over to the Bahá'ís by the contractor. [BW13:737; MC15]

10 Dec The trial of the 14 Bahá'ís imprisoned in Morocco on charges of sedition opens. [BW13:289; BW14:97]

- The prosecution makes no attempt to prove the charges against the accused. [BW13:289; BW14:97]

14 Dec The Regional Court of Nador gives its verdict in the case of the 14 Bahá'ís imprisoned in Morocco on charges of sedition: four are acquitted on the grounds that they claim to be Muslims; one is acquitted apparently through family connections; one is released on 15 years' probation owing to his diabetes; five are committed to life imprisonment; and three are condemned to death. [BBRSM174; MC18–19]

- The sentences are appealed to the Supreme Court. [BW13:289; BW14:97; MC19]

17 Dec The Custodians ask the Bahá'í International Community to issue press releases deploring Morocco's persecution of religious minorities and pointing out its failure to adhere to the UN charter condemning religious intolerance. [MC397]

21 Dec Telegrams are sent to 35 United Nations delegations appealing for help under the Genocide Convention for the Bahá'ís sentenced to death and imprisoned for life in Morocco. [BW13:794]

23 Dec The Custodians ask national spiritual assemblies to cable Secretary General of the United Nations U Thant requesting his intervention on behalf of the Bahá'ís under sentence of death and imprisoned for life in Morocco. [BW13:794; MC397–8]

27 Dec The Custodians ask national and local spiritual assemblies to write to the Moroccan ambassador in their respective countries pleading for justice and religious freedom. [MC398–9]

31 Dec The first indigenous local spiritual assembly in Venezuela is formed among the Yaruro Indians of Apure state in the village of Agua Linda.

1963

In the year In Angola, Antonio Francesco Ebo and seven other Bahá'ís are arrested and imprisoned in a penal colony off the coast of southern Angola.

- They remain in confinement for eight years.

1 Jan The Custodians ask all national and local spiritual assemblies to cable the King of Morocco appealing for justice for the Bahá'ís under sentence of death and imprisoned for life in his country. [BW14:97; MC19]

31 Jan Roger Baldwin, Chairman of the International League for the Rights of Man, appears before the UN sub-commission on Prevention of Discrimination and Protection of Minorities and states that, as far they know, the Bahá'í prisoners in Morocco are the only example in recent history where members of a religion have been condemned to death solely for holding and expressing religious views regarded as heretical. [MC415–16]

31 Mar King Hassan II of Morocco states in a televised interview in the United States that the Bahá'í Faith is not a religion and is 'against good order and also morals'. [MC415]

2 Apr King Hassan II of Morocco makes a public statement promising that if the Supreme Court upholds the decision condemning three Bahá'í prisoners to death, he will grant them a royal pardon. [MC416]

4 Apr The Custodians issue a statement of information to the national spiritual assemblies of the United States and Europe regarding the Bahá'ís imprisoned in Morocco and under threat of death, reminding them that clemency or a pardon are not sufficient, as the condemned Bahá'ís cannot be pardoned for a crime they did not commit. [MC414]

- For text of statement see MC414–20.

9 Apr The sixth Conclave of the Hands of the Cause of God is convened at Bahjí.

- For the agenda see MC404.

- For cabled message from the Conclave see MC420.

20 Apr The Ten Year Crusade is successfully completed.

- For a summary of achievements during the Crusade see BW13:459–60.

- For countries opened to the Faith during the Crusade see BW13:461–2.

- For number of localities in which Bahá'ís reside in different parts of the world see BW13:462.

- For languages into which Bahá'í literature has been translated see BW13:462–4.

- For races represented in the Bahá'í world community see BW13:464.

- For national spiritual assemblies at the end of the plan see BW13:468–9.

1963

21–3 Apr The First International Convention is convened in Haifa. [MC424]

- For programme see MC424–5.
- For details of the Convention and pictures see BW14:425–30.

21 Apr The Universal House of Justice is elected for the first time. [BW14:427; MC424]

- The election is held at 9:30 in the morning at the home of 'Abdu'l-Bahá, 7 Haparsim Street, Haifa. [BW14:427; MC425]
- Ballots are received from all 56 national spiritual assemblies. [BW14:427]
- 288 members of 51 national spiritual assemblies are present at the election. [BW14:427]
- For a list of the electors see MC406–13.
- For details of the election see BW14:425–9 and MC20–1.

22 Apr The results of the election of the Universal House of Justice are announced at the close of the morning session of the International Convention: Charles Wolcott, 'Alí Nakhjavání, H. Borrah Kavelin, Ian Semple, Luṭfu'lláh Ḥakím, David Hofman, Hugh Chance, Amoz Gibson and Ḥushmand Fatheazam. [BBD231–3; BBRSM131; BW14:425; MC425; SS50; VVXI-XII]

- For a picture of the Hands of the Cause of God with the Universal House of Justice see ZK123.

23 Apr Two Hands of the Cause and two members of the Universal House of Justice attend, on behalf of the House of Justice, the State funeral of Izhak Ben Zvi, second President of Israel. [BW14:92–3]

- This is the first official act of the Universal House of Justice. [BW14:92–3]

28 Apr–2 May The first Bahá'í World Congress, the 'Most Great Jubilee', is held in London to celebrate the centenary of the declaration of Bahá'u'lláh. [BW14:57]

Members of the first Universal House of Justice

- For a detailed account and many pictures see BW14:57–80.
- For the programme of speakers see BW14:60–1.
- Some 6000 Bahá'ís attend.

30 Apr The members of the Universal House of Justice are presented to the World Congress and the first statement of the House of Justice is read by David Hofman. [BW 14:68]

- For the text of the statement see BW14:431–2 and WG1–3.

7 May The Universal House of Justice issues its first message to national conventions. [WG4–8]

- It pays tribute to the Hands of the Cause. [WG5]
- It announces that the body has no officers and that its communications will be signed 'Universal House of Justice' over an embossed seal. [WG6]

9 May The Hands of the Cause of God pass a resolution regarding the principles that will apply between the body of the Hands and the Hands Residing in the Holy Land and the activities of the Hands in the Holy Land. [MC426]

Above left: The Royal Albert Hall, London, site of the first Bahá'í World Congress

Above right: Hand of the Cause Amatu'l-Bahá Rúḥíyyih Khánum addresses the first Bahá'í World Congress

Below left: African Bahá'ís singing *Alláhu-u-Abhá* at the first Bahá'í World Congress

Below right: The son of one of the Bahá'ís imprisoned in Morocco recites a prayer at the first Bahá'í World Congress

- Five Hands of the Cause are assigned to the Holy Land.

19 May The Hands of the Cause cable the annual conventions with the names of the five Hands chosen to reside in the Holy Land: Amatu'l-Bahá Rúḥíyyih Khánum, Leroy Ioas, 'Alí-Akbar Furútan, Paul Haney and Abu'l-Qásim Faizí. [MC427]

5 Jun onwards Throughout Iran, advantage is taken of the general anti-government disorder to launch attacks on Bahá'ís in several localities under the cover of these disturbances. [BW18:391]

- The Bahá'í cemetery in Ṭihrán is attacked, its buildings burnt and graves desecrated. [BW18:391]
- Bahá'í houses are attacked and burned at Árán and the local Bahá'í centre attacked. [BW18:391]
- The Bahá'í centre at Iṣfahán is attacked. [BW18:391]
- Several Bahá'í homes and businesses are attacked in Shíráz. [BW18:391]
- An attack on the House of the Báb in Shíráz is attempted. [BW18:391]
- Bahá'ís are dismissed from government employment. [BW18:391]

7 Jun The Custodians publish a Declaration 'releasing all their functions, rights and powers conferred upon them by the Declaration of the Hands, November 25, 1957, to the Universal House of Justice'. [MC433]

- This is in accordance with the terms of the original document which provided for the Hands to exercise these functions until the election of the Universal House of Justice. [MC431]

16 Jun The Universal House of Justice announces that it will for the present use the Western Pilgrim House at 10 Haparsim Street, Haifa, as its seat. [WG9]

25 Aug The Universal House of Justice announces the demolition by the Soviet authorities of the House of Worship in 'Ishqábád owing to earthquake damage. [BBD122; BW14:479–81]

• For a picture of the damaged Temple see BW14:481.

Oct The Universal House of Justice announces the launching at Riḍván 1964 of the Nine Year Plan. [WG14]

• As a preliminary step 19 new national spiritual assemblies are to formed at Riḍván 1964. [WG15–17]

• The next election of the Universal House of Justice will be in spring 1968. [WG17]

• The Faith has now entered the third epoch of the formative age. [WG17]

6 Oct The Universal House of Justice cables that it finds that 'there is no way to appoint or to legislate to make it possible to appoint a second Guardian to succeed Shoghi Effendi'. [WG11]

1 Nov The first person on Saipan to become a Bahá'í, Patience Robinson, enrols.

23 Nov At the request of the Universal House of Justice, Bahá'ís around the world pray at the Feast of Qawl for favourable action to be taken in the case of the Bahá'ís under threat of death and imprisoned in Morocco. [BW14:98]

• Shortly after the Feast the Moroccan Supreme Court heard the appeals, reversed the decision of the trial court and ordered the release of the prisoners. [BW14:98]

13 Dec The Bahá'í prisoners in Morocco are released on order of the Supreme Court. [BW14:98; MC19]

• For a picture of the release of the Moroccan Bahá'í prisoners see BW14:97.

1964

In the year Four new believers in Cambodia are arrested and imprisoned as the Bahá'í Faith is not formally recognized and the Bahá'ís do not have permission to teach it.

3 Feb Hand of the Cause Amatu'l-Bahá Rúḥíyyih Khánum and her companion Violette Nakhjavání leave Haifa at the start of their 55,000 mile, 9–month journey through India, Ceylon, Nepal and Sikkim. [AVI14; VVII]

22 Mar The Faith is brought to St Vincent for the first time by Shirley Jackson, who returns to the island the day after having become a Bahá'í while on a visit to her native home in Grenada.

- Later in the year she enrols the first Bahá'ís on St Vincent.

Apr The chief of the Arpushana clan of the Guajiros, Francisco Pimienta Arpushana, becomes a Bahá'í in Colombia and teaching work begins among his people. [BW14:319]

Riḍván The National Spiritual Assembly of North West Africa is formed with its seat in Tunis.

The National Spiritual Assembly of West Africa is formed with its seat in Monrovia.

The National Spiritual Assembly of West Central Africa is formed with its seat in Victoria, Cameroon.

The National Spiritual Assembly of Uganda and Central Africa is formed with its seat in Kampala.

The National Spiritual Assembly of Kenya is formed with its seat in Nairobi.

The National Spiritual Assembly of Tanganyika and Zanzibar is formed with its seat in Dar-es-Salaam.

The National Spiritual Assembly of South Central Africa is formed with its seat in Salisbury.

The National Spiritual Assembly of the Bahá'ís of South and West Africa is formed with its seat in Johannesburg.

The National Spiritual Assembly of the Indian Ocean is formed with its seat in Port Louis.

The National Spiritual Assembly of the Bahá'ís of the Hawaiian

Islands is formed with its seat in Honolulu.

The National Spiritual Assembly of the South Pacific Ocean is formed with its seat in Suva.

The National Spiritual Assembly of the South West Pacific Ocean is formed with its seat in Honiara.

The National Spiritual Assembly of North East Asia is formed with its seat in Tokyo.

The National Spiritual Assembly of Korea is formed with its seat in Seoul.

The National Spiritual Assembly of Malaysia is formed with its seat in Kuala Lumpur.

The National Spiritual Assembly of Indonesia is formed with its seat in Djakarta.

The National Spiritual Assembly of Viet Nam is formed with its seat in Saigon.

The National Spiritual Assembly of Thailand is formed with its seat in Bangkok.

The National Spiritual Assembly of the Philippines is formed with its seat in Manila.

The Nine Year Plan is launched. [BBRSM159; BW14:101; VV1; WG22–7]

- This marks the beginning of the second epoch of 'Abdu'l-Bahá's Divine Plan. [AWH178]
- For letter of the Universal House of Justice announcing the Plan see BW14:102–4.
- For an analysis of the details of the national plans sent to 69 national spiritual assemblies see BW14:104–23.

The Universal House of Justice releases statistics on the growth and spread of the Bahá'í Faith at Riḍván. [BW14:124–35]

Jun Isaac Eziukwu, a Nigerian who had become a Bahá'í in Bangui, Central African Republic, in 1956, arrives in Libreville, Gabon, the first pioneer to the country. [BW16:522–3]

4 Jul The House of Worship in Langenhain, Germany, is dedicated. [BW14:483–4]

The House of Worship in Langenhain, Germany

- For the message of the Universal House of Justice see BW14:485–6.
- For pictures see BW14:482, 483, 485, 491.
- For a description of the teaching conference accompanying the dedication see BW14:586–8.

See also MC14–15; PP432–4.

19 Sep Prince Sihanouk Norodom, Head of State, and Prince Kantol Norodom, Prime Minister, sign a decree authorizing the exercise of the Bahá'í Faith in Cambodia and recognizing the Bahá'í World Centre in Haifa.

Nov The Universal House of Justice announces that 'there is no way to appoint, or to legislate to make it possible to appoint, Hands of the Cause of God'. [WG41]

- For decisions of the Universal House of Justice regarding the development of the institution of the Hands of the Cause of God see WG40–3.

5 Nov Followers of Charles Mason Remey file suit in the United States District Court for Northern Illinois against the National Spiritual Assembly of the United States, claiming they are the rightful owners of all Bahá'í properties and funds in the United States. [BW14:95]

- The National Spiritual Assembly of the United States files a counter claim asking the court to restrain the Covenant-breakers from using Bahá'í names and symbols protected by trademark. [BW14:95]

1965

In the year Emma Reinert, the first Faroese to become a Bahá'í, enrols.

The first pioneer to the San Andrés and Providencia Islands settles there briefly.

William Carr visits Alert Bay in Canada, only 800 km. from the North Pole and the most northerly inhabited location in the world.

Nils and Sigrid Rutfjäll, the first Samer (Lapps) to become Bahá'ís, enrol in northern Norway. [BW 5:483]

Feb Jean and Ivanie Désert and their three children arrive in Guadeloupe from Haiti, the first Bahá'ís to settle on the island.

23 Mar The case filed by the followers of Charles Mason Remey against the National Spiritual Assembly of the United States is dismissed on technical grounds. [BW14:95]

- The Covenant-breakers file a further suit. [BW14:95]

Apr Franklin Bozor, an agricultural labourer, and Pierre Defoe, the first to become Bahá'ís in Guadeloupe, enrol.

Riḍván The first local spiritual assembly in Iceland is formed in Reykjavík.

15 Jul Hendrik Olsen, the first indigenous Greenlander to become a Bahá'í, enrols.

22 Jul Leroy Ioas, Hand of the Cause of God, dies in Haifa. [BW14:291; VV7]

• For his obituary see BW14:291–300.

• For cable of the Universal House of Justice see WG157.

Aug Thaddeus Smith, Clara Smith, Nando Valle, Evert Scott, Gloria Scott, Thomas Seymour and Lawrence Jebbers, the first to become Bahá'ís in the Cayman Islands, enrol in George Town owing to the efforts of Ivan A. Graham, a Jamaican Bahá'í.

1 Aug Mrs Ridvan Sadeghzadeh and Mrs Parvine Djoneidi and their children arrive in Niamey, Niger, from Ṭihrán, the first Bahá'ís to settle in the country.

19 Sep Walter Garland and Miss Annie Lourie Williams, the first to become Bahá'ís on Grand Turk Island, enrol.

Oct Alice Grey, the first person to become a Bahá'í on South Caicos Island, enrols.

11 Nov The Universal House of Justice announces that the 'final step' in the 'process' of the 'purification' of the Bahá'í properties in Bahjí has been taken with the removal of the remains of the Covenant-breaker Mírzá Ḍiyá'u'lláh from a room within the Shrine of Bahá'u'lláh. [BW14:82–3]

12 Nov Mr Jazy Souleymane, a teacher and the first person in Niger to become a Bahá'í, enrols.

late in the year The Bahá'í International Community establishes its own offices in the United Nations Plaza Building in New York. [BW14:90]

1966

c. 1966–7 The island of Niue is opened to the Bahá'í Faith for the first time.

In the year Florence Parry, the first to become a Bahá'í in the West Leeward Islands, enrols.

Tommy Kabu, a prominent person from the village of Ara'ava in the Gulf Province and the first in the Territory of Papua to become a Bahá'í, enrols. [BW15:459–60]

Jesus Blas Manibusan of Sinajana, Guam, the first Chamorro to become a Bahá'í, enrols.

Mm. Marion Magnée arrives in Mali from Belgium, the first Bahá'í to settle in the country.

Feb The first members of the Yao tribe become Bahá'ís in Laos. [BW14:150]

8 Mar The second suit brought against the National Spiritual Assembly of the United States by the followers of Charles Mason Remey, who claim to be the lawful owners of all Bahá'í properties and funds in the United States, is dismissed. [BW14:95]

11 Mar Eduardo Duarte Vieira is arrested in Portuguese Guinea following a period of increasing pressure and harassment instigated by the clergy. [BW14:390]

- He had been detained, maltreated and brutally beaten on several occasions since becoming a Bahá'í. [BW14:390]

22 Mar Napoleon Bergamaschi, an Alaskan Eskimo, and his three children open St Lawrence Island to the Bahá'í Faith. [BW14:146]

31 Mar Eduardo Duarte Vieira dies in prison in Portuguese Guinea and is named the first African martyr. [BW14:390; BW16:568]

- For his obituary see BW14:389–90.
- For the messages to his wife and children he scratched on a biscuit box see BW14:390–1.

14 Apr Jessie Revell, formerly a member of the International Bahá'í Council, dies in Haifa. [BW14:300]

- For her obituary see BW14:300–3.

17 April Ivor Ellard, a British resident of the United States, arrives in Dominica, the first pioneer to the island.

- Two days later William Nedden settles on the island.

Riḍván The National Spiritual Assembly of the South West Pacific Ocean is

Jessie Revell, centre, with Hand of the Cause Amatu'l-Bahá Rúḥíyyih K͟hánum and 'Alí Nak͟hjavání

formed with its seat in Honiara, Solomon Islands.

The National Spiritual Assembly of Brunei is formed with its seat in Brunei town. [BW14:99]

The first local spiritual assembly in Senegal is formed in Dakar.

The first local spiritual assembly in Suriname is formed in Paramaribo.

19 May The first legally recognized Bahá'í wedding in Europe takes place in Finland. [BW14:154]

1 Jun The counter-claim of the National Spiritual Assembly of the United States against the followers of Charles Mason Remey, restraining them from using Bahá'í names and symbols, is upheld when the Covenant-breakers fail to appear at the trial. [BW14:95]

10 Jun The Universal House of Justice addresses its first letter to 'Bahá'í Youth in Every Land'. [BW15:324; WG92–7]

29 Sep Frances A. Foss, the first pioneer on St Maarten, arrives in Philipsburg.

7 Nov The first local spiritual assembly in Niger is formed in Niamey.

late in the year Lorraine Landau arrives on Saba in the West Leeward Islands, the first Bahá'í to settle on the island.

Dec A campaign is launched against the Bahá'ís of Saysán, Ádharbáyján, by Mullá Mihdí Sulṭánpúr. [BW18:391]

1967

c. 1967 Egbert Barrett arrives on Carriacou from Grenada, the first pioneer to the island.

Mr O. T. Shelton arrives on St Eustatius in the West Leeward Islands, the first pioneer to the island.

In the year Victor de Araujo is appointed by the Universal House of Justice as the full-time Accredited Representative of the Bahá'í International Community to the United Nations; Mildred Mottahedeh is appointed Alternate Representative. [BW14:88–9; BW15:364]

• For picture see BW15:365.

The first Mataco Indians to become Bahá'ís enrol in Argentina. [BW14:150]

1 Jan A Bahá'í is beaten to death by a mob in Saysán, Ádharbáyján, and other Bahá'ís are attacked and beaten. [BW18:391]

21 Feb The Universal House of Justice establishes the International Bahá'í Audio-Visual Centre in Victor, New York. [BW14:91–2]

Mar The first Bahá'í summer school in Liberia begins. [BW14:174]

Riḍván The Universal House of Justice calls upon the Bahá'ís to launch a global campaign proclaiming the message of Bahá'u'lláh to every stratum of society. [BW14:211]

The National Spiritual Assembly of Laos is formed with its seat in Vientiane. [BW14:99]

The National Spiritual Assembly of Sikkim is formed with its seat in Gangtok. [BW14:99]

The National Spiritual Assembly of Taiwan is formed with its seat in Taipeh. [BW14:99]

The National Spiritual Assembly of the Cameroon Republic is formed with its seat in Victoria. [BW14:96]

The National Spiritual Assembly of Swaziland, Lesotho and Mozambique is formed with its seat in Mbabane. [BW14:96]

The National Spiritual Assembly of Zambia is formed with its seat in Lusaka. [BW14:97]

The National Spiritual Assembly of the Leeward, Windward and Virgin Islands is formed with its seat in Charlotte Amalie. [BW14:93]

The National Spiritual Assembly of Eastern and Central Arabia is formed with its seat in Bahrain.

The National Spiritual Assembly of the Gilbert and Ellice Islands is formed with its seat in Tarawa. [BW14:99]

The National Spiritual Assembly of Algeria and Tunisia is formed with its seat in Algiers. [BW14:96]

The National Spiritual Assembly of Belize is formed with its seat in the city of Belize. [BW14:93]

3 May Patsy Vincent, a youth from Castries and the first St Lucian to become a Bahá'í, enrols.

Oct A special edition of *The Proclamation of Bahá'u'lláh* is published by the Universal House of Justice for presentation to 140 heads of state. [BW14:204–6; CB406]

- For a picture of the book see BW14:194.
- For pictures and descriptions of some of the rulers addressed by Bahá'u'lláh see BW14:196–203.
- For responses from present-day leaders to the book, and pictures, see BW14:207–10.

5–10 Oct Six Intercontinental Conferences are held simultaneously in Panama City, Wilmette, Sydney, Kampala, Frankfurt and New Delhi to celebrate the centenary of the proclamation of Bahá'u'lláh to the kings and rulers of the world. [BW14:221]

H.E. Sir Bruce Greatbatch, Governor and Commander-in-Chief of Seychelles, second from left, receives Bahá'ís in his office on the occasion of their presentation to him of *The Proclamation of Bahá'u'lláh*

- For the message of the Universal House of Justice to the conferences see BW14:221–2.

- For descriptions of each conference see BW14:223–58.

- The six Hands of the Cause representing the Universal House of Justice at the conferences travelled to Adrianople to visit the House of Bahá'u'lláh before dispersing to the conferences. [BW14:236, 458; VV2]

8 Oct The foundation stone of the Mother Temple of Latin America is laid by Hand of the Cause Rúḥíyyih Khánum in Panama City. [BW14:494]

1967–8 Rhoda Vaughn arrives on Bonaire, remaining for nine months, the first Bahá'í to visit the island.

Cleophas Koko Vava, a Togolese employed at the American Cultural Centre as a librarian to the United States Information Service and the first person to become a Bahá'í in Chad, enrols.

1968

In the year Ernest Ndouba (GBeadoumadji Moadoumgar) of the Sara ethnic group and the first Chadian to become a Bahá'í, enrols in Ndjamena.

The Bahá'í Publishing Committee based in Karachi develops into a Bahá'í Publishing Trust responsible for translation and publication into Urdu, English, Persian, Arabic, Sindhi, Pushtu, Balochi, Gojri, Balti and other regional languages.

Over a thousand new believers enrol in Ethiopia. [BW15:186]

26 Jan A Moroccan Bahá'í is arrested, tried and convicted on the charges of having abused the sacredness of Islam and using deceptive methods to convert people to another religion; he is sentenced to three years' imprisonment. [BW15:172]

19 Feb His Highness Malietoa Tanumafili II of Western Samoa, the first reigning monarch to become a Bahá'í, writes to the Universal House of Justice confirming his acceptance of the Faith. [BW15: 180–3]

Riḍvan The Universal House of Justice is elected for a second time. [BW15:557]

- Dr David Ruhe is elected to replace Dr Hakím, who resigned for reasons of ill health. [VV3]

- For a description of the second international convention and pictures see BW14:564–8.

The first local spiritual assembly in French Guiana is formed at Cayenne.

His Highness Malietoa Tanumafili II of Western Samoa, right, with Hand of the Cause Dr Ugo Giachery

The first local spiritual assemblies of Equatorial Guinea are formed in Bata and Santa Isabel.

The first local spiritual assembly of the Cayman Islands is formed in George Town.

21 Jun The Universal House of Justice establishes the Continental Boards of Counsellors to continue into the future the functions of the Hands of the Cause in the protection and propagation of the Faith. [BBD58–9, 97; BW15:611–13; BW17:319; MUHJ4–5; WG141]

- For details of the eleven Boards and their membership see BW15:612 and WG140–4.

Members of the Universal House of Justice elected at Riḍván 1968

• For pictures of the Counsellors see BW15:614, 615, 618, 619, 622, 623, 625, 627.

22–3 Jun The first National Youth Conference of the Bahá'ís of the United States opens in Wilmette, Illinois. [BW15:327–8]

• For picture see BW15:325.

summer The first summer school to be held in Ireland begins.

Jul Christian and Elanzo Callwood, Norris Duport and Ethien Chinnery, the first people to become Bahá'ís on the island of Jost Van Dyke in the British Virgin Islands, enrol.

Louis Joseph, the first Bahá'í indigenous to Dominica, enrols in Roseau.

7 Jul Hermann Grossman, Hand of the Cause of God, dies in Germany. [BW15:416]

• For his obituary see BW15:416–21.

• For cable of the Universal House of Justice see BW15:416 and WG157–8.

27–8 Jul The first National Youth Conference of Honduras opens in Santa Rosa de Copán. [BW15:328–9]

10 Aug Dr Luṭfu'lláh Ḥakím, former member of the Universal House of Justice, dies in Haifa. [BW15:434]

- For his obituary see BW15:430–4.

- For cable of the Universal House of Justice see BW15:434 and WG158.

23–5 Aug The first Oceanic Conference takes place in Palermo, Sicily, to commemorate the arrival of Bahá'u'lláh in the Holy Land. [BW15:73, 178; VV3]

- It is attended by some 2,300 Bahá'ís from 67 countries. [BW15:73]

Bahá'ís mounting the staircase to the Shrine of the Báb at the commemoration of the Centenary of Bahá'u'lláh's arrival in the Holy Land

• For details of the conference, maps and pictures see BW15:72–80.

26–31 Aug The centenary of the arrival of Bahá'u'lláh in the Holy Land is commemorated at the World Centre. [BW15:81–4]

• For details of the commemoration, the pilgrimage to follow and pictures see BW15:81–6.

2 Sep Ṭaráẓu'lláh Samandarí, Hand of the Cause of God, dies in Haifa. [BW15:416]

• For his obituary see BW15:410–16.

• For cable of the Universal House of Justice see BW15:416 and WG158–9.

9 Sep Gerald (Jerry) Van Deusen, a 24–year-old American Bahá'í from the Windward, Leeward and Virgin Islands and the first pioneer to Upper Volta, arrives in Ouagadougou.

9 Oct The Universal House of Justice addresses its second letter to Bahá'í Youth. [BW15:324; WG152–4]

The widowed mother of seven children is sentenced to six months' imprisonment in Morocco for refusing to deny her faith. [BW15:172]

• Despite the efforts of national spiritual assemblies to secure justice for her through their embassies and cables to the King of Morocco, she is made to serve the entire sentence. [BW15:172]

24 Oct The Moroccan Bahá'í sentenced to three years' imprisonment in January 1968 appeals and his sentence is extended to four years. [BW15:172]

• Despite the efforts of national spiritual assemblies to secure justice for him through their embassies and cables to the King of Morocco, he is made to serve the entire sentence. [BW15:172]

Nov Mohammed Brimer (Mohammed Braimah Belem), the first person to become a Bahá'í in Upper Volta, enrols.

4 Nov Following the participation of Algerian Bahá'ís in the first Oceanic Conference in Palermo, Sicily, and subsequent international news coverage, foreign Bahá'ís in Algeria are summoned by the police and interrogated. [BW15:172]

7 Nov Sixteen Persian Bahá'ís in Algeria are expelled from the country and their properties confiscated; native Algerian Bahá'ís are put under restrictions and five are exiled to the Sahara and the eastern mountain regions. [BW15:172]

- Following appeals, the confiscated properties are returned and the order of banishment for the local believers is gradually relaxed. [BW15:172]

Dec George Howard arrives on Union Island, the first person to take the Bahá'í Faith to the Grenadine Islands.

late in the year Two Chilean Bahá'ís, Aníbal Soto, a telegraph operator in the Chilean Navy, and his wife, Norma Soto, are posted to a Chilean base in Antarctica.

1969

1968–9 Throughout Iran, pressure on Bahá'ís intensifies. [BW18:391]

- Applications for government employment are refused. [BW18:391]
- Bahá'ís are refused admission to colleges and universities. [BW18:391]
- Bahá'í centres are closed. [BW18:391]
- Individual Bahá'ís are attacked. [BW18:391]

In the year Owing to the increased flow of pilgrims, the pilgrim house in Haifa is converted to a pilgrim centre and the decision taken to accommodate pilgrims in hotels. [DH178]

Fifteen youth enrol at Mayaguez, Puerto Rico, the beginning of a process in which over 300 people become Bahá'ís. [BW15:218]

Apr The Bahá'í Faith is banned in Algeria by official decree, all Bahá'í institutions are disbanded and the National Spiritual Assembly dissolved. [BW15:189; BW19:41]

3–6 Apr The first European Youth Conference opens in Madrid, Spain. [BW15:329]

4–6 Apr The first National Youth Conference of Australia opens at Bolton Place summer School. [BW15:329]

- For picture see BW15:328.

Riḍván The National Spiritual Assembly of Burundi and Rwanda is formed. [BW15:205]

- For picture see BW15:142.

The National Spiritual Assembly of Papua New Guinea is formed with its seat in Lae. [BW15:265]

- For picture see BW15:142.

The first local spiritual assembly of Upper Volta is formed in Ouagadougou.

24–5 May The first Bahá'í Youth Conference of Japan opens on Jogashima Island. [BW15:329]

Aug The first 12 new Bahá'ís enrol on Union Island in the Grenadines during a visit of Patricia Paccassi and her daughter Judith.

The Bahá'í Faith is legally recognized in Lebanon when the Local Spiritual Assembly of Beirut is incorporated. [BW15:173]

- This is the first time any Arab government has granted the Faith recognition. [BW15:173]

5 Aug Hand of the Cause Amatu'l-Bahá Rúḥíyyih Khánum and her companion, Violette Nakhjavání, arrive in Kampala, Uganda, at the start of the 'Great Safari'. [BW15:59]

- For details of the safari and pictures see BW15:588–607.

29 Dec–2 Jan 1970 The First Pacific Area Bahá'í Youth Conference takes place in Apia, Western Samoa. [BW15:329-30]

- For picture see BW15:330.

1970

In the year The first Gypsy in Spain to become a Bahá'í, Maria Camacho Martinez, enrols in Sabadell.

The first native of Mauritania to become a Bahá'í enrols.

A Bahá'í International Youth Conference is held in Abidjan, Ivory Coast.

Botswana holds its first National Youth School. [BW15:329]

The House of Bahá'u'lláh in Ṭihrán undergoes major repair and a fundamental restoration of both exterior and interior parts.

1970–early 1971 Over 20,000 Afro-Americans from the rural areas of the south-eastern United States become Bahá'ís. [BBRSM187]

25 Jan Valde Nyman, the first full Gypsy in Finland to become a Bahá'í, enrols in Helsinki.

Apr–Aug More than 6,000 people become Bahá'ís in Bolivia. [BW15:232]

Riḍván The National Spiritual Assembly of Botswana is formed with its seat in Gaborone. [BW15:199]

- For picture see BW15:144.

The National Spiritual Assembly of Dahomey, Togo and Niger is formed with its seat in Cotonou, Dahomey. [BW15:189]

- For picture see BW15:144.

The National Spiritual Assembly of Ghana is formed with its seat in Accra. [BW15:192]

- For picture see BW15:144.

The National Spiritual Assembly of Nigeria is formed. [BW15:192]

The National Spiritual Assembly of Malawi is formed with its seat in Limbe. [BW15:201]

• For picture see BW15:146.

The National Spiritual Assembly of Rhodesia is formed. [BW15:200]

The National Spiritual Assembly of Central Africa is formed with its seat in Bangui. [BW15:206]

The National Spiritual Assembly of Upper West Africa is formed with its seat in Banjul, The Gambia. [BW15:193]

• For picture see BW15:147.

The National Spiritual Assembly of Zaire is formed with its seat in Kinshasa. [BW15:205]

• For picture see BW15:147.

The National Spiritual Assembly of the Near East is formed with its seat in Beirut, Lebanon. [BW15:146; BW16:264]

• For picture see BW15:146.

The National Spiritual Assembly of Guyana, Surinam and French Guiana is formed with its seat in Georgetown, Guyana. [BW15:238]

• For picture see BW15:144.

The National Spiritual Assembly of Samoa is formed with its seat in Apia. [BW15:274]

• For picture see BW15:146.

The National Spiritual Assembly of Tonga and the Cook Islands is formed with its seat in Nuku'alofa. [BW15:275]

• For picture see BW15:146.

The National Spiritual Assembly of Fiji is formed with its seat in Suva. [BW15:271]

The first Local Spiritual Assembly of Nouakchott, Mauritania is formed.

1970

May The Iraqi government issues a decree disbanding all Bahá'í institutions and banning all Bahá'í activities. [BBRSM174; BW15:173; BW16:137]

One thousand Guajiro Indians become Bahá'ís in Venezuela. [BW15:241]

27 May The Bahá'í International Community is granted consultative status, category II, by the Economic and Social Council (ECOSOC) of the United Nations. [BBRSM149; BW15:178, 366; BW16:333; BW19:30; VV54]

• As a result, the Bahá'í International Community begins to be represented at sessions of UN bodies addressing a wide range of issues of particular interest to Bahá'ís, including human rights, social development, status of women, environment, human settlements, agriculture, science and technology, new and renewable resources, population, law of the sea, crime prevention, narcotic drugs, children, youth, the family, disabled persons, the ageing, the United Nations University anddisarmament.

• At such sessions the Bahá'í International Community offers statements on the Bahá'í position on the subject under discussion.

19–21 Jun Rúḥíyyih Khánum interrupts her African teaching safari to meet with more than 2,000 youth at the National Youth Conference in the United States. [BW15:331–2; VV10]

23 Jun The centenary of the death of Mírzá Mihdí is commemorated with a day of prayer by Bahá'ís around the world and in the Holy Land with a pilgrimage to the barracks in 'Akká, Bahjí and to his monument. [BW15:162–3]

14 Aug–5 Sep 1971 Eight Oceanic and Continental Conferences are held. [BW15:296–323]

• For many pictures see BW15:296–316.

14–16 Aug The Oceanic Conference is held in Rose Hill, Mauritius. [BW15:317; VV5]

• For pictures see BW15:299–301.

The Continental Conference is held in La Paz, Bolivia. [BW15:317; VV5]

• For pictures see BW15:301–2.

12 Nov Bahá'ís in the Central African Republic are arrested at a meeting to commemorate the anniversary of the birth of Bahá'u'lláh and Bahá'í activities are banned when a disaffected Bahá'í denounces the Faith as a political movement to the authorities. [BW15:207]

Dec Canadian Bahá'ís hold a Victory Conference in Iceland to prepare the community to achieve assembly status in 1972. [BW15:335]

25 Dec– 3 Jan 1971 The First International Bahá'í Youth winter School takes place in Salzburg, Austria, attended by 600 people from 25 countries. [BW15:332]

• For picture see BW15:332.

1971

c. 1971 The first local spiritual assembly in Ciskei is formed in Mdantsane.

In the year Following the prohibition of Bahá'í activity in Egypt in 1960, Egyptian Bahá'ís put forward a petition to the Supreme Constitutional Court seeking to overturn the presidential decree as unconstitutional.

The first summer school in Singapore is held.

The first local spiritual assembly in Mali is formed in Bamako.

The first three people to become Bahá'ís in Guinea enrol. [BINS45]

The first Amerindian to become a Bahá'í in French Guiana enrols.

The first Gypsies, six adults and six youth, to become Bahá'ís in France enrol at a campsite near Le Bourget airport.

The first Pingelapese to become a Bahá'í enrols in the East Caroline Islands.

1971

Over 500 people become Bahá'ís in Bangladesh. [BINS86]

The 'Lake Victoria Plan', a joint venture among the National Spiritual Assemblies of Uganda, Kenya, Tanzania and Burundi designed to carry the Faith to all the peoples and tribes living within Africa's largest lake basin, is inaugurated at the suggestion of Hand of the Cause Dr Muhájir. [DM96–8]

Jan Thirty people enrol in Iceland as a result of the Victory Conference held in December, doubling the number of Icelandic believers. [BW15:335]

1 Jan Agnes Alexander, Hand of the Cause of God, dies in Honolulu. [BW15:423; VV8]

- For her obituary see BW15:423–30.

1–3 Jan The Oceanic Conference of the South China Seas is held in the Victoria Memorial Hall in Singapore. [BW15:319; VV5]

- For pictures see BW15:302–3 and VV6.

The Continental Conference of Africa is held in Monrovia, Liberia. [BW15:318; VV5]

- For pictures see BW15:304–5.

13 Feb Following the ban imposed by the government of the Central African Republic on Bahá'í activities in November 1970 and subsequent representations made by the international Bahá'í lawyer Dr Aziz Navidi, the ban is lifted and the Bahá'í Faith officially recognized.

- This is broadcast in every news bulletin on government radio for the next 24 hours, the first public proclamation of the Bahá'í Faith in the country.

Apr The International Bahá'í Youth Conference takes places at Oteppe-Namur, Belgium, launching a two-year youth campaign for Europe. [BW15:333–4]

- For picture see BW15:334.

Riḍván The National Spiritual Assembly of the Central African Republic is formed with its seat in Bangui. [BW15:207]

• For picture see BW15:148.

The National Spiritual Assembly of Chad is formed with its seat in Fort Lamy. [BW15:207]

• For picture see BW15:148.

The National Spiritual Assembly of Congo and Gabon is formed with its seat in Brazzaville, the Congo. [BW15:206]

• For picture see BW15:148.

The National Spiritual Assembly of Lesotho is formed with its seat in Maseru. [BW15:202]

• For picture see BW15:148.

The National Spiritual Assembly of Ivory Coast, Mali and Upper Volta is formed with its seat in Abidjan, Ivory Coast. [BW15:193]

• For picture see BW15:150.

The National Spiritual Assembly of Sudan is formed. [BW15:187]

• For picture see BW15:150.

The National Spiritual Assembly of Trinidad and Tobago is formed with its seat in Port-of-Spain. [BW15:219, 242]

The National Spiritual Assembly of the Solomon Islands is formed with its seat in Honiara. [BW15:269]

The first local spiritual assemblies in Guam are formed in Dededo, Inarajan, Mangilao and Tamuning.

May The first National Teaching Committee of Sierra Leone is appointed by the Regional Spiritual Assembly of West Africa.

21–3 May The Caribbean Conference is held in Kingston, Jamaica. [BW15:218, 319–20; VV5–6]

The National Spiritual Assembly of Trinidad and Tobago in 1971

• For pictures see BW15:304–8 and VV6.

The South Pacific Oceanic Conference is held in Suva, Fiji. BW15:320–1; VV6.

• For pictures see BW15:308–9.

Youth at the Fiesch Conference release balloons bearing messages about the Bahá'í Faith

31 Jul–11 Aug The European Youth Conference takes place in Fiesch, Switzerland, attended by 1,200 youth from 50 countries. [BW15:336–8]

- About 200 people enrol in the Bahá'í Faith during the conference. [BW15:336]
- For pictures see BW15:337.

Aug The Universal House of Justice erects an obelisk on the site of the future House of Worship of the Holy Land. [BBD172; BW15:177–8; DH175; MUHJ83–4]

The obelisk erected on the site of the future House of Worship of the Holy Land

4 Aug The first Bahá'í College Club of Latin America is formed at the University of the Americas, Puebla, Mexico. [BW15:215]

27–30 Aug The first Bahá'í Youth Conference for Western Asia takes place in New Delhi. [BW15:335]

- Two thousand people enrol during the conference and the week following. [BW15:335]

3–5 Sep The North Pacific Oceanic Conference is held in Sapporo, Japan. [BW15:321–2; VV6]

- For pictures see BW15:312–14 and VV5.

1971–1972

The North Atlantic Oceanic Conference is held in Reykjavik, Iceland. [BW15:322–3; VV6]

- For pictures see BW15:309–12.

4 Sep Músá Banání, Hand of the Cause of God, dies in Kampala, Uganda. [BW15:42; VV7]

- For his obituary see BW15:421–3.

13 Oct Following the banning of Bahá'í activities in Egypt in 1960, Egyptian Bahá'ís submit a petition to the Supreme Constitutional Court asking for redress and for justice to be upheld. [BW15:173]

- The opinion of one Mandatory of the government is that the 1960 decree is unconstitutional. [BW15:173]

Nov The first Bahá'í Youth Conference of the Antilles takes place in the Dominican Republic. [BW15:217]

26–8 Nov The fiftieth anniversary of the passing of 'Abdu'l-Bahá is commemorated. [BW15:125–8; VV14]

- For text of the letters of the Universal House of Justice see BW15:125–6 and MUHJ76–7.

Dec–Jan 1972 The first youth summer school for southern Africa is held at the Leroy Ioas Teacher Training Institute in Mbabane and is attended by 67 people from eight countries.

1972

In the year The first Summer School of Jamaica is held. [BW15:218]

The first Winter School of Luxembourg is held in Pétange. [BW15:284]

The first West African Bahá'í Youth conference is held in The Gambia.

Derek and Sally Dacey, the first resident pioneers on Montserrat in the East Leeward Islands, arrive at their pioneer post.

In Indonesia the Attorney-General confirms the 1962 ban on Bahá'í administrative institutions and adds a further prohibition against organized Bahá'í teaching activities. [BW19:41]

The first Bahá'í studies seminar is held in London.

- For an account of the development of these seminars see BW18:204 and BW19:368.

Jan The first Bahá'í Youth Summer School in Southern Africa takes place in Swaziland, attended by 70 youth from eight countries. [BW15:338]

- For picture see BW15:340.

Mar A thousand children attend a Bahá'í school in Esmeraldas, Ecuador. [BW15:237]

Riḍván The National Spiritual Assembly of Afghanistan is formed with its seat in Kabul. [BW15:243]

- For picture see BW15:151.

The National Spiritual Assembly of the Arabian Peninsula is formed.

- For picture see BW15:151.

The National Spiritual Assembly of Bangladesh is formed with its seat in Dacca. [BW15:243]

- For picture see BW15:153.

The National Spiritual Assembly of Iceland is formed with its seat in Reykjavik. [BW15:225, 281]

- For picture see BW15:153.

The National Spiritual Assembly of the Republic of Ireland is formed with its seat in Dublin. [BW15:283]

- For picture see BW15:153.

- The National Spiritual Assembly of the British Isles is renamed the National Spiritual Assembly of the United Kingdom. [BW15:290]

The National Spiritual Assembly of the Malagasy Republic is formed with its seat in Tananarive. [BW15:199]

• For pictures see BW15:153, 198.

The National Spiritual Assembly of Nepal is formed with its seat in Kathmandu. [BW15:249]

• For pictures see BW15:155, 248.

The first national spiritual assembly in Micronesia, the National Spiritual Assembly of the North West Pacific Ocean, is formed with its seat in Ponape. [BW15:268]

• For picture see BW15:155.

The National Spiritual Assembly of Puerto Rico is formed with its seat in San Juan. [BW15:218]

• For picture see BW15:155.

The National Spiritual Assembly of Réunion is formed with its seat in St Pierre. [BW15:199]

• For picture see BW15:155.

The National Spiritual Assembly of Rwanda is formed. [BW15:205]

• For picture see BW15:157.

The National Spiritual Assembly of Burundi is formed with its seat in Bujumbura. [BW15:205]

• Because of disturbances in the country, the assembly is dissolved in the same year and the affairs of the Faith placed under an administrative committee. [BW15:205]

The National Spiritual Assembly of Seychelles is formed with its seat in Victoria. [BW16:156]

• For picture see BW15:157.

The National Spiritual Assembly of Gabon is formed. [BW15:206]

The National Spiritual Assembly of Singapore is formed with its seat in Singapore. [BW15:257]

• For picture see BW15:157.

The National Spiritual Assembly of Eastern Malaysia and Brunei is formed with its seat in Kuching, Sarawak. [BW15:253]

• For picture see BW15:254.

The National Spiritual Assembly of the Windward Islands is formed with its seat in St Lawrence, Barbados. [BW15:220]

• For picture see BW15:157.

The National Spiritual Assembly of Tunisia is formed.

The first local spiritual assembly in the Republic of San Marino is formed.

28 Apr–2 May An international teaching conference is held in conjunction with the dedication of the Mother Temple of Latin America in Panama. [BW15:633–42]

• For pictures see BW15:632–49.

29 Apr The House of Worship in Panama is dedicated in a series of ceremonies held throughout the day attended by Hands of the Cause Amatu'l-Bahá Rúḥíyyih Khánum, Ugo Giachery and Dhikru'lláh Khádem and four thousand Bahá'ís. [BW15:634; VV14]

• For the history of the House of Worship see BW15:643–6.

• For statistics on the House of Worship see BW15:647–9.

30 Apr The House of Worship in Panama is publicly dedicated by Amatu'l-Bahá Rúḥíyyih Khánum in two sessions. [BW15:634]

1 May The international teaching conference in Panama held in conjunc-

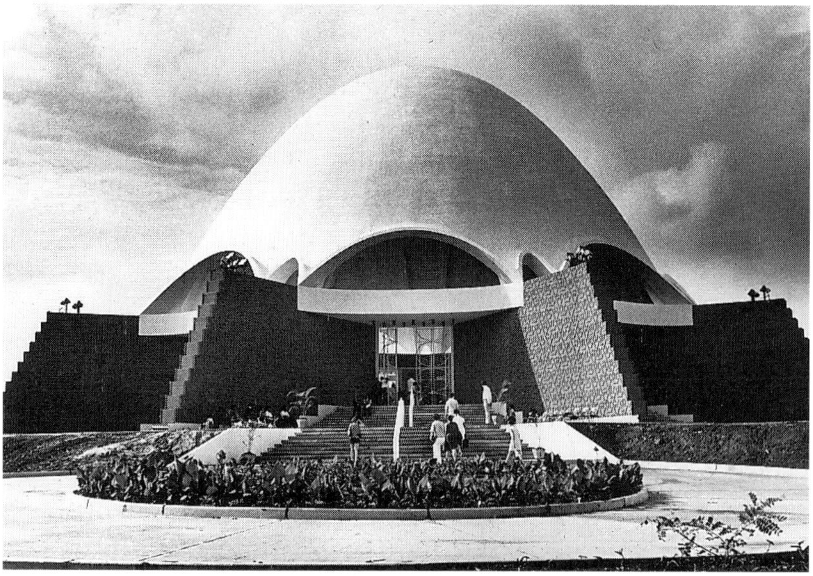

The Panama House of Worship

tion with the dedication of the House of Worship opens. [BW15:635]

• For the message of the Universal House of Justice see BW15:635–7.

May The northeast and southeast quadrants of the gardens at Bahjí are completed and the southern gardens are extended to 'Abdu'l-Bahá's Tea House.

7 Jun The Universal House of Justice announces the decision to construct its Seat. [DH172; MUHJ98–9; VV37]

19 Jun The government of Indonesia re-affirms the ban on the Bahá'í Faith.

• Following this a number of Bahá'ís lose their jobs.

summer Over 150 American youth join European youth in Operation Hand-in-Hand, a joint teaching project. [BW15:338]

• For picture see BW15:347.

30 Jul Parvíz Ṣádiqí, Farámarz Vujdání and Parvíz Furúghí, Iranian youth pioneers, are murdered near Mindanao, Philippines, by Muslims. [BW15:257; DM316–17]

Bahjí in 1973, showing the completed northeast and southeast quandrants of the gardens

• For their obituaries see BW15:514–16.

6 Aug 'Abdu'l-Ḥamíd Ishráq-Khávarí, Iranian scholar, author, translator and promoter of the Bahá'í Faith, dies. [BW15:520]

• For his obituary see BW15:518–20.

Sep The Bahá'í Publishing Trust of Taiwan is established and registered. [BW15:262]

7 Sep The first local spiritual assembly in Malta is formed.

Oct The first local spiritual assembly in the Falkland Islands is formed. [BW15:650]

Nov Thirty-two people enrol in Corsica.

26 Nov The constitution of the Universal House of Justice is adopted. [BW15:169; BBRSM132, 138; VV14]

• For full text of the constitution see BW15:555–64.

Dec The first International Youth Conference of Surinam takes places in Paramaribo. [BW15:341]

The first winter school in Bangladesh takes place. [BW15:245]

1973

In the year The first International Youth Conference of Mexico takes place in Puebla City, attended by 200 youth from five countries. [BW15:343]

The House of Bahá'u'lláh in Ṭihrán and its adjacent bírúní (reception area) are completely restored to their original structure, design and elegance.

The first local spiritual assembly in St Helena is formed.

The first local spiritual assembly in the Faroes is formed in Tórshavn.

Jan The Bahá'ís of The Gambia are granted freedom of worship by the Secretary-General of the Gambian government. [BW15:193]

19 Jan *The Synopsis and Codification of the Kitáb-i-Aqdas* is completed. [BW15:169]

Feb Hand of the Cause Amatu'l-Bahá Rúḥíyyih Khánum and her companion Violette Nakhjavání complete their tour of Africa. [BW15:605]

- They have driven some 36,000 miles to visit more than 30 countries. [BW15:596; VV12]
- For details of the safari see BW15:593–607.
- See BW15:606–7 for the countries, islands and territories visited and the heads of state and other dignitaries who received them.

15 Mar The mansion at Mazra'ih is purchased. [BW15:169; BW16:136; DH94; VV14]

1 Apr The Bahá'ís of the Central African Republic broadcast the first of their weekly radio programmes on Radio Bangui. [BW16:141]

7 Apr Following the return to stability in Burundi, the Bahá'í Faith is granted formal recognition by the government. [BW16:137]

The mansion at Mazra'ih, shown here in 1989

Riḍván The Nine Year Plan is successfully completed. [BW16:131]

• For the growth of the Bahá'í Faith in this period see BW16:130.

The Synopsis and Codification of the Kitáb-i-Aqdas is published. [BBRSM138; MUHJ105; VV14]

The Universal House of Justice is elected for the third time. [VV14]

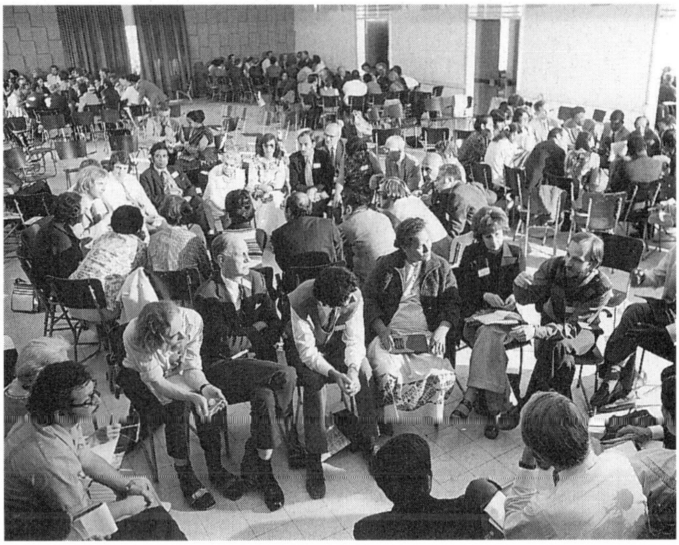

Some of the delegates attending the third International Convention to elect the Universal House of Justice

5 Jun The International Teaching Centre is established at the Bahá'í World Centre. [BBD118–19; BBRSM132–3; BW16:134, 411–14; BW17: 322–5; VV16]

- For cable of the Universal House of Justice see BW16:413.
- Hands of the Cause Amatu'l-Bahá Rúḥíyyih Khánum, 'Alí-Akbar Furútan, Paul Haney and Abu'l-Qásim Faizí and Counsellor members Hooper Dunbar, Florence Mayberry and Aziz Yazdi are appointed. [BW16:413]
- For pictures see BW16:412 and VV16.

The Universal House of Justice asks the Bahá'ís to commemorate on the Feast of Núr the one hundredth anniversary of Bahá'u'lláh's departure from 'Akká and move to Mazra'ih. [VV21]

8 Jun The Universal House of Justice permits the Continental Boards of Counsellors to authorize individual Auxiliary Board members to appoint assistants. [BW17:322]

14 Jun The International Teaching Centre meets for the first time. [VV16]

Jul The National Spiritual Assembly of Equatorial Guinea is formed. [BW16:141]

- Owing to local circumstances, it is disbanded within the year. [BW16:141]

5 Sep John Ferraby, Hand of the Cause of God, dies in Cambridge, England. [BW16:511; VV8]

- For his obituary see BW16:511–12.

18 Sep Ḥusayn Amánat is appointed architect of the Seat of the Universal House of Justice. [BW16:133; DH172; VV37]

Nov The first youth conference of Papua New Guinea takes place in Sogeri with 40 youth and visitors. [BW16:276]

Dec A teenaged Muslim student defends the Bahá'í Faith in a school in Baghdád, causing her arrest and the arrest of three Bahá'í girl students. [BW16:138]

• Over the next months nearly 50 Bahá'ís are arrested. [BW16:138]

The National Spiritual Assembly of Puerto Rico holds its first Bahá'í school. [BW16:194]

4 Dec The Universal House of Justice announces the completion of the final, southwestern quadrant of the gardens at Bahjí. [BW16:135–6; DH122]

1974

In the year The Canadian Association for Studies on the Bahá'í Faith is created. [BW16:200]

• For its history, terms of reference and programmes and publications see BW17:197–201.

The National Spiritual Assembly of the Leeward and Virgin Islands holds its first annual National Teaching Conference. [BW16:187]

The National Television Network of Ghana broadcasts an interview with Dr William Maxwell, the first mention of the Bahá'í Faith on television in the country. [BW16:168]

As a result of an intervention by the Egyptian chargé d'affaires, Bahá'í activities in Burundi are banned. [BW16:137]

The first International Bahá'í Youth Conference to be held in Botswana takes place in Mahalapye. [BW16:150]

Owing to the failure of the Indonesian Bahá'ís to obtain religious liberty, the Universal House of Justice instructs that the national convention not be held.

Owing to difficulties within the Bahá'í community, the National Spiritual Assembly of Thailand is disbanded.

The first Native Council takes place in Haines, Alaska, attended by 50 native Bahá'ís.

The Bahá'í Publishing Trust of Japan is established.

1974

The Bahá'í Publishing Trust of Malaysia is established.

7 Feb The construction of the Seat of the Universal House of Justice is initiated with the acceptance of the design conceived by architect Ḥusayn Amánat. [BW17:73]

4 Mar Following the arrest of more than 50 Bahá'ís in Iraq, their trial opens and the Bahá'ís are exonerated. [BW16:138]

- The Revolutionary Council is dissatisfied with this result and the case is ordered to be reopened in a military court, with the death sentence requested for all the detainees. [BW16:138]

Mar The Bahá'í Publishing Trust of the Philippines is established in Manila. [DM318]

21 Mar The Universal House of Justice launches the Five Year Plan. [BBD181; BBRSM159; BW16:107; VV17]

- For the message of the Universal House of Justice setting out the broad objectives of the Plan see BW16:107–9.

- For details of the national plans see BW16:111–29.

Riḍván The National Spiritual Assembly of Hong Kong is formed. [BW16:251]

- For picture see BW16:452.

The National Spiritual Assembly of Japan is formed with its seat in Tokyo. [BW16:233]

The National Spiritual Assembly of Morocco is formed.

The first local spiritual assembly of Kotzebue, an Iñupiat Eskimo community situated north of the Arctic Circle, is formed.

23 Apr At the trial of nearly 50 Bahá'ís in Bag͟hdád, the Iraqi military court sentences 13 men and one girl to life imprisonment, one man and two girls to 15 years' imprisonment, and two men and seven women to ten years' imprisonment; 13 Bahá'ís are fined and released. [BW16:138]

c. May The first National Youth Conference of Burma takes place during the visit of Hand of the Cause Amatu'l-Bahá Rúḥíyyih Khánum. [BW16:251]

20 May The Iraqi military court trying nearly 50 Bahá'ís hands down *in absentia* sentences of life imprisonment on ten Bahá'ís, two of whom are deceased and a number of whom are of other nationalities or Iraqis not resident in Iraq. [BW16:138]

- In the weeks following, 24 Bahá'ís have their property confiscated, one Bahá'í is sentenced to ten years' imprisonment and another to 20 years. [BW16:138]

Jun The first Alacalufe Indians to become Bahá'ís enrol in Puerto Eden, Chile. [BW16:215]

Aug The first Bahá'í to settle on Christmas Island, Stanley Foo, arrives from Malaysia.

The first local spiritual assembly in Andorra is formed at Andorra la Vella.

4–8 Aug The first International Youth Conference, the largest conference ever held in Hawaii to date, takes place in Hilo. [BW16:229]

- For picture see BW16:232.

11–18 Aug The first Teaching Conference of the Arctic and sub-Arctic regions of Europe take place in Tórshavn, Faroe Islands. [BW16:110]

18 Aug Laura Clifford Dreyfus-Barney, compiler of *Some Answered Questions*, dies in Paris. [BW16:296]

- For her obituary see BW16:535–8.

28 Aug–2 Sep The conference held in St Louis, Missouri, to launch the Five Year Plan in the United States attracts some 10,000 Bahá'ís, the largest gathering of Bahá'ís to take place anywhere in the world to date. [BW16:203; VV40]

11 Sep Annemarie Krüger arrives in Moldavia on the first of many teaching trips.

• In 1985 she is named a Knight of Bahá'u'lláh by the Universal House of Justice, although she never lived in the country.

1975

In the year

The first Bahá'í summer school to be held in Antigua takes place. [BW16:187]

• For picture see BW16:188.

Owing to the continuing ban on Bahá'í activities and institutions, the national spiritual assembly and all local spiritual assemblies are disbanded in Indonesia.

The ban imposed on the Bahá'í Faith in Burundi in 1974 is lifted. [BW16:137]

• Bahá'í activities continue to be restricted, particularly in provincial areas. [BW16:137]

The first international Quechua conference is held in Cusco, Peru, attended by Bahá'ís from Peru, Bolivia and Ecuador.

The Supreme Constitutional Court of Egypt decides that the 1960 decree of President Nasser banning all Bahá'í activities is constitutional and the application of the Bahá'ís for annulment of the decree is dismissed. [BW16:137]

The Bahá'í Publishing Trust of Fiji is established.

The Bahá'í Publishing Trust of Australia is established.

Following the creation of the Rastákhíz political party by the Sháh of Iran and the refusal of the Bahá'ís to join it, although membership in it is compulsory, Bahá'ís throughout Iran are put under pressure. [BW18:391]

• Many Bahá'ís lose their jobs. [BW18:391]

In Indonesia several Bahá'ís are arrested, given light sentences and released for violating the 1962 and 1972 bans on Bahá'í activity. [BW19:41]

• A few months later four Bahá'ís are sentenced to five years' imprisonment; they remain in prison for the full five years. [BW19:41]

Jan A Bahá'í is arrested in Iraq and sentenced to ten years' imprisonment. [BW16:138]

1 Jan Shidan and Susan Kouchekzadeh, an Iranian-British couple pioneering in Sierra Leone, arrive in Conakry, the first Bahá'ís to settle in Guinea.

2–4 Jan The first annual meeting of the Association for Bahá'í Studies is held at Cedar Glen, Bolton, Ontario. [BW17:198]

See also BBD201–2; VV23–5.

14 Jan The house of 'Abdu'lláh Páshá is purchased after lengthy and delicate negotiations. [BBD108; BW16:103, 133; BW17:82 DH73; VV39]

• For a history of the house see BW16:103–6.

Feb The first National Teaching Conference in Sierra Leone takes place in Bo. [BW16:172]

The first Bahá'í Women's Conference of the Solomon Islands takes place at Auki, Malaita Island, attended by more than 90 women. [BW16:282]

The Arab Boycott Office, at its meeting in Cairo, announces that the Bahá'í Faith has been placed on its blacklist. [BW16:136; BW17:78]

Feb–Aug Hand of the Cause Amatu'l-Bahá Rúḥíyyih Khánum sets out on the Green Light Expedition to visit the indigenous peoples of the Amazon Basin in South America. [VV30–2]

• For a pictorial description of the expedition see BW16:419–48.

5 Feb A strip of land facing the resting place of Shoghi Effendi is bought by the Universal House of Justice to ensure protection of the site. [BW16:134; BW17:82; VV22]

Mar The only Bahá'í to visit the continent in the 1970s, John R. Peiniger, an Australian, is stationed in Antarctica for a brief time.

Above: The *Queen Mary*, the boat used by Amatu'l-Bahá Rúḥíyyih Khánum on the Green Light Expedition

Below: Members of the Green Light Expedition consult with Bahá'ís of a Bush Negro village in Surinam

29 Mar The first Bahá'í Youth Conference of the Canary Islands is held in Santa Cruz. [BW16:313]

Riḍván The National Spiritual Assembly of Niger is formed with its seat in Niamey. [BW16:141]

The National Spiritual Assembly of Sierra Leone is formed with its seat in Freetown. [BW16:141]

The first national convention of Sierra Leone. Hand of the Cause Enoch Olinga is seated at the front centre

The National Spiritual Assembly of Togo is formed with its seat in Lomé. [BW16:141]

The National Spiritual Assembly of Upper West Africa is formed with its seat in Dakar, Senegal. [BW16:141]

The National Spiritual Assembly of The Gambia is formed with its seat in Banjul. [BW16:165]

The National Spiritual Assembly of Ethiopia is formed. [BW16:144]

The National Spiritual Assembly of Jordan is formed with its seat in Amman. [BW16:264]

• For picture see BW16:452.

The first local spiritual assembly to be elected among the Meo tribes, Laotian refugees in northern Thailand, is formed. [BW16:262]

25 Apr A revolution in Portugal removes the ban on Bahá'í meetings and teaching activities.

2 May The first teaching institute of the Bahamas takes place in Nassau. [BW16:207]

Jun Elti Kunak of Papua New Guinea is awarded the British Empire Medal for her work with women's clubs in the Bismarck Archipelago. [BW16:278]

5 Jun Excavation of the site of the Seat of the Universal House of Justice begins. [BW16: 133; BW18:465]

- See BW16:399–404 for an article on the Seat by architect Ḥusayn Amánat.
- See BW17:301 for the significance of the seat.

Elti Kunak

19 Jun–2 Jul Two Bahá'í women represent the Bahá'í International Community at the first World Conference on Women in Mexico City; nine Bahá'ís represent the Bahá'í International Community at the parallel NGO Tribune.

21 Jun Following the revolution in Portugal in April, the National Spiritual Assembly is officially recognized.

- The process of incorporation began in 1951.

Jul In Iraq, a partial amnesty reducing the terms of the Bahá'ís imprisoned by 15 per cent is granted. [BW16:138]

The first Katio Indians to become Bahá'ís enrol in northern Colombia. [BW16:217]

9–12 Jul The first International Bahá'í Youth Conference of Iceland takes place in Njardvik with youth from nine countries. [BW16:301]

c. Sep In Iraq, a young Bahá'í is detained, interrogated, beaten and asked to recant his faith when he specifies his religion on a form. [BW16:138]

• When he refuses to recant his faith he is tried by a revolutionary court and sentenced to ten years' imprisonment. [BW16:138]

Oct The New Era Rural Development Project, the first project of its kind in the world, begins in the villages around Panchgani, India. [BW17:227–8]

31 Oct The Secretary of Religious Affairs in the President's Office of Uganda informs the Bahá'ís that the Bahá'í Faith is not among those religions prohibited to practise in the country. [BW16:147]

Nov In Iran, the house of the maternal uncle of the Báb and the adjacent house in which the Báb was born are destroyed on the pretext that the sites need to be cleared. [BW17:79]

The land for the Samoan House of Worship is purchased on a site overlooking Apia. [BW18:104]

Dec The first International Youth School to be held in Rhodesia takes place near Bulawayo. [BW16:155]

The first National Teaching Conference to be held in Senegal takes place in Dakar. [BW16:175]

end of the year The Bahá'ís of the Central African Republic begin to televise regular semi-weekly programmes. [BW16:141]

1976

In the year The government of Equatorial Guinea outlaws all religions and the national spiritual assembly is dissolved.

• It is re-formed in 1984.

Following the conquest of South Vietnam by North Vietnam, an anti-religion policy is implemented and the Bahá'í Faith, along with all other religions, is banned.

The Bahá'í Publishing Trust of Norway is established.

Jan Bahá'ís in Jamaica initiate a weekly 15-minute radio programme. [BW16:186]

1976

10 Jan The most northerly-located local spiritual assembly in the world is formed in the Iñupiat community of Barrow, Alaska.

10–15 Jan The first National Bahá'í Children's School to be held in Rhodesia takes place in Salisbury. [BW16:155]

Feb The Bahá'í Publishing Trust of Korea is established. [BW16:237]

8 Mar The Bahá'í International Community is granted consultative status with the United Nations Children's Fund (UNICEF). [BW16:337–8; VV54]

24–5 Mar The first Continental Youth Conference of Western Asia takes place in Karachi, Pakistan. [BW16:265]

24 Apr Mark Tobey, Bahá'í and well-known American painter, dies in Basel, Switzerland. [VV119]

- For his obituary see BW17:401–4.

May Bahá'í activities in Mali are restricted by order of the government and the decree of recognition of the Faith suspended. [BW17:81]

7 May Saichiro Fujita, the second Japanese to become a Bahá'í, dies in Haifa. [BW17:406]

- For his obituary see BW17:406–8.

5–8 Jul An International Teaching Conference is held in Helsinki, Finland, attended by some 950 Bahá'ís. [BW17:81; VV33]

- For the message of the Universal House of Justice see BW17:129–30.

- For pictures see BW17:109, 112, 114–15.

9–11 Jul An International Youth Conference is held in Ivory Coast, attended by nearly 200 Bahá'ís. [BW17:150, 153]

23–5 Jul An International Teaching Conference is held in Anchorage, Alaska, attended by 1,005 Bahá'ís. [BW17:81]

- For the message of the Universal House of Justice see BW17:130–1.

• For pictures see BW17:110, 113, 116–17.

3–6 Aug An International Teaching Conference is held in Paris, attended by some 5,700 Bahá'ís. [BW17:81; DM416; VV33]

• For the message of the Universal House of Justice see BW17:131–2.

• For the message of Kurt Waldheim, Secretary-General of the United Nations, see BW17:140.

• For pictures see BW17:109, 117–19.

12 Sep His Highness Malietoa Tanumafili II of Western Samoa visits the resting place of Shoghi Effendi. [BW17:69; VV22]

15–17 Oct An International Teaching Conference is held in Nairobi, Kenya, attended by 1,363 Bahá'ís. [BW17:81; VV33]

• For the message of the Universal House of Justice see BW17:133–4.

• For pictures see BW17:110, 119–21.

6–7 Nov The first Canadian Bahá'í Native Council is held in Tyendinaga, Ontario. [BW17:162]

27–30 Nov An International Teaching Conference is held in Hong Kong, attended by 506 Bahá'ís. [BW17:81; VV33]

• For the message of the Universal House of Justice see BW17:135–6.

• For pictures see BW17:110, 111, 121–2.

Dec The first Bahá'í Winter School in Cyprus is held in Nicosia.

27 Dec The first local spiritual assembly in Dominica is formed in St George.

1977

In the year The Hemispheric Bahá'í Radio and Television Conference is held in Panama, with 125 participants from 24 countries. [BW17:219]

Participants at the Cyprus Winter School; Hand of the Cause Adelbert Mühlschlegel is in the centre

The National Spiritual Assembly of Thailand is re-formed.

The first Macuxi people to become Bahá'ís enrol in the northern state of Roraima, Brazil.

19–22 Jan An International Teaching Conference is held in Auckland, New Zealand, attended by 1,195 Bahá'ís. [BW17:81; VV33]

• For the message of the Universal House of Justice see BW17:136–7.

• For pictures see BW17:111, 122–4.

27–30 Jan An International Teaching Conference is held in Bahia, Brazil, attended by 1,300 Bahá'ís, the largest such gathering of Bahá'ís to date in Brazil. [BW17:81; VV33]

• For the message of the Universal House of Justice see BW17:137–8.

• For pictures see BW17:110, 124–5.

4–6 Feb An International Teaching Conference is held in Mérida, Mexico, attended by more than 2,000 Bahá'ís. [BW17:81; VV33]

• For the message of the Universal House of Justice see BW17:139.

• For pictures see BW17:112, 126–7.

Notes VV33 *says this was 2–6 Feb.*

24 Mar In a cabled message, the Universal House of Justice calls upon Bahá'í women around the world to arise and play an active role in the service of the Faith. [BW17:202]

• For the report of the response to this call see BW17:202–14.

Apr The first National Bahá'í Children's Conference of Samoa takes place. [BW17:211]

16–17 Apr The first annual Bahá'í Studies Seminar supported by the Departments of Religious Studies and of Sociology at the University of Lancaster, England, takes place. [BW18:204]

Riḍván The National Spiritual Assembly of Surinam and French Guiana is formed with its seat in Paramaribo. [BW16:219].

The National Spiritual Assembly of Upper Volta is formed with its seat in Ouagadougou. [BW17:141]

The National Spiritual Assembly of the Marshall Islands is formed with its seat in Majuro. [BW17:174]

The National Spiritual Assembly of the New Hebrides is formed with its seat in Port Vila. [BW17:186]

The National Spiritual Assembly of Greece is formed with its seat in Athens. [BW16:287; BW17:190]

May The Himalayan Conference is held in Gangtok, Sikkim. [BW17:180–2]

Paul and Jane Jensen arrive on Andros Island in the Bahamas, the first Bahá'ís to reside on the island.

14 May The house of a Bahá'í in Fáḍilábád, Iran, is attacked; the Bahá'í is killed and his sister severely injured. [BW18:391]

Notes BW17:79 *says this was June.*

1977

31 May Joe Rabess, the first Carib to become a Bahá'í, enrols in Dominica.

Jun At the behest of the Universal House of Justice, two conferences are held for Persian-speaking Bahá'ís resident in Europe, one in Germany and one in London. [BW17:194]

11 Jun The centenary of the termination of Bahá'u'lláh's confinement in 'Akká is commemorated at the World Centre. [BW17:64]

Hands of the Cause of God, members of the Universal House of Justice and members of the International Teaching Centre at the Garden of Riḍván to commemorate the centenary of the end of Bahá'u'lláh's confinement in 'Akká

Jul The first Bahá'í summer school of Ecuador is held in Cuenca. [BW17:170]

19 Jul The National Spiritual Assembly of Ecuador is granted permission to operate a radio station at Otavalo. [BW17:169]

12–14 Aug An International Bahá'í Youth Conference is held in Enugu, Nigeria, attended by over 250 Bahá'ís from 19 countries. [BW17:150, 153]

14 Sep The first local spiritual assembly in the Galapogos Islands is formed on Santa Cruz.

16 Sep In Uganda, 27 religious organizations are banned, including the Bahá'í Faith, and the Bahá'í House of Worship is closed. [BW17:81]

- The national spiritual assembly and all 1,550 local assemblies are dissolved. [BW17:141]

12 Oct The first Bahá'í educational and cultural radio station, HCRN–1 Radio Bahá'í del Ecuador, makes its inaugural broadcast in Spanish and Quechua. [BBD193; BW17:169, 215–17; BW19:120; VV77]

- For pictures see BW17:216, 218 and VV77.

See also *Hein,* RADIO BAHÁ Í ECUADOR.

13–16 Oct The Asian Bahá'í Women's Conference is held in New Delhi, attended by more than a thousand women from across Asia. [BW17:180]

- For picture see BW17:212.

17 Oct At the end of the Asian Bahá'í Women's Conference Hand of the Cause Amatu'l-Bahá Rúḥíyyih Khánum lays the foundation stone of the Mother Temple of the Indian Subcontinent. [BW17:85, 180, 368–70; VV35]

Dec The restoration of the house of 'Abdu'lláh Páshá begins. [BW17:84]

Properties confiscated by the Iraqi government belonging to individual Bahá'ís are returned; properties and funds belonging to the Faith are turned over to the Ministry of the Interior for disposal. [BW17:80]

The first International Conference of Bahá'í Women in South America is held in Lima, Peru, attended by 200 women from 12 countries. [BW17:172]

- For picture see BW17:211.

27–30 Dec The first Bahá'í summer school of Sierra Leone is held in Magburaka. [BW17:151]

1978

In the year The National Spiritual Assembly of Burundi is re-formed. [BW16:137; BW17:141]

The Bahá'ís of Vietnam are prohibited by the government from meeting and practising their religion. [BW17:81; BW19:50]

- Bahá'í centres throughout the country are closed or confiscated;
- The national ḥaẓíratu'l-quds in Ho Chi Minh City is seized and made into an orphanage;
- Two members of the national spiritual assembly are arrested and sent to 're-education' camps.
- One is released in 1982, owing to ill health.

The first local spiritual assembly in Bonaire is formed.

- It never functions and is dissolved in 1989.

See also *West*, LETTERS FROM BONAIRE.

In Iran, many local Bahá'í centres are seized by armed men of the revolutionary committees, along with files and membership lists. [BW17:79–80]

Ten Bahá'ís are killed in Iran, seven by mobs. [BW18:291]

- For the response of Bahá'í institutions to the persecution of the Bahá'ís in Iran see BW18:337.

15 Jan The first National Bahá'í Women's Conference of Niger takes place.

Feb The government of the Congo bans the majority of smaller religious groups, including the Bahá'í Faith; [BW17:141]

- The national ḥaẓíratu'l-quds is confiscated and the assemblies dissolved.

Mar The first Bahá'í-owned school in Pakistan, the New Day Montessori, opens in Karachi.

4 Mar Christaline Francis, the first woman of the Caribs to become a Bahá'í, enrols in Dominica.

Apr Dorothy Francis, a Salteaux Indian, is awarded the Order of Canada for her services to Canadian native peoples and her efforts to preserve their culture. [BW17:103; VV29]

• For a picture see BW17:103.

Riḍván The Universal House of Justice is elected for the fourth time at the International Convention held in Haifa. [BW17:293]

• For details of the International Convention and pictures see BW17:293–300.

The National Spiritual Assembly of Mauritania is formed with its seat in Nouakchott. [BW17:141; BW19:49]

The National Spiritual Assembly of Cyprus is formed with its seat in Nicosia. [BW17:190]

The first local assembly in the British Virgin Islands is formed on Tortola.

20 May The National Spiritual Assembly of the Bahamas is formed with its seat in Nassau. [BW17:162]

23 May The House of Worship in Wilmette is included in the register of historic places in the United States. [BW17:166, 375]

• For picture see BW17:165.

26 May The National Spiritual Assembly of the Mariana Islands is formed with its seat in Guam. [BW17:174–5; DM348, 386]

• For picture see DM387.

Jul In Niger, an announcement is made on the national radio banning 'the Bahá'ist sect and the Nineteen Day Feast' throughout the country; immediately, all Bahá'í administrative activities are stopped and the national spiritual assembly is dissolved. [BW17:147]

• Mr Djoneidi is called into police-headquarters in Niger for questioning and is held for three days; upon his release, unharmed, other Bahá'ís are also called in.

Aug An International Bahá'í Youth Conference is held in Yaoundé, Cameroon, attended by some 380 Bahá'ís from 19 countries. [BW17:150, 153]

4 Sep The Bahá'í Publishing Trust of Japan is established.

Dec Two hundred Bahá'í homes near Shíráz are burned and the Bahá'ís driven from them, property is stolen and many Bahá'ís are beaten. [BW17:79; BW19:42]

- At one point 700 Bahá'ís are homeless and their means of livelihood destroyed. [BW17:79]

Bahá'í homes in Andarún, Iran, are besieged; one Bahá'í is badly beaten. [BW18:275–6]

The first Bahá'í Winter School of Malta takes place. [BW17:192]

15 Dec A cabled message is sent to 93 national spiritual assemblies stating that the Bahá'ís in Iran and the Holy Places in Ṭihrán and Shíráz are in peril. [BW17:79]

23 Dec Helmut Winkelbach, a German Bahá'í, arrives in Bobrujsk, Belarus, and is named a Knight of Bahá'u'lláh. [ELA-D COMMITTEE OF GERMANY RECORDS]

28–30 Dec The West African Bahá'í Women's Conference is held in Monrovia, Liberia. [BW17:154]

1979

In the year Five Bahá'ís are killed in Iran, two by execution. [BW18:291]

- For the response of Bahá'í institutions to the persecution of the Bahá'ís in Iran see BW18:337–9.

The House of Bahá'u'lláh in Ṭihrán is confiscated by the revolutionary government of Iran. [BW17:79]

Bahá'í cemeteries across Iran are confiscated, including the cemetery in Ṭihrán, which contains the graves of several Hands of the Cause and other distinguished Bahá'ís and several thousand other graves of Bahá'ís.

• Many graves are desecrated and the gravestones smashed.

The Bahá'í cemetery at Shíráz is destroyed

The Síyáh-Chál in Ṭihrán and the houses of Quddús and Ḥujjat are seized and occupied by members of the revolutionary committees. [BW17:79–80]

The National Spiritual Assembly of Afghanistan is disbanded owing to persecution of the Bahá'ís and the political instability of the country.

12 Jan Bahá'í members of the Sádát-Maḥmúdí clan of the Buyr-Aḥmad tribe of central Iran are driven from their homes by other clan members. [BW18:271]

• For the report of this incident and its aftermath see BW18:271–4.

• For a picture see BW18:272.

27 Jan In Samoa, His Highness Malietoa Tanumafili II and Hand of the

Cause of God Amatu'l-Bahá Rúḥíyyih Khánum lay the cornerstone of the first Bahá'í House of Worship of the Pacific Islands. [BW17:188, 371; VV36]

- For the text of the address delivered by His Highness Malietoa Tanumafili II see BW17:372.
- For excerpts from the address of Hand of the Cause of God Amatu'l-Bahá Rúḥíyyih Khánum see BW17:373.
- For pictures see BW17:374.

Feb A mob of some 5,000 armed with hatchets, spades and pickaxes converge on Ḥisár, Iran, intent on harming the Bahá'ís; the mob is prevented from doing so. [BW18:275]

- Shortly afterwards the home of Mr Ma'naví is looted and he is carried off; it appears he was beaten to death. [BW18:275]

Revolutionary Guards raid the offices of Nawnahálán, a Bahá'í investment company, and the Umaná' Corporation, a foundation for the purchase and maintenance of Bahá'í properties, and impound the keys. [BW18:252]

- In the weeks following, the offices are occupied by the Revolutionary Guards and the staff are dismissed. [BW18:252]

In Iran, Bahá'í representatives meet with high-ranking clergy in Shíráz, Qum and Mashhad to combat the widespread accusation that the Bahá'ís of Iran had supported the regime of the Sháh. [BW18:252]

15 Feb The National Ḥaẓíratu'l-Quds of Iran is seized by the Revolutionary Guards. [BW18:250]

- All the records of the National Spiritual Assembly, including a membership list of all the Bahá'ís in Iran, are confiscated by the government. [BW19:43]

Mar Yúsif Subḥání, a well-known Bahá'í businessman, is imprisoned in Ṭihrán. [BW18:278]

21 Mar The Universal House of Justice outlines the broad goals of the

Seven Year Plan to be launched at Riḍván 1979. [BW18:81–5]

spring The House of Bahá'u'lláh in Tákur, Iran, is confiscated by the Revolutionary Government. [BW18:289]

Apr Revolutionary Guards in Iran occupy the House of the Báb in Shíráz and neighbouring Bahá'í properties, explaining that it is a temporary measure intended to protect the building. [BW17:79]

The ban against the Bahá'í Faith in Uganda is lifted and the House of Worship in Kampala is re-opened for worship. [BW17:141]

17 Apr The first local spiritual assembly in Greenland is formed in Nuuk.

The first Local Spiritual Assembly of Nuuk

20 Apr The Bahá'í World Centre reports that ten countries or territories have a Bahá'í population that exceeds one percent of the general population. [BW17:99]

Riḍván The Seven Year Plan is launched. [BBD181; BBRSM159; BW17:71]

The first local spiritual assembly in Lappland is formed in Kemi, Finland.

6 May Bernard Leach CBE, internationally known potter, artist and author, dies in St Ives, Cornwall. [BW18:669–71]

Bernard Leach

24 May Shaykh Muḥammad Muvaḥḥid, a well-known Bahá'í, is kidnapped in Ṭihrán. [BW18:254, 294]

summer In Iran, the offices of Nawnahálán and the Umaná' Corporation are taken over by Revolutionary Guards. [BW18: 252]

25–6 Aug An Administrative Committee for Uganda is appointed by the Universal House of Justice to prepare the Bahá'í community for the re-establishment of the national spiritual assembly.

Sep Bahár Vujdání is executed in Mahábád, Iran. [BW18: 255]

Revolutionary committees in Shahsavár, 'Ábádán and Tabríz, Iran, order the arrest of Bahá'ís. [BW18:255]

- Among those arrested are members of local spiritual assemblies. [BW18:255]
- Bahá'í homes in Tabríz are raided and literature seized. [BW18:255]

8–10 Sep The House of the Báb in Shíráz is attacked and substantially demolished by a crowd accompanied by 25 Revolutionary Guards

The House of the Báb is attacked

apparently under the clergyman in charge of the local religious endowments department. [BBD108; B111; BW18:253]

16 Sep Enoch Olinga – Hand of the Cause of God and Knight of Bahá'u'lláh – his wife and three of his children are murdered in Kampala, Uganda. [BBD172; BW18:633]

- For his obituary see BW18:618–35.

Oct The first Bahá'í summer school for Quechua-speakers is held in Cachaco, Imbabura, Ecuador. [BW17:170]

In Iran, Bahá'ís in the ministries of education, health and social administration are dismissed from their jobs. [BW18:255]

Nov Bahá'í meetings are prohibited in Shasavár, Iran. [BW18:255]

11 Nov Dr 'Alímurád Dávúdí, a member of the National Spiritual Assembly of Iran, is kidnapped in Ṭihrán and presumed dead. [BW18:254, 294]

Dec Work on the demolition of the House of the Báb in Shíráz is resumed and the building almost razed to the ground. [BW18:255]

'Aẓamatu'lláh Fahandizh is executed in Ṭihrán. [BW18:255]

The House of the Báb during demolition

Dec The Constitution of the Islamic Republic of Iran, from which all civil rights stem and which does not give recognition to the Bahá'í Faith, is adopted by referendum. [BI11]

29 Dec Raḥmatu'lláh Muhájir, Hand of the Cause of God and Knight of Bahá'u'lláh, dies in Quito, Ecuador. [BW18:486, 651]

- For his obituary see BW 18:651–9.

Hand of the Cause Dr Muhájir

See also *Muhájir*, DR MUHAJIR: HAND OF THE CAUSE OF GOD, KNIGHT OF BAHÁ'U'LLÁH.

end of the year In Iran, Nawnahálán and the Umaná' Corporation are stripped of their assets and non-Bahá'í directors, inimical to the aims of the companies, are appointed. [BW18:252]

1980

In the year The persecution of the Bahá'ís of Iran continues throughout the year. [BW18:92]

- Twenty-four Bahá'ís are executed or otherwise killed. [BW19: 229–30]

Notes BW18:291–2 *shows a slightly different, incorrect list.*

- For pictures of the martyrs see BW18:295–305 and BW19:236–46.

- For accounts of some of the martyrdoms see BW18:275–81.

- Twelve Bahá'ís disappear and are presumed dead. [BW19:235]

- For a list of resolutions adopted by the United Nations, regional bodies, national and provincial governments, and other actions taken, see BW18:92–6.

- For a list of the actions taken by the Bahá'í International Community, Bahá'í institutions and others see BW18:339–41, 415–17.

The first local spiritual assemblies in Guinea are formed.

Yee Wah Sing, the first Fiji-born person to become a Bahá'í in Fiji, enrols. [BN596:14]

Feb The persecution of the Bahá'ís in Iran enters a new, more dangerous phase. [BW18:255]

- Prominent Bahá'ís are abducted. [BW18:256]

- The homes of members of the National Spiritual Assembly are raided. [BW18:256]

12 Feb Hasan M. Balyuzi, Hand of the Cause of God, dies in London. [BW18:635; VV52]

- For his obituary see BW18:635–51 and SBBR5:XI-XX.

25 Feb Robert Hayden, much-honoured American poet, dies in Ann Arbor, Michigan. [BW18:717]

Robert Hayden

• For his obituary see BW18:715–17.

See also *Hatcher*, FROM THE AURORAL DARKNESS: THE LIFE AND POETRY OF ROBERT HAYDEN.

Mar The first Bahá'í Summer School of the Cameroon Republic is held in Victoria. [BW18:166]

Apr Eight Bahá'ís are arrested in Tabríz; five are released after signing an agreement not to take part in Bahá'í administrative activities. [BW18:256]

• Two of the others, members of the local assembly, are put on trial and executed on 14 July 1982. [BW18:256]

Riḍván The National Spiritual Assembly of Transkei is formed with its seat in Umtata. [BW18:107, 163]

2 May The Bahá'ís of India commemorate the centenary of the founding of the Bahá'í Faith in their country with a reception attended by about 400 guests, including the Minister of Foreign Affairs. [BW18:246–7]

The first Bahá'í International Conference on Health and Healing is held in Ottawa, Canada, under the sponsorship of the Association for Bahá'í Studies. [BW18:201]

14 Jul Two of the Bahá'ís arrested in Tabríz in April are executed. [BW18:256]

29 Jul Adelbert Mühlschlegel, Hand of the Cause of God, dies at his pioneer post in Athens, Greece. [BW18:613; VV52]

- For his obituary see BW18:611–13.

21 Aug The members of the National Spiritual Assembly of Iran are arrested; they disappear without trace and are presumed dead. [BW19:43, 235]

The National Spiritual Assembly of Iran before its members disappear in August 1980

Sep Additional land is acquired in the southwestern area of the Ḥaram-i-Aqdas, permitting the completion of the fourth quadrant. [BW18:99; DH122]

1980

The European Parliament, the Parliamentary Assembly of the Council of Europe and the United Nations Sub-Commission on Prevention of Discrimination and Protection of Minorities adopt resolutions on the plight of the Bahá'ís in Iran. [BW19:38]

Building work begins on the Samoan House of Worship. [BW18:104]

17 Oct Leonora Armstrong, the 'spiritual mother of South America' and the first Latin American pioneer, dies in Bahia, Brazil. [BW18:738; VV32]

• For her obituary see BW18:733–8.

20 Nov Abu'l-Qásim Faizí, Hand of the Cause of God, dies in Haifa. [BW18:659; VV52]

• For his obituary see BW18:659–65.

Hand of the Cause Abu'l-Qásim Faizí

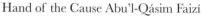

1981

In the year The persecution of the Bahá'ís of Iran continues throughout the year. [BW18:92]

- Forty-six Bahá'ís are executed and two assassinated. [BW18:292–3; BW19:230–1]

Seven Bahá'ís executed in Hamadán on 14 June 1981

- For pictures of the martyrs see BW18:295–305 and BW19:236–46.
- For accounts of some of the martyrdoms see BW18:277–8, 281–4.
- For excerpts from the wills of some of the martyrs see BW18:284–9.
- For a list of resolutions adopted by the United Nations, regional bodies, national and provincial governments, and other actions taken, see BW18:92–6 and BW19:44–6.
- For a list of the actions taken by the Bahá'í International Community, Bahá'í institutions and others see BW18:341–5, 417–20.

The European branch office of the Bahá'í International Community is established in Geneva. [BW19:33; VV54]

The Comunicación Intercambio y Radiodifusión Bahá'í para America Latina y el Caribe (CIRBAL) is established by the Universal House of Justice to promote the development of Bahá'í radio and mass media activities in Latin America. [BW19:59]

The site of the House of the Báb, destroyed by a mob in 1979, is made into a road and public square. [BBD108]

The National Assembly of Zaire is dissolved temporarily and three administrative committees are appointed in its place. [BW19:62, 147]

Apr In Pakistan a constitutional amendment names the Bahá'í Faith among the non-Muslim faiths of the country, thus according it legal recognition. [BW18:107; VV67]

The Canadian Association for Studies on the Bahá'í Faith is renamed the Association for Bahá'í Studies. [BBD202; VV24–5]

Riḍván The National Spiritual Assembly of Bophuthatswana is formed with its seat in Mmbatho. [BW18:107, 163]

The National Spiritual Assembly of South West Africa/Namibia is formed with its seat in Windhoek. [BW18:107, 163]

The National Spiritual Assembly of South WestAfrica/Namibia

The National Spiritual Assembly of Bermuda is formed with its seat in Hamilton. [BW18:107, 171]

The National Spiritual Assembly of the Leeward Islands is formed with its seat in St John's, Antigua. [BW18:107, 171]

The National Spiritual Assembly of the Windward Islands is formed with its seat in Kingstown, St Vincent. [BW18:171]

The National Spiritual Assembly of Tuvalu is formed with its seat in Funafuti. [BW18:107; BW19:62]

The National Spiritual Assembly of Uganda is re-formed after a period of 19 months during which the Faith was banned. [BW18:107, 163]

23 May Helmut Winkelbach, Knight of Bahá'u'lláh for Belarus, marries Olga Grigorevna Dolganova, a Russian, their wedding ceremony being the first Bahá'í wedding in the Soviet Union.

Jul The reconstituted Bahá'í Publishing Trust of Uganda meets for the first time. [BW18:112]

An International Chinese Teaching Committee is appointed by the Universal House of Justice. [BW19:76]

10 Dec The Universal House of Justice announces that the House of Bahá'u'lláh in Tákur, Núr, Iran, confiscated by the Revolutionary Government in the spring of 1979, has been totally demolished and the site offered for sale by auction. [BW18:289; BW19:42]

27 Dec Eight of the nine members of the National Spiritual Assembly of Iran are executed. [BI13; BW19:43]

1982

In the year The persecution of the Bahá'ís of Iran continues throughout the year. [BW18:92]

- Thirty-two Bahá'ís are executed or otherwise killed. [BW19:232]

Notes BW18:293–4 *shows a slightly different, incorrect list.*

- For pictures of the martyrs see BW18:295–305 and BW19:236–46.

• For a list of resolutions adopted by the United Nations, regional bodies, national and provincial governments, and other actions taken, see BW18:92–6 and BW19:44–6.

• For a list of the actions taken by the Bahá'í International Community, Bahá'í institutions and others see BW18:345–52, 420–4.

One of the members of the National Spiritual Assembly of Vietnam sent to a 're-education' camp is released owing to ill health; the other remains in detention. [BW18:96]

The Canadian Bahá'í International Development Service is established. [BBRSM154]

The National Spiritual Assembly of Laos is re-established after a lapse of six years. [BW18:96]

Jan After a lapse of six years, the first formal meeting of the Spiritual Assembly of Laos is held at the Bahá'í Centre. [BW19:49]

9–12 Apr The first conference on Bahá'í scholarship to be held in Australia takes place at Yerrinbool Bahá'í School in New South Wales. [BW18:202]

10–11 Apr The Bahá'í International Health Agency is established as an affiliate of the Association for Bahá'í Studies. [BW18:201; VV25]

The National Spiritual Assembly of Panama petitions its government to issue a stamp in commemoration of the dedication of the Mother Temple of Latin America. [BW18:172–3]

Riḍván The National Spiritual Assembly of Nepal is re-formed. [BW18:107, 181]

14 May Amoz Gibson, a member of the Universal House of Justice from 1963 until 1982, dies in Haifa. [BW18:669; VV52]

• For his obituary see BW18:665–9.

25 May The Subcommittee on Human Rights and International Organizations of the Foreign Affairs Committee of the United States House of Representatives hears the testimony of six witnesses concerning the persecution of the Bahá'ís in Iran. [BW18:172]

19–20 Jun The teaching project *Camino Del Sol* (Trail of Light), comprising indigenous believers from North America, is formed on the Navajo Reservation in Arizona, United States. [BW18:239]

Amoz Gibson

- The team travels through Central and South America in a programme of cultural exchange. [BW18:172]
- For a report of the project and pictures see BW18:239–45 and BW19:74–6.

25–7 Jun An International Conference to mark the fiftieth anniversary of the passing of the Greatest Holy Leaf is held in Dublin, Ireland, attended by some 1,900 Bahá'ís from 60 countries. [BW18:100; VV61]

- For the message of the Universal House of Justice see BW18:156–7.

Members of the Universal House of Justice carry the coffin of Amoz Gibson

Hand of the Cause John Robarts addresses the International Conference in Dublin

• For a pictorial report see BW18:138–40.

27 Jun The Bahá'í Youth Academy is established in Panchgani, India. [BW18:230–2]

15 Jul In commemoration of the fiftieth anniversary of the passing of Bahíyyih Khánum, the Greatest Holy Leaf, Bahá'ís at the World Centre pray at midnight at the Shrine of the Báb and at the tomb of the Greatest Holy Leaf; commemoration services are held in many parts of the world. [BW18:53, 102]

• For a list of references to the Greatest Holy Leaf found in English-language works see BW18:55–6.

• For a list of works published to commemorate this anniversary see BW18:57–8.

• For an article about her life and service see BW18:68–73.

• Five international conferences and their satellites, held in June, August and September, are dedicated to her memory. [BW18:102]

17 Jul A seminar on the life of Bahíyyih Khánum, the Greatest Holy Leaf, is conducted at the Seat of the Universal House of Justice, the first gathering held in the building. [BW18:53–4; VV62]

• For excerpts from the talk by 'Alí Nakhjavání on this occasion see BW18:59–66.

Aug Shakontala ('Shaku') Aswani, the first Gibraltan to become a Bahá'í, enrols in Northern Ireland, shortly afterwards returning to Gibraltar.

6–8 Aug An International Conference to mark the fiftieth anniversary of the passing of the Greatest Holy Leaf is held in Quito, Ecuador, attended by some 1,450 Bahá'ís from 43 countries. [BW18:100; VV61]

• For the message of the Universal House of Justice see BW18:157–8.

• For a pictorial report see BW18:141–3.

19–22 Aug An International Conference to mark the fiftieth anniversary of the passing of the Greatest Holy Leaf is held in Lagos, Nigeria, attended by some 1,110 Bahá'ís from 46 countries representing some 90 ethnic groups. [BW18:100; VV61]

• For the message of the Universal House of Justice see BW18:158–9.

• For a pictorial report see BW18:144–6.

2–5 Sep An International Conference to mark the fiftieth anniversary of the passing of the Greatest Holy Leaf is held in Canberra, Australia, attended by some 2,400 Bahá'ís, twice as many as were expected, from 45 countries. [BW18:100; VV61]

• For the message of the Universal House of Justice see BW18:159–60.

• For a pictorial report see BW18:147–50.

An International Conference to mark the fiftieth anniversary of the passing of the Greatest Holy Leaf is held in Montreal, Canada, attended by 9,400 Bahá'ís from 101 countries. [BW18:100; VV61]

• For the message of the Universal House of Justice see BW18:161–2.

• For a pictorial report see BW18:151–4.

Nov The West African Centre for Bahá'í Studies is established in Nigeria. [BW18:167; BW19:366]

- For a report of its activities see BW19:366–7.

3 Dec Paul Haney, Hand of the Cause of God, dies in Haifa in an automobile accident. [BW18:617; VV52]

- For his obituary see BW18:613–18.

1983

In the year The persecution of the Bahá'ís of Iran continues throughout the year. [BW18:92; BW19:177–226]

- Twenty-nine Bahá'ís are executed or otherwise killed. [BW19: 232–3]
- For pictures of the martyrs see BW18:295–305 and BW19:236–46.
- For a list of resolutions adopted by the United Nations, regional bodies, national and provincial governments, and other actions taken, see BW18:92–6 and BW19:44–6.
- For a list of the actions taken by the Bahá'í International Community, Bahá'í institutions and others see BW18:352–6, 424–5.

The Association for Bahá'í Studies, German-Speaking Europe, is established in Austria. [BW19:357–8]

The Association for Bahá'í Studies, India, is established. [BW19: 360]

The Association for Bahá'í Studies, English-Speaking Europe, is established in the Republic of Ireland.

- Responsibility for the Association is transferred to the United Kingdom in 1989.

The Association for Bahá'í Studies of Francophone Europe is established in Switzerland.

c. Jan–Feb The Seat of the Universal House of Justice is completed; the Universal House of Justice formally occupies it. [BBD204; BW19:23; VV62]

- For a description and history of the building see BW19:24–6.

The Seat of the Universal House of Justice

• For pictures see BW18:466–72.

Mar Five local and two pioneer Bahá'ís are arrested, interrogated and held briefly in prison in Mauritania. [BW19:49]

• The National Assembly is dissolved. [BW19:49]

The first International Youth Camp of Surinam is held in Nw. Nickerie, attended by 130 Bahá'ís. [BW18:176]

Apr The Government of Morocco prohibits all Bahá'í meetings. [BW19:49]

Riḍván The renovation of the House of 'Abdu'lláh Pá<u>sh</u>á in 'Akká is completed. [BW18:77]

• Delegates attending the fifth International Convention are the first pilgrims to visit it. [BW18:77]

The central hall of the newly renovated House of 'Abdu'lláh Pá<u>sh</u>á

• For pictures see BW18:78–80.

The National Spiritual Assembly of Dominica is formed with its seat in Roseau. [BW18:107, 171]

The National Spiritual Assembly of St Lucia is formed with its seat in Castries. [BW18:107, 171]

The National Spiritual Assembly of St Vincent and Grenada is formed. [BW18:107]

29 Apr–2 May The Universal House of Justice is elected for the fifth time at the International Convention held in Haifa.

• The National Spiritual Assembly of Iran is unable to attend but sends 133 red roses as its gift to its sister Assemblies. [BW18:461]

• For a report of the Convention see BW18:461–4.

• See BW18:462, 464 for pictures.

May The number of members of the International Teaching Centre is raised to nine. [BW19:27]

23 May A five year term for the Counsellor members of the International Teaching Centre is established. [BW19:27]

18 Jun In S͟híráz, 10 Bahá'í women ranging in age from 17 to 57 are hanged after months of imprisonment and torture. [BW19:180; VV56]

Below: Four of the women hanged in S͟híráz in June 1983

Clockwise from top left: S͟hírín Dálvand, 'Izzat Jánami Is͟hráqí, Símín Ṣábirí Is͟hráqí, Mahs͟híd Nírúmand

• For the story of the martyrs see BW19:180–7.

• For their obituaries see BW19:596–607.

• For pictures of the martyred women see BW19:240–1.

24 Jun In response to the hanging of 10 Bahá'í women in Shíráz, the Universal House of Justice addresses a cable to the Bahá'í youth throughout the world, urging them to re-dedicate themselves to the Cause. [BW19:187–8, 297]

Jul The Office of Social and Economic Development is opened at the Bahá'í World Centre. [AWH8; BBD70; BBRSM154; BW19:58; VV78]

• See BW19:351–5 for a survey of Bahá'í social and economic projects.

5–7 Aug The first Los Angeles Bahá'í History Conference is held at the University of California at Los Angeles. [BW19:369–70]

29 Aug The Bahá'í Faith is banned in Iran and membership of Bahá'í institutions made a criminal offence. [BW19:43]

• The National Spiritual Assembly dissolves all Bahá'í institutions throughout the country. [BW19:43]

3 Sep The National Spiritual Assembly of Iran sends an open letter to the Prosecutor General of the Islamic Revolution refuting the false charges made against the Bahá'ís and informing him of their willingness to obey the government. [BW19:43]

• The National Spiritual Assembly is dissolved. [BW19:62]

20 Oct The Universal House of Justice outlines the Bahá'í principles of social and economic development in a letter addressed to the Bahá'ís of the world. [AWH6–10; BW19:153]

• For the response of the Bahá'í world to the letter see BW19:112–13.

See also *Vick,* SOCIAL AND ECONOMIC DEVELOPMENT: A BAHÁ'Í APPROACH.

21 Oct The Republic of Panama issues a postage stamp bearing the picture of the House of Worship in Panama. [BW19:157]

Dec Bahá'ís are arrested in Mohammadieh and Casablanca, Morocco. [BW19:49]

- The Bahá'ís in Mohammadieh are convicted of violating the ban on Bahá'í meetings, are sentenced to two years' imprisonment but are released. [BW19:49]

1984

In the year The persecution of the Bahá'ís of Iran continues throughout the year. [BW19:177–226]

- Thirty Bahá'ís are executed or otherwise killed. [BW19:233–4]
- For pictures of the martyrs see BW18:295–305 and BW19:236–46.
- For a list of resolutions adopted by the United Nations, regional bodies, national and provincial governments and other actions taken, see BW19:44–6.

Four Bahá'ís, one of whom had already spent five years in prison, are imprisoned in Indonesia, convicted of membership in a banned religious organization, with teaching the Bahá'í Faith and with insulting Islam. [BW19:42]

- The prison terms range from one to five years. [BW19:42]

The first Bahá'í university, Universidad Núr, opens in Santa Cruz, Bolivia. [VV82–3]

3 Jan The Universal House of Justice addresses a letter to the Bahá'í youth of the world encouraging them to volunteer a period of service to the Bahá'í Faith. [AWH14–17; BW19:297–8, 299, 311–13; VV116]

Riḍván The National Spiritual Assembly of Equatorial Guinea is re-formed with its seat in Malabo. [BW19:62, 147]

- See BW19:521 for picture.

The National Spiritual Assembly of the Andaman and Nicobar Islands is formed with its seat in Port Blair. [BW19:62, 162]

• See BW19:520 for picture.

The National Spiritual Assembly of the Canary Islands is formed with its seat in Santa Cruz. [BW19:62, 169]

• See BW19:520 for picture.

The National Spiritual Assembly of Cape Verde is formed with its seat in Praia. [BW19:62, 147]

• See BW19:521 for picture.

The National Spiritual Assembly of French Guiana is formed with its seat in Cayenne. [BW19:62, 155]

• See BW19:522 for picture.

The National Spiritual Assembly of Gabon is formed with its seat in Libreville. [BW19:62, 147]

• See BW19:522 for picture.

The National Spiritual Assembly of Grenada is formed with its seat in St George's. [BW19:62, 155]

• See BW19:523 for picture.

The National Spiritual Assembly of Martinique is formed with its seat in Fort-de-France. [BW19:62, 155]

• See BW19:523 for picture.

The National Spiritual Assembly of Yemen (North) is formed. [BW19:524]

Delegates at the United States National Convention petition the Universal House of Justice requesting that the law of Ḥuqúqu'lláh be made binding on the American Bahá'ís. [AWH30; ZK146–77]

• The Universal House of Justice replies that it is not yet the time to take this step. [AWH30]

Jun A Bahá'í in Tetuan, Morocco, is arrested and sentenced to three years' imprisonment for violating the 1983 ban on Bahá'í meetings. [BW19:49]

• An appeal to the Supreme Court is unsuccessful. [BW19:49]

The Association for Bahá'í Studies, Australia, is established in Perth. [BW19:356]

4 Jun Vladimir Malai, the first Moldovan to become a Bahá'í in Moldova, enrols.

30 Aug–2 Sep An International Teaching Conference is held to coincide with the dedication of the House of Worship at Apia, Western Samoa. [BW19:548–54; VV64]

• For a report of the conference see BW19:548–54.

• For the message of the Universal House of Justice see BW19:555–6.

• For pictures see BW19:475, 547–57 and VV64.

1 Sep The House of Worship in Apia, Western Samoa, the Mother Temple of the Pacific, is dedicated in the presence of Hand of the Cause of God Amatu'l-Bahá Rúḥíyyih Khánum, Hand of the Cause Dr Ugo Giachery, His Highness Malietoa Tanumafili II and more than a thousand Bahá'ís from 45 countries. [BW19:100–1; VV64]

The House of Worship in Apia, Samoa

- For a report of the dedication see BW19:552–3.

- For the text of the address of His Highness Malietoa Tanumafili II see BW19:556.

- For pictures see BW19:553 and VV64.

Oct In Tunisia, the activities of the Faith are curtailed and Bahá'ís are interrogated. [BW19:50]

21 Oct His Excellency Chaim Herzog, President of the State of Israel, pays an official visit to the Bahá'í World Centre at the invitation of the Universal House of Justice. [BW19:377; VV88]

- This is the first visit by a head of state to the Seat of the House of Justice. [VV88]

Nov The International Bahá'í Refugee Office, responsible for coordinating efforts to resettle Iranian Bahá'í refugees, is established by the National Spiritual Assembly of Canada at the request of the Universal House of Justice. [BW19:50]

- For a report of the work of the Office see BW19:50–3.

9 Nov The Universal House of Justice meets with representatives of the Bahá'í International Community and various national spiritual assemblies at the World Centre.

16 Nov Shu'á'u'lláh 'Alá'í, Hand of the Cause of God, dies in Scottsdale, Arizona. [BW19:594; VV123]

Notes BW19:159 *says this was 17 November.*

- For his obituary see BW19:593–5.

28–30 Dec The first National Bahá'í Youth Conference to be held in Greece takes place in Athens. [BW19:319]

1985

In the year The persecution of the Bahá'ís of Iran continues throughout the year. [BW19:177–226]

Members of the Universal House of Justice with members of the Bahá'í International Community and various National Assemblies

• Seven Bahá'ís are executed or otherwise killed. [BW19:234]

• For pictures of the martyrs see BW18:295–305 and BW19:236–46.

• For the actions taken by the Bahá'í International Community see BW19:39.

A regional office of the Bahá'í International Community affiliated with the Economic and Social Commission for Asia and the Pacific (ESCAP) is established in Bangkok. [BW19:161–2]

To support the United Nations International Youth Year Bahá'í communities undertake a variety of activities. [BW19:301–10]

Annemarie Krüger, who began travelling to Moldavia to teach the Bahá'í Faith in 1974, is named a Knight of Bahá'u'lláh by the Universal House of Justice, although she never lived in the country.

23 Jan The plans of the Universal House of Justice for the International Year of Peace are outlined to national spiritual assemblies. [AHW31–4; VV86]

23 Feb Forty-one Bahá'ís from various parts of Egypt are arrested, charged with offences against laws introduced in 1960 banning activities of Bahá'í institutions. [BW19:41, 283]

- For an account of the event, its aftermath and the press campaign surrounding it see BW19:283–7.

5–8 Apr An International Youth Conference to support the United Nations International Youth Year is held in Bophuthatswana, attended by 198 people. [BW19:300]

Riḍván The National Spiritual Assembly of Ciskei is formed with its seat in Mdantsane. [BW19:62]

Notes BW19:147 *says the seat is in Bisho. However, it was not possible to obtain a site in Bisho, the capital, and so the offices of the National Spiritual Assembly were built in Mdantsane in 1990.*

- See BW19:524 for picture.

The National Spiritual Assembly of the Cook Islands is formed with its seat in Rarotonga. [BW19:62, 168]

The National Spiritual Assembly of Mali is formed with its seat in Bamako. [BW19:62, 147]

The National Spiritual Assembly of the Cook Islands

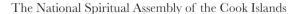

• See BW19:525 for picture.

The National Spiritual Assembly of Mozambique is formed with its seat in Maputo. [BW19:62, 147]

• See BW19:526 for picture.

The National Spiritual Assembly of the Western Caroline Islands is formed with its seat in Colonia, Yap. [BW19:62, 168]

• See BW19:526 for picture.

The National Spiritual Assembly of the Eastern Caroline Islands is formed with its seat in Pohnpei. [BW19:168]

30 Apr–1 May The first annual conference of the Association for Bahá'í Studies, Brazil, takes place in Saõ Paulo. [BW19:358]

May The Office of Public Information is established at the Bahá'í World Centre. [BBD38; BW19:58–9; VV54]

7 May The court hearings open on the cases of the Bahá'ís arrested in Egypt in February on charges of disregarding the 1960 ban on Bahá'í activity. [BW19:285]

• The cases are adjourned until 7 October to allow time for the defence lawyer to study the files numbering about a thousand pages. [BW19:285]

Jul Three Bahá'í youths in Mentawai are imprisoned for having married according to Bahá'í law. [BW19:42]

3–7 Jul An International Youth Conference to support the United Nations International Youth Year is held in Columbus, Ohio, United States, attended by more than 3,200 youth from 42 nations. [BW19:300]

15–26 Jul Ten representatives of the Bahá'í International Community attend the World Conference to Review and Appraise the Achievements of the United Nations Decade for Women and Forum '85 in Nairobi. [BW19:147–8, 412; VV28–9]

• For a report of the Bahá'í participation see BW19:412–15.

• For pictures see BW19:413, 415.

26–9 Jul An International Youth Conference to support the United Nations International Youth Year is held in Antwerp, Belgium, attended by some 1,450 youth from 45 nations. [BW19:301]

• For picture see BW19:315.

Aug An International Youth Conference to support the United Nations International Youth Year is held in Molepolole, Botswana, attended by 119 youth from six countries. [BW19:300]

• For picture see BW19:320.

An International Youth Conference to support the United Nations International Youth Year is held in New Delhi, India, attended by more than 550 youth from 24 countries. [BW19:300]

1–4 Aug An International Youth Conference to support the United Nations International Youth Year is held in Port Dickson, Malaysia, attended by 1,300 youth from 15 countries, the largest gathering of Bahá'ís ever held in Malaysia. [BW19:301]

2–5 Aug An International Youth Conference to support the United Nations International Youth Year is held in Lima, Peru, attended by 500 youth from 18 countries and representing four native tribes. [BW19:300]

• For picture see BW19:322.

8–11 Aug An International Youth Conference to support the United Nations International Youth Year is held in Kauai, Hawaii, attended by 300 youth from nine Pacific countries. [BW19:301]

• For picture see BW19:321.

Sep The first Bahá'í Studies conference in Hawaii takes place at the national Bahá'í centre. [BW19:360]

The first National Bahá'í Youth Conference in Nepal takes place, attended by 120 Bahá'ís, the largest Bahá'í gathering ever held in the country. [BW19:161]

Notes VV74 *says this was in October.*

7 Oct The court cases against the Bahá'ís arrested in Egypt for contravening the 1960 ban on Bahá'í activities, due to be heard today, are adjourned until 3 February 1986 owing to adverse and unfair reports appearing in today's newspapers. [BW19:286]

18 Oct The remains of Mírzá Muḥammad-Qulí and 11 members of his family are re-interred in a new Bahá'í cemetery near the original grave site. [BW19:56]

19 Oct The Association for Bahá'í Studies, Chile, is established in Santiago. [BW19:358–9]

24 Oct On the fortieth anniversary of the United Nations and in anticipation of the United Nations International Year of Peace, the Universal House of Justice addresses a statement to the peoples of the world, *The Promise of World Peace*, on the theme of universal peace. [BBD174, 187–8; BW19:139, 155; VV59, 86–8]

- Within six months national spiritual assemblies present copies to 167 world leaders, including 140 to leaders of independent countries. [BW19:139, 334–6]
- For pictures see BW19:337–44.
- For text see BW19:324–33.

22 Nov *The Promise of World Peace* is presented to the Secretary-General of the United Nations Javier Perez de Cuellar by Hand of the Cause Amatu'l-Bahá Rúḥíyyih Khánum and representatives of the Bahá'í International Community. [BW19:33, 382; VV87]

13 Dec For the first time, the United Nations General Assembly adopts a resolution on the human rights situation in Iran which contains specific references to the Bahá'ís. [BW19:38; VV55]

27 Dec–2 Jan 1986 The Universal House of Justice convenes a Counsellors' Conference at the Bahá'í World Centre. [AWH39; BW19:29; VV122]

- The gathering, held in the Seat of the Universal House of Justice, consulted on the opportunities and challenges facing the Bahá'í world community. [BW19:29]
- See BW19:494, 504 for pictures.

The Counsellors' Conference

1986

In the year The persecution of the Bahá'ís of Iran continues throughout the year. [BW19:177–226]

- One Bahá'í, 15-year-old Paymán Subḥání, is killed. [BW19:225–6, 234]
- For his picture see BW19:246.
- For the actions taken by the Bahá'í International Community see BW19:38.

Hundreds of members of the Aeta tribe in Tarlac and Pampanga, Philippines, become Bahá'ís. [BINS158:13]

Community-based Bahá'í health care programmes are launched in Kenya, Uganda and Swaziland, spearheaded by Dr Ethel Martens of Canada.

The Sri Lanka post office issues a commemorative postage stamp featuring the Bahá'í-sponsored World Religion Day. [BINS176:4]

The first local spiritual assembly of San Salvador Island, mentioned in the *Tablets of the Divine Plan* as Watling Island, is formed.

The Bahá'í Association for Arts (BAFA) is formed with its base in the Netherlands.

2 Jan The Universal House of Justice ends the Counsellors' Conference at the Bahá'í World Centre by announcing in a letter that the Bahá'í world has entered the fourth epoch in the Formative Age of the Cause. [AWH39–42; BBD79, 85; BW19:29; VV91]

- The seven major objectives of the Six Year Plan, to begin at Riḍván 1986, are outlined. [AWH40]

- The year from Riḍván 1992 is designated a Holy Year. [AWH40–1]

21 Jan The Islamic Research Academy at the Azhar University in Cairo publishes in a number of newspapers a lengthy opinion about the Bahá'í Faith in advance of the court cases of Bahá'ís due to be heard in February. [BW19:286]

- For a refutation of this statement by the Bahá'í International Community, see BW19:288–96.

13 Mar The United Nations Commission on Human Rights adopts a resolution asking its chairman to appoint a new special representative to report to the General Assembly in November 1986 on the human rights situation in Iran, including the situation of the Bahá'ís. [BINS153:12]

Apr The first province-wide gathering of Bahá'í youth in Northern Ireland convenes. [BINS154:15]

20 Apr The Seven Year Plan is successfully completed. [BW19:23]

- For a graph showing the growth of the Bahá'í Faith in this period see BW19:23.

- For statistics on the Bahá'í Faith at this date see BINS155:13 and BW19:61–98, 112–46.

1986

21 Apr The Six Year Plan is launched. [AWH40, 42–4; BBRSM159; VV91]

23 May Fourteen State Bahá'í Councils are elected in India by members of local spiritual assemblies. [BW19:162; VV99–100]

- For a description of the Councils and their responsibilities see BW19:162–4.

Jul Jack Malardy, 88-year-old tribal leader of the Karradjarrie people of Australia, and his wife Lilly become Bahá'ís in Lagrange, Australia. [BINS156:3; BINS179:1]

18–24 Jul The European Bahá'í Youth Movement is launched at the Bahá'í Youth School, Landegg Conference Centre, Switzerland. [BINS157:9–10; BINS158:10]

3–4 Aug The Honourable Sir Thomas David, Prime Minister of the Cook Islands, at his request, consults with the Universal House of Justice at the Bahá'í World Centre about world peace, 'the most concrete response to date by a political leader to the Peace Statement'. [BINS157:1; VV88]

- For picture see VV86.

The Honourable Sir Thomas David, Prime Minister of the Cook Islands, front row centre, with members of the Universal House of Justice

6 Aug The Indo-Chinese Refugee Committee of Thailand estimates that five to six thousand people are Bahá'ís in the refugee camps on the Thai border. [BINS158:17]

The Brazilian Society of Physicians for Peace is formed by Bahá'í physicians in Pôrto Alegre at a ceremony attended by 120 medical professionals. [BINS159:2–3]

19 Oct Lorraine Kahn of Pine Springs, Arizona, is elected a delegate to the United States National Convention, the first Navajo woman to serve in this capacity. [BINS161:19]

13 Nov Zikrullah Khadem (Dhikru'lláh Khádem), Hand of the Cause of God, dies in Skokie, Illinois. [VV123; ZK151]

See also *Khadem,* ZIKRULLAH KHADEM: THE ITINERANT HAND OF THE CAUSE OF GOD.

Dec The National Spiritual Assembly of Mauritania and all ten local spiritual assemblies in the country are dissolved.

7 Dec Radio Bahá'í Liberia, the first Bahá'í radio station in Africa, makes its test broadcast. [BINS164:6]

24 Dec The House of Worship in New Delhi, India, is dedicated in the presence of Hand of the Cause Amatu'l-Bahá Rúḥíyyih Khánum and more than 8,000 Bahá'ís from all continents. [AWH47; BINS161; BW19:102; VV92]

• See VV93–4 for pictures.

1987

In the year The first conference on the production of Bahá'í literature in Spanish is held in Argentina.

The first Pygmy local spiritual assembly in the Central African Republic is formed. [BINS173:1]

The Bayan Hospital, the first Bahá'í hospital in Honduras, opens in Palacios.

The first conference on Ḥuqúqu'lláh is held at the Bahá'í World Centre.

The House of Worship in India

The first National Children's Camp in Australia is held in Yerrinbool School with 36 children between 9 and 13 years of age in attendance. [BINS173:10]

16–17 Jan The first Youth Conference of the Bahamas is held with representation from three islands. [BINS173:9]

26 Jan Charles Wolcott, member of the Universal House of Justice, dies in Haifa. [BINS162:1; VV97]

6–8 Feb Maori women hold the first National Women's Hui in the tribal area of Ngati Tuwaretoa, New Zealand. [BINS163:8]

24–8 Feb The Bahá'í Cultural Centre is opened in the Guaymi area of Panama.

The Guaymi Cultural Centre in Boca de Soloy, Chiriqui, Panama

Mar The first Bahá'í Winter School held on San Salvador Island, Bahamas, takes place. [BINS164:11]

24 Mar Radio Bahá'í of Liberia, the first Bahá'í radio station in Africa, is inaugurated in Maynesville. [BINS164:6; BW19:121; VV77]

Riḍván The National Spiritual Assembly of Zaire is re-formed. [AWH48]

The National Convention of Turkey is held for the first time with the official permission of the Turkish government.

A reorganization of the areas of jurisdiction of local spiritual assemblies in India results in the loss of 5,000 assemblies, substantially reducing the over-all number of local assemblies in the world.

22 Apr A ceremony is held to sign a 'status agreement' between the Bahá'í International Community and the Government of Israel defining the relationship of the Bahá'í World Centre with the State of Israel. [LETTER OF THE UNIVERSAL HOUSE OF JUSTICE, 30 APR 87]

- Shimon Peres, Vice-President and Foreign Minister, represents the Government of Israel while Donald Barrett signs the agreement in his capacity as Secretary-General of the Bahá'í International Community. [LETTER OF THE UNIVERSAL HOUSE OF JUSTICE 30 APR 87]

Above: Counsellor Wingi Mabuku, representative of the Universal House of Justice, right, and Counsellor Hushang Ahdieh at the Convention to re-form the National Spiritual Assembly of Zaïre

Below: The National Convention in Turkey, 1987

30 Apr The Universal House of Justice indicates that the way is open to erect the remaining buildings on the arc at the Bahá'í World Centre. [AWH51]

31 Aug The Universal House of Justice calls for the erection of the remaining three buildings along the arc at the Bahá'í World Centre – the

Centre for the Study of the Sacred Texts, the Seat of the International Teaching Centre and the International Bahá'í Library – as well as an expansion of the International Archives building and the creation of 19 monumental terraces from the foot of Mount Carmel to its crest. [AWH50–4, 90; BBD21; VV96]

Sep The United Nations Secretary-General designates the Bahá'í International Community and the National Spiritual Assemblies of Australia, Belgium, Brazil, Kenya and Lesotho as Peace Messengers, an honour given to only 300 organizations worldwide for their support of the UN Year of Peace 1986. [BINS173:4]

c. Oct The first local spiritual assembly on the island of São Tomé is formed at São Tomé.

autumn The National Spiritual Assembly of Brazil submits proposals based on Bahá'í principles such as human rights to the National Constitutional Assembly drafting the new constitution. [BINS174:2]

- Favourable responses are received from 46 Senators and Deputies. [BINS174:2]

The Post Office of the United Kingdom issues a commemorative stamp honouring Bernard Leach, Bahá'í and world-renowned potter. [BINS173:8]

3 Oct The Bahá'í International Community joins the Network on Conservation and Religion of the World Wide Fund for Nature, the sixth major religion to do so. [AWH56; BBD38; VV106]

Nov Representatives of 17 national spiritual assemblies in Europe and North America, together with senior representatives of the Offices of the Bahá'í International Community, meet in Germany to discuss their external affairs. [AWH56; VV105]

Dec The first Children's Conference of Uganda is held in Kikaaya, Kampala. [BINS173:7]

1988

In the year The Bahá'í International Community becomes a founding member of 'Advocates for African Food Security: Lessening the Burden for

Women', a coalition of agencies and organizations formed to act on behalf of farm women in Africa, and is convener for 1988–92.

The government of Niger authorizes the resumption of Bahá'í activities and Bahá'í administration under an administrative committee.

The first Caribbean Bahá'í Women's conference takes place in Antigua.

Branches of the Bahá'í International Community's Office of Public Information are established in Paris and London. [VV54]

'Arts for Nature', a fund-raising programme held to benefit the work of the World Wide Fund for Nature, is held in London with the collaboration of the Bahá'í International Community. [AWH61; VV106]

Hand of the Cause Rúḥíyyih Khánum addresses the Arts for Nature audience

HRH Prince Philip, the Duke of Edinburgh, left of centre, examines the Arts for Nature book produced by Bahá'í Peter Maguire, standing opposite

More than a thousand people become Bahá'ís in Taiwan as a result of the Muhajír Teaching Project. [BINS187:4]

Jan A teaching campaign is launched in Chad, resulting in 1,340 new Bahá'ís and 33 new local spiritual assemblies. [BINS187:1]

8 Mar Shirin Fozdar, ardent champion of women's rights and influential women's leader, is honoured for her work for equality and women's advancement at a ceremony organized by the Singapore Council of Women, which she founded in 1952. [BINS176:7]

Riḍván The Universal House of Justice is elected for the sixth time at the International Convention held in Haifa. [BINS176; VV97]

- David Hofman and H. Borrah Kavelin announce their retirement. [VV97]

The National Spiritual Assembly of Guinea is formed with its seat in Conakry. [BINS178:8]

Jun Over 100,000 people, including large numbers of women, youth and families, become Bahá'ís in Uttar Pradesh, India. [BINS179:4]

30 Jun–3 Jul The Bahá'í Arts Council, Canada, holds the first arts festival, 'Invitation 88: A Festival of the Human Spirit' at the University of Western Ontario, London, Ontario. [BINS179:2]

Jul Nearly 50 people become Bahá'ís in Saipan, Mariana Islands. [BINS181:5]

• Later reports indicate 91 people have enrolled by October 1988.

Eighty-nine people become Bahá'ís in Belize. [BINS186:2]

In 18 days of teaching, 876 adults, youth and children become Bahá'ís in Haiti. [BINS181:7]

• Reports from the National Spiritual Assembly in September indicate that 2,371 people enrolled in the first phase of the teaching campaign.

Jul–Aug Over 500 people become Bahá'ís in Liberia. [BINS184:8]

7–10 Jul The first Youth Convention of Spain is held in Madrid. [BINS180:5]

14–17 Jul The Bahá'í Association for Arts (BAFA) holds its first arts festival at the Bahá'í conference centre De Poort, Netherlands. [BINS180:4]

15 Jul The first International Women's Conference of Paraguay opens, attended by 130 women from seven countries. [BINS180:5]

Aug A 20–day teaching project in Coro, Falcon State, Venezuela, enrols 120 people in the first two days. [BINS182:7]

3–7 Aug The first Iberian Youth Conference is held in Lisbon, attended by 120 Bahá'ís from nine European countries. [BINS181:6]

Sep An intensive teaching campaign in Kenya enrols 448 new Bahá'ís. [BINS184:8]

A five-day teaching project in the Lake Titicaca region of Peru enrols 738 youth and 1,026 adults, almost half of whom are women. [BINS184:10]

• A later report gives the figure as over 2,000. [BINS185:8]

A teaching project in Maddhya Pradesh, India, enrols 20,000 new Bahá'ís in Morena District. [BINS185:4]

10 Sep A three-month teaching project is launched in Colombia, resulting in 1,245 people becoming Bahá'ís. [BINS193:1]

24 Sep The six-week Manicaland Teaching Campaign is launched in Zimbabwe, reporting 166 enrolments in the first three weeks. [BINS188:8]

24–5 Sep The first annual Bahá'í Studies Conference of Spain is held in Barcelona. [BINS192:5]

Oct Thirteen Romanies become Bahá'ís in northern Spain. [BINS186:7]

In the State of Orissa, India, 2,600 people become Bahá'ís and 16 new local spiritual assemblies are formed in 15 days.

One hundred and twenty people in Hong Kong and 280 in Macau become Bahá'ís as a result of teaching institutes. [BINS189:8]

- A later report states that more than 600 people in Macau have become Bahá'ís. [BINS194:3]

c. Nov Pietro Pandolfini, the first from the Albanian minority in Sicily to become a Bahá'í, enrols. [BINS189:5]

Nov More than 2,500 people enrol in Bangladesh. [BINS190:5]

- A later report indicates that over 5,000 people have become Bahá'ís and 108 new local spiritual assemblies formed. [BINS192:1]

Nov–Dec Six hundred people become Bahá'ís in West Bengal and 5,150 in Orissa, India. [BINS189:4–5]

The first members of the Jhana tribe to become Bahá'ís enrol in India. [BINS189:5]

One thousand one hundred people become Bahá'ís in the State of Gujarat, India. [BINS190:5]

Nov–Feb 1989 Teaching projects are launched in the Philippines, resulting in 3,847 people becoming Bahá'ís. [BINS195:4]

26 Nov–4 Dec Over a thousand people become Bahá'ís in Bolivia during a teaching project. [BINS189:2]

- A later report indicates that over 2,000 people have become Bahá'ís. [BINS195:1]

30 Nov The Bahá'í International Community is elected Secretary of the Board of the 'Conference on Non-Governmental Organizations in consultative status with the Economic and Social Council of the United Nations' (CONGO) for the period 1988–91. [BINS189:2]

c. Dec The Government of Western Samoa publishes a Christmas issue of four stamps of religious buildings, among them the Bahá'í House of Worship in Samoa. [BINS196:8]

4 Dec A two-week teaching project is launched, resulting in 414 people becoming Bahá'ís, including ten chiefs. [BINS192:4]

8 Dec The plenary session of the General Assembly of the United Nations adopts a resolution concerning human rights in Iran which specifically mentions the suffering of the Bahá'ís. [BINS189:2]

18 Dec H. Borrah Kavelin, former member of the first House of Justice, dies in Albuquerque, New Mexico. [VV97]

24 Dec The first National Youth Conference of Côte d'Ivoire takes place. [BINS196:9]

28 Dec Sean Hinton, a British Bahá'í youth of 22 years, arrives in Ulaan Baator, Mongolia, as an official research scholar in ethnomusicology from the University of Cambridge, the first Bahá'í to reside in Mongolia. [VV101]

- Seven months later he is named a Knight of Bahá'u'lláh by the Universal House of Justice.

- See VV101 for a picture.

29 Dec The Universal House of Justice issues a letter to the Bahá'ís in the United States published as *Individual Rights and Freedoms in the World Order of Bahá'u'lláh.*

30 Dec– 1 Jan 1989 Senior officers of the Bahá'í International Community in the Holy Land, Geneva and New York meet with representatives of five national spiritual assemblies to discuss their collaboration with the United Nations, its agencies and their governments.

Members of the Bahá'í International Community and of various National Spiritual Assemblies in 1988

1989

In the year A branch of the Bahá'í International Community's Office of Public Information is established in Hong Kong in anticipation of the time when the Bahá'í Faith can be proclaimed on the mainland of China. [AWH61; VV54]

More than 250 people become Bahá'ís in Zambia in the first three months of the year. [BINS201:6]

During a three-week teaching effort on the island of Tobago, 450 people become Bahá'ís. [BINS201:7]

The first travel teachers to visit Albania since World War II arrive from Italy.

Fourteen-year-old Olga Anatolevna Kirushkin becomes a Bahá'í in Minsk, the first known native person to become a Bahá'í in Belarus.

Three International Music Festivals are held in Africa. [BINS215]

Jan Three per cent of the population of North Tarawa, Kiribati, 70 people, become Bahá'ís. [BINS193:3]

1989

7 Jan A week-long teaching project is launched in the Andaman and Nicobar Islands resulting in 43 enrolments and the re-formation of two local spiritual assemblies. [BINS191:7]

9 Mar The Commission on Human Rights adopts a resolution expressing grave concern at human rights violations in Iran, mentioning the Bahá'ís three times. [BINS195:1]

17 Mar The Bahá'í International Community enters into a 'working relationship' with the World Health Organization (WHO) for the period 1989–91. [AWH61; BINS201:1]

23–6 Mar The First National Women's Conference of Spain is held in Madrid. [BINS201:6]

24–7 Mar The first All-Ireland Youth Spring School is held in Closkelt, Northern Ireland. [BINS197:5]

Apr The Association for Bahá'í Studies of Malaysia is established. [BINS206:8]

Riḍván The National Spiritual Assembly of Macau is formed. [AWH62; BINS199:1; VV104]

The National Spiritual Assembly of Macau with Hand of the Cause Rúḥíyyih Khánum, centre

Above: The National Spiritual Assembly of Guinea-Bissau

Below: The Local Spiritual Assembly of ‘Ishqábád

The National Spiritual Assembly of Guinea-Bissau is formed. [AWH62; BINS199:1, 4]

The Local Spiritual Assembly of ‘Ishqábád is re-formed after a lapse of 61 years, the first local assembly to be formed in the Soviet Union. [AWH73; VVIII]

The Universal House of Justice reports that nearly half a million people became Bahá'ís in the past year. [AWH60]

The Universal House of Justice announces the release of the vast majority of the Bahá'í prisoners held in Iran. [AWH62]

May Nearly 880 people become Bahá'ís in Guyana. [BINS202:8]

The Olinga Teaching Project is launched in Fiji, resulting in over a thousand people becoming Bahá'ís. [BINS204:3]

6 May The Bahá'í World Centre receives one of six awards given by the Council for a Beautiful Israel in a ceremony in Jerusalem. [BINS199:2]

Jul Sean Hinton, the first Bahá'í to reside in Mongolia, is named a Knight of Bahá'u'lláh by the Universal House of Justice.

Jul–Aug Five European Regional 'Peace Moves' Youth Conferences are held in different parts of the continent.

1–2 Jul The first European Bahá'í Women's Conference is held at De Poort Conference Centre, the Netherlands. [BINS203:2]

The funeral of Hand of the Cause Dr Ugo Giachery

5 Jul Dr Ugo Giachery, Hand of the Cause of God, dies while on a visit to Western Samoa. [BINS204:1; VV123]

• For the cable of the Universal House of Justice see BINS204:1.

23 Jul The first meeting of Bahá'í women in Mauritius takes place at the Bahá'í Institute. [BINS215:6]

Aug The first Mongolian to become a Bahá'í, Ms Oyundelger, a 22-year-old English-language pupil of Sean Hinton, enrols in Ulaan Baator. [VV101]

Forty Bahá'ís from Réunion, Mauritius, Seychelles and France join a teaching campaign in Madagascar during which 724 people become Bahá'ís. [BINS217:4]

3 Aug The first Latvian resident in Latvia to become a Bahá'í, Lilita Postaza, a renowned tapestry artist, enrols after visiting the Bahá'í temple in India.

Sep The Bahá'í Office of the Environment is established as part of the Bahá'í International Community in New York. [AWH75; VV54, 106]

16–17 Sep Bahá'ís in Liechtenstein mount a display of Bahá'í books and an exhibition at an international festival for peace, justice and the preservation of creation held in Balzers, the first time they have been allowed to have a booth or stand of any kind in public. [BINS209:8]

Oct The National Spiritual Assembly of Bangladesh reports the enrolment of 7,500 people in the year since November 1988. [BINS210:1]

21–2 Oct The Southern African Bahá'í Association for the Advancement of Women is formed in Johannesburg. [BINS210:8]

Oct–Nov In India, 4,300 people become Bahá'ís in the State of Orissa, [BINS213:3]

4–6 Nov The European Bahá'í Youth Council, comprising seven youth and appointed by the Universal House of Justice to coordinate those European youth activities that have a continental impact, meets for the first time, in London. [BINS213:4; BW93–4:121]

1989–1990

15 Dec A World Forestry Charter Gathering organized by the Offices of Public Information in London and New York takes place in London. [AWH75; BINS214:1–2]

- It commemorates the centenary of the birth of Richard St Barbe Baker, the Bahá'í environmentalist who founded the Gatherings in 1945.

18 Dec–2 Jan 1990 West Berlin Bahá'í communities are joined by 26 Bahá'ís from six European countries and the United States in proclamation and teaching activities among East Germans. [BINS215:2]

- More than 50,000 copies of a shortened version of the Peace Statement and other Bahá'í materials are distributed at four major border check-points in West Berlin and at the Brandenburg Gate. [BINS215:2]

- During the Youth Winter School in Traben-Trarback participants from 12 countries including East Germany, Romania, Hungary and the Soviet Union gather for the first time since the Second World War. [BINS215:2]

25–9 Dec The first International Bahá'í Summer School of Bophuthatswana is held at the Pilanesberg National Game Reserve, attended by 263 people from 12 countries. [BINS215:1–2]

1990

In the year The Council of Agriculture of the Executive Yuan (Senate) of Taiwan co-sponsors with the National Spiritual Assembly a Bahá'í educational programme on environmental protection. [BINS218:5]

- This is the first formal joint effort between the Bahá'ís of Taiwan and the government authorities.

The National Spiritual Assembly of Taiwan opens a permanent Bahá'í Office of the Environment for Taiwan in Taipei. [BINS221:5]

An Association for Bahá'í Studies is established in Kenya.

The Italian Association for Bahá'í Studies is established in Rome. [BINS232:5]

• It lapses in 1991 but is re-established in 1992.

The first Adam Benke Project is organized by the Bahá'í European Youth Council in Bulgaria.

• The first semi-public talks and lectures in Bulgaria are given in restaurants, where people are invited to private meetings.

• Eleven people become Bahá'ís.

The Purest Branch Project in Belize results in over a thousand people becoming Bahá'ís from the Garifuna population around Dangriga.

With the approval of the Universal House of Justice, the Bahá'í administrative institutions of the eastern and western parts of Germany are re-united. [BINS230:2]

For the first time a representative of the United Nations officially meets with a representative of the Bahá'í community in Iran. [AWH76]

Amata Kabua, President of the Marshall Islands, visits the Bahá'í World Centre. [BW94–5:83]

26 Jan The Bahá'í Chair for World Peace is established at the University of Maryland's Centre for International Development and Conflict Management at the official signing of the Memorandum of Understanding. [AWH76; BINS217:7; VV108]

• Professor Suheil Bushrui is appointed to the Chair in 1992.

• For picture see VV108.

Feb The Brazilian Society of Educators for Peace, conceived and initiated by Bahá'ís, is officially recognized by the Amazonas State Government. [BINS219:3]

The first local spiritual assembly comprised entirely of newly enrolled Bahá'ís of Ahmadiyyah background is formed in Chak No. 8P Katta, Pakistan. [BINS219:5]

21 Feb Jalál Kházeh, Hand of the Cause of God, dies in Toronto. [BINS219:90]

Notes VV123 *says it was 20 February.*

24–5 Feb The first All-Union Bahá'í Conference takes place in Moscow, the first national Bahá'í conference held in the USSR in about 60 years. [BINS224:8; VV112]

The first All-Union Bahá'í Conference, Moscow

Mar The Haifa District Town Planning Commission approves the plan submitted by the World Centre for the building projects on Mount Carmel. [AWH76]

21 Mar The first local spiritual assembly formed in Eastern Europe since the Second World War is elected in Cluj, Romania. [AWH73; BINS221:4]

24 Mar 'Abbás and Rezvánieh Katirai arrive on Sakhalin Island, the last remaining unopened territory of the Ten Year Crusade, and are named Knights of Bahá'u'lláh by the Universal House of Justice. [AWH73; BINS221:3; BINS226:2; VV112]

29 Mar–1 Apr The first Bahá'í International Chinese Symposium is held in San Francisco, California, attended by 362 Bahá'ís from eight countries. [BINS222:6]

9 Apr The first professorial Chair in Bahá'í Studies is established at Indore University, India. [BINS222:8; VV108]

Riḍván In its Riḍván message the Universal House of Justice announces that in the previous two years almost two million people have become Bahá'ís. [AWH79]

The first local spiritual assembly in Estonia is formed at Tallinn. [BINS223:3]

The first local assembly to be formed in Hungary since before the Second World War is elected in Budapest. [BINS223:4]

• The assembly was first elected in 1939 but lapsed during the war. [BINS223:4]

The first indigenous local spiritual assembly of Amazonas State, Brazil, is formed among the Mura tribe in Beruri. [BINS223:7]

Maureen Nakekea and Marao Teem are elected to the National Spiritual Assembly of Kiribati, the first indigenous women to be elected to the institution. [BINS224:7]

For the first time, two Bush Negro women delegates attend the national convention of Surinam. [BINS226:6]

The Local Spiritual Assembly of Moscow is re-formed after a lapse of six decades. [VVIII–12]

A subsidiary Two Year Teaching Plan for Eastern Bloc countries is launched by the Universal House of Justice. [AWH70–2]

18–20 May The first of seven European women's conferences sponsored by the Continental Board of Counsellors is held in Iskenderun, Turkey. [BINS230:1]

23 May Work begins on the terraces above and below the Shrine of the Báb. [AWH83, 102; BINS227:1]

Jun Nicolai Gejnze, from Bishkek and a crew member in one of three boats in which Bahá'ís made a trip down the Volga River in June and July 1990, enrols, the first person from Kirgizia known to have become a Bahá'í.

4 Jun The first International Exposition on Education for Peace, inaugurated by the National Spiritual Assembly of Brazil, takes place in Brasilia. [BINS226:1]

Hands of the Cause Amatu'l-Bahá Rúḥíyyih Khánum and 'Alí-Akbar Furútan, members of the Universal House of Justice and Counsellor members of the International Teaching Centre listen to Fariburz Sabha, Mount Carmel Projects manager, explain the work to be done on the Terraces

9 Jun The first local spiritual assembly in Czechoslovakia is formed at Prague. [BINS226:1]

10 Jun The Paraguay International Chinese Teaching Symposium, the first of its kind in South America, is held in Asuncion, attended by 80 people from 10 countries. [BINS226:4]

Jul The first youth conference of Estonia is held in Kabli, near Parnu, attended by some 113 participants from all parts of Europe.

3 Jul The National Spiritual Assembly of Guyana announces that the Bahá'ís constitute about five percent of the total population of the country. [BINS228:1]

- In some towns over 20 percent of the people are Bahá'ís. [BINS228:1]

8–11 Jul The first summer school of Czechoslovakia is held in Jindrichuv Hradec, attended by 24 Bahá'ís from eight countries. [BINS230:2]

end of Jul The first Polish summer school is held in Hajdany. [BINS233:6]

6 Aug The first local spiritual assembly in the Ukraine is formed in Kiev.

Sep The first International Dialogue on the Transition to a Global Society, co-sponsored by the University of Maryland, the Vienna Academy for the Study of the Future and Landegg Academy, is held at Landegg Academy, Switzerland, attended by 80 leaders of thought from around the world. [VV109]

1–2 Sep The European Bahá'í Business Forum is formed at a meeting in Chamonix, France, attended by people from eight countries. [BINS244:8; VV115]

- For picture see VV115.

6 Sep The Bahá'í International Community opens a branch of its United Nations Office for the Pacific region in Suva, Fiji. [AWH76; BINS233:4–5; VV54]

8 Sep The first local spiritual assembly on Sakhalin Island is formed in Yuzhno. [BINS232:5]

29 Sep Collis Featherstone, Hand of the Cause of God, dies in Kathmandu, Nepal. [BINS232:8; VV123]

- For picture see VV124.

19–21 Oct The first National Children's Conference of Nicaragua is held in Retiro, Aurora, Managua, attended by more than 40 children. [BINS243:8]

The first summer school of Cape Verde is held in Tarrafal, attended by 30 people. [BINS247:8]

11 Nov For the first time in 45 years, a Bahá'í meeting is held in a public building in Bulgaria. [BINS236:2]

30 Nov–2 Dec The First National Teaching Conference of Romania is held near Poiana Brasov, in the Carpathian mountains.

Dec The first week-long residential Bahá'í study school of Guinea is held in Guéckédou.

Monument over the resting place of Hand of the Cause Collis Featherstone, Kathmandu

8–9 Dec The first All-Union Bahá'í Consultative Conference is held in Moscow. [BINS238:6]

22–6 Dec The First European Bahá'í Youth Encounter is held in the Canary Islands, attended by over 150 people from eight countries. [BINS239:1]

1991

In the year The first major public statement of the National Spiritual Assembly of the Bahá'ís of the United States, *The Vision of Race Unity: America's Most Challenging Issue*, is published and disseminated widely throughout the country.

The administration of the Bahá'í Faith in Zaire is devolved to a system of subordinate regional councils.

Jan The first local spiritual assembly in Slovakia is formed in Bratislava.

2 Jan The first local spiritual assembly in Bulgaria is formed in Plovdiv. [BINS239:2]

20 Jan The first World Religion Day to be held in Bophuthatswana takes place in Mmabatho. [BINS244:1]

25 Jan The first local spiritual assembly in Latvia is formed in Riga. [BINS241:3]

26–7 Jan The first National Teaching Conference of Yugoslavia is held in Belgrade. [BINS243:3]

8–14 Feb The first Bahá'í Winter School of Romania is held in Felix, attended by 80 Bahá'ís. [BINS241:3]

12 Apr The Local Spiritual Assembly of Tashkent, Uzbekistan, is re-formed.

Riḍván The Universal House of Justice announces that the law of Ḥuqúqu'lláh will become universally applicable at Riḍván 1992. [AWH91–2, 174]

Hand of the Cause Amatu'l-Bahá Rúḥíyyih Khánum, centre, with members of the National Spiritual Assembly of Romania

National Spiritual Assembly of the Soviet Union

The National Spiritual Assembly of Romania is formed with its seat in Bucharest. [AWH86; BINS246:1; VV113]

The National Spiritual Assembly of the Soviet Union is formed with its seat in Moscow. [AWH86; BINS246:1–3; VV113]

The National Spiritual Assembly of Czechoslovakia is formed with its seat in Prague. [AWH86; BINS246:3–4; VV113]

The National Spiritual Assembly of the West Leeward Islands is formed. [AWH86; BINS246:1; VV113]

May The first local spiritual assembly in Moldova is formed in Kishinev.

14 May The first local spiritual assembly in Armenia is formed at Yerevan.

National Spiritual Assembly of Czechoslovakia with Hand of the Cause Dr Varqá, centre back

National Spiritual Assembly of the West Leeward Islands, with Counsellor Ruth Pringle, far left, and William Roberts, far right

16 Jun The first local spiritual assembly in Albania is formed at Tirana.

18 Jun John Aldham Robarts, Hand of the Cause of God, Knight of Bahá'u'lláh, dies in Rawdon, Quebec. [BINS250:10; VV124]

- For his obituary see BINS250:10.
- For picture see VV124.

21 Jun The first local spiritual assembly in Kirgizia is formed in Bishkek.

15–21 Jul The first European Bahá'í Youth Conference of Romania is held in Neptune. [BINS253:9; VV74]

- For picture see VV74.

19–21 Jul The first summer school of Sikkim is held in Saramsa. [BINS257:6]

15–22 Aug The first summer school of Tajikistan takes place in Varzoub Gorge.

2 Oct The first local spiritual assembly in Belarus is formed at Minsk.

25–7 Oct The first National Teaching Conference of Bulgaria is held in Plovdiv. [BINS258:2–3]

12 Nov The first Bahá'í meeting to be held in a public location in Mongolia takes place in the theatre of the former Lenin Museum.

1991–1992

Dec The first Music Festival for Youth of Zaire is held. [BINS288:8]

20 Dec A Bahá'í Monument for Peace is inaugurated in a ceremony held in Florianopolis, Brazil. [BINS266:1]

27–31 Dec The first winter school of Hungary is held in Miskolc. [BINS266:2]

31 Dec The National Spiritual Assembly of Niger is given permission by the Ministry of the Interior to engage in Bahá'í activities. [BINS261:6]

1992

In the year The annotated English translation of the Kitáb-i-Aqdas is printed. [KAIV; VV142]

Notes *The date of copyright is 1992 but the book is not available until Riḍván 1993.*

The Universal House of Justice announces its decision to establish an Office for the Advancement of Women at the headquarters of the Bahá'í International Community in New York. [VV29, 54]

Jan The first teaching conference of Southern Yugoslavia is held, attended by 40 Bahá'ís representing 12 nationalities. [BINS264:8]

2–5 Jan The first European Conference on Bahá'í Activities in Universities is held in Brno, Czechoslovakia. [BINS263:2]

- BINS290:2 gives a second report of this event, incorrectly implying it was held in January 1993.

10–11 Jan The first teaching conference of Croatia and Slovenia is held in Kranj. [BINS263:1–2]

1 Feb The Local Spiritual Assembly of Zanzibar Island is formed. [BINS267:6]

- This is the first administrative body on the island since the revolution of 12 January 1964. [BINS267:6]

3–6 Feb The Association of Bahá'í Publishers and Distributors is established at a Bahá'í Publishers' Conference in Oakham, England, with its headquarters in the Netherlands. [BINS273:4–5; VV71]

7 Mar The first local spiritual assembly in Eastern Germany is formed in Erfurt. [BINS267:3]

18 Mar Bahman Samandarí is executed in Evin prison, Ṭihrán, the first execution of a Bahá'í in Iran in three-and-a-half years. [AWH118–19; BINS273:1; VV126]

25 Mar William Sears, Hand of the Cause of God, dies in Tucson, Arizona. [BINS267; VV124]

Apr The first Bahá'í Youth School of Romania is held in Curtea de Arges, attended by 60 Bahá'ís. [BINS269:5]

Above: Bahman Samandarí

Hand of the Cause William Sears, shown here in October 1991

1992

4–5 Apr The first Children's Festival and Family Conference of Turkey is held in Cankaya, Ankara. [BINS269:5–6]

20 Apr The Six Year Plan is successfully completed.

- For the major accomplishments of the Plan see AWH97–102, 187–8 and VV126.

Riḍván Holy Year commences. [AWH40, 90, 95–6; BW92–3:20; VV127, 133]

- For the purpose of the Holy Year see AWH96–7, 107–9 and BW92–3:20, 29–30.

- For the significance of Holy Year see BW92–3:95–6.

The law of Ḥuqúqu'lláh becomes universally applicable. [AWH106, 175; BW92–3:28]

The Regional Spiritual Assembly of Russia, Georgia and Armenia is formed. [BW92–3:119; VV121]

The National Spiritual Assembly of Albania is formed with its seat in Tirana. [BINS270:3–4; BW92–3:119; VV121]

Hand of the Cause Amatu'l-Bahá Rúḥíyyih Khánum, seated second from left, with the National Spiritual Assembly of Poland

The National Spiritual Assembly of Hungary

• For picture see BINS279:9.

The National Spiritual Assembly of Bulgaria is formed with its seat in Sofia. [BINS270:1; BW92–3:119; VV121]

• For picture see BINS279:9.

The National Spiritual Assembly of Poland is formed with its seat in Warsaw. [BINS270:2; BW92–3:119; VV121]

The National Spiritual Assembly of Central Asia

The National Spiritual Assembly of Azerbaijan, with Counsellor Mas'úd Khamsí, right of centre

The Regional Spiritual Assembly of the Baltic States is formed with its seat in Tallinn. [BINS270:2; BW92–3:119; VV121]

• For picture see BINS282:9.

The National Spiritual Assembly of Hungary is formed with its seat in Budapest. [BINS270:2–3; BW92–3:119; VV121]

The Regional Spiritual Assembly of Central Asia (comprising the

The National Spiritual Assembly of Angola

Hand of the Cause Dr Varqá, centre, with the National Spiritual Assembly of Greenland

republics of Kazakhstan, Kirgizia, Tadjikistan, Turkmenistan and Uzbekistan) is formed with its seat in Ashkhabad. [BINS270:4–5; BW92–3:119; BW94–5:29; VV121]

The Regional Spiritual Assembly of Ukraine, Belarus and Moldova is formed with its seat in Kiev. [BW92–3:119; VV121]

The National Spiritual Assembly of Azerbaijan is re-formed after half a century of prohibition and persecution. [BINS270:4; BW92–3:119; VV121]

The National Spiritual Assembly of Angola is formed. [BINS270:4; BW92–3:119; VV121]

The National Spiritual Assembly of Greenland is formed with is seat in Nuuk. [BINS270:3; BW92–3:119; VV121]

The National Spiritual Assembly of the Congo Republic is re-formed after 14 years' suspension of the Bahá'í Faith. [BINS270:5; BW92–3:119; VV121]

- For picture see BINS275:7

The National Spiritual Assembly of Niger is re-formed after a 14–year interruption. [BINS270:5; BW92–3:119; VV121]

The National Spiritual Assembly of Niger

The first local spiritual assembly in Mongolia is formed in Ulaan Baatar. [BINS269:4]

- The local assembly was understood to have been formed in the spring of 1991 but this was found to have been a mistake.

The government of Trinidad and Tobago issues a postage stamp in recognition of the Bahá'í Holy Year. [BW92–3:119; VV133]

- For picture see BW92–3:121.

27 Apr After a ten-year struggle, the Faith's legal Chinese name in Taiwan is changed from 'Ta Tong Giao' (Religion of Great Harmony), used for 70 years, to 'Bahá'í Faith'. [BINS271:6]

Apr–May Fifteen people become Bahá'ís in Barentsburg, Spitzbergen. [BINS271:4–5]

May The Bahá'í International Community issues a statement on Bahá'u'lláh at the request of the Universal House of Justice. [BW92–3:47]

- For the text see BW92–3:47–94.

27–30 May Three thousand Bahá'ís representing approximately 200 countries and territories, gather at the Bahá'í World Centre to mark the Centenary of the Ascension of Bahá'u'lláh. [BINS271:1–2; BW92–3:96–8, 121]

- Countries and territories with national spiritual assemblies send 19 representatives each; those without national spiritual assemblies send nine each.

- For pictures see BINS271:10 and BW92–3:97.

27 May One hundred thirteen Knights of Bahá'u'lláh attend a reception at the Seat of the Universal House of Justice to view the Roll of Honour. [BINS271:1]

Knights of Bahá'u'lláh view the Roll ofHonour bearing their names

- For pictures see BINS271:9.

28 May The original scroll bearing the Roll of Honour of the Knights of Bahá'u'lláh is placed by Hand of the Cause Amatu'l-Bahá Rúḥíyyih Khánum in a chamber at the entrance door of the inner sanctuary of the most holy shrine. [AWH90, 105; BINS271:1; BW92–3:98; VV128]

- For pictures see BINS271:9 and VV127, 128.

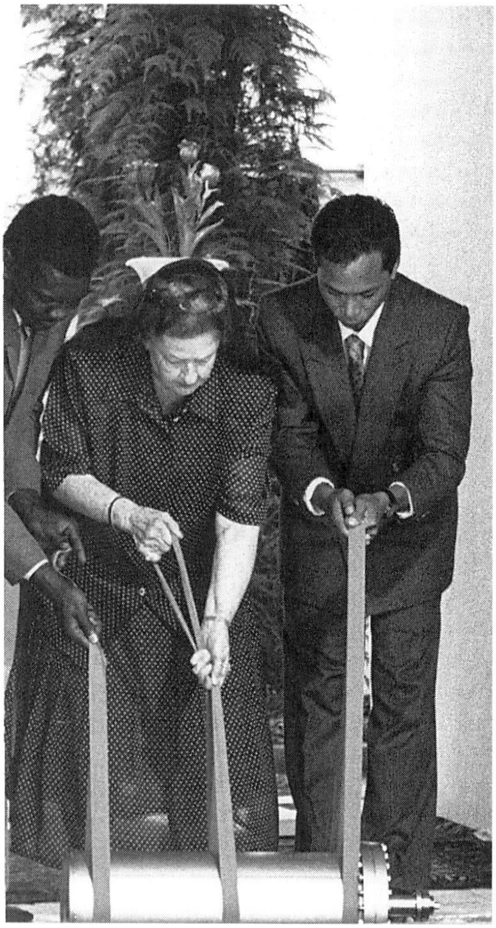

Hand of the Cause Amatu'l-Bahá Rúḥíyyih Khánum places the scroll of the Roll of Honour at the entrance to the Shrine of Bahá'u'lláh

Ibsen Valls Pinheiro, President of the Federal Chamber of Deputies, opens a special session of the Chamber called to observe the Centenary of the Ascension of Bahá'u'lláh, attended by 45 federal deputies. [BINS271:2; BW92–3:121]

• For picture see BW92–3:122.

Notes VV133 *says this was 29 May.*

29 May The Centenary of the Ascension of Bahá'u'lláh is commemorated at Bahjí in a candle-lit programme of prayers and readings. [BINS271:1–2; ; BW92–3:96–7; VV129–30]

Representatives of the Bahá'ís of the world circumambulate the Shrine of Bahá'u'lláh at the end of the service commemorating the Centenary of the Ascension of Bahá'u'lláh

- For the tribute to Bahá'u'lláh by the Universal House of Justice see BW92–3:31–6.

- For pictures see BINS271:10 and VV129, 130.

A series of postage stamps overprinted with 'Bahá'í Holy Year' is released by the postal service in Guyana. [BW92–3:122]

The Centenary of the Ascension of Bahá'u'lláh is commemorated at the Guardian's Resting Place in London.

1–14 Jun Bahá'ís from many countries participate in the United Nations Conference on the Environment (UNCED), known as the Earth Summit, and the Global Forum for non-governmental organizations in Rio de Janeiro, Brazil. [BINS272:1–3; BW92–3:124; VV110]

- For a report of the Bahá'í involvement at the Earth Summit see BW92–3:177–89.

- For the text of the statement of the Bahá'í International Community read at the plenary session see BW92–3:191–2.

Hundreds of Bahá'ís gather at the Guardian's Resting Place to commemorate the Centenary of the Ascension of Bahá'u'lláh

The Bahá'í International Community stand at
the Earth Summit

• For pictures see BW92–3:179, 183, 186.

5 Jun The Bahá'í Vocational Institute for Rural Women, a non-profit education project based in Indore, India, is one of 74 individuals and institutions presented with the United Nations Environment Programme 'Global 500' award in Rio de Janeiro. [BINS272:5; BW92–3:125; VV110]

• For picture see BW92–3:183.

9 Jul The National Post Office of Panama issues a commemorative envelope to mark the centenary of the Ascension of Bahá'u'lláh. [BW92–3:127]

• For picture see BW92–3:127.

27 Jul The National Spiritual Assembly of Tonga broadcasts the first of its weekly 30–minute television programmes. [BINS281:5]

21–3 Aug The first National Summer School of Bulgaria is held in Stara Zagora, attended by 75 people. [BINS278:1–2]

23–9 Aug The first Bahá'í summer school to be held in Croatia takes place in Pula, Istria, attended by a hundred Bahá'ís from nine countries. [BINS278:2; BINS287:10]

17 Sep The Bahá'í Professional Society of Hong Kong is inaugurated. [BINS292:8; BW92–3:129]

25–7 Sep The first Bahá'í Youth Conference of Lithuania takes places in Kaunas, attended by 32 Bahá'ís. [BINS281:1]

24–8 Oct The first Bahá'í Autumn School of Central Asia is held in Bishkek, Kyrgyzstan, attended by more than 200 Bahá'ís and many others. [BINS284:2]

25 Oct–11 Nov Prince Alfred von Lichtenstein tours ten cities in Japan delivering memorial lectures celebrating the centenary of the Ascension of Bahá'u'lláh. [BW92–3:132]

22–3 Nov The Bahá'í Faith is mentioned in the media of Mozambique for the first time with three write-ups in *Notices*, the only newspaper in Maputo, and announcements on Radio Maputo and Radio Mozambique. [BINS292:7]

23–6 Nov The second Bahá'í World Congress is held in New York City. [BINS283:1–2; BINS287:6; BW92–3:98–101, 136; VV136–41]

- Nine auxiliary conferences are held in Buenos Aires, Sydney, New Delhi, Nairobi, Panama City, Bucharest, Moscow, Apia and Singapore. [BINS283:3–4]

The Jacob Javits Centre, site of the second Bahá'í World Congress

Musicians from around the world perform at the second Bahá'í World Congress

Tapestries sent by Bahá'ís from many countries to the World Congress

• For pictures see BINS283:9–10, BW92–3:100 and VV136–41.

26 Nov Bahá'ís around the world are linked together by a live satellite broadcast serving the second Bahá'í World Congress, nine auxiliary conferences and the Bahá'í World Centre and is received by those with access to satellite dish antennas. [BINS283:1–5, 8; BINS286:10; BINS287:4]

Living on five continents, a family reunites at the World Congress

• For the message of the Universal House of Justice read on the satellite link see BW92–3:37–4.

Dec The Universal House of Justice announces the establishment of the Office for the Advancement of Women in New York. [BW92–3:136; VV29]

26–30 Dec The first National Bahá'í Winter School of Bulgaria is held in Lovech, attended by 130 Bahá'ís. [BINS286:1–2]

1993

In the year More than 10,000 people become Bahá'ís in Bangladesh. [BINS318:8; BINS319:1]

Jan Reynaldo Galindo Pohl, the United Nations' special representative in charge of monitoring the human rights situation in Iran, reveals a secret document written by Iran's Supreme Revolutionary Cultural Council providing evidence that the Iranian Government has formulated a plan to oppress and persecute the Bahá'í community both in Iran and abroad. [BW92–3:139; BW93–4:154]

17 Jan The first World Religion Day commemoration to be held in Mozambique takes place in Maputo. [BINS290:5; BW92–3:140]

19 Jan The Bahá'í Chair for World Peace at the University of Maryland is inaugurated. [BW92–3:140–1]

29–31 Jan The first Latin American Bahá'í Social and Economic Development Seminar takes place in Santa Cruz, Bolivia. [BINS308:2; BW92–3:139]

16 Feb A stamp featuring the Seat of the Universal House of Justice is issued by the Philatelic Service of the Israel Postal Authority. [BW92–3:142]

- For picture see BW92–3:143.

19–21 Feb The first Bahá'í Winter School of Slovenia and Croatia, the first Bahá'í school to be held in Slovenia, takes place in Mozirje, Slovenia, attended by 20 adults and seven children. [BINS289:5–6]

20 Feb The first National Youth Conference of Hungary is held in Debrecen, attended by 60 youth. [BINS289:3]

22 Feb At the 49th session of the UN Commission on Human Rights, Reynaldo Galindo Pohl, special representative in charge of monitoring the human rights situation in Iran, highlights the contents of the secret document written by Iran's Supreme Revolutionary Cultural

The Kitáb-i-Aqdas arrives at the Bahá'í Centre on Goodenough Island, Papua New Guinea, carried on a bed of flowers

Council outlining its plans for the treatment of Bahá'ís. [BW92–3:139; BW94–5:134]

Mar The English translation of the Kitáb-i-Aqdas is published. [BW92–3:44]

- For the significance of its publication see BW92–3:45–6.
- For its place in Bahá'í literature see BW92–3:105–18.

13 Mar Three Bahá'ís are assassinated at the Bahá'í Centre in Mdantsane, Ciskei, in a racially-motivated attack. [BW93–4:147–50]

10–12 Apr The first Bahá'í Congress of Catalunya takes place in Barcelona. [BW92–3:146]

Riḍván The Three Year Plan is launched. [VV142]

- For statistics about the Bahá'í Faith at the beginning of the Plan see BW92–3:311–14 and BW93–4:323–6.

The Local Spiritual Assembly of Tbilisi (Tiflis), Georgian Republic, is re-formed. [BINS298:8; BW93–4:82]

- An assembly existed in the city in the 1930s. [BW93–4:82]

The Local Spiritual Assembly of Leipzig, Germany, is re-formed 56 years after its dissolution during the time the Faith was banned. [BW93–4:82]

The first person resident on Norfolk Island to become a Bahá'í enrols. [BINS293:8]

29 Apr–2 May The Universal House of Justice is elected for the seventh time at the Bahá'í International Convention in Haifa. [BINS295]

- Hugh Chance and David Ruhe announce their retirement. [BINS295]
- For a report of the Convention see BW93–4:51–8.
- For pictures see BW93–4:52, 53, 54, 57.

Delegates at the Seventh International Convention

23 May The first general conference of Health for Humanity, an association of health professionals sponsored by the National Spiritual Assembly of the United States, is held in Evanston, Illinois. [BINS298:7; BW93–4:104]

26 May The Office for the Advancement of Women officially opens at the headquarters of the Bahá'í International Community in New York. [BINS296:2; BW93–4:83–9; VV29]

• For pictures see BW93–4:83, 86.

Jun The bodies of Bahá'ís buried in the Bahá'í section of a Ṭihrán cemetery are exhumed and taken by lorry to unknown destinations. [BW93–4:153]

10–25 Jun The Bahá'í International Community and Bahá'ís from 11 countries participate in the United Nations World Conference on Human Rights in Vienna and the parallel meeting for non-governmental organizations. [BINS298:1–2]

The Hon. Sir Julius Chan, centre front, with members of the Universal House of Justice

12 Jun The Honourable Sir Julius Chan, KBE, Deputy Prime Minister of Papua New Guinea consults with the Universal House of Justice on the future role of his country as an emerging nation and on the destiny of the Pacific region. [BINS297:9; BW93–4:78]

• For pictures see BINS297:9 and BW93–4:78

Jul A section of the Bahá'í cemetery in Ṭihrán is bulldozed to make way for the construction of an Islamic cultural centre. [BW93–4:140]

• It is first thought that about two thousand Bahá'í graves are desecrated but later revealed that 15,000 graves are destroyed. [BW93–4:140; BW94–5:133]

The first Bahá'í Youth Symposium of the Marshall Islands is held in Majuro, attended by youth from six island groups. [BW93–4:124]

25–30 Jul The first summer school of Albania is held in Gdem, attended by about 400 Bahá'ís. [BINS299:3]

Aug The first International Bahá'í Youth Conference of Belarus is held, attended by 164 people from 16 countries. [BINS299:8; BINS306:7; BW93–4:123]

Oct The Australian Bahá'í community and the Arrente Aboriginal tribe co-sponsor an intercultural celebration of indigenous peoples, 'Heart of Australia Calling' in Alice Springs to mark UN International Year for the World's Indigenous Peoples. [BW93–4:90]

The first European Bahá'í Medical Conference is held in De Poort, Netherlands, attended by people from 26 countries. [BW93–4:104–5]

Notes BINS302:4 *says it was attended by 19 people from nine countries.*

29–31 Oct The founding conference of the Association for Bahá'í Studies in Russia is held in St Petersburg. [BINS305:5]

26 Nov The National Spiritual Assembly of the Marshall Islands signs a Memorandum of Understanding with the Majuro local government in which the operation of administration of five elementary schools is legally handed over to the National Spiritual Assembly. [BINS307:4–5; BW93–4:101]

8 Dec In Iran, death sentences are pronounced against two Bahá'ís on the grounds of their membership in the Bahá'í community. [BW93–4:141–2]

24–6 Dec The first summer school of Angola is held in Luanda, attended by more than 20 Bahá'ís. [BINS309:1]

1994

In the year His Highness King Malietoa Tanumafili II of Samoa receives the

Kitáb-i-Aqdas from Tongan Bahá'ís Sohrab and Soheyla Bolouri. [BINS314:9]

His Highness Malietoa Tanumafili II is presented with the Kitáb-i-Aqdas

Jan The first winter school of Mongolia is held in Songino, near Ulaan Baatar. [BINS310:6]

30 Jan The first worldwide fireside on the Internet, 'Pioneering in Cyberspace – the Bahá'í Faith and the Internet', is held, with a live audience in the Bahá'í Centre in New York City communicating electronically with people all over the United States and in two other countries.

The Dalai Lama at the Bahá'í World Centre

17–20 Feb The first Bahá'í ASEAN (Association of South East Asian Nations) Forum is held in Bangkok. [BINS312:6]

24 Mar The Dalai Lama visits the Bahá'í World Centre. [BW93–4:78]

The National Spiritual Assembly of Cambodia is

Riḍván formed with its seat in Phnom Penh. [BINS317:1; BW93–4:82; BW94–5:25, 30–1]

The National Spiritual Assembly of Mongolia is formed with its seat in Ulaan Baatar. [BINS317:1–2; BW93–4:82; BW94–5:25, 31–2]

Above: Hand of the Cause Amatu'l-Bahá Rúḥíyyih Khánum, seated centre, with members of the Continental Board of Counsellors Lee Lee Ludher and Shantha Sundram, with Violette Nakhjavání and members of the National Spiritual Assembly of Cambodia

Below: The National Spiritual Assembly of Mongolia. Knight of Bahá'u'lláh Sean Hinton is kneeling at the far left

The National Spiritual Assembly of Slovenia and Croatia is formed with its seat in Ljubljana, Slovenia. [BINS317:2; BW93–4:82; BW94–5:25, 33–6]

• For picture see BINS320:9 and BW94–5:35.

The National Spiritual Assembly of Kazakhstan is formed. [BINS317:2–3; BW93–4:82; BW94–5:25, 29–30]

• For picture see BW94–5:28.

The National Spiritual Assembly of Kyrgyzstan is formed. [BINS317:3; BW93–4:82; BW94–5:25, 29]

The National Spiritual Assembly of Tajikistan is formed. [BINS317:3; BW93–4:82; BW94–5:26, 29–30]

The National Spiritual Assembly of Tajikistan

The National Spiritual Assembly of Uzbekistan is formed. [BINS317:3–4; BW93–4:82; BW94–5:26, 29–30]

• For picture see BINS328:9 and BW94–5:30.

19 May The first National Bahá'í Conference of Armenia is held in Yerevan. [BINS318:5–6]

22 May The first Bahá'í Children and Youth Conference of Martinique is held in Fort-de-France, attended by 22 people. [BINS318:4–5]

Jun The first National Youth School of Mongolia is held in Darkhan, attended by 34 youth. [BINS321:4]

11–12 Jun The first Bahá'í conference to be held in the Republic of Georgia takes place in Tbilisi, attended by over a hundred people from 11 countries. [BINS319:5]

13 Jun The Prime Minister of Israel, Yitzhak Rabin, visits the Bahá'í World Centre to view the Terraces Project. [BW94–5:77]

Yitzhak Rabin, front row centre, is escorted to the Terraces by the Bahá'í World Centre's Deputy Secretary-General, Albert Lincoln, front right, and Project Manager, Fariborz Sabha, front left

6–10 Jul The first Children's Bahá'í Summer School of Pakistan is held in Abbottabad, attended by 13 children. [BINS324:5]

20–5 Jul The European Bahá'í Youth Council sponsors five regional 'Shaping Europe' conferences, in Berlin, Bucharest, St Petersburg, Barcelona and Wolverhampton, United Kingdom. [BINS323:3–5; BW94–5:177–8, 189]

22–3 Jul His Excellency France Albert René, President of the Republic of Seychelles, consults with the Universal House of Justice. [BINS322:9; BW94–5:76–7]

28 Jul The World Forestry Charter Gatherings, established by Richard St

His Excellency France Albert René, centre front, and members of the Universal House of Justice

Barbe Baker in 1945, are re-instituted by the Bahá'í International Community's Office of the Environment at a luncheon at St James's Palace, London. [AWH75; BW94–5:112–13, 142–3; OC6,2:1; VV106]

• For pictures see BW94–5:143 and OC6,2:1, 12.

4 Aug Shimon Peres, Israel's Minister of Foreign Affairs, makes an official visit to the Bahá'í World Centre. [BW94–5:77]

5–13 Sep The Bahá'í International Community attends the United Nations International Conference on Population of Development and the parallel Non-Governmental Organizations' Forum in Cairo. [BINS328:1]

Shimon Peres, centre, views the model of the Mount Carmel Projects

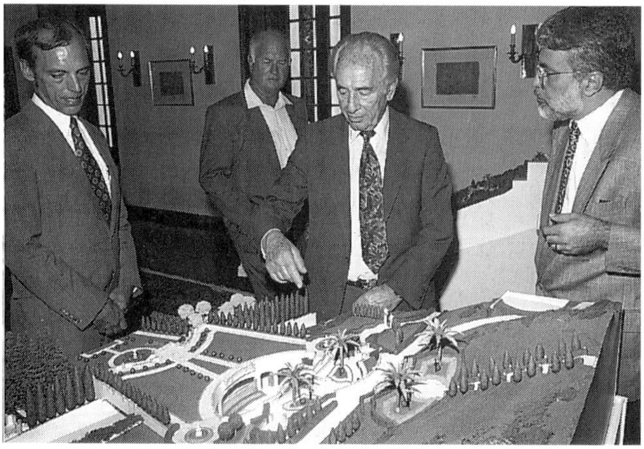

9–11 Sep The first National Youth Conference of Liberia is held, attended by 75 youth. [BW94–5:188–9]

- For picture see BW94–5:189.

Oct The Bahá'í Health Association for Central and Eastern Europe and the European Bahá'í Dental Association are formed at the second Bahá'í Health Conference held at De Poort, Netherlands. [BW94–5:116]

7–9 Dec The first World Press Exhibition is held by the Information and Public Relations Committees of the National Spiritual Assembly of El Salvador to mark the International Day of Peace. [BINS335:2]

1995

In the year The Association for Latin American Bahá'í Writers and Authors is formed at the fifth Latin American Seminar for External Affairs in Cali, Colombia. [BINS336:2]

Jan The first National Teaching Conference of Cambodia is held in Phnom Penh, attended by more than 50 Bahá'ís. [BINS334:2]

The first meeting of the Association of Bahá'í Doctors and Health Professionals in India takes place. [BW94–5:116]

Feb Jacinto Pcynado, Vice President of the Dominican Republic, visits the Bahá'í World Centre. [BW94–5:77]

3–12 Mar The Bahá'í International Community and Bahá'ís from many countries participate in the United Nations World Summit for Social Development and the parallel Forum '95 for non-governmental organizations in Copenhagen. [BINS337:1–2]

- For a report of the Bahá'í involvement in the Summit see BW94–5: 37–6.

- For the text of *The Prosperity of Humankind*, the Bahá'í International Community statement released at the Summit, see BW94–5: 273–96.

- For pictures see BW94–5:39, 43, 45.

Bambi Betts, right, explains the Bahá'í concept of moral education at one of the many workshops sponsored by the Bahá'ís at the World Summit for Social Development

The National Spiritual Assembly of Georgia with member of the Continental Board of Counsellors Abbas Katirai, seated centre

Riḍván The National Spiritual Assembly of Georgia is formed with its seat in Tbilisi. [BINS341:1]

The National Spiritual Assembly of Armenia is formed. [BINS342:2]

The National Spiritual Assembly of Belarus is formed. [BINS341:2]

The National Spiritual Assembly of Eritrea is formed. [BINS341:2]

The National Spiritual Assembly of Armenia with Counsellor Abbas Katirai, seated centre

The National Spiritual Assembly of Belarus

The National Spiritual Assembly of Sicily, with Hand of the Cause Dr Varqá, seated centre

The National Spiritual Assembly of Sicily is formed. [BINS341:1–2]

14 May The Universal House of Justice representative Mr 'Alí Nakhjavání begins his tour of major Bahá'í communities to discuss the significance of the Arc projects on Mount Carmel.

Mr 'Alí Nakhjavání addresses more than a thousand Bahá'ís in London

30 May–1 Jun The first International Medical/Surgical Conference of Tirana is held under the auspices of Health for Humanity and the University of Tirana, attended by more than 400 Albanian physicians. [BINS343:2–3]

8–11 Jun The first European Bahá'í Conference on Law and International Order is held at De Poort Conference Centre, Netherlands. [BINS345:4]

c. Jul The first Bahá'í summer school of Lithuania is held in Ukmerge, attended by 20 people. [BINS346:1]

26 Jul The inaugural meeting of the Association for Bahá'í Studies of Ghana is held in Accra. [BINS348:3]

Aug More than 7,000 people become Bahá'ís in Haiti in two weeks. [BINS348:3]

28 Aug–14 Sep The Bahá'í International Community and about 500 Bahá'ís from many countries attend the Fourth United Nations International

The First Conference on Law and International Order, the Netherlands

Some of the 500 Bahá'ís at an informal gathering at the NGO Forum in Huairou, near Beijing

Conference on Women and the parallel Non-Governmental Organization Forum in Beijing.

Oct–Dec More than a million people visit the Bahá'í House of Worship in India in this period. [BINS357:5]

20 Oct The first local spiritual assembly in the Komi Republic is formed at Syktyvkar. [BINS357:8]

14 Dec A Chair for Bahá'í Studies is inaugurated at the University of Lucknow. [BINS354:3]

Notes *The* BINS *number is wrongly given as* 254; *the correct number is* 354 (15 JAN 1996).

28–30 Dec The first teaching conference of Lithuania is held in Vilnius, attended by Bahá'ís from five countries. [BINS355:1]

1996

Feb By now, approximately 1,250 people have enrolled in the Bahá'í Faith in Guinea-Bissau as a result of the Luz Local Teaching Project and the William Sears project. [BINS356:8]

9–11 Feb The first National Bahá'í Winter School of Belarus is held near Minsk. [BINS358:3]

23–4 Mar The first National Women's Seminar of Bulgaria is held in Sofia, organized by the European Task Force for Women. [BINS365:8]

20 Apr The Three Year Plan is successfully completed.

Riḍván The Four Year Plan is launched.

The National Spiritual Assembly of Sao Tomé and Principe is formed. [BINS363:1]

• For picture see BINS366:9.

The National Spiritual Assembly of Moldova is formed. [BINS363:1–2]

The terraces below the Shrine of the Báb are completed and open to pilgrims.

Pilgrims climb the terraces to the Shrine of the Báb

Above: The 'Highway of the Kings'

Below: Dr Wally N'Dow, Secretary-General of the Habitat II Conference, second from right, and Mrs N'Dow, right, are guests of the National Spiritual Assembly of the United Kingdom at a reception in London

1996

30 May–14 Jun The Bahá'í International Community and 150 Bahá'ís from many countries participate in the Second United Nations Conference on Human Settlements (Habitat II) and the parallel Non-Governmental Organization Forum in Istanbul. [BINS365:5]

Right: Member of the Continental Board of Counsellors Ilhan Sezgin inspires the 150-strong Bahá'í delegation to Habitat II

Below right: Bahá'í delegates to Habitat II, the Hon. Barney Leith of the United Kingdom and Dr Beth Bowen, representing Health for Humanity, facilitate the participation of NGOs at the government negotiations

Below: Lawrence Arturo, Director of the Bahá'í Office for the Environment, Bahá'í International Community, welcomes Bahá'í participants to Habitat II

Index

The entries are indexed word by word, thus Chan Lie Kun precedes Chance, Hugh. Hyphens are treated as spaces; connecting letters -i- and y-i- are ignored; titles such as Áqá and Mírzá precede names such as Kámil; 'of', 'on' 'and', and 'for' in titles are ignored.

Figures refer to month (where relevant) and year, thus 5:1863 indicates May 1863.